SEPTEMBER 2005–AUG

MW00805387

DAVID C. COOK
LESSON
COMMENTARY

GENERAL EDITOR: DR. DANIEL LIOY

CONTRIBUTING EDITORS: KERRY KRYCHO AND BONNIE PRESTEL

COOK COMMUNICATIONS MINISTRIES CURRICULUM
COLORADO SPRINGS, COLORADO/PARIS, ONTARIO

DAVID C. COOK LESSON COMMENTARY © 2005 Cook Communications Ministries, 4050 Lee Vance View, Colorado Springs, CO 80918, U.S.A. All rights reserved. Printed in U.S.A. May not be reproduced without permission.

Editorial Manager: Douglas C. Schmidt

General Editor: Daniel Lioy, Ph.D.

Contributing Editors: Kerry Krycho and Bonnie Prestel

Designer: Ty Pauls

Cover Design by Ty Pauls

Cover photography © 1998 by Dan Stultz

ISBN: 0781442354

CONTENTS

A Word to the Teacher v
Commentary Use vi

■

SEPTEMBER, OCTOBER, NOVEMBER 2005

1	September 4	**Making the Right Choices** 1
2	September 11	**Choosing the Right Values** 9
3	September 18	**Leading with Respect** 17
4	September 25	**The Success Trap** 25
5	October 2	**The Choice is Yours** 33
6	October 9	**Heeding What We Hear** 41
7	October 16	**Better Than You Expected** 49
8	October 23	**A Heart for Worship** 57
9	October 30	**Never Beyond His Reach** 65
10	November 6	**The Mark of a Christian Leader** 73
11	November 13	**Learning to Listen** 81
12	November 20	**The Harvest of Sin** 89
13	November 27	**Sliding down the Slippery Slope** 97

■

DECEMBER 2005, JANUARY, FEBRUARY 2006

1	December 4	**Encouraging Others** 105
2	December 11	**Say 'Yes' to God** 113
3	December 18	**Not Without Opposition** 121
4	December 25	**Share the News** 129
5	January 1	**A Commitment to Change** 137
6	January 8	**Overcoming Rejection** 145
7	January 15	**Changed Hearts, Changed Homes** 153
8	January 22	**Turn Right toward God** 161
9	January 29	**A Whole-Life Plan** 169
10	February 5	**Power-full Living** 177
11	February 12	**Right in His Sight** 185
12	February 19	**Promises to Live By** 193
13	February 26	**Hope to Hold On** 201

CONTENTS

MARCH, APRIL, MAY 2006

1	March 5	**God Moves Hearts**	209
2	March 12	**Living in God's Present**	217
3	March 19	**Let's Celebrate**	225
4	March 26	**Radical Change Required**	233
5	April 2	**Taking the Lead**	241
6	April 9	**Setting Up Our Defenses**	249
7	April 16	**All Fear Is Gone**	257
8	April 23	**Be Confident in the Lord**	265
9	April 30	**Hearing God Again**	273
10	May 7	**Actions Follow Beliefs**	281
11	May 14	**Finding the Celebration**	289
12	May 21	**The Problems of Obedience**	297
13	May 28	**What's Right — Regardless!**	305

JUNE, JULY, AUGUST 2006

1	June 4	**Share the Blessings**	313
2	June 11	**The Right Reflection**	321
3	June 18	**Stop Worrying**	329
4	June 25	**The Sweet Fragrance of Forgiveness**	337
5	July 2	**Made for Each Other**	345
6	July 9	**Deceit's Destructive Force**	353
7	July 16	**The Folly of Favoritism**	361
8	July 23	**God Means It for Good**	369
9	July 30	**A Perfect Imitation**	377
10	August 6	**Showers of Blessings**	385
11	August 13	**All Together Now**	393
12	August 20	**Body Building**	401
13	August 27	**The Battle Belongs to the Lord**	409

In *The Quiet Hour*, the story is told of a harried mom whose four-year-old son who thrust a paper-towel tube in her hand, and challenged her to a sword-fight. He tossed his security-blanket cape behind his back and assumed the position of a would-be musketeer.

Distracted by her own personal battle with coupons scattered across the table, she simply held the sword in her hand as she continued her scavenger hunt for any overlooked savings. In response to the whacks of her son's bigger sword, she half-heartedly waved her own in his general direction.

Suddenly, he pressed his little palms against her face to be sure she was looking him in the eye.

"Mom," he said, "you have to act like you believe."

This year you will also have the opportunity to encourage your students to "act like they believe." May the Lord continue to bless you through this often-challenging task.

Your Co-Laborer in Christ,

Doug Schmidt

This commentary was created specifically to supplement the lessons in David C. Cook's Bible-in-Life Adult Curriculum for the September 2005 — August 2006 Sunday School year.

Making the Right Choices

DEVOTIONAL READING

Psalm 119:10-19

DAILY BIBLE READINGS

Monday August 29
*Proverbs 3:13-20 Blessed
Is the Person Who Finds
Wisdom*

Tuesday August 30
*1 Kings 2:1-6 David
Blesses Solomon*

Wednesday August 31
*1 Kings 2:7-12 David Tells
Solomon He is a Man of
Wisdom*

Thursday September 1
*1 Kings 3:1-6 Solomon
Offered Offerings to God*

Friday September 2
*1 Kings 3:7-15 Solomon
Asks God for Wisdom*

Saturday September 3
*Mark 10:17-25 A Young
Man Chooses Riches
instead of Jesus*

Sunday September 4
*Luke 6:46-49 A Wise
Person Obeys Jesus' Words*

Scripture

Background Scripture: *1 Kings 2:1-4; 3:1-15;
1 Chronicles 29:22-25; 2 Chronicles 1:1-13*
Scripture Lesson: *1 Kings 2:1-4; 3:3-10*
Key Verse: *"So give your servant a discerning heart to
govern your people and to distinguish between right and
wrong" 1 Kings 3:9a.*

Lesson Aim

A discerning heart is better than power or riches.

Lesson Setting

Time: 980 B.C.
Place: Jerusalem and Gibeon (which was six miles away)

Lesson Outline

Making the Right Choices

   I. David's Charge to Solomon: 1 Kings 2:1-4
      A. *Be Strong: vss. 1-2*
      B. *Keep God's Laws: vs. 3*
      C. *Remember God's Promise: vs. 4*
  II. Solomon's Request: 1 Kings 3:3-10
      A. *Solomon's Sacrifices at Gibeon: vss. 3-4*
      B. *God's Generous Offer: vs. 5*
      C. *Solomon's Thankfulness: vs. 6*
      D. *Solomon's Admission: vs. 7*
      E. *Solomon's Need: vss. 8-9*
      F. *God's Pleasure: vs. 10*

Introduction

When Tasks Overwhelm

Most of us at one time or another have thrown up our hands in despair and shouted, "It's impossible!" That's a normal human response. Perhaps it's a situation at work in which our boss has demanded more from us than is physically possible for us to accomplish. Or maybe we're expected to do a job for which we lack the training and experience. Another scenario may involve our impatience in dealing with personal problems that appear unending.

Slick advertisers try to capitalize on our frustration by telling us no problem is too big for us to handle. Supposedly it's possible for us to get rich, be popular, and command respect. And if we buy certain products or use particular medications, all our problems will magically go away. And why not, since we're number one (or so we're told).

Christians know these are bogus claims. We also recognize that such promises draw us away from trusting in God. In fact, the Bible rarely promises quick, easy answers to the vexing issues of life. Rather, as Paul said, "I can do everything through him who gives me strength" (Phil. 4:13). Thus, our confidence is in Jesus, not in ourselves or others. When we feel overwhelmed, we can go to Him for the strength, hope, and courage we need to live.

Lesson Commentary

I. David's Charge to Solomon: I Kings 2:1-4

A. Be Strong: vss. 1-2

When the time drew near for David to die, he gave a charge to Solomon his son. "I am about to go the way of all the earth," he said. "So be strong, show yourself a man."

After David's sin with Bathsheba and his murder of Uriah, his reign was marked by troubles within his family. For instance, his son Absalom rebelled, and this drove David from Jerusalem. After Absalom's death, David was restored to the throne. He then sinned in taking a census, which led to a plague wiping out 70,000 people (2 Sam. 13—24).

As David's life drew to a close, he recognized the need to install his successor to the throne. David's first son, Amnon, had been killed by Absalom for having raped his sister (13:20-33). David's second son, Daniel, is mentioned only in the genealogy of 1 Chronicles 3:1, and may have died by this time. David's third son, Absalom, died in an earlier rebellion (2 Sam. 18:1-18).

Adonijah was David's fourth son and the logical choice to be the next king. Though many expected him to be the new ruler, David planned to install Solomon as Israel's next monarch (1 Kings 1:5, 29-30). Eventually Solomon had Adonijah executed for trying to usurp the throne (2:23-25).

In ancient times it was customary for a leader to pass on instructions to his successors. Thus before his death, David gave Solomon a final exhortation. He would face many challenges and enemies as Israel's king. It was no time for him to be timid and squeamish. Rather, he needed to be a person of courage, determination, and decisiveness. David's charge to Solomon was reminiscent of Moses' words to the Israelites (Deut. 31:6) and the Lord's admonition to Joshua (Josh. 1:6-7, 9).

B. Keep God's Laws: vs. 3

"And observe what the LORD your God requires: Walk in his ways, and keep his decrees and commands, his laws and requirements, as written in the Law of Moses, so that you may prosper in all you do and wherever you go."

David next turned to Solomon's need for spiritual guidance. It was not enough for him to rule with power. He also needed to understand and obey the Mosaic law. Even if he were strong in the execution of his office, he would fail if he disregarded the Word of God.

David's admonition is summed up in the different verbs he used: "observe," "walk," and "keep" (vs. 3). He also used different nouns to describe God's law: "decrees," "commands," "laws," and "requirements." David's instructions echo the standards of righteousness recorded in the Mosaic covenant (Deut. 5:33; 8:6, 11; 11:1, 22).

Solomon could not claim that he had never seen the law or that he did not have access to it, for the decrees of God were recorded

---

2:2 "be strong"—

The verb has several possible nuances. It can describe those who summoned their strength (Gen. 48:2). It can refer to gaining political strength (2 Sam. 3:6; cf. 2 Chron. 13:21; 27:6). In the present passage, as David passes on the rulership of Israel to Solomon, he exhorts his son to "be strong" in the face of the weighty demands of being king.

in His Word. Thus, the law was readily available to him (Rom. 10:6-8).

Solomon's success as king not only depended on knowing God's Word but also applying it to his life. It was not enough for him to have an intellectual grasp of the Bible's content. He also had to use properly what God had commanded in the law.

Thus, there were two paths that Solomon could take. If he chose the way of disobedience, he would fail as Israel's king and plunge the nation into turmoil. But if he chose the path of obedience, God would enable him to succeed in all that he did and wherever he went as king. Solomon was truly wise if he chose the path of uprightness, not evil.

The king's responsibilities were both personal and national. His own welfare and that of Israel depended on his unwavering commitment to God. Regardless of what other skills and abilities he had, Solomon's continued success would depend upon his faithfulness to the Mosaic covenant.

C. Remember God's Promise: vs. 4

"And that the LORD may keep his promise to me: 'If your descendants watch how they live, and if they walk faithfully before me with all their heart and soul, you will never fail to have a man on the throne of Israel.' "

God had made an unconditional covenant with David in which He promised that David's line would continue forever (2 Sam. 7:12-16; 1 Chron. 17:11-14). Though the Davidic covenant was an unending and sacred promise, individual kings through their evil behavior could fail to receive the benefits of the covenant (Ps. 89:3-4, 14-24, 27-37).

Solomon learned that he had to follow God faithfully with all his "heart and soul" (1 Kings 2:4). These words are an allusion to Deuteronomy 4:29 and 6:5. The implication is that Solomon and his descendants would remain in office as kings only when they honored and obeyed God.

The Old Testament reveals that the throne of David was marked more by vice than by virtue. Only David's greatest descendant—Jesus Christ—would succeed where all others had failed (Isa. 9:6-7).

II. Solomon's Request:
I Kings 3:3-10

A. Solomon's Sacrifices at Gibeon: vss. 3-4

Solomon showed his love for the LORD by walking according to the statutes of his father David, except that he offered sacrifices and burned incense on the high places. The king went to Gibeon to offer sacrifices, for that was the most important high place, and Solomon offered a thousand burnt offerings on that altar.

Solomon began his reign well. He loved the Lord and followed all the instructions of David. The one key area of failure, however, concerned Solomon's worship at the high places. These were either specially constructed enclosures or open-air sanctuaries on prominent hills.

The Mosaic law said that the Israelites could make sacrifices only in specified places (Deut. 12:13-14). This was to prevent the people from establishing their own methods of worship and allowing pagan practices to creep into their ceremonies. Sadly, many Israelites—including Solomon—made sacrifices in the surrounding hills. Though Solomon loved God, his use of the hilltop shrines was sin.

The most important of these altars was at Gibeon, a town about seven miles northwest of Jerusalem. This is where the tabernacle and the original bronze altar were located (1 Chron. 21:29; 2 Chron. 1:2-6). There Solomon sacrificed 1,000 burnt offerings, which were typically used to give thanks and atone for sin (Lev. 6:8-13)

B. God's Generous Offer: vs. 5

At Gibeon the LORD appeared to Solomon during the night in a dream, and God said, "Ask for whatever you want me to give you."

While Solomon was at Gibeon, God appeared to him in a dream. This dream sets the stage for the first major period in Solomon's tenure as king. In the dream, God made a generous offer. He invited Solomon to ask for anything he wanted. Such an offer was sure to test the new king's priorities as well as his devotion to the Lord.

2:3 "walk"—

The verb most frequently employed to describe the act or process of living. In addition to signifying literal walking or going, it can refer figuratively to the pursuit of human life (Pss. 23:4; 142:3 [Heb. 142:4]; Isa. 50:10). It regularly occurs to designate life that is lived in obedience or disobedience to God's covenant expectations. "To walk after" refers to loyalty to God and to his covenant or his commandments (1 Kings 14:8; 2 Chron. 34:31) with the metaphor of a path or way underlying it (Deut. 11:28; 28:14).

C. Solomon's Thankfulness: vs. 6

Solomon answered, "You have shown great kindness to your servant, my father David, because he was faithful to you and righteous and upright in heart. You have continued this great kindness to him and have given him a son to sit on his throne this very day."

Solomon responded by first praising and thanking God for His goodness both to him and his father. Solomon then acknowledged that apart from God's blessing, he would not be the king of Israel. He gave God the credit and took no glory for himself.

Solomon's thanksgiving centered on what God had done for David. Two times Solomon called it God's "great kindness" (vs. 6). Though the king said that his father was faithful, righteous, and upright, he nevertheless attributed David's success to the goodness of the Lord.

Not only had God blessed David's reign, but also God had provided a son to succeed David on the throne. Solomon acknowledged that God's hand was on him, especially because he had survived some serious obstacles to his succession. For this he offered praise to the Lord.

D. Solomon's Admission: vs. 7

"Now, O LORD my God, you have made your servant king in place of my father David. But I am only a little child and do not know how to carry out my duties."

The term rendered "child" (vs. 7) was often used to refer to a servant or to an inexperienced person still in training for a profession (1 Kings 19:21; 2 Kings 4:12). In this case, Solomon saw himself as being relatively young and inexperienced to shoulder the awesome responsibility of ruling Israel. (He was possibly 20 years old when he became king.) His willingness to admit his lack of qualification was a demonstration of true humility.

E. Solomon's Need: vss. 8-9

"Your servant is here among the people you have chosen, a great people, too numerous to count or number. So give your servant a discerning heart to govern your people and to distinguish

between right and wrong. For who is able to govern this great people of yours?"

Solomon prefaced his request by noting that governing Israel was a huge task. Since the Israelites' departure from Egypt, they had grown in population. This large number of people would give any leader considerable challenges. That's why, when given an opportunity to have anything in the world, Solomon asked for wisdom—"a discerning heart" (vs. 9)—in order to lead well and make sensible decisions.

The phrase "discerning heart" implies both a willingness to listen and the patience to consider all sides of an issue. Also implied is the desire to think through difficult matters in a reasonable way. Solomon would put such abilities to good use as he made decisions about good and evil, right and wrong, and justice and injustice. He sensed that only God could enable him to succeed in carrying out such complex tasks.

F. God's Pleasure: vs. 10

The LORD was pleased that Solomon had asked for this.

Solomon's admission of his need and his request for wisdom pleased the Lord. God knew that Solomon had his priorities straight. For instance, the king put the interests of God and the needs of the Israelites before his own desires. He truly wanted to do what was best for the nation.

The Lord demonstrated His satisfaction with Solomon's request by granting it. God said He would give the king a "wise and discerning heart" (vs. 12). In fact, his abilities in these areas would be unmatched.

In addition, the Lord promised to give Solomon what he had not asked for, namely, riches and honor. The king would have no equal among the rulers of the world (vs. 13). God also pledged to give Solomon a long life, especially if he followed the Lord and obeyed His commands (vs. 14).

When Solomon woke up, he realized that he had been dreaming. He returned to Jerusalem, stood before the ark of the covenant, and sacrificed a variety of offerings to God. Then he invited all his officials to a sumptuous banquet to celebrate the goodness of the Lord in his life (vs. 15).

Discussion Questions

1. What did David urge his son Solomon to observe? Why?
2. What promise had God made to David concerning his descendants?
3. As Solomon began his reign as king, what characterized his relationship with God?
4. What did Solomon do at Gibeon?
5. Why did Solomon ask for wisdom?
6. How did God respond to Solomon's request?

Now Ask Yourself . . .

What is the most important piece of spiritual advice I need to follow at this point?

What is the most important piece of commonsense advice I need to implement today?

How can I be more perceptive of spiritual dangers around me without becoming overly fearful?

In what kinds of circumstances might I be tempted to change my loyalties to protect my job or my popularity?

What are some ways I have rationalized sin so it didn't seem so bad?

What boundaries has God established in my life? What is likely to happen if I cross them?

Illustrations

Solomon's reign got off to a good start. He received great advice from his father. He had sense enough to accept his inadequacies. And he knew he needed wisdom from the Lord, especially to succeed as king of Israel.

When we face awesome responsibilities for which we feel unqualified, we can either avoid them or seek God's help. We may not ever have to ask Him how to be a wise ruler of a whole nation, but we still need wisdom to lead our families, churches, and communities.

Oftentimes what we think we need to live differs from what God thinks. Society says we should have lots of money, power, and popularity. But God's Word says our foremost concern should be His kingdom (Matt. 6:33). We can put God and His work first, for He has promised to supply all our needs from His glorious riches, which have been given to us in Christ (Phil. 4:19).

Therefore, our main focus should be on spiritually maturing as believers. This involves growing wiser, becoming more patient, demonstrating unconditional love to others, and obeying God in whatever we do (1 Cor. 13:4-7). It means manifesting the fruit of the Spirit, rather than the acts of the sinful nature (Gal. 5:19-23).

Setting our sights on riches will only leave us dissatisfied, for even if we get the material possessions we crave, we will still want something more. But if we seek wisdom from God, He will provide it in abundance (Jas. 1:5).

Choosing the Right Values

DEVOTIONAL READING
Nahum 1:2-8

DAILY BIBLE READINGS

Monday September 5
*2 Corinthians 6:14-18
Compromise Can Weaken
Our Faith*

Tuesday September 6
*Psalm 1 Do Not Follow
Those Who Have No Use
for God*

Wednesday September 7
*1 Kings 11:1-8 Solomon's
Heart Turns Away from
God*

Thursday September 8
*1 Kings 11:9-13
Solomon's Actions Anger
God*

Friday September 9
*1 Kings 11:14-25 God
Raises Up Enemies*

Saturday September 10
*1 Kings 11:26-33 The
Prophet Ahijah Speaks to
Jeroboam*

Sunday September 11
*1 Kings 11:34-43 God
Makes a Promise to
Jeroboam*

Scripture

Background Scripture: *1 Kings 11*
Scripture Lesson: *1 Kings 11:1-13*
Key Verse: *As Solomon grew old, his wives turned his heart after other gods, and his heart was not fully devoted to the LORD his God, as the heart of David his father had been. 1 Kings 11:4.*

Lesson Aim

Compromise with the world's values means abandoning God's values.

Lesson Setting

Time: 940 B.C.
Place: Jerusalem

Lesson Outline

Choosing the Right Values

    I. Solomon's Foreign Wives: 1 Kings 11:1-8
       A. *God's Injunction: vss. 1-2a*
       B. *Solomon's Willful Disobedience: vss. 2b-3*
       C. *Solomon's Divided Loyalties: vs. 4*
       D. *Solomon's Corrupted Worship: vss. 5-8*
    II. God's Displeasure: 1 Kings 11:9-13
       A. *Solomon's Refusal to Listen: vss. 9-10*
       B. *God's Discipline of Solomon: vss. 11-13*

Introduction

When Compromise Ruins

Obedience to God's Word has been compared to following a diet. We know that we shouldn't eat certain foods, because they're harmful to our physical health. But when something enticing is set before us, we make excuses for why we should break our diet. Similarly, when temptation strikes, we may rationalize why it's all right to give in to a forbidden desire. Of course, this is detrimental to our spiritual health.

Solomon tried to keep one foot in the camp of God and the other foot in the camp of idols. He utterly failed, however, in his attempt to pull this off. We should not be surprised, for Jesus said, "No one can serve two masters" (Matt. 6:24). John likewise warned, "Keep yourselves from idols" (1 John 5:21).

Solomon did not understand that friendship with the world makes one an enemy of God (Jas. 4:4). The king also did not realize that the world is fading away, along with everything it craves (1 John 2:17). May we not fall into the same errors as Solomon.

Lesson Commentary

I. Solomon's Foreign Wives: I Kings 11:1-8

A. God's Injunction: vss. 1-2a

King Solomon, however, loved many foreign women besides Pharaoh's daughter—Moabites, Ammonites, Edomites, Sidonians and Hittites. They were from nations about which the LORD had told the Israelites, "You must not intermarry with them, because they will surely turn your hearts after their gods."

The "however" in this record is one of the most tragic in the Bible, for it reflects the seriousness of the fall of Israel's great king. It means that despite Solomon's promising beginning, his rich heritage, his prayer for wisdom from God, his building of the temple, and his accumulation of enormous wealth and power, he had one fatal flaw that ruined everything. He loved many women who were idolaters.

Scripture presents monogamy (namely, marital union between one man and one woman at a time) as the divine ideal (Gen. 2:22-24; Matt. 19:4-6; 1 Cor. 6:16). Perhaps polygamy, like divorce, was tolerated because of the hardness of people's hearts (Matt. 19:8).

Though the Bible never justifies polygamy, ancient kings frequently undertook multiple marriages for political reasons. For instance, a king would marry the daughter of another king in order to create a stronger alliance. The larger a king's harem, the more prestige he enjoyed (11:3).

David had numerous wives, and negative results inevitably followed his multiple marriages (2 Sam. 3:2-5). For example, David's son Amnon violated his half-sister Tamar, then was killed by her avenging brother, Absalom. That led to a bitter estrangement between Absalom and his father that resulted in the treason and, ultimately, the death of Absalom—all to David's great regret (2 Sam. 13—18). Later Adonijah tried to usurp the throne from Solomon to whom it had been promised (1 Kings 1:5–10).

David's polygamy also set a poor example for his successor, Solomon. By taking foreign wives, he violated the Lord's prohibitions against marrying Canaanite women (Exod. 34:12-17; Deut. 7:1-3). Solomon's yielding to the customs of the day had disastrous spiritual consequences for himself and the Israelites.

The Lord had clearly explained why His people must not intermarry among the surrounding pagan nations. The women they married would lead them to the worship of idols (Deut. 7:4). For instance, the Moabites venerated Chemosh, a savage war-god. The Ammonites worshiped Molech (or Milcom), an astral deity. The Edomites venerated Qaus, a fertility deity. The Sidonians worshiped Ashtoreth, a Canaanite goddess of love and war. And the Hittites venerated Tesub (a storm god) and Hepat (a sun goddess).

Marriage is one the most intimate of relationships. By joining himself to idolatrous women, Solomon made himself vulnerable to their ungodly influences. God banned such marriages because the purity of Israelite worship had to be maintained at all costs. Though Solomon was extremely wise in most other areas of life, he was foolish in exchanging his allegiance to God for idols.

11:2 "turn your hearts after"—

This verb signifies stretching something outward or spreading something out. It can describe straying from a path or route (Num. 20:17; 21:22; 2 Sam. 6:10). In 1 and 2 Kings this verb occurs to describe spiritual direction. As part of a commentary on the ultimate direction of Solomon's reign, the biblical historian affirmed that Solomon's many wives caused his heart to incline after their false gods (1 Kings 11:2-4).

B. Solomon's Willful Disobedience: vss. 2b-3

Nevertheless, Solomon held fast to them in love. He had seven hundred wives of royal birth and three hundred concubines, and his wives led him astray.

"Nevertheless" (vs. 2) is a severe indictment of Solomon. He sinned, not in ignorance of God's commands, but despite them.

The king allowed his love for pagan women to compromise his devotion to God.

The number of Solomon's wives seems mind-boggling to us, but we have no reason to question the text's accuracy. The biblical record clearly shows that regardless of whether it was gold, horses, or women, Solomon acquired them in excess (1 Kings 9:26-28; 10:14-29; Eccles. 2:1-8). Even if the number of the king's wives was 70 and not 700, it would still reveal an utterly sensual heart, one that could not be satisfied with anything less than gross indulgence.

God's warning came true. Solomon did not convert his many wives to faith in the Lord. Rather, they led him astray. The seed of idolatry that was planted in the heart of Solomon would soon bear fruit in the lives of the Israelites and eventually lead to their exile from the land (2 Kings 17:16-20).

C. Solomon's Divided Loyalties: vs. 4

As Solomon grew old, his wives turned his heart after other gods, and his heart was not fully devoted to the LORD his God, as the heart of David his father had been.

Solomon did not immediately become an idolater. Rather, he gradually drifted away from the Lord. As the king grew richer and more powerful, he began to act like the rulers of the surrounding pagan nations.

Verse 4 makes an astute comparison between Solomon and his father David. David fell into terrible sin, but he did not exchange his faith in God for a life of sexual abandon with hundreds of women. The crucial issue was the direction of the heart. Unlike Solomon, David put God first.

Solomon did far more than the occasional transgression. He turned his heart completely away from the Lord toward idols. That never happened to David. His faith in God remained rock solid to his dying day.

Solomon's apostasy is hard to understand, especially in light of his remarkable wisdom. He should have been able to see what was happening to him. Did he argue with his wives about who was the greatest, the God of Israel or some idol? If so, Solomon could have easily won those debates.

Solomon's downfall stemmed from his failure to use his spiritual gifts. His wisdom was useless when he caved in to his love for women. They eroded his moral foundation and sucked whatever spiritual life he had out of him.

The crucial expression is "fully devoted" (vs. 4). We cannot follow the world's idols and still remain a faithful believer in the Lord. Perhaps at first Solomon resisted the pressures from his wives to compromise his faith. Then he may have tolerated a more widespread practice of idolatry. Eventually, he became involved in idolatry, perhaps rationalizing away the danger to himself and the nation.

God requires that we love Him with all of our heart, soul, and mind. That is the first and greatest commandment (Deut. 6:4-5; Matt. 22:36-40).

D. Solomon's Corrupted Worship: vss. 5-8

He followed Ashtoreth the goddess of the Sidonians, and Molech the detestable god of the Ammonites. So Solomon did evil in the eyes of the LORD; he did not follow the LORD completely, as David his father had done. On a hill east of Jerusalem, Solomon built a high place for Chemosh the detestable god of Moab, and for Molech the detestable god of the Ammonites. He did the same for all his foreign wives, who burned incense and offered sacrifices to their gods.

Ashtoreth and Molech were two of Solomon's idols. Moses had warned Israel about these pagan deities (Exod. 34:13; Lev. 20:2-5). The worship of Molech was especially repugnant because it included sacrificing infants.

Solomon's idolatry was evil in God's eyes, for it denied His supremacy. The issue was mixed allegiances. Perhaps outwardly the king appeared to be a faithful worshiper. For instance, three times a year Solomon offered burnt offerings and peace offerings to the Lord (1 Kings 9:25). But inwardly Solomon had embraced the worship of idols, something abhorrent to God.

David is again presented as the standard by which other kings were to act and be judged. This was not because David had not sinned, but rather because he repented appropriately from his sin, and because sin did not continue as the pattern of his life.

Unlike David, Solomon had the audacity to build pagan shrines on the Mount of Olives, east of Jerusalem. The king built such

---

11:5 "detestable"—

This noun, based on the verb (to regard as or make abominable), occurs 28 times in the OT and refers to everything detestable from the perspective of true Yahweh worship. Five of the six occurrences of this noun in 1 and 2 Kings refer to the idols that Solomon erected in the vicinity of Jerusalem. In 1 Kings 11 they are mentioned as evidences of Solomon's covenant treachery.

idolatrous centers of worship for all his foreign wives to use for burning incense and sacrificing to their gods.

Though Solomon successfully handled great pressures in running the government, he could not bear the pressure from his wives who wanted him to venerate their gods and goddesses. Whether he married to strengthen political alliances or to gain personal pleasure, Solomon became an open idolater. He woshiped images of wood and stone in the sight of the temple. Ironically, this was the sanctuary that the king had built in his early years to the one true God.

Solomon's actions encouraged Israel to jettison the true worship of God for powerless, lifeless objects. Solomon thus became the father of Israel's syncretistic worship. This is the blending of the false and true, the worship of idols and the Lord. This eventually led to the destruction of the nation.

II. God's Displeasure: I Kings 11:9-13

A. Solomon's Refusal to Listen: vss. 9-10

The LORD became angry with Solomon because his heart had turned away from the LORD, the God of Israel, who had appeared to him twice. Although he had forbidden Solomon to follow other gods, Solomon did not keep the LORD's command.

The word rendered "angry" (vs. 9) is a strong term denoting intense displeasure. The Lord was indignant with Solomon because he willfully violated the law. When the Lord first appeared to him at Gibeon, He told Solomon that if he obeyed the law, he would live a long time (3:4-14). Part of God's decree would have included a ban on idolatry (Deut. 5:7-8).

When the Lord appeared a second time to Solomon at Jerusalem, He urged the king to remain obedient, honest, and fair in all that he did. God also warned that if either Solomon or any of his descendants started worshiping idols, it would be a disastrous course. The Lord would allow the temple to be destroyed and His people removed from the land (1 Kings 9:1-9).

Solomon's venture into idolatry was inexcusable. Most likely he didn't turn away from God all at once or in a brief moment. Rather, he grew spiritually cold over an extended period of time.

Perhaps at first it was a minor infraction of God's laws. But as the years rolled along, the sins became more numerous and severe. This eventually led to Solomon's downfall.

B. God's Discipline of Solomon: vss. 11-13

So the LORD said to Solomon, "Since this is your attitude and you have not kept my covenant and my decrees, which I commanded you, I will most certainly tear the kingdom away from you and give it to one of your subordinates. Nevertheless, for the sake of David your father, I will not do it during your lifetime. I will tear it out of the hand of your son. Yet I will not tear the whole king-dom from him, but will give him one tribe for the sake of David my servant and for the sake of Jerusalem, which I have chosen."

Because Solomon had become divided in his loyalties, the Lord would cause his kingdom to become divided. One of the king's officials named Jeroboam would gain control of the 10 northern tribes (11:26; 12:20). God's great love for David prompted Him to temper His judgment with mercy by not disrupting the kingdom in Solomon's lifetime (11:34).

The Lord also declared that the throne of David would still rule one tribe, namely, Judah. (Simeon had assimilated with Judah by this time.) God extended this grace because He had not forgotten that David had served Him with unwavering devotion. Also, the Lord had chosen Jerusalem as the place where His name would dwell forever (9:3). Therefore, Jerusalem and its temple would remain so that the divine promise might stand.

God's response to Solomon was a reflection of His righteous character. How could the Holy One of Israel stand by and let the nation's king get away with flagrant violations of the Mosaic covenant (Isa. 54:5)? It was in love that God disciplined Solomon (Prov. 3:11-12). The Lord's firm and righteous response would send a clear message to His people that not even the king was above the law.

Discussion Questions

1. What led to Solomon's downfall?
2. Why did Solomon depart from his rich spiritual heritage?
3. What are some of the challenges to our faith that often confront us?
4. What steps can we take to keep from falling into sin?
5. What part does God's discipline of us serve in helping us to remain faithful to Him?
6. What can we do to ensure that our hearts and lives remain fully devoted to the Lord?

Now Ask Yourself . . .

Do I love anything or anyone more than I love the Lord?

What kinds of "gods" have tried to get my attention recently?

How would I know if my commitment to God was waning?

What kind of trouble could I expect if I were to step outside the will of God?

How do I know my plans for the future will please God?

Illustrations

A false sense of security has led to the downfall of empires, businesses, families, churches, and individuals. Consider Solomon. He thought he had everything going for him. So what did it matter if he married several hundred foreign women? He imagined he could worship God in the temple and participate in the idolatrous rituals of his pagan wives. Solomon failed to see that his sinful actions would bring tragic consequences to him and the Israelites.

We need to check ourselves rigorously to be sure that our devotion to Christ does not wane. Even so-called little missteps can lead us away from Jesus. That's why each day demands accountability to God. When we allow ourselves to drift away even in minor matters from the truths of Scripture, we court disaster.

It's not the sins we don't know about but the sins we excuse that cause us the greatest trouble. That's why we should not let any sin go unchallenged. Accountability groups and trusted friends can help us remain unwavering in our commitment to the Lord. Beyond this we should confess our sin to God and ask Him for the strength to resist temptation when it arises.

Leading with Respect

DEVOTIONAL READING

Matthew 11:27-30

DAILY BIBLE READINGS

Monday September 12
Isaiah 3:1-8 Good Leaders Are Hard to Find

Tuesday September 13
Isaiah 3:9-12 Some Leaders Mislead Their People

Wednesday September 14
Exodus 18:13-20 Wise Leadership Listens

Thursday September 15
Exodus 18:21-26 Wise Leadership Shares Responsibility

Friday September 16
1 Kings 12:1-5 The People Ask King Rehoboam for Favor

Saturday September 17
1 Kings 12:6-11 King Rehoboam Ignores Wise Advice

Sunday September 18
1 Kings 12:12-19 The People of Israel Rebel against Rehoboam

Scripture

Background Scripture: *1 Kings 12; 2 Chronicles 10:1—11:12*

Scripture Lesson: *1 Kings 12:3-4, 6-11, 13-14a, 16*

Key Verse: *"If today you will be a servant to these people and serve them and give them a favorable answer, they will always be your servants." 1 Kings 12:7.*

Lesson Aim

Wise leadership respects all people.

Lesson Setting

Time: Shortly before 900 B.C.

Place: Shechem

Lesson Outline

Leading with Respect

   I. The Request of the People: 1 Kings 12:3-4

  II. The Counsel of the Elders: 1 Kings 12:6-7

 III. The Counsel of the Young Men: 1 Kings 12:8-11

 IV. The People's Response: 1 Kings 12:13-14a, 16

Introduction

Choose Wisely

Solomon asked God for wisdom, and he became the wisest ruler on earth in his day (1 Kings 3:9-12). But he forsook God's wisdom and paid dearly (11:9-13). Solomon's son, Rehoboam [ree-uh-BOW-uhm], apparently was as idolatrous and power-hungry as his father. And when it came time to act wisely, Rehoboam foolishly adopted the plans of those who only wanted to perpetuate the power of the royal court. This in turn led to the division of the nation.

We all face considerable pressures when we make important decisions. For instance, our unsaved acquaintances tell us it's foolish to follow Christ. They also urge us to to look out for ourselves. Scripture, however, directs us to reject such worldly ways of thinking and acting. Instead, we must pursue what is true, right, and good (Phil. 4:8). This is the mark of true wisdom (Jas. 3:17-18).

Lesson Commentary

I. The Request of the People: I Kings 12:3-4

So they sent for Jeroboam, and he and the whole assembly of Israel went to Rehoboam and said to him: "Your father put a heavy yoke on us, but now lighten the harsh labor and the heavy yoke he put on us, and we will serve you."

The lessons to be studied this quarter trace Israel's history from Solomon's death and the division of the united kingdom to the fall of the northern kingdom in 722 b.c. This particular time period was marked by struggles for political power and national security. It was also a period marked by injustice, oppression, and Israel's violation of God's covenant with their ancestors.

The downward spiral for the Israelites really began with the apostasy of Solomon. In the closing years of his reign, the king—though formerly renowned for his God-given wisdom—failed to remain faithful to God. Though the Lord had chosen Solomon to lead, he slipped away from the Lord's ways through the idolatrous influences of his many wives and consorts, who were steeped in paganism (1 Kings 11:1-8).

The Lord was disheartened by the king's faithlessness. To honor the memory of David, God allowed Solomon to reign until the end of his days. However, the consequence of Solomon's apostasy would be the dividing of the nation (vss. 9-13). And that's what we see happening in chapter 12. (A parallel account of this narrative can be found in 2 Chronicles 10 and 11.)

After Solomon's death in 931 b.c., his 41-year-old son, Rehoboam, journeyed to Shechem to be anointed king over Israel (1 Kings 12:1). Shechem was a key city in Ephraim, located in a beautiful valley 31 miles north of Jerusalem. This city had a rich spiritual heritage, which may have been why Shechem had been chosen as the site of Rehoboam's coronation.

When Jeroboam heard of Solomon's death, he returned from Egypt, where he had fled during Solomon's reign (vs. 2). Jeroboam is first mentioned in 11:26-28. There we read that he was a capable leader. In fact, when Solomon found out how industrious he was, the king placed him in charge of the labor force from the tribes of Ephraim and Manasseh.

Jeroboam was perfectly positioned to hear the complaints of Israel's forced laborers. He realized that Solomon's kingdom rested on a shaky foundation. In fact, in this soil were planted the bitter seeds of discontentment and revolt.

The biblical text reveals that one day, as Jeroboam was leaving Jerusalem, a prophet named Ahijah [uh-HIGH-juh] from Shiloh met him on the road. Ahijah took the new cloak he was wearing, tore it into 12 pieces, and declared that the Lord would tear the united kingdom from the hand of Solomon and give 10 tribes to Jeroboam (vss. 29-31).

When Solomon learned of this prophecy, he tried to kill Jeroboam. But the future leader of the 10 northern tribes fled to Egypt, where Shishak I (the monarch at the time) granted him political asylum (vs. 40). Only after Solomon's death did Jeroboam risk returning to his native Palestine.

It would have been normal to anoint a new king in Jerusalem, the capital city. But apparently Rehoboam saw trouble brewing with Jeroboam. Thus, Rehoboam went north to try to maintain good relations with the northern tribes. They in turn sent for

---

12:4 "serve"—

The verb "to serve" can simply refer to work (Gen. 2:5; 4:2, 12; Exod. 20:9; Deut. 28:39; 2 Sam. 9:10) and can signify the service rendered by one person for another (as a servant) (Exod. 21:2, 6; Lev. 25:39-46; Deut. 15:12). It can also describe service rendered in a political realm.

Jeroboam, and then the whole assembly of Israel went to speak with Rehoboam (12:3).

Though the kingdom of Israel was united under David and Solomon, the tensions between north and south were never resolved. The jealously and animosity are evident in the statement recorded in verse 4. The leaders of the 10 northern tribes complained that Solomon had been a hard taskmaster. They thus demanded that Rehoboam lighten the harsh labor demands and heavy taxes imposed on them by his father. If he agreed to this, the people would be his loyal subjects.

Rehoboam, who was a new and inexperienced leader, listened to the concerns of his people. Then he called for a three-day recess, a break that would allow him time to consider their request as well as perhaps to summon his advisers, who may have remained behind in Jerusalem (vs. 5). Though Rehoboam did not have his father's wisdom, he was smart enough to seek counsel before making a major decision.

II. The Counsel of the Elders: 1 Kings 12:6-7

Then King Rehoboam consulted the elders who had served his father Solomon during his lifetime. "How would you advise me to answer these people?" he asked. They replied, "If today you will be a servant to these people and serve them and give them a favorable answer, they will always be your servants."

King Rehoboam took the people's request to the older men who had advised his father (1 Kings 12:6). These probably included priests, commanders, counselors, and district governors. They were well acquainted with the traditions of Israel and understood how the monarchy affected the lives of ordinary citizens. They thus were a rich source of insight and wise counsel, people whom a discerning leader would take seriously.

The elders got it right when they framed Rehoboam's ruling responsibility as one of a servant to the people of Israel. Such a mentality conveys an attitude of humility, compassion, and sensitivity. It's one that would seek to the give the people "a favorable answer" (vs. 7).

The Hebrew word rendered "favorable" literally means "good." In this context, it suggests that Rehoboam needed to be kind and agreeable with his subjects. The elders seemed to be advising that the king do more than just grant the people's request. He needed to do so in such a way that the people saw how much he cared for them and their plight. This sentiment is echoed in Proverbs 15:1, which says, "A gentle answer turns away wrath, but a harsh word stirs up anger."

The elders knew that the oppressive conditions, if left unchecked, would erupt into rebellion. Thus the key to a successful reign was Rehoboam's willingness to humbly minister to the Israelites. In this case, that meant acceding to their request for relief from excessive taxation and work.

III. The Counsel of the Young Men: 1 Kings 12:8-11

But Rehoboam rejected the advice the elders gave him and consulted the young men who had grown up with him and were serving him. He asked them, "What is your advice? How should we answer these people who say to me, 'Lighten the yoke your father put on us'?" The young men who had grown up with him replied, "Tell these people who have said to you, 'Your father put a heavy yoke on us, but make our yoke lighter'—tell them, 'My little finger is thicker than my father's waist. My father laid on you a heavy yoke; I will make it even heavier. My father scourged you with whips; I will scourge you with scorpions.' "

Rehoboam flatly rejected the counsel of the older men. Perhaps the new king didn't want to accept the truth that the wise use of authority requires an attitude of humble service. The king may have also seen Jeroboam as a threat to his throne.

In any case, Rehoboam turned to his peers—those young men with whom he had long, established friendships. The Hebrew root of the term rendered "were serving him" (1 Kings 12:8) carries the meaning of employment or appointment. This suggests that Rehoboam had already given his friends positions of authority within the new administration.

Whereas the elders had advised the new king to be accommodating, his buddies recommended a hard-line approach that involved boasting and vowing to outdo his father (vss. 10-11). With this advice, the younger men flattered their king and appealed to his vanity and greed. Perhaps they thought that ingratiating

Rehoboam in this way they would ensure their status within the royal court.

The younger men first wanted Rehoboam to quote a proverb to the effect that his little finger was larger than his father's "waist" (vs. 10). This may have been a reference to Solomon's hips, which was basically the broadest part of a person's body. In other words, the new king was encouraged to boast of the superior power he wielded.

Rehoboam's young advisers also wanted him to say that the people's yokes—primarily in the form of forced labor and excessive taxes—would get heavier. Furthermore, the whips the people had endured would be replaced with "scorpions" (vs. 11). This is a reference to leather lashes spiked with pieces of sharp metal.

The intent of this message was painfully clear. Governmental burdens and punishment alike would be increased.

IV.   The People's Response: I Kings 12:13-14a, 16

The king answered the people harshly. Rejecting the advice given him by the elders, he followed the advice of the young men. . . . When all Israel saw that the king refused to listen to them, they answered the king: "What share do we have in David, what part in Jesse's son? To your tents, O Israel! Look after your own house, O David!"

Three days later, Jeroboam and all the leaders of the 10 northern tribes returned to hear the king's decision (1 Kings 12:12). Had Rehoboam been a man of wisdom, he could have realized that this was not the time to play the role of a big shot. Sadly, however, he chose the foolish advice of his younger colleagues.

On that appointed day, the delegates did not receive the news for which they had hoped. Instead, Rehoboam sharply rebuked them, telling them exactly what his young advisers had suggested. The brash king had nothing but a cold heart for the people (vss. 13-14). This turn of events was the will of the Lord, for it fulfilled what He had revealed to Jeroboam through the prophet Ahijah from Shiloh (vs. 15).

At this point the Israelites rejected the new king, realizing they could not bear his leadership. Those who were not members of the tribes of Judah and Benjamin did not see why they had to remain

---

12:16 "share"—

The noun "inheritance" translated here as "share" occurs 221 times in the OT and most frequently refers to land (in the Promised Land) that belonged to an individual Israelite and his household (Lev. 25:23; Num. 32:18; Deut. 19:14). This noun can also signify a national relationship. In the present passage, when the ten northern tribes broke off from the other two tribes at the beginning of Rehoboam's reign, they seem to be saying that they had no familial relationship with David that benefited them (providing a motivation to stay with the other two tribes) or required their continued commitment. From their perspective, they were being treated like outsiders.

devoted to Rehoboam, since he was part of the Davidic dynasty. They refused to suffer under another king from the tribe of Judah (vs. 16). Evidently the tribe of Benjamin remained under Judah's control because it was too weak and too close to Judah to break away with the other tribes (vs. 17).

Animosity among the tribes had been brewing for many years. And most people from the northern tribes realized there was nothing to be gained by remaining under Rehoboam's leadership. Thus the cry arose for the people to return to their tents. In other words, they were ready to turn their back on Judah's king and go home.

After his envoy to the Israelites was stoned to death, Rehoboam realized how dangerous it was for him to remain at Shechem. He thus fled to Jerusalem. There he gathered an army to attack the Israelites who had rejected his kingship. During this time, the Israelites of the 10 northern tribes named Jeroboam their new king (vss. 18-21).

Before Rehoboam could face Jeroboam in battle, the Lord spoke through Shemaiah [she-MAY-yah], a prophet, and commanded Rehoboam and the tribes of Judah and Benjamin not to fight. When the people heard God's message, they put away their weapons and returned to their homes (vss. 22-24).

Rehoboam's rash decision spelled the end of national unity, which had always been somewhat tenuous. (Even in King David's time rebellion had erupted under Absalom.) But the final division of the nation was a direct consequence of Solomon's idolatry and oppression. As the king and people strayed further and further from God, conditions deteriorated. Thus, as Samuel had warned, if the nation and its king forsook the Lord, calamity would surely follow (1 Sam. 12:14-15).

Discussion Questions

1. Why did the people of the 10 northern tribes appeal to Rehoboam for relief?
2. Why did Rehoboam reject the advice of his elders?
3. Why did Rehoboam follow the advice of his younger colleagues? What does this say about his character?
4. How did Rehoboam's decision sit with the 10 northern tribes? What were the consequences for the nation?
5. How was God involved in Rehoboam's decision making?
6. In what circumstances do believers sometimes find it hard to make wise and sensible decisions?

Ask Yourself . . .

Are there times when I need to seek relief and don't get it from the authority I am seeking it from?

How do I respond when I don't get the answer that seems like it would be most just?

How can I remain true to God when I face unjust decisions?

Who do I look to for advice and counsel? To my peers or to those older than me?

Who does the Bible encourage us to seek counsel from?

Illustrations

Perhaps you've met people similar to Rehoboam, people who so relish authority that they foolishly make life miserable for others. The danger with having authority is that it can subtly slip away from being responsible leadership to self-motivated control. But control is not what wise authority is about.

If we're honest with ourselves, we know that none of us is immune to the tempting power of authority. In ways big and small, it touches us all. Anyone can make people obey if they have enough authority. Shaming or embarrassing people into action can also be quite effective. Yet it takes wise and dedicated people to give up the display of power in favor of servanthood.

Rehoboam's actions show us that wisdom is not passed down from one generation to the next. The wise use of authority requires a willingness to seek out experienced counselors, and the humility to consider their advice, even when it may rub us the wrong way.

Christian leaders who serve their people well are less likely to misuse their authority. These servant-leaders cultivate a deep sense of trust and loyalty in those who work with them. These spiritual shepherds are more effective because they imitate Christ's style of leadership (Matt. 20:27-28).

The Success Trap

DEVOTIONAL READING
Matthew 27:15-26

DAILY BIBLE READINGS
Monday September 19
*1 Kings 12:20-24
Jeroboam Is Made King of
Israel*

Tuesday September 20
*1 Kings 12:25-33
Jeroboam Turns Away
from God*

Wednesday September 21
*James 4:1-6 Don't Be
Friends with This World*

Thursday September 22
*1 Timothy 6:6-10 Don't Be
Tempted by Earthly Riches*

Friday September 23
*Matthew 19:16-22 An
Ungodly Rich Man Is
Successful, but Not
Satisfied*

Saturday September 24
*Matthew 19:23-30 Jesus
Explains True Success*

Sunday September 25
*Matthew 23:1-12 The
Pharisees Only Desire
Worldly Success*

Scripture

Background Scripture: *1 Kings 12*
Scripture Lesson: *1 Kings 12:20, 25-33*
Key Verse: *After seeking advice, the king made two golden calves. He said to the people, "It is too much for you to go up to Jerusalem. Here are your gods, O Israel, who brought you up out of Egypt." 1 Kings 12:28.*

Lesson Aim

The desire for success can lead to spiritual compromise.

Lesson Setting

Time: About 900 B.C.
Place: The city of Shechem, about 25 miles north of Jerusalem.

Lesson Outline

The Success Trap

   I. Jeroboam's Inauguration: 1 Kings 12:20, 25
      A. The People Crowned Him: vs. 20
      B. He Fortified Shechem: vs. 25
  II. Jeroboam's Apostasy: 1 Kings 12:26-30
      A. His Fear: vss. 26-27
      B. His Idols: vss. 28-30
III. Jeroboam's Corrupt Worship: 1 Kings 12:31-33
      A. The High Places: vs. 31
      B. The Festival: vss. 32-33

Introduction

Anything to Keep Power

Nations and their people have always suffered because of foolish power plays made by their political leaders. Libraries are filled with books detailing unwise decisions in the past. Why did Hitler decide that he had to conquer Europe? Why did Japan attack Pearl Harbor? Reasons for war are complicated, but millions of people suffer and die because of sins committed by national leaders.

It is easy to blame powerful people for what appears to be their sins. But what about our sins? In recent years a strange notion has spread through out society suggesting that what we do is a private matter. Whatever we do—if no one gets hurt—is said to be okay. Christians have to stand against such unwise thinking.

Nationally, as the people of Israel learned, there are serious repercussions from sins at the top. The same principle works in our personal affairs, no matter how small we might think our influence is. God's Word calls us to faithful obedience to His standards. Nothing is to be gained, and much is to be lost, if we follow Jeroboam's example and violate God's will to save our positions.

Lesson Commentary

I. Jeroboam's Inauguration: I Kings 12:20, 25

A. The People Crowned Him: vs. 20

When all the Israelites heard that Jeroboam had returned, they sent and called him to the assembly and made him king over all Israel. Only the tribe of Judah remained loyal to the house of David.

Jeroboam gained Israel's throne because of a foolish decision on the part of Solomon's son Rehoboam. At his father's death, Rehoboam could have enjoyed the support of all Israel. But there was trouble coming in the person of Jeroboam, who earlier had fomented a revolt against Solomon and had been exiled to Egypt.

Jeroboam was one of a contingent drafted by Solomon when he built the bastion called Millo, a part of the fortifications of Jerusalem which seems to have been left unfinished by David. Jeroboam's zeal and skill in this work were noted by Solomon, and the king promoted him to be at the head of all the workmen from the tribes of Ephraim and Manasseh.

In this position Jeroboam heard the mutterings of the bands of unwilling laborers, saw on what a hollow foundation the splendors of Solomon rested, and began to cherish in his impetuous soul the patriotic indignation and the towering personal ambition which were to bear such momentous fruit in the future.

Jeroboam returned from Egypt and led a group of people in making a request of the new king. Tragically, the king rejected the advice of his experienced advisers and turned aside the appeal of Jeroboam and his supporters with harsh words.

The people decided to revolt (12:16) and Rehoboam fled to Jerusalem. They made Jeroboam their king. Thankfully, Rehoboam listened to a man of God, and did not start a civil war (12:22-24).

B. He Fortified Shechem: vs. 25
Then Jeroboam fortified Shechem in the hill country of Ephraim and lived there. From there he went out and built up Peniel.

Jeroboam established his capital in the city of Shechem in the territory of Ephraim. Jerusalem had been the religious center of the united kingdom. Jeroboam opened the way for not only a rival political center but also for a religious one. Peniel was the site of an important pass. Gideon destroyed the tower there and Jeroboam rebuilt the city, probably to protect Shechem from invaders from the east.

II. Jeroboam's Apostasy: 1 Kings 12:26-30

A. His Fear: vss. 26-27
Jeroboam thought to himself, "The kingdom will now likely revert to the house of David. If these people go up to offer sacrifices at the temple of the LORD in Jerusalem, they will again give their allegiance to their lord, Rehoboam king of Judah. They will kill me and return to King Rehoboam."

Jeroboam established his capital in the city of Shechem in the tribal territory of Ephraim. This was a smart move because Ephraim in particular envied Judah's power. A split had threatened in David's time (2 Sam. 20). Jerusalem had been the religious center of the united kingdom. Jeroboam opened the way not only for a rival capital, but also for a rival religious center. The secret of national unity and strength always lay in the bond of common worship of the one true God. The monarchy itself was no substitute.

The prophet Ahijah had told Jeroboam that God would make him king over 10 tribes. His dynasty was guaranteed if he obeyed the Lord (1 Kings 11:35-39). However, once he got into power, Jeroboam carried out his own plans to preserve his throne, rather than trusting God to preserve it for him.

He feared the loss of his kingdom if he permitted his people to worship at Jerusalem. He knew that their strong emotional attachment to Jerusalem and to Solomon's magnificent temple would cause the people to revert to Rehoboam.

Politically, his fears were well grounded. If Jerusalem continued to be the center of national worship, if the Levites from all parts of Israel continued to take their turns in the temple services, and if the Israelites continued to flock to the "Holy Place" three times a year—as the law commanded them to do—of course a strong reaction could set in, and they might want to unite their country.

So, what Jeroboam did is understandable. The record tells us nothing of Jeroboam's faith and trust in God. Therefore, it's not surprising that he succumbed to the temptation to try to do what he could to save his throne rather than trusting God to do it for him. If he had been a person of deep faith, he would have been content to trust the promise God had given him earlier.

12:30 "sin"—

The basic meaning of this verb is to miss the intended mark or way. A person who sins misses the standard or goal God has set for him or falls short of spiritual wholeness. Although a given deed may be deemed "sin" because it represents a violation of a standard or divine law, "to sin" has relational implications. A person sins against another person or against God (1 Sam. 2:25; Jer. 16:10-12; 1 Kings 8:46; 18:9).

B. His Idols: vss. 28-30

After seeking advice, the king made two golden calves. He said to the people, "It is too much for you to go up to Jerusalem. Here are your gods, O Israel, who brought you up out of Egypt." One he set up in Bethel, and the other in Dan. And this thing became a sin; the people went even as far as Dan to worship the one there.

Instead of preserving his kingdom by staying true to God, Jeroboam did the one thing that was certain to bring about his doom and the doom of his nation. He made two idols—calves of gold—and told two lies: (1) that it was too much trouble to go to Jerusalem to worship, and (2) that the idols were Israel's gods who had delivered them from bondage in Egypt. It presses our credulity to think that he and the people actually believed this.

The second lie actually was blasphemy, because it attributed the work of God to an idol. Regardless of how unbelievable this seems to us, Jeroboam carried out his plan.

Having started on this road of idolatry, Jeroboam never recovered. The golden calves were well-known Canaanite idols. He put one shrine at Bethel, only 12 miles north of Jerusalem, on the main road of pilgrims going to Jerusalem. The other one was at Dan, the most northerly Israelite city.

Apparently the king, who had spent time in Egypt, was not as much influenced by the idolatry he had seen there as he was by his conviction that the people needed visible objects to worship. He did not have any of the old objects of reverence that were in the temple in Jerusalem. But he did have some history to go on: Aaron's golden calf (Exod. 32:4). In fact, Jeroboam made almost the same claim to his people that Aaron had spoken before—the idol had delivered them from Egypt.

Jeroboam also appealed to the fact that it would be more convenient to worship in the north. He reminded them of how troublesome it was to travel to the temple, no doubt appealing to their love of ease and convenience.

Putting a shrine at Bethel was a master stroke. Not only did Bethel guard his southern flank, it was also a very special place in Israel's history. The Lord appeared to Jacob twice at Bethel, and Jacob raised an altar to the Lord there. During the times of the judges the ark of the covenant was kept at Bethel. Samuel held his solemn gatherings there.

The name Bethel ("house of God") means that God dwelled there in a special way. Therefore, the Israelites would conclude that their worship would be acceptable at a place that Jacob had called "the house of God . . . the gate of heaven" (Gen. 28:17).

Jeroboam put his second shrine at Dan, in Israel's extreme north, at one of the sources of the Jordan River where there was a Canaanite place of worship. Although not as important religiously as Bethel, Dan did have the reputation of being a holy city, because a shrine had been established there by Moses' grandson Jonathan and his descendants (Judg. 18:30). Along with Bethel, Dan remained a national sanctuary until Israel fell into captivity to the Assyrians in 722 b.c.

The conclusion of the king's cleverness was stunning from God's viewpoint: "And this thing became a sin" (vs. 30). By building these idols and shrines Jeroboam violated the basic concept of Israel's worship of the one true God. The worship of God was intended to set Israel apart from other peoples and nations. Their religions were incompatible with that revealed to Abraham, Jacob, and Moses.

Idolatry was forbidden by the Ten Commandments. Moses taught that Israel's religion was not based on any "form" that looked like God (Deut. 4:12). Thus, the second commandment was unique in the world. No idol of the one true God has ever been uncovered, while idols have abounded in every other religion.

Jeroboam violated the heart of Israel's faith when he built the golden calves. When Israel turned to idolatry, it was always necessary to borrow the trappings from the local pagans. Did Jeroboam think the calves actually represented God? Probably not. More likely he thought of them as a pedestal over which God was enthroned.

Nevertheless, his idolatry was a grievous sin because although the idol itself was nothing, it was a demonic spiritual force to be reckoned with. There are spiritual forces of evil, and idolatry brings people into deadly contact with these forces.

Isaiah said you cannot touch an idol and not be affected (Isa. 44:8-20). Contact with false gods infects worshipers with spiritual blindness of heart and mind. Those who worship idols become like them (Ps. 115:8; Jer. 2:5; Hos. 9:10). Because of the reality of evil power behind the idol, it is an abomination to God (Deut. 7:25). Idolatry is spiritual adultery and prostitution; it is called the gravest of sins (Deut. 31:16; Judg. 2:17; Hos. 1:2).

The consequences of Jeroboam's sin were far-reaching, leading to Israel's downfall. His idolatry set the pattern for all the kings who followed him until the Assyrians destroyed Israel. The record of 1 and 2 Kings shows that the kings who succeeded Jeroboam followed in his footsteps.

12:31 "high places"—

Although this noun can generally refer to "heights" (Deut. 32:13; Job 9:8; Isa. 58:14; Amos 4:13; Hab. 3:19), it primarily designates a place of worship. These locations represented a serious threat to the pure worship of Yahweh because they represented conflicting loyalties.

III. Jeroboam's Corrupt Worship: I Kings 12:31-33

A. The High Places: vs. 31
Jeroboam built shrines on high places and appointed priests from all sorts of people, even though they were not Levites.

Jeroboam's sin did not stop with the two golden calves at Bethel and Dan. He went throughout Israel and built pagan shrines at "high places." These were hilltops on which altars were built, sometimes for the worship of God (1 Sam. 9:12). Solomon sacrificed a thousand rams at Gibeon, "the great high place."

However, after the building of the temple at Jerusalem and Jeroboam's rebellion, "high places" became the settings of idolatrous worship. Perhaps Jeroboam invoked God's name to placate the people. However, he was severely rebuked for his sin by a man of God (1 Kings 13:1-6). Tragically, Judah also fell into idolatry at the same time under Rehoboam (1 Kings 14:23).

Jeroboam further broke the law by bringing unqualified priests into what he set up as the worship of God. This was another futile attempt to paper over his departure from the Lord.

B. The Festival: vss. 32-33

He instituted a festival on the fifteenth day of the eighth month, like the festival held in Judah, and offered sacrifices on the altar. This he did in Bethel, sacrificing to the calves he had made. And at Bethel he also installed priests at the high places he had made. On the fifteenth day of the eighth month, a month of his own choosing, he offered sacrifices on the altar he had built at Bethel. So he instituted the festival for the Israelites and went up to the altar to make offerings.

Jeroboam went the whole way in his effort to give his northern kingdom the pretext of authentic worship. He established a regular religious festival at which he made sacrifices to the golden calves. The corruption was complete, with his chosen priests presiding at pagan worship.

Jeroboam himself assumed the functions of the high priest (vs. 33), at least at the great festivals. He probably had seen the king of Egypt combine the roles of king and priest. The office of high priest was too important to be left to one of his own subjects.

"A month of his own choosing" summarizes the character of Jeroboam. Rather than choosing to follow the Lord and His instructions for worship, he established ceremonies and services that were entirely of his own devising. (For a graphic picture of the hideous practices that came to pass in Israel as a result of Jeroboam's sin, read 2 Kings 17:7-23.)

Discussion Questions

1. Why do you think Jeroboam was so fearful of losing his power?
2. Why did he turn to idols for stability in his kingdom, instead of to God?
3. What are we tempted to do in similar situations, when our security is threatened?
4. What kinds of false religion grip people today?
5. What do you learn from the fact that all the kings who succeeded Jeroboam followed his wicked ways?

Ask Yourself . . .

How do I know when I'm getting bad advice?

Have I ever retaliated when I should have compromised? If so, what were the results?

Am I holding any grudges against anyone in my biological or church family?

Have I ever attributed my successes in life to anyone but God?

How can we help people to trust completely in the Lord Jesus Christ without leaning on mixtures of superstition and false religions?

Illustrations

Too often when we read sad stories like this one about Jeroboam's sin, we think that nothing like that could ever happen to us. We would never betray God for the sake of some dumb idol. We're too smart for that, we tell ourselves.

On the other hand, every issue in which we have to make moral and spiritual choices is like the issue Jeroboam faced when he looked around and worried about how he could keep his new kingdom. He panicked, and instead of asking God for help, or seeking the wise counsel of a prophet, he pulled two golden calves out of his hat, so to speak.

If the church is to be faithful to Christ, we cannot mix our faith in Him with other strange ideas of "truth" that float about. Christians must be unequivocal in their declaration that Jesus alone saves. We cannot try to combine Christian faith with the so-called good elements in other religions. Jeroboam's sorry example is a strict warning that in a day when all religions supposedly lead to God we have to be true to God's commands. He alone is worthy of our worship, and He revealed Himself in Jesus Christ alone.

The Choice Is Yours

DEVOTIONAL READING
Joshua 24:14-18

DAILY BIBLE READINGS

Monday September 26
Joshua 24:14-24 Decide Today Whom You Will Serve

Tuesday September 27
1 Kings 18:1-8 Obadiah Protects the Lord's Prophets

Wednesday September 28
1 Kings 18:9-15 Elijah Asks Obadiah to Tell King Ahab He Is Here

Thursday September 29
1 Kings 18:16-24 Everyone Meets on Mount Carmel

Friday September 30
1 Kings 18:25-29 Baal Does Not Answer His Prophets

Saturday October 1
1 Kings 18:30-40 The Lord Does What Elijah Asks

Sunday October 2
Matthew 8:18-22 Are You Ready to Follow Jesus Today?

Scripture

Background Scripture: *1 Kings 18*
Scripture Lesson: *1 Kings 18:20-21, 30-39*
Key Verse: *Elijah went before the people and said, "How long will you waver between two opinions? If the L*ORD* is God, follow him; but if Baal is God, follow him." But the people said nothing. 1 Kings 18:21.*

Lesson Aim

Decide today to be committed only to God.

Lesson Setting

Time: 874–853 B.C.
Place: Mount Carmel

Lesson Outline

The Choice Is Yours

   I. Elijah's Challenge: 1 Kings 18:20-21
  II. Elijah's Careful Preparations: 1 Kings 18:30-35
      A. *The Altar and the Stones: vss. 30-31*
      B. *The Trench and the Water: vss. 32-35*
 III. God's Powerful Response: 1 Kings 18:36-39
      A. *The Prayer of Elijah: vss. 36-37*
      B. *The Fire of the Lord: vs. 38*
      C. *The Declaration of the People: vs. 39*

Introduction

Remain Committed

We often wonder how it was possible for the Israelites to fall under the sway of idols. After all, we would never do such a foolish thing. But the Scripture passage we will study in this week's lesson (1 Kings 18:20-21, 30-39) serves as a warning of how easy it is for us to drift away from God.

Lest we grow too smug, we need to remember that anything which siphons off our allegiance to Christ is an idol. Therefore, we have to take precautionary steps to avoid the various false gods that would entice us. Taking spiritual inventory of ourselves is one useful exercise. For instance, are we growing in our faith and worship, or are we losing our zeal and love for God, His church, and His will?

Our idols are subtler than the statues and poles venerated by the ancient Israelites. Nevertheless, idolatry is still alive and well in the West. Yes, we have to work hard to identify the idols in our culture. And though they might seem very appealing, they will defile our soul.

Lesson Commentary

I. Elijah's Challenge:
1 Kings 18:20-21

So Ahab sent word throughout all Israel and assembled the prophets on Mount Carmel. Elijah went before the people and said, "How long will you waver between two opinions? If the LORD is God, follow him; but if Baal is God, follow him." But the people said nothing.

The northern kingdom had become idolatrous. The worship of Baal (the principal Canaanite fertility deity) and Asherah [uh-SHEER-uh] (a Canaanite fertility goddess) had the official endorsement of King Ahab and Queen Jezebel (1 Kings 16:29-33).

During the reign of King Ahab, a severe famine gripped the land. Then, in the third year of the drought, the Lord commanded Elijah to go to Ahab and announce that God would soon send rain. The prophet did as he was told (18:1-2).

Sometime after that, Elijah met Obadiah (one of Ahab's palace officials) and agreed to see the king (vss. 7-16). When Ahab went out to meet the prophet, the king sarcastically asked, "Is that you, you troubler of Israel?" (vs. 17). By this Ahab implied that Elijah was nothing more than a rogue and a threat to the normal functioning of Israelite society, as seen in the severe drought the nation had to endure.

Elijah wasn't afraid to challenge Ahab's statement. The prophet declared that instead of worshiping the true God, Ahab and his pagan wife, Jezebel, venerated Baal (vs. 18). (A Baal idol was often made in the shape of a bull, representing strength and fertility and reflecting lust for power and sensual pleasure.)

Tragically, at the instructions of Jezebel, the Lord's prophets were being executed (vs. 4). One of the few prophets left to survive was Elijah. He challenged Ahab to gather the prophets of Baal and Asherah on Mount Carmel, where he would contest their power (vs. 19).

The Carmel range of mountains rises to 1,800 feet at its highest point and extends about 30 miles to the southeast from the shores of the Mediterranean Sea into the southern part of the Jezreel Valley. The series of rounded peaks and valleys in the Carmel range became a symbol of beauty and fruitfulness because of its lush tree coverage. It's not known at exactly what point along this range the contest between Elijah and the false prophets took place.

Mount Carmel was one of the heights on which places of worship to Baal had been built. In choosing this place for the coming encounter, Elijah moved into Baal's home territory. There once was also an altar of the Lord there, but Baal worshipers evidently had torn it down (vs. 30).

Ahab accepted Elijah's challenge, and summoned the 850 pagan prophets to Mount Carmel (vs. 20). Then Elijah stood in front of them and asked, "How long will you waver between two opinions?" (vs. 21). This phrase might literally be rendered, "limp along on (or between) two twigs." The idea is that Israel had not totally rejected the Lord but rather was seeking to combine worship of Him with the worship of Baal. It's almost as if the nation was doing a wild and frantic dance to appease both entities.

Elijah was forcing the Israelites to make a choice. Either the Lord was God or Baal was god, but not both of them. And the Israelites needed to decide whether they would worship and serve the Lord or Baal exclusively. Elijah made it clear that the Israelites couldn't have it both ways.

18:21 "follow"—

The text reads literally "walked after." When used metaphorically, as here, it can depict allegiance and loyalty.

Elijah's challenge was met with stony silence. So he proposed a test to reveal whether the Lord or Baal was the true God. First, the false prophets would prepare a bull to be sacrificed. They were to cut the animal in pieces and lay it on the wood of their altar, but without setting fire to it. In the meantime, Elijah would prepare the other bull and lay it on the wood of his altar, again without setting fire to it (vss. 22-23).

The false prophets would call on the name of their god, and Elijah would call on the name of the Lord. The god who answered by setting fire to the wood would be the true God. All the people agreed to this plan (vs. 24).

Elijah invited the false prophets to go first. All morning and afternoon they shouted to Baal, danced, and even injured themselves. But, perhaps to their amazement, no fire came. So now it was Elijah's turn, and the stage was set for the Lord's awesome display of power (vss. 25-29).

II. Elijah's Careful Preparations: I Kings 18:30-35

A. The Altar and the Stones: vss. 30-31

Then Elijah said to all the people, "Come here to me." They came to him, and he repaired the altar of the LORD, which was in ruins. Elijah took 12 stones, one for each of the tribes descended from Jacob, to whom the word of the LORD had come, saying, "Your name shall be Israel."

After this vivid evidence of Baal's impotence, Elijah called for the people to come while he repaired the altar of the Lord (1 Kings 18:30). The prophet did not build a new one, but instead repaired the old one that had been torn down. Evidently the Israelites had not used this altar for quite some time, and either the effects of time or some enemies had ruined it.

During this period in Israel's history, God's people existed as two separate nations—the northern and southern kingdoms. The Lord originally had intended them to be united, not divided. Elijah called attention to the covenant God had with all 12 tribes by taking 12 stones, one representing each tribe of the sons of Jacob, and building the altar with them.

Verse 31 makes reference to an incident involving Jacob that is recorded in Genesis 32:28. The Lord changed his name to Israel, which signified that the patriarch was under His ownership. Similarly, the descendants of Jacob were under God's ownership. They were to trust, obey, and follow Him, not false gods.

B.   The Trench and the Water: vss. 32-35

With the stones he built an altar in the name of the LORD, and he dug a trench around it large enough to hold two seahs of seed. He arranged the wood, cut the bull into pieces and laid it on the wood. Then he said to them, "Fill four large jars with water and pour it on the offering and on the wood." "Do it again," he said, and they did it again. "Do it a third time," he ordered, and they did it the third time. The water ran down around the altar and even filled the trench.

Elijah built an altar "in the name of the LORD" (1 Kings 18:32). This is significant, for many Israelites had been worshiping Baal. Elijah, through his actions, was refocusing their attention on the one true and living God.

Next, Elijah made a trench around the altar. It was large enough to hold "two seahs of seed." In our terms, the amount was perhaps about 13 quarts. After digging the trench, Elijah arranged the wood on the altar. He then cut a young bull into pieces and laid those pieces on the wood (vs. 33).

Elijah instructed the people to completely soak the animal pieces and wood resting on the altar he had made. Four large jarfuls of water were poured on the sacrifice and on the wood. This procedure was performed a second time and a third time, until the water was not only running off all sides of the altar, but even filled the trench (vss. 34-35).

From a human perspective, it seemed counterproductive to thoroughly drench the altar and all that was on it with water. Elijah wanted to ensure that nothing short of a genuine miracle would accomplish the burning up of the sacrifice and the wood on the altar. No one would be able to accuse the prophet of trying to deceive the people.

III. God's Powerful Response: I Kings 18:36-39

18:37 "answer"—

A. The Prayer of Elijah: vss. 36-37

At the time of sacrifice, the prophet Elijah stepped forward and prayed: "O LORD, God of Abraham, Isaac and Israel, let it be known today that you are God in Israel and that I am your servant and have done all these things at your command. Answer me, O LORD, answer me, so these people will know that you, O LORD, are God, and that you are turning their hearts back again."

In the sight of all the people, Elijah approached the altar he had made (1 Kings 18:36). This took place at the customary time when the Israelites offered the evening sacrifice; this would have been around 3:00 p.m.

The prophet did not pray to Baal or any other pagan deity. Instead, he spoke to the Lord, the God of Abraham, Isaac, and Israel (Jacob). The Israelites had forgotten who was the true God of Israel. Elijah asked Yahweh [YAH-weh] (as the Hebrews called the Lord) to make it clear that Israel's God was not Baal but Yahweh Himself.

In addition, Elijah prayed that the people would know he had faithfully followed and served the Lord. Elijah wanted God to validate him as His prophet, as the one who had foretold the drought and called for this contest at God's command.

Elijah asked the Lord to "answer" (vs. 37), or positively respond to, his request. The prophet's goal was not to make a name for himself, but for the people to repent and return to the Lord. Elijah's address underscored that God is personal, knowable, and alive. Also, the Lord had not abandoned His people, but rather they had turned their backs on Him.

The people needed to realize that Baal worship was corrupt, immoral, and disgraceful. They also needed to see that Baal was a powerless, lifeless idol, a worthless object that couldn't do anything for them. Only the God of Israel was worthy of their trust, obedience, and worship.

18:37 "answer"—

The basic meaning of this verb is to answer or reply. The issue of God answering his servant received focused attention in the context of Elijah's conflict with the prophets of Baal on Mount Carmel. After laying down the ground rules, Elijah affirmed that "the god who answers by fire—he is God." (1 Kings 18:24). The prophets of Baal cried to their "god" to no avail. There was no answer; all was silent (1 Kings 18:26, 29). When Elijah's turn came, he cried out, "Answer me" (1 Kings 18:37). The Lord answered by sending fire from heaven and consuming the sacrifice on the altar.

B. The Fire of the Lord: vs. 38

Then the fire of the LORD fell and burned up the sacrifice, the wood, the stones and the soil, and also licked up the water in the trench.

Elijah did not have to spend long hours ranting and raving like the prophets of Baal to get God to answer with fire. After Elijah had prayed, the fire of the Lord fell (1 Kings 18:38). Some think God may have struck the altar and the area around it with a bolt of lightning.

Despite all the water that had been poured over everything, fire consumed not only the sacrifice and the wood it was laid upon, but the stone altar and the soil around it as well. So that there would be no doubt concerning the power of the Lord, fire also "licked up the water in the trench." In this way God showed Himself to be true and the pagan deities of Canaan to be false.

C. The Declaration of the People: vs. 39

When all the people saw this, they fell prostrate and cried, "The LORD—he is God! The LORD—he is God!"

When the Israelites saw the Lord's awesome display of power, they fell on their faces in worship. They did not give homage to Elijah, but to the God of Israel, crying out twice, "The LORD—he is God" (1 Kings 18:39). For that moment and in that place, the Lord turned the hearts of the people back to Him.

Elijah's name means "the LORD is my God." The prophet's job was to oppose in word and deed both Baal worship and those engaged in it. Elijah succeeded in doing this while on Mount Carmel.

Discussion Questions

1. What would a victory over Baal prove to the people of Israel?
2. Why did Elijah go to great lengths to convince the people that the Lord was the one true God?
3. Why did Elijah refer to the Lord as the God of Abraham, Isaac, and Israel?
4. Why was the immediacy of God's response to Elijah's prayer important?
5. Why are the false gods of the world a poor substitute for the one true God?

Ask Yourself . . .

Does anything hinder my ability to worship God?

If I were going to convince people around me that the Lord is truly God, how would I do that?

How do I react to the times when God requires me to take a stand alone for Him?

How can I identify the false things I worship that come up in my life?

How can I keep God first in my life?

How can we prevent our lives from becoming substitutes for God?

Illustrations

When the fire fell and consumed Elijah's sacrifice and the altar, the people cried out their profession, "The LORD—he is God!" (1 Kings 18:39). In our evangelistic efforts today, we often wish for such a dramatic outpouring of God's power and the consequent spiritual turnaround. We somehow think that unbelievers will be impressed by dramatic signs. Some are and some aren't.

Jesus and the apostles made it clear that signs aren't the main issue, because God has already revealed Himself so clearly that there is no excuse for not worshiping Him. Today we have a lot more reasons to encourage our faith than the people on Mount Carmel did. We have the evidence of God's power in the resurrection of the Lord Jesus Christ. We have the record of His life and teachings. We have the offer of abundant grace and forgiveness.

Therefore, we can with confidence invite people to choose the Lord. We can invite them to investigate the claims, love, and deeds of Jesus with us. People have the right to consider the evidence before they choose Jesus. Today when the fire falls it often is in response to our prayers, our love, and our deeds on behalf of those who have yet to come to faith in Christ.

Heeding What We Hear

DEVOTIONAL READING
Proverbs 12:13-22

DAILY BIBLE READINGS
Monday October 3
*Deuteronomy 30:11-20
Listen and Obey the Word
of God*

Tuesday October 4
*Jonah 3 The People of
Nineveh Obey God's Word
from Jonah*

Wednesday October 5
*1 Kings 22:1-12
Jehoshaphat and Ahab Ask
the Prophets If They Will
Win*

Thursday October 6
*1 Kings 22:13-18 Micaiah
Is Called to Prophesize*

Friday October 7
*1 Kings 22:19-28 Micaiah
Prophesies Ahab's Death*

Saturday October 8
*1 Kings 22:29-40 King
Ahab Dies*

Sunday October 9
*John 14:15-24 If We Love
Jesus, We Will Obey Him*

Scripture
Background Scripture: *1 Kings 22:1-40*
Scripture Lesson: *1 Kings 22:15-23, 26-28*
Key Verse: *Micaiah said, "As surely as the LORD lives, I
can tell him only what the LORD tells me." 1 Kings 22:14.*

Lesson Aim
God's Word must be heeded as well as heard.

Lesson Setting
Time: 854 or 853 b.c.
Place: Samaria

Lesson Outline
Heeding What We Hear
I. Disaster Foretold: 1 Kings 22:15-23
   A. A Sarcastic Response: vss. 15-16
   B. A Pronouncement of Doom: vss. 17-18
   C. A Lying Spirit: vss. 19-23
II. Defeat Assured: 1 Kings 22:26-28
   A. The King's Order: vss. 26-27
   B. The Prophet's Assertion: vs. 28

Introduction

Speak Truth

"I can't be bought," declared the candidate for public office. However, after being elected, he found himself under great pressure from various special interest groups and also from individuals wanting favors. Consequently, his job became increasingly difficult.

Christians, too, find themselves under considerable pressure to conform to public expectations. Public opinion polls seem to indicate that if the majority favor doing something, then it must be okay. This is called morality by popular opinion, rather than by following God's standards.

Ultimately, our conduct must be shaped by our biblical convictions. And our confession of Jesus as Lord requires us to follow His standards, not those of the unsaved. Like the prophet Micaiah, we should ask God to give us the courage we need to stand for His truth.

Lesson Commentary

I. Disaster Foretold: 1 Kings 22:15-23

A. A Sarcastic Response: vss. 15-16

When he arrived, the king asked him, "Micaiah, shall we go to war against Ramoth Gilead, or shall I refrain?" "Attack and be victorious," he answered, "for the LORD will give it into the king's hand." The king said to him, "How many times must I make you swear to tell me nothing but the truth in the name of the LORD?"

The account of Micaiah [mih-KAY-uh] involved Ahab, king of Israel (874–853 b.c.), and Jehoshaphat [jih-HOSH-uh-fat], king of Judah (872–848 b.c.). Jehoshaphat's son Jehoram had married Ahab's daughter Athaliah (2 Chron. 21:6). During this time, Israel and Judah were allied against Aram, or Syria (1 Kings 22:44; 2 Chron. 18:1).

Ahab and Jehoshaphat were poles apart because Ahab was exceedingly wicked while Jehoshaphat followed the Lord

(1 Kings 22:43). For three years there had not been war between Aram and Israel. Then during the third year (around 854 to 853 b.c.), Jehoshaphat went to visit Ahab. During the visit, Ahab asked Jehoshaphat if he would join in fighting against the Arameans, who controlled Ramoth Gilead (vss. 1-4).

In Bible times, Ramoth Gilead (which means "heights of Gilead") was an important city in the territory of Gad near the border of Israel and Aram. It was about 25 miles east of the Jordan River. In the time of Solomon, one the king's 12 district officers was stationed at Ramoth Gilead to secure food for the king's household, for the city was a center of commerce (4:13). Because of its strategic location, Ramoth Gilead frequently became the scene of battles between Israel and Aram.

The king of Judah said he would join in the fight. Jehoshaphat apparently was influenced by the apparent weakness of the Syrians, by his family ties with Ahab, and by Ahab's domineering personality. But Jehoshaphat also wanted to know the Lord's will in the matter (22:5).

Ahab thus summoned his prophets, which numbered about 400, and asked them whether Israel and Judah should go to war against Aram to free Ramoth Gilead. They all approved the idea and declared that God would give His people great victory in battle. But Jehoshaphat seemed uneasy with such an ingratiating response. He knew that prophets were supposed to speak the word of the Lord, not simply what kings wanted to hear (Ezek. 13:2-3). He thus wanted to know whether there was a real prophet of the Lord, one who would give an honest answer (1 Kings 22:6-7).

Ahab noted that Micaiah was such a prophet. But the king disliked him because he consistently prophesied calamity for Ahab. Despite Ahab's personal thoughts, Jehoshaphat wanted to hear what Micaiah had to say, so a messenger was dispatched to get him (vss. 8-9).

The scene was one of great pomp. Ahab and Jehoshaphat were dressed in their royal robes and sitting on their thrones at the threshing floor near the gate of Samaria, the capital of the northern kingdom. (Threshing floors were placed in elevated areas to allow the wind to blow away the discarded hulls of grain.) Ahab's false prophets were declaring that his armies would route the Arameans in battle and free Ramoth Gilead from the hand of

22:10 "prophesying"—

In the hithpael stem the denominative verb ("to prophesy") appears 28 times. In a number of these occurrences this word describes one who makes prophetic utterances, apparently while in an ecstatic state (Num. 11:25-27). This word for prophesying is used in the Hebrew Bible not only to describe the ministry of true prophets of Yahweh who convey divine revelation, but it may also be used of false prophets whose message does not originate with the Lord at all.

the enemy (vss. 10-12).

Meanwhile, the messenger sent by the king found Micaiah and told him that all the other prophets were foretelling victory for the king. The messenger urged Micaiah to make a similar pronouncement. In other words, the king wasn't seeking guidance but rather assurance of victory. Micaiah declared that he would only state what the Lord had revealed to him (vss. 13-14).

When Micaiah arrived before the king, Ahab pointedly asked him whether Israel should go to war against Aram to free Ramoth Gilead from the enemy's control. Micaiah answered in words similar to those of the false prophets (vs. 15). However, his mocking tone of voice must have angered Ahab, who sensed this was not really the word from the Lord.

Ahab's statement in verse 16 clearly indicates that he and Micaiah had had similar encounters before. The king demanded that Micaiah speak only the truth as the Lord had revealed it to him.

22:17 "sheep without a shepherd"—

A common simile used in biblical imagery is that of sheep representing people and of a shepherd representing a leader. In this verse, the fact that the sheep are portrayed as scattered and as left without a shepherd signals that the flock of Israel had been left exposed and vulnerable to threatening circumstances.

B. A Pronouncement of Doom: vss. 17-18

Then Micaiah answered, "I saw all Israel scattered on the hills like sheep without a shepherd, and the LORD said, 'These people have no master. Let each one go home in peace.'" The king of Israel said to Jehoshaphat, "Didn't I tell you that he never prophesies anything good about me, but only bad?"

Ahab had demanded a straight answer and Micaiah gave it. He prophesied in solemn and majestic language a disastrous outcome for the military expedition. Micaiah saw all of Israel's warriors scattered in confusion on the mountains of Gilead "like sheep without a shepherd" (1 Kings 22:17). The idea is that the enemy would kill Ahab in battle and cause the Israelites to retreat in defeat.

Ahab got the message. He turned to Jehoshaphat and reminded him of what he had said earlier about Micaiah (vs. 18). Ahab implied that the prophet had spoken out of personal hatred, not with divine authority. Ahab tried to convince Jehoshaphat to disregard Micaiah and instead trust what the other prophets had said.

C. A Lying Spirit: vss. 19-23

Micaiah continued, "Therefore hear the word of the LORD: I saw the LORD sitting on his throne with all the host of heaven standing around him on his right and on his left. And the LORD said, 'Who will entice Ahab into attacking Ramoth Gilead and going to his death there?' One suggested this, and another that. Finally, a spirit came forward, stood before the LORD and said, 'I will entice him.' 'By what means?' the LORD asked. 'I will go out and be a lying spirit in the mouths of all his prophets,' he said. 'You will succeed in enticing him,' said the LORD. 'Go and do it.' So now the LORD has put a lying spirit in the mouths of all these prophets of yours. The LORD has decreed disaster for you."

Micaiah noted that he saw the Lord sitting on His throne with all the armies of heaven "standing around him on his right and on his left" (1 Kings 22:19). The vision the prophet saw was either a picture of a real incident in heaven or a parable of what was happening on earth, illustrating that the seductive influence of the false prophets would be part of God's judgment on Ahab.

In this scene of God's celestial court, He asked those around Him who could be sent to entice Ahab to go into battle against the Arameans so that the king would die in the conflict. There were many suggestions, but none apparently were acceptable (vs. 20). Then a spirit approached the royal throne and said, "I will entice him" (vs. 21). The Lord asked the spirit how it would deceive Ahab. In the response, the spirit said it would go out and inspire all the prophets of the king to speak lies. The Lord approved the plan and authorized the spirit to make it happen (vs. 22).

Micaiah told Ahab that God had put "a lying spirit" (vs. 23) in the mouths of all the king's prophets so that he might be enticed to go to war against the Arameans. In other words, God wanted the king to be killed in battle.

There are differing views about the exact identity of the lying spirit. Some think it was either Satan or one of his demonic cohorts. Another option is that a spirit from God played the role of a deceitful spirit. (But that idea might contradict 1 Samuel 15:29.) A third possibility is that the spirit merely represented the power of lies to deceive people. In this case, Ahab's 400 prophets rejected God and His truth, declaring instead fabrications of their heart.

45

Thus the Lord allowed them to be seduced by lies and in turn lead Ahab astray.

Some wonder how God could use a lying spirit to entice Ahab and bring about his death. It goes without saying that God Himself is righteous (Ps. 11:7). He also hates all evil and will one day do away with it completely and forever (Rev. 20:10-15). Moreover, He does not entice anyone to become evil (Jas. 1:13-15). Rather, people such as Ahab choose the path of wickedness. In the king's case, the Lord permitted a lying spirit to influence Ahab to decide on a course of action that hastened his deserved judgment (1 Pet. 2:7-8).

It's best not to press all the details of what Micaiah said. Perhaps to some extent God was accommodating to our limited human understanding. Despite the unanswered questions we might have, we can remain confident of God's absolute control over evil and His total goodness toward us.

II. Defeat Assured: I Kings 22:26-28

A. The King's Order: vss. 26-27

The king of Israel then ordered, "Take Micaiah and send him back to Amon the ruler of the city and to Joash the king's son and say, 'This is what the king says: Put this fellow in prison and give him nothing but bread and water until I return safely.'"

Micaiah paid dearly for his fearless declaration of the truth. A person named Zedekiah [zedd-ih-KEYE-uh] walked up and slapped him across the face. (Zedekiah apparently was the leader of the 400 false prophets.) Then the antagonist made a sarcastic remark in which he implied that Micaiah was just as much of a liar as anyone else present (1 Kings 22:24).

In response, Micaiah declared that Zedekiah would learn soon enough who was telling the truth when he found himself disgraced and seeking refuge in a secret spot (vs. 25). This turn of events would vindicate Micaiah. Despite the pressure he faced, Micaiah never wavered in his trust in God.

Ahab, by now thoroughly disgusted with Micaiah, ordered that the prophet be arrested and taken back to Amon, the governor of Samaria, and to the king's son, Joash (vs. 26). (Evidently Joash was in charge of the prison in the city.) Micaiah was only to be fed a diet of bread and water until Ahab returned safely from the battle.

In making this statement, Ahab showed how much contempt he had for what the prophet had said. However, the ultimate test of who was correct would come during the battle with the Arameans.

B. The Prophet's Assertion: vs. 28

Micaiah declared, "If you ever return safely, the LORD has not spoken through me." Then he added, "Mark my words, all you people!"

Micaiah could have changed his message to spare himself from further abuse and anguish. But instead, he courageously affirmed what the Lord had revealed to him. Remaining ever confident in God, Micaiah declared that if Ahab returned safely from the battle, then the Lord had not spoken through the prophet.

This wasn't idle boasting on Micaiah's part. At stake were life and death outcomes. So serious was the matter that the prophet declared, "Mark my words, all you people!" (1 Kings 22:28).

Verses 29 through 38 reveal that Micaiah was correct in what he had predicted. Despite Ahab's efforts to conceal his presence, an arrow (which an Aramean soldier had randomly shot) hit the king and brought about his eventual death. In the end, Ahab could not escape God's judgment.

Discussion Questions

1. Why did Micaiah at first respond in a sarcastic way to Ahab?
2. How did Micaiah depict Ahab's defeat and death in battle?
3. Why did God send a lying spirit to deceive Ahab?
4. How did Micaiah respond when Ahab ordered him to be imprisoned?
5. How do you account for Micaiah's courage in the presence of Ahab?
6. Why is it important for us to remain faithful to God despite the pressures we might face to do otherwise?

Ask Yourself . . .

What situations am I facing in my life that might be pressuring me to not remain faithful to the Lord?

Where do I have a hard time speaking the truth of God's word in spite of opposition?

How strong do I stand for God when I feel threatened for stating the truth?

What can give me courage in difficult circumstances?

Illustrations

Perhaps Micaiah is not as well known to us as some of the other prophets in the Old Testament. Nevertheless, his encounter with King Ahab gives us a vivid glimpse of what it was like to remain faithful to God while living in an evil, idolatrous society. Micaiah's life serves as a forceful lesson of how important it is for us to remain faithful to God despite the pressures we might face to do otherwise.

With so much wickedness in the world, it's sometimes hard for us to discern how God is working through various circumstances. Perhaps at times we feel upset or discouraged by the crime and hatred all around us. God's answer to us is the same as it was for His people in the Old Testament. He wants us to be patient and trust Him to bring about His perfect justice.

Admittedly it's not always easy for us to be patient when we see a multitude of wrongs taking place all around us. We should remember that God is in full control and that His timing, not ours, is perfect. If we find the sinful activities of the world abhorrent, He does even more. As the all-powerful and just Lord, He cannot allow iniquity to go unpunished forever. At the right time He will deal with all who have rebelled. Until then we need to continue to trust Him fully, even when we cannot figure out why He has allowed certain events to take place.

We can rest assured that the Lord is directing all things according to His wise plans, that He is always in control. We also know that He will never let us down, regardless of how difficult our times might be.

Better Than You Expected

DEVOTIONAL READING

1 Samuel 12:1-15

DAILY BIBLE READINGS

Monday October 10
  *Isaiah 55:6-11 God's Ways
  Are Not Our Ways*

Tuesday October 11
  *Haggai 1:5-11 Give
  Careful Thought to Your
  Plans*

Wednesday October 12
  *2 Kings 5:1-6 Naaman
  Wants to be Cured of
  Leprosy*

Thursday October 13
  *2 Kings 5:7-12 Naaman
  Doesn't Like What He Is
  Told*

Friday October 14
  *2 Kings 5:13-18 Naaman
  Asks for Forgiveness of His
  Unbelief*

Saturday October 15
  *Proverbs 19:16-21 The
  Lord's Purpose Prevails*

Sunday October 16
  *Luke 12:13-21 The Parable
  of the Rich Fool*

Scripture

Background Scripture: *2 Kings 5:1-19*
Scripture Lesson: *2 Kings 5:2-6, 9-14*
Key Verse: *Many are the plans in a man's heart, but it is
the LORD's purpose that prevails. Proverbs 19:21.*

Lesson Aim

God's plan for us may not match our expectations.

Lesson Setting

Time: About 840 B.C.
Place: The city of Samaria, the capital of Israel.

Lesson Outline

Better Than You Expected

I. Naaman Goes to Israel: 2 Kings 5:2-6
  A. *The Slave Girl's Advice: vss. 2-3*
  B. *The King's Permission: vss. 4-6*
II. Naaman Is Healed: 2 Kings 5:9-14
  A. *Elisha's Command: vss. 9-10*
  B. *Naaman's Anger: vss. 11-12*
  C. *Naaman's Obedience: vss. 13-14*

Introduction

Healing in
Unexpected Ways

Naaman fits our impression of generals, except for one thing: his eventual humility. We usually expect military leaders to be like General George Patton. It is questionable whether he would have done what Naaman did.

But in this story we have to get beyond the trappings to see what God was doing. God is the God of the unexpected. He touches us in ways that defy our usual thinking. No one could have scripted what happened to Naaman through the advice of a slave girl. No one could have scripted that he would change his mind and get over his anger.

But God's word is powerful. God's word releases the Holy Spirit to do unexpected things. Our faith is tested when we face what seem to be unreasonable demands from the Lord. Naaman's story encourages us to keep going, trusting that God's promises will be fulfilled.

Lesson Commentary

I. Naaman Goes to Israel: 2 Kings 5:2-6

A. The Slave Girl's Advice: vss. 2-3

Now bands from Aram had gone out and had taken captive a young girl from Israel, and she served Naaman's wife. She said to her mistress, "If only my master would see the prophet who is in Samaria! He would cure him of his leprosy."

After King Jeroboam's rebellion and apostasy, a succession of wicked kings followed him. The worship of God in Israel reached an all-time low during the 22-year reign of King Ahab (874–853 b.c.). He and his wife Jezebel introduced the corrupt worship of Baal and brought in hundreds of prophets of Baal which gradually became the focus of religious life in Israel.

At this desperate time, God sent His prophet Elijah to Israel. His preaching, confrontations with Israel's wicked kings, and miracles are recorded in 1 Kings 17—21 and 2 Kings 1. Elisha was Elijah's attendant (2 Kings 3:11), his disciple, and ultimately his successor. Elisha was an ordinary farmer until one day when he was plowing Elijah suddenly confronted him and threw his cloak around him, a signal that he was supposed to assume the prophetic mantle.

Elisha ran after Elijah and begged to kiss his parents good-bye. Elijah told him to go back home, where he butchered his oxen and cooked the meat over the fire provided by his burning plow. Then Elisha left to follow Elijah (1 Kings 19:19-21). He saw the whirlwind that caught up Elijah and saw the fiery chariot and horses (2 Kings 2:1-12).

Left standing alone in the desert, Elisha took up his work right away. He began his ministry during the reign of King Jehoram (852–841 b.c.) and prophesied in Israel for 55 years, covering the reigns of four kings. Some eighteen episodes in his life are told in 2 Kings 2—13.

Elisha revealed to King Jehoshaphat the winning strategy over the Moabites; he provided oil for a poor widow to use and sell so her sons would not be taken as slaves; he restored the Shunammite's son to life; he saved the prophets from poisoned stew; he fed one hundred men; then he met and healed the Syrian general Naaman.

Naaman was a remarkable individual (vs. 1). He commanded the army of Ben Hadad, king of Damascus and sworn enemy of Israel. He had risen in the king's estimation because of the battles he had won "through the Lord." (This phrase shows that the biblical writers saw God's control over all such events.) Naaman was a brave, courageous fighter, but he suffered from a skin disease. This was not necessarily what we know as leprosy today, because the Hebrew word covered various skin diseases.

Whatever it was, it carried not only physical but also social consequences, in Israel at least. People who suffered with skin diseases were avoided at all cost, out of fear of becoming contaminated (Lev. 13:14). Consequently, they became social outcasts. But in Syria the disease did not keep Naaman from holding high office.

Of course, he could not hide his affliction and probably talked about it around the house enough for the servants to be aware of it. The general enjoyed a good reputation at home, too, because one of the slave girls who served there had compassion on him and suggested how he could be cured.

This girl had been taken captive in one of the ongoing fights between the Syrians (or Arameans) and the Israelites. That was the traditional way of treating the losers; you took their women and girls for whatever purposes you wanted.

But this young girl knew something Naaman did not. Somehow

> **5:1 "respect"—**
>
> *Based on the general meaning of the verb "to lift up," to "lift up the face of . . ." carries various meanings. A person who was "lifted of face" like Naaman, was an esteemed and respected individual.*

she had heard about the miracles being performed by Elisha (2 Kings 3—4). Either the girl had witnessed a miracle herself, or she had heard about one of them from her friends and relatives before she had been taken to Syria.

There was no doubt she was convinced that Elisha was God's prophet and that he could heal her master Naaman. Of course, she could not tell this to the general directly, so she sent the word through his wife.

This is a remarkable example of faith and compassion joined in one God-fearing person who overlooked hatred, resentment, revenge, and racial animosity for the sake of bringing hope and healing to a sick enemy. When Jesus said, "Love your enemies," this is what He was talking about.

Of course, the girl needed great courage, too. What is faith if it does not incorporate courage? She could have been accused of impertinence, or worse, even to make such an impossible suggestion. It was totally unrealistic to expect Israel's enemy commander to cross the lines for the sake of trying to heal his disease.

B. The King's Permission: vss. 4-6

Naaman went to his master and told him what the girl from Israel had said. "By all means, go," the king of Aram replied. "I will send a letter to the king of Israel." So Naaman left, taking with him ten talents of silver, six thousand shekels of gold and ten sets of clothing. The letter that he took to the king of Israel read: "With this letter I am sending my servant Naaman to you so that you may cure him of his leprosy."

Amazingly, Naaman's wife told him what her servant girl had said, and he in turn swallowed his pride to do this. Imagine going to the king and saying, "This young Israelite girl told me how to be healed."

On the other hand, news of what Elisha had been doing swept across political boundaries. The prophet by this time was a man of renown, even among the Syrians. So perhaps the servant's advice was not so strange after all.

However the discussion progressed, the outcome was clear: "By all means, go." What did Naaman have to lose? He certainly was not going to be healed in Syria. Who knows how many cures he had tried over the years?

Of course, the risky thing was to gain safe passage to the king of Israel. Somehow, the king of Aram got the young girl's message mixed up. He wrote to the king of Israel and appealed to him to heal Naaman's leprosy. Naaman made sure the king of Israel would be open to the idea by taking a peace offering of considerable worth: about 750 pounds of silver, 150 pounds of gold, and ten changes of clothing. At today's prices we're talking close to a million dollars. This lavish gift demonstrates the way things were done at that time. The more lavish the gift, the better your chances of getting what you want.

II. Naaman Is Healed: 2 Kings 5:9-14

A. Elisha's Command: vss. 9-10
So Naaman went with his horses and chariots and stopped at the door of Elisha's house. Elisha sent a messenger to say to him, "Go, wash yourself seven times in the Jordan, and your flesh will be restored and you will be cleansed."

The king of Israel is not named in the story. It could have been Joram or Jehu, both ungodly men. Anyway, the king took the letter as an insult and as an invitation to a fight (vs. 7). He rightly understood that he could not heal anyone, and tore his robes in disgust. Why would Naaman walk into his palace with such a request?

Word of the king's distress and anger reached Elisha (vs. 8). He told him to calm down and send Naaman to his house. Elisha sensed that Naaman represented another opportunity for the world to know that God had not abandoned Israel. In this case, Elisha explained that Naaman would know the truth.

Naaman was not an Israelite, but a pagan Gentile, hardly a prime candidate for a word from the Lord. Of course, from the call of Abraham it was clear that God's people were supposed to be a light to the nations. But instead they found themselves fighting and killing the Gentiles most of the time.

Naaman accepted the invitation and pulled up at Elisha's house with his entourage from Syria. So far so good for Naaman, but now he faced some problems. First, the prophet Elisha did not greet him at the door—a social snub no doubt. Second, Elisha sent a messenger with a very insulting command.

53

5:11 "Invoke" the name of
the Lord his God—

*The verb "to call" basically
means to get someone's
attention through the sound
of the voice in order
to establish contact. In a
context where the speaker
desires or expects some form
of divine intervention, the
phrase might mean "to ask
for Yahweh's help" or "to
intercede with Yahweh." In
the present passage, Naaman
expected that Elisha would
intercede with Yahweh on his
behalf with some beautiful
and impressive prayer.*

He told Naaman to go to the Jordan River and wash seven times in it, and then he would be healed. This, of course, was not what Naaman had expected. This was no way to treat a visiting dignitary who had fought and won many battles.

Elisha's word was a command and a promise. It was a take-it-or-leave-it proposition. Now the ball was in Naaman's court.

B. Naaman's Anger: vss. 11-12

But Naaman went away angry and said, "I thought that he would surely come out to me and stand and call on the name of the LORD his God, wave his hand over the spot and cure me of my leprosy. Are not Abana and Pharpar, the rivers of Damascus, better than any of the waters of Israel? Couldn't I wash in them and be cleansed?" So he turned and went off in a rage.

Naaman's anger and rage are understandable. He knew he had been snubbed: "I thought that he would surely come out to me . . ." He had not even been greeted properly by the prophet. How could the prophet tell what was wrong with him if he had not even laid eyes on him?

Naaman's anticipated treatment had been scorned: "I thought that he would . . . call on the name of the LORD his God, wave his hand over the spot and cure me of my leprosy." Wasn't that the way the priests did it in Damascus? Not so with Elisha.

Naaman's pride had been insulted: "Are not . . . the rivers of Damascus better than any of the waters of Israel?" In other words, what makes the Jordan River so special? Now it's your river versus ours. And ours are cleaner than yours, so if I want to take a bath, I'll take it in my own river.

This is where Naaman stumbled. He was willing to listen to a young slave girl. He was willing to take gifts to an enemy king. He was willing to call on an enemy prophet. But the prophet's instructions were too humiliating. Naaman would not play the fool for any Hebrew prophet. In his rage he decided to pack it up and go home.

C. Naaman's Obedience: vss. 13-14

Naaman's servants went to him and said, "My father, if the prophet had told you to do some great thing, would you not have done it? How much more, then, when he tells you, 'Wash and be cleansed'!" So he went down and dipped himself in the Jordan seven times, as the man of God had told him, and his flesh was restored and became clean like that of a young boy.

The story took an amazing turn. Before Naaman had a chance to leave Samaria, his servants pleaded with him. Was the young girl among them? Perhaps. But if not, some other servants who had come under her influence had traveled with Naaman's party.

The strong ties of love and trust came to the surface, and they boldly interceded. They took a great risk in approaching a general in a rage. Nevertheless, they went to him with commonsense.

They appealed to his sense of logic. After all, the prophet had not demanded "some great thing." Naaman was not required to tear his clothes, repent, and wail on some ash heap for a week. All he had to do was wash in the Jordan. What could be easier than that?

What he had to do didn't require physical courage, but it was just as tough. He not only had to take a bath seven times, but also swallow his pride and his humiliation at not being received by Elisha. That's harder than fighting sometimes.

How long did it take Naaman to decide? We don't really know. But in the end, Naaman decided to believe Elisha. He bathed seven times in the Jordan and he was healed. The healing was so complete that his skin was "like that of a young boy" (vs. 14). God had accomplished a mighty miracle through the words of Elisha the prophet. But his words became effective only by faith. Naaman's humiliation became the key to his restoration.

Perhaps Elisha was at the river also, because afterwards Naaman and his party went back to him. At last Naaman got to see the prophet, who did not wave his hands over him or even cry out to God for healing. Did Naaman learn anything from his healing? He confessed to Elisha, "Now I know that there is no God in all the world except in Israel" (vs. 15). That was what he was supposed to discover.

The story of Naaman's healing shows how God revealed Himself in Israel, even in the midst of apostasy and corruption. It also shows how God revealed Himself to Gentiles. This point was cited by Jesus (Luke 4:27) as proof that the good news had come to Gentiles as well as to Jews.

Discussion Questions

1. How do you account for the slave girl's boldness?
2. What risks did she take?
3. Why do you think Elisha rebuffed Naaman when he came to his door?
4. From this story, what do you find are some obstacles to faith and obedience?
5. How do we learn from those whom God sends us today?
6. How does the Word of God work today to bring people to faith in Christ?

Ask Yourself . . .

How would I respond in a circumstance that required me to step out and boldly tell someone what God is saying?

What risks am I willing to take to encourage someone to take God at His word?

How do I respond when I have to humble myself to receive what God has for me?

What should my response be when God's plan does not match my expectations?

Illustrations

Naaman's story shows how easy it is to stumble over little things that seem foolish to us. The apostle Paul said the Greeks (the wise people of his day) considered his talk about Jesus as foolishness. Too simple, they said. How could God raise anyone from the dead?

Sophistication and power stand in the way of faith that leads to salvation. Jesus said we have to become like little children to be saved. We must humble ourselves before Him. That's what Naaman must have looked like to his peers.

The church needs to stand against the wisdom of the world in declaring its message of hope and healing. Many people despair of finding help in the church because they find the message confusing, or they worry about keeping rules and coming up to the church's social expectations.

We need never be embarrassed by offering a simple Gospel "for it is the very power of salvation to those who are believing." We must always guard against adding things that would scare people away. Faith in Jesus alone is the way to salvation and heaven.

October 23, 2005
Royalty and Loyalty

A Heart for Worship

DEVOTIONAL READING
Psalm 122:1-9

DAILY BIBLE READINGS

Monday October 17
2 Chronicles 30:1-9
Hezekiah and the People
Plan to Celebrate Passover

Tuesday October 18
2 Chronicles 30:10-20 The
People Reluctantly Come
to the Celebration

Wednesday October 19
2 Chronicles 30:21-27 The
Lord Blesses Their
Celebration of Worship

Thursday October 20
Colossians 3:12-17 Act As
God's Chosen People

Friday October 21
Romans 12:1-8 Change
Your Thinking and
Worship God

Saturday October 22
John 4:4-14 Jesus Talks
with a Samaritan Woman

Sunday October 23
John 4:15-26 True
Worshipers Will Worship
in Spirit and Truth

Scripture

Background Scripture: *2 Chronicles 29—30; 2 Kings 18—20*
Scripture Lesson: *2 Chronicles 30:1-6, 8-12*
Key Verse: May the LORD, *who is good, pardon everyone who sets his heart on seeking God. 2 Chronicles 30:18b-19a.*

Lesson Aim

A changed heart brings you to worship.

Lesson Setting

Time: Around 715 B.C.
Place: Judah and Jerusalem

Lesson Outline

A Heart for Worship

I. The King's Decision: 2 Chronicles 30:1-5
   A. *Celebrate the Passover: vss. 1-3*
   B. *Proclaim the Decision in Israel: vss. 4-5*

II. The King's Letter: 2 Chronicles 30:6, 8-9
   A. *Return to the Lord: vs. 6*
   B. *Serve the Lord: vs. 8*
   C. *Receive God's Grace: vs. 9*

III. The People's Response: 2 Chronicles 30:10-12
   A. *Some Refused: vs. 10*
   B. *Others Repented: vss. 11-12*

Introduction

A Time to Decide

Suppose you sent out invitations to a party and no one came. How would you feel? What questions would come to your mind? Probably you would ask yourself, "What's wrong with me since no one came?" God's people often have to ask the same question. Why are we not more interested in serving the Lord? All of the institutions and programs of the church are in place, but we seem to have more important things to do.

Early in Hezekiah's reign, time, pride, idolatry, and wickedness kept the people from following the Lord. The king sensed that a profound spiritual malaise existed among his people. Hezekiah thus started a program of bold reforms, but when it came to observing the Passover, the people had to decide whether they would return to the Lord. God is also calling us to choose life with Him, not death apart from Him.

Lesson Commentary

I. The King's Decision: 2 Chronicles 30:1-5

A.   Celebrate the Passover: vss. 1-3

Hezekiah sent word to all Israel and Judah and also wrote letters to Ephraim and Manasseh, inviting them to come to the temple of the LORD in Jerusalem and celebrate the Passover to the LORD, the God of Israel. The king and his officials and the whole assembly in Jerusalem decided to celebrate the Passover in the second month. They had not been able to celebrate it at the regular time because not enough priests had consecrated themselves and the people had not assembled in Jerusalem.

Our studies this quarter cover the time from King Hezekiah in Judah to the fall of Jerusalem in 586 b.c. It was a period of momentous struggle between obedience to God and moral and spiritual failure. In the end, the people rejected God's law, His warnings about coming judgment, and His calls to repentance and faith.

Repentance and renewal came under the leadership of King Hezekiah (715–686 b.c.). He was one of Judah's most noteworthy rulers. Perhaps the greatest test of his faith arose when the Assyrians—who had conquered the northern kingdom of Israel—

also attacked the southern kingdom of Judah in 701 b.c. (This was during the fourteenth year of Hezekiah's reign.) The king prayed for deliverance, and God saved His people from their invaders (2 Chron. 32:1-23).

Hezekiah began his reign after Ahaz, his wicked and idolatrous father, died (28:27). Right from the start, Hezekiah sought to follow the Lord (29:2). This was a wise decision, for the king recognized that disobedience to the law had brought God's judgment. Hezekiah first repaired the temple and removed all forms of defilement from it. He then rededicated the sanctuary to the Lord (vss. 3-36).

The king next sent a message to everyone in Israel and Judah, including those in the territories of Ephraim and west Manasseh. Hezekiah invited them to the temple in Jerusalem for the celebration of the Passover in honor of "the LORD, the God of Israel" (30:1).

Passover was the first of the three great festivals of the Israelite people. It was normally observed in every household on the fourteenth day of the first month of the religious year (Exod. 12:16, 18). It involved the slaying and eating of a lamb, together with bitter herbs and bread made without any yeast. Passover was designed to commemorate Israel's deliverance from Egypt.

It's important to note that Hezekiah's invitation included Israelites living throughout the land of Canaan. Although the Assyrians had already exiled the northern kingdom (in 722 b.c.), Hezekiah still wanted to include the Israelites remaining in that region to come to the Passover observance. This is because the king never lost sight of the fact that God's covenant had been made with all 12 tribes and that His promises included them all (Ezek. 37:15-28).

At this time, the repair and consecration of the temple was still underway. Thus the people were not ready to observe the Passover at the prescribed time. The law made provision for the festival to be postponed if a person was absent on an important journey or was ritually defiled (Num. 9:9-12). Evidently Hezekiah interpreted this ordinance to include the priests who had not yet consecrated themselves to ministry (2 Chron. 29:34). In any case, all the people of Israel had not had time to gather to assemble at Jerusalem (30:3). Thus, it was necessary to delay the celebration until "the second month" (vs. 2).

Hezekiah's devotion to God was not merely an external matter; he also wholeheartedly trusted in the Lord. He looked to God for help and relied on Him to bring deliverance in times of affliction. The extent of Hezekiah's trust in the Lord was unparalleled. In fact, no king of Judah who preceded him and none who came after him remained as committed to God. When we consider how steadfast Hezekiah was in his faith, it is little wonder that the Lord was with him (2 Kings 18:5-7).

B. Proclaim the Decision in Israel: vss. 4-5

The plan seemed right both to the king and to the whole assembly. They decided to send a proclamation throughout Israel, from Beersheba to Dan, calling the people to come to Jerusalem and celebrate the Passover to the LORD, the God of Israel. It had not been celebrated in large numbers according to what was written.

Pagan influences and practices abounded when Hezekiah became Judah's king. For example, his father was guilty of offering sacrifices and burning incense at the high places where false gods were worshiped (2 Kings 16:4). Many of the people openly practiced idolatry, prostitution, and child sacrifice. When we realize the moral climate of Hezekiah's day, it is amazing he enacted policies that were pleasing to God and met with His approval.

Some of the sweeping changes implemented during Hezekiah's reign included destroying the local pagan shrines, demolishing the stone pillars representing foreign gods, and cutting down the carved wooden figures of the Canaanite goddess Asherah (18:4). For many years the Israelites had been burning incense to a bronze snake that Moses had made (Num. 21:4-9). As part of his reform efforts, Hezekiah had the bronze snake demolished. This cultic object was called Nehushtan, which may mean "bronze thing" (that is, a piece of bronze; 2 Kings 18:4).

Perhaps one of Hezekiah's most noteworthy reforms was the celebration of the Passover. The plans for observing it in the second month of the Hebrew religious calendar, rather than the first month (2 Chron. 30:1-3), met with the approval of the king and his officials (vs. 4). They thus sent a proclamation throughout all Israel, from the town of Beersheba in the south to Dan in the north. Everyone was invited to come to Jerusalem for the festival (vs. 5).

According to official records kept at the time, this was the largest crowd of people that had ever observed the event. The fact that Israelites throughout Canaan were included indicates that there were many followers of God left in what used to be the territory of the northern kingdom. This remained true despite more than two centuries of backsliding and the Assyrian invasion.

II. The King's Letter: 2 Chronicles 30:6, 8-9

A. Return to the Lord: vs. 6

At the king's command, couriers went throughout Israel and Judah with letters from the king and from his officials, which read: "People of Israel, return to the Lord, the God of Abraham, Isaac and Israel, that he may return to you who are left, who have escaped from the hand of the kings of Assyria."

The messengers Hezekiah dispatched went everywhere in Canaan with an official letter from him. The document reminded the people that many of their ancestors and Israelite relatives to the north had been unfaithful to the Lord, and He punished them horribly for their rebellion (2 Chron. 30:7). The letter also said that, for those who had survived the invasion of the Assyrians, it was time to turn back to "the Lord, the God of Abraham, Isaac and Israel" (vs. 6).

Here we find Hezekiah appealing to the remnant (namely, those who had survived Assyrian slaughter and deportation) on the basis of the Abrahamic covenant. While the kingdom had been divided and many Israelites endured the hardship of exile far from their homeland, God's promises remained in effect. Thus, the king urged them to worship the Lord. If they did, He would relent from His anger.

B. Serve the Lord: vs. 8

"Do not be stiff-necked, as your fathers were; submit to the Lord. Come to the sanctuary, which he has consecrated forever. Serve the Lord your God, so that his fierce anger will turn away from you."

In the past, the Israelites had stubbornly refused to follow the

30:8 "stiff-necked"—

Like the similar expressions "to turn the face from" and "to turn the back on," the expression "to be stiff-necked" is a common biblical metaphor for refusal to obey the Lord. It means to be or become obstinate. It suggests an attitude of recalcitrance and rejection of sound advice or counsel on the part of those who should be open to correction.

Lord and heed His commands. The official document Hezekiah had drafted spelled out concrete ways the people could get right with God.

First, the remnant needed to "submit to the LORD" (2 Chron. 30:8). This is the opposite of rebellion. It meant overcoming pride, which is the heart of sin. It also meant humbling oneself, which is the heart of obedience.

Second, God's people needed to "come to the sanctuary." As one of three annual pilgrim festivals, Passover required attendance at the Jerusalem temple. Thus, it made sense for the Israelites to show their devotion to the Lord by coming to the structure that He had set apart as holy forever.

The king urged the Israelites to serve, or worship, "the LORD your God." If they did, His righteous indignation—His "fierce anger"—against them would be "[turned] away." In other words, He would discontinue judging them for their past transgressions.

30:9 "gracious"—

The adjective used here for "gracious" occurs 13 times in the Hebrew Bible. The cognate verb ("to be gracious") is more common, appearing 78 times. The various forms of this root describe a beneficent action undertaken on behalf of a recipient who is viewed with tender concern by one who is in a position of superiority over him. This gracious action is motivated only by a desire to improve the lot of a person or object that stands in dire need.

C. Receive God's Grace: vs. 9

"If you return to the LORD, then your brothers and your children will be shown compassion by their captors and will come back to this land, for the LORD your God is gracious and compassionate. He will not turn his face from you if you return to him."

Hezekiah stated in his letter that if the remnant returned to the Lord, the enemies that had captured their families would show pity and send them back home (2 Chron. 30:9). The king declared that Israel's God, unlike the idols they had worshiped in the past, was "gracious and compassionate." If the people turned back to Him, He would no longer turn His back on them.

The invitation to the Passover revealed that Hezekiah had much more in mind than a national celebration. His letter underscored the heart of the issue—repentance, faith, and obedience. God is both just and merciful. He had judged Israel's sin (vs. 7) and now He wanted to forgive and restore His people (vs. 9).

The Gospel reveals that all of us have sinned and deserve God's judgment. We also learn that Jesus died on the cross for our sins. When we repent of our transgressions and put our trust in Him, we experience God's mercy, grace, and love.

III. The People's Response:
2 Chronicles 30:10-12

A. Some Refused: vs. 10

The couriers went from town to town in Ephraim and Manasseh, as far as Zebulun, but the people scorned and ridiculed them.

Hezekiah's invitation forced people to make a decision. Tragically, some of the people not only refused his invitation, but also scorned and ridiculed the messengers who had brought it. They revealed by their actions that they had no desire to worship and serve the Lord. Instead, they wanted to remain enslaved to their powerless and lifeless idols.

It is still this way today. No matter how kind and merciful God promises to be, some people remain entrenched in their sin. Rather than repenting, they redouble their efforts to do wrong. The passing pleasure of sin means more to them than the eternal joy found in Christ.

B. Others Repented: vss. 11-12

Nevertheless, some men of Asher, Manasseh and Zebulun humbled themselves and went to Jerusalem. Also in Judah the hand of God was on the people to give them unity of mind to carry out what the king and his officials had ordered, following the word of the LORD.

Thankfully not everyone from the former northern kingdom rejected Hezekiah's invitation. Some from the territories once belonging to "Asher, Manasseh and Zebulun" (2 Chron. 30:11) were willing to humble themselves and make the trip south to Jerusalem. The Lord undoubtedly blessed them for their obedience.

The response in Judah was much more favorable to Hezekiah's invitation. God gave many people a strong desire to unite in obeying the orders of the king and his officials. After all, they were "following the word of the LORD" (vs. 12). Here we see God's grace at work in the efforts of His people to please Him. It still remains true today that the hand of the Lord is seen at work in those who choose to follow His will in their daily lives.

Discussion Questions

1. What did Hezekiah ask the people of Israel to do?
2. Why did the king decide to celebrate Passover a month later than usual?
3. To whom was the invitation sent to observe the religious festival?
4. What did Hezekiah, in his official letter, urge the people to do? What varying responses did he get?
5. What are some specific ways we can rekindle our love and devotion to God?

Ask Yourself . . .

In what areas is God inviting me to come back to Him?

Are there some areas of my life from which the Lord is asking for me to repent?

Have I truly received His mercy and grace?

Do I know the Lord as a God of compassion? How can I show that to others around me?

How can my godly life influence those around me?

Illustrations

This week's lesson teaches us that holding fast to the Lord brings the greatest security. Just as Hezekiah found, all other forms of security, regardless of what they are, can never give us the peace, joy, and satisfaction He provides. The more we rely on Him to meet our needs and to bring us through our pressing trials, the more joyful and godly we will become.

God wants us to look to Him for assurance and confidence. When we encounter problems that seem too great to handle or experience anguish that feels unbearable, we can rely on Him to bring us through the ordeal. We can rest assured that He will uphold us and watch over us every step of the way, remembering that He is full of compassion for us.

It is not always easy to hold fast to the Lord in those difficult moments in our lives. We must reject the false forms of security we might be tempted to rely on. We can do so knowing that the hope and assurance God provides are real and lasting.

Never Beyond His Reach

DEVOTIONAL READING
2 Chronicles 6:36-42

DAILY BIBLE READINGS

Monday October 24
  Acts 9:1-9 Saul, Killer of the Lord's Followers, Is Called by Jesus

Tuesday October 25
  Acts 9:10-19 Saul Is Visited by Ananias and Baptized

Wednesday October 26
  Acts 9:20-31 Saul Is Accepted and Begins Evangelizing

Thursday October 27
  2 Chronicles 33:1-6 Manasseh Does Evil in the Eyes of the Lord

Friday October 28
  2 Chronicles 33:7-13 Manasseh Turns toward God

Saturday October 29
  2 Chronicles 33:14-20 Manasseh Serves God

Sunday October 30
  Romans 8:1-11 Jesus Sets Us Free from Sin

Scripture

Background Scripture: *2 Chronicles 33:1-20; 2 Kings 21*
Scripture Lesson: *2 Chronicles 33:1-13*
Key Verse: *And when he prayed to him, the LORD was moved by his entreaty and listened to his plea; so he brought him back to Jerusalem and to his kingdom. Then Manasseh knew that the LORD is God.*
2 Chronicles 33:13.

Lesson Aim

No one is beyond redemption.

Lesson Setting

Time: 696–642 B.C.
Place: Judah and Jerusalem

Lesson Outline

Never Beyond His Reach
  I. Idolatry Sanctioned: 2 Chronicles 33:1-6
      A. *Detestable Practices: vss. 1-2*
      B. *Idolatrous Worship: vss. 3-5*
      C. *Depraved Actions: vs. 6*
  II. Wickedness Approved: 2 Chronicles 33:7-9
      A. *Total Apostasy: vss. 7-8*
      B. *Unrestrained Evil: vs. 9*
  III. Divine Punishment Experienced:
        2 Chronicles 33:10-13
      A. *Warnings Ignored: vs. 10*
      B. *Captivity Experienced: vss. 11-12*
      C. *Divine Mercy Encountered: vs. 13*

Introduction

Learning the Hard Way

What are the lessons we have learned the hard way? What stories could we tell about how we suffered because we thought we knew better? It is humbling to admit that we blew it because we were too proud and stubborn to listen to someone's advice or to the wisdom of God's Word.

Nevertheless, how thankful we are that God often delivers us from our follies. Also, how wonderful it is to tell others about His grace. We should mention not just our mistakes, but also God's mercies and goodness.

Imagine King Manasseh assembling the people in Jerusalem, acknowledging his wrongdoing to them, and thanking God for restoring him. Now that would send a powerful and unforgettable message!

Lesson Commentary

I. Idolatry Sanctioned: 2 Chronicles 33:1-6

A. Detestable Practices: vss. 1-2

Manasseh was twelve years old when he became king, and he reigned in Jerusalem fifty-five years. He did evil in the eyes of the LORD, following the detestable practices of the nations the LORD had driven out before the Israelites.

King Hezekiah's reign, which lasted from 715–686 b.c., was marked by sweeping religious reforms in the southern kingdom of Judah and its capital, Jerusalem (2 Chron. 31). It was also during this time that Assyria invaded Judah. Despite the Assyrian threat, the Lord delivered His people from the enemy (32:1-23). Around that time, when Hezekiah became deathly ill, God healed him. The Lord also materially blessed the king (vss. 24-32).

When Hezekiah died, the people of Judah and Jerusalem honored him. Then his son, Manasseh, was crowned the next king (vs. 33). He was 12 years old when he ascended the throne as the fourteenth monarch of Judah (33:1), though it's possible he co-reigned with Hezekiah for about a decade. Manasseh ruled longer than any other king (55 years, until 642 b.c.). He also had the dubious distinction of being the nation's most wicked monarch.

Despite Hezekiah's godly influence, Manasseh reverted to the evil ways of his grandfather, Ahaz. For instance, Manasseh fell into the practices of the Canaanites whom God had driven out in the days of Joshua (vs. 2). Canaanite worship was "detestable" to God because it included the veneration of idols (prohibited by the Ten Commandments) and degenerate sexual practices.

Despite Hezekiah's reforms, idolatry, immorality, and injustice had not been completely eradicated from the Israelite psyche. No matter how much the prophets preached against these iniquities, the people reverted to pagan practices again and again. In fact, not long after Hezekiah's death, idol worship was easily revived in Judah.

Perhaps one of the hardest questions to answer is how the son of one of Judah's most godly kings could turn out to be its most notorious idolater. One explanation is that seeds of Manasseh's debauchery were sown in the soil of pride evident in Hezekiah's waning years. We read in 32:25 that "Hezekiah's heart was proud." And even though he repented (vs. 26), the episode involving the Babylonian envoys was laced with insecurity and arrogance (2 Kings 20:12-19; 2 Chron. 32:31).

A second explanation hinges on the fact that kingly families in ancient times encountered unique pressures because of polygamy (especially with respect to the king's harem). There was also constant infighting between the many wives and children of a king, especially over who would get royal favors and eventually accede to the throne.

A third explanation, which is related to the other two, notes that the sons of a king were often waited on, flattered, courted, and treated as superior beings whose ways should never be checked. Given no hard work, their self-conceit was fostered at every turn. Perhaps all three of these explanations applied to Manasseh.

In addition, some think that there were a cadre of princes and aristocrats in Judah and Jerusalem who never really embraced Hezekiah's sweeping reforms. Thus, upon his death, they seized the opportunity to reintroduce idolatry in Judah and to win Manasseh's approval of its practice.

It's appropriate that Manasseh's name means "causing to forget," for the new king chose to ignore the high moral values of his father. In fact, the overarching theme of Manasseh's reign is that "he did evil in the eyes of the Lord" (2 Chron. 33:2). God wanted

Judah to be a witness and blessing to the whole world. Sadly, however, Manasseh rejected this goal. Instead, he chose the path of wickedness and brought his nation to the brink of destruction. Tradition holds that he even executed Isaiah the prophet by having him sawn in two (Heb. 11:37).

B. Idolatrous Worship: vss. 3-5

He rebuilt the high places his father Hezekiah had demolished; he also erected altars to the Baals and made Asherah poles. He bowed down to all the starry hosts and worshiped them. He built altars in the temple of the LORD, of which the LORD had said, "My Name will remain in Jerusalem forever." In both courts of the temple of the LORD, he built altars to all the starry hosts.

During Hezekiah's reign, he destroyed the local shrines, which were used to venerate idols. But when Manasseh came to power, he rebuilt these centers of pagan worship. What's more, the king constructed altars for the images of Baal (the supreme fertility god of the Canaanites) and set up sacred poles for worshiping Asherah (the goddess of fertility). Moreover, Manasseh bowed down before all the stars in the sky and "worshiped them" (2 Chron. 33:3).

Judah's king didn't stop there. Inside the temple, where only the Lord was supposed to be worshiped, Manasseh built altars for pagan gods and for the stars (vs. 4). He also placed these altars in both courtyards of the temple, namely, the court of the priests and Levites and the court open to the public (4:9; 33:5). Thus the Jerusalem sanctuary no longer was the exclusive dwelling place for the Lord; instead, it became the haunt of lifeless idols.

Manasseh, by his actions, not only defiled the temple, but also disgraced and dishonored God's name, which represents truth, beauty, holiness, and righteousness. The king put his idols on a par with the Lord, and did all he could to keep the people from worshiping the true God.

C. Depraved Actions: vs. 6

He sacrificed his sons in the fire in the Valley of Ben Hinnom, practiced sorcery, divination and witchcraft, and consulted mediums and spiritists. He did much evil in the eyes of the LORD, provoking him to anger.

33:6 "sorcery"—

This practice was expressly forbidden in the Torah. These acts of religious apostasy were profoundly influential in leading Judah astray from orthodoxy. The first of several words used in 2 Chronicles 33:6 for these offensive religious practices refers to a type of magical practice that included the interpreting of alleged signs. This word is used only 10 times in the Hebrew Bible to refer to the practice of soothsaying.

Like Ahaz, his grandfather (2 Chron. 28:3), Manasseh practiced human sacrifice (33:6), perhaps in veneration of the Ammonite god Molech. Judah's king even went so far as to offer up his own children in "the Valley of Ben Hinnom." This was located just outside the western wall of Jerusalem. It was a dumping ground for all kinds of refuse, much of which was burned. The valley itself became a symbol of impurity.

Manasseh did many other sinful things that aroused the Lord's anger. For instance, the king practiced sorcery, divination, and witchcraft, and he consulted with mediums and spiritists (2 Chron. 33:6). Divination involved the inspection of animal entrails, smoke, oil in water, the flights of birds, and phenomena in the sky. These were done in an attempt to determine the plans and purposes of the gods so that their hostility could be avoided and their favor gained. Sorcery and witchcraft used magical or mystical rituals to bring about desired results. And mediums and spiritists claimed to be able to contact and consult with the dead.

God had strictly forbidden all of these practices (Deut. 18:9-12), for He saw them as pagan substitutes for Him. Manasseh, rather than depend on the Lord for guidance and grace, made use of occult means. In effect, the king was denying God's power, wisdom, and love. It's no wonder the Lord was provoked to anger.

II. Wickedness Approved: 2 Chronicles 33:7-9

A. Total Apostasy: vss. 7-8

He took the carved image he had made and put it in God's temple, of which God had said to David and to his son Solomon, "In this temple and in Jerusalem, which I have chosen out of all the tribes of Israel, I will put my Name forever. I will not again make the feet of the Israelites leave the land I assigned to your forefathers, if only they will be careful to do everything I commanded them concerning all the laws, decrees and ordinances given through Moses."

Previously Ahaz had closed the temple to any use and placed his altars and idols elsewhere (2 Chron. 28:23-25). Manasseh's wickedness surpassed even this when he set up a stone image of a foreign god in the temple (33:7). In other words, the king defiled the place

---

33:6 "witchcraft"—

The denominative verb is used only six times in the Hebrew Bible. Apart from 2 Chronicles 33:6, where it describes King Manasseh's sinful participation in sorcery, this word appears elsewhere as a substantive to mean "sorcerer." Sorcerers employed such things as spells, incantations, charms, amulets, and various rituals in order to acquire secret knowledge that set them apart as those who could interpret the present and predict the future.

reserved exclusively for Yahweh's name. Manasseh thus flouted God's promise of blessing for obedience. He also ignored the warnings of exile for disobedience to the law (vs. 8).

B. Unrestrained Evil: vs. 9

But Manasseh led Judah and the people of Jerusalem astray, so that they did more evil than the nations the LORD had destroyed before the Israelites.

God had pledged to never remove the people of Israel from the land they had inherited. This promise, of course, was preconditioned on their obedience to all the stipulations of the covenant. The atrocities Manasseh committed greatly jeopardized the presence of the people in the land (2 Chron. 33:9). They listened to him and did even more sinful things than the nations the Lord had wiped out when the Israelites entered Canaan.

III. Divine Punishment Experienced: 2 Chronicles 33:10-13

A. Warnings Ignored: vs. 10

The LORD spoke to Manasseh and his people, but they paid no attention.

In the midst of all of this corruption, God used various prophets to warn Manasseh and his subjects about the disastrous consequences of idolatry, immorality, and injustice. Undoubtedly these spokespersons for God also urged the people to repent. Tragically, no one paid any attention (2 Chron. 33:10).

B. Captivity Experienced: vss. 11-12

So the LORD brought against them the army commanders of the king of Assyria, who took Manasseh prisoner, put a hook in his nose, bound him with bronze shackles and took him to Babylon. In his distress he sought the favor of the LORD his God and humbled himself greatly before the God of his fathers.

This was a time of tremendous change and power struggles on the international scene. God used these events to punish and humble Manasseh. The Lord allowed Assyrian army commanders to invade Judah and capture their king. In accordance with the customs of the day, they put a hook in Manasseh's nose, tied him up in chains, and took him to Babylon, which was under Assyrian control at that time (2 Chron. 33:11).

Judah's king, in his dire situation, could see that the pagan gods and goddesses he had been venerating were nothing more than powerless and lifeless objects. They could not prevent his captivity and they were unable to bring about his release. Thus, in Manasseh's moment of dire need, he asked the Lord for forgiveness and help (vs. 12).

C.   Divine Mercy Encountered: vs. 13

And when he prayed to him, the LORD was moved by his entreaty and listened to his plea; so he brought him back to Jerusalem and to his kingdom. Then Manasseh knew that the LORD is God.

According to 2 Chronicles 7:14 (which is part of Solomon's prayer), when God's people humbly prayed, turned back to Him, and abandoned their sin, He would forgive them and make their land fertile once again. We find this happening to some extent in the life of Manasseh. The Lord listened to his prayer, saw how repentant he was, and allowed him to go back to Jerusalem and rule as king.

From this we see that God was not just punishing Manasseh for his transgressions. The Lord was also seeking a higher goal. Through the king's plight, he gained a fresh understanding of God's absolute sovereignty (33:13). The genuineness of Manasseh's repentance is seen in the reforms he enacted after returning to Jerusalem (vss. 15-16).

Manasseh's experiences anticipated those of the people of Judah. The king's abominations resulted in invasion and captivity, while his repentance brought him relief and restoration to the land. To some extent the experience of God's people would parallel this.

Discussion Questions

1. In what ways was Manasseh's reign different from that of Hezekiah?
2. What are some of the detestable practices associated with Manasseh's reign?
3. What did God allow to happen to Manasseh as a result of his evil deeds?
4. How did Manasseh respond to the way God dealt with him?
5. Why is repenting of our sin, rather than wallowing in it, always the best course of action we can take?

Ask Yourself . . .

How can I deal with some of the detestable practices I see in my world today?

What do I see as consequences from God for those evil deeds?

How do I respond when God deals strictly with my sin?

Do I ever find myself pouting in my sin when God brings me correction? How can I learn to respond in repentance more quickly?

Illustrations

After many years of sin, Manasseh decided to seek the Lord. But what does it mean to seek the Lord? Some people believe all one has to do is recite a pious-sounding prayer and that is the end of it.

More accurately, seeking the Lord is a process in which God's people individually and collectively turn their hearts to Him in unwavering devotion. It means they go out into the world and make His presence known through their words and deeds. Seeking the Lord means they dedicate every aspect of their lives to His service. It is done through spending time reading the Bible and in prayer before Him.

When we seek the Lord fully, we figuratively hand Him a blank sheet to fill in, with our name signed at the bottom. We orient our minds and hearts to His will. We effectively say no to our sinful ways and yes to His holy desires. At times we might not feel inclined to seek the Lord as much as we ought. It is in those moments that we should pray to God for a willing mind and heart.

We should not think that seeking the Lord is an entirely personal matter. God wants us to encourage one another to remain spiritually in tune to Him. For instance, when we see our fellow Christians spiritually struggling, we can stand by their side and offer consolation and support. We can also remember to pray for one another and ask that God would enable us to remain loyal to Him and His people.

Seeking the Lord is the only viable option we have, especially after we repent of our misdeeds. When we leave behind habitual sinful practices, the void in our lives has to be filled with something. The unwholesome things of the world are an unworthy alternative, however. We should seek to replace sinful actions with a lifestyle that is wholesome and pure. Over time we will discover that repenting of sin and turning to the Lord is the best decision we could ever make.

The Mark of a Christian Leader

DEVOTIONAL READING
Psalm 119:1-8

DAILY BIBLE READINGS
Monday October 31
  Genesis 12:1-9 Abraham Honors God with Obedience
Tuesday November 1
  Genesis 45:1-11 Joseph Sees His Leadership as a Gift from God
Wednesday November 2
  2 Chronicles 34:1-13 Josiah's Reign Follows the Lord
Thursday November 3
  2 Chronicles 34:14-21 The Book of the Law Is Found
Friday November 4
  2 Chronicles 34:22-28 Huldah, the Prophetess, Explains What the Law Says
Saturday November 5
  2 Chronicles 34:29-33 Josiah Vows to Honor the Covenant of the Lord
Sunday November 6
  Luke 22:24-30 Jesus Explains How to Be a Leader

Scripture

Background Scripture: *2 Chronicles 34—35; 2 Kings 22—23*
Scripture Lesson: *2 Chronicles 34:1-3, 21, 29-33*
Key Verse: *Because your heart was responsive and you humbled yourself before God when you heard what he spoke against this place and its people, and because you humbled yourself before me and tore your robes and wept in my presence, I have heard you, declares the* LORD. *2 Chronicles 34:27.*

Lesson Aim

Godly leaders honor the Lord.

Lesson Setting

Time: 640–609 B.C.
Place: Judah and Jerusalem

Lesson Outline

The Mark of a Christian Leader
  I. Josiah's Religious Reforms: 2 Chronicles 34:1-3, 21
      A. *Josiah's Reign: vss. 1-2*
      B. *Josiah's Actions: vs. 3*
      C. *Josiah's Directive: vs. 21*
  II. Josiah's Covenant: 2 Chronicles 34:29-33
      A. *The Covenant Read: vss. 29-30*
      B. *The King's Pledge: vs. 31*
      C. *The People's Pledge: vs. 32*
      D. *The King's Legacy: vs. 33*

73

Introduction

What You Don't Know Can Hurt You

The adage is true. What we don't know can hurt us. This even applies to our spiritual renewal. The tenth edition of Merriam-Webster's Collegiate Dictionary says that renewal involves restoring something to freshness or vigor. The process is so thorough that what had become deteriorated is now new.

How can adults experience spiritual renewal, especially in their relationship with God? As this week's lesson indicates, it requires specific, costly steps. This is especially true in terms of the energy spent, the time invested, and the personal sacrifices made. Often both individual and group activities will help foster spiritual renewal and encourage one to make difficult choices and tough decisions.

Most Christians who have sought to renew their relationship with God would agree that the change, though in their best interests, was not easy. They also would concur that the benefits they obtained were worth the effort.

Lesson Commentary

I. Josiah's Religious Reforms: 2 Chronicles 34:1-3, 21

A. Josiah's Reign: vss. 1-2

Josiah was eight years old when he became king, and he reigned in Jerusalem thirty-one years. He did what was right in the eyes of the LORD and walked in the ways of his father David, not turning aside to the right or to the left.

Josiah was the sixteenth king of Judah, the son of Amon, and the grandson of Manasseh. He was eight years old when his reign began, and his rule lasted 31 years (from 640–609 b.c.; 2 Chron. 34:1). Unlike his father and grandfather, Josiah did what was pleasing in the Lord's sight. In this regard, he followed the example of his ancestor David by seeking to obey the Lord (vs. 2). That a wicked king such as Amon could have such a godly son and successor such as Josiah is a testimony to the grace of God at work.

B. Josiah's Actions: vs. 3

In the eighth year of his reign, while he was still young, he began to seek the God of his father David. In his twelfth year he began to purge Judah and Jerusalem of high places, Asherah poles, carved idols and cast images.

Josiah's reforms took place in three stages. When he was crowned as Judah's king, the young monarch was evidently blessed with wise advisors who despised the idolatrous ways of Amon. Perhaps due to their influence, Josiah, at the age of 16, began worshiping God, just his ancestor David had done (2 Chron. 34:3).

Then, four years later, when Josiah was 20, he decided to destroy the local shrines in Judah and Jerusalem. He also sought to demolish the sacred poles for worshiping Asherah along with the carved idols and cast images of foreign gods (vss. 3-5). Josiah's reform was even more extensive than that of Hezekiah. For instance, Josiah extended his cleansing of the land into the territory that once belonged to northern kingdom of Israel (vss. 6-7).

Josiah took such harsh and drastic measures because he knew that pagan practices were deeply ingrained in the lives of Judah's citizens. He understood that if his renewal efforts were to have any lasting impact, he would have to weed out all ungodly practices. His sincere desire was that everyone under his rule would worship and serve the Lord rather than the things of the world.

The third stage of the king's reforms took place when he was 26, during the eighteenth year of his reign (vs. 8). Josiah ordered that the temple be repaired under the supervision of Hilkiah the high priest (vs. 9). Monies were collected to fund the work (vss. 10-11), and the laborers performed their tasks honestly (vs. 12).

The three decades of Josiah's reign were characterized by peace and prosperity as well as spiritual reform. Given the years preceding and following it, Josiah's tenure as Judah's monarch were among the most pleasant experienced by the nation.

C. Josiah's Directive: vs. 21

"Go and inquire of the LORD for me and for the remnant in Israel and Judah about what is written in this book that has been found. Great is the LORD's anger that is poured out on us because our fathers have not kept the word of the LORD; they have not acted in accordance with all that is written in this book."

While the monies that had been collected were being given to various supervisors, Hilkiah found a copy of "the Book of the Law"

34:3 "purge"—

This verb has traditionally been understood as meaning "burn away, purge." The term, as used here, appears to have a Deuteronomic flavor (Deut. 17:12; 19:13; 22:22).

(2 Chron. 34:14). This portion of Scripture contained the ordinances and directives that the Lord had given to Moses. Apparently it had somehow become either lost or misplaced during the ungodly tenures of Manasseh and Amon.

It did not take Hilkiah long to recognize how valuable and important this document was. He gave it Shaphan, the court secretary (vs. 15). Shaphan, in turn, took the scroll to Josiah and reported that all the officials were doing the tasks the king had assigned to them (vs. 16). For instance, the collected revenues had been given to the supervisors and workers (vs. 17). Also, Shaphan mentioned the discovery of a scroll in the temple (vs. 18).

When the king heard about the document, he directed his official to read it to him. Shaphan then read everything, including the blessings and curses associated with the Mosaic covenant. When Josiah heard what was written in God's Word, he tore his clothes in sorrow (vs. 19). He then summoned several of his trusted officials and related his concerns (vs. 21).

The king ordered the priest and his company to "inquire of the LORD" about the future of kingdom, including the remnant in Israel and Judah. Josiah figured out that his ancestors had disobeyed the Lord and violated His commands. They thus deserved God's righteous judgment.

Josiah's confession was based on what he had heard in God's law. He could easily discern how far the Lord's people had fallen from His holy standards. Judah's king did not offer any excuses. He could see that God's wrath had resulted in the destruction of the northern kingdom and the dispersion of its people. Josiah sensed that the same end would befall Judah. Therefore, he confessed and sought God's will.

When we first become Christians, our relationship with God feels strong. We are eager to do whatever He asks and we desire to conform our lives to His will. Over time, however, our devotion may wane. We start worrying about our problems and become distracted by the pressures of life. Before long we realize that we are not as close to the Lord as we wanted to be.

This common situation underscores the importance of renewing our relationship with God. In Romans 12:1, Paul urged us to do this very thing. Because of all the Lord has done for us in Christ, we are to give ourselves fully to Him in service for His glory. As we renew our relationship with God, we will be pure and pleasing sacrifices to Him.

If our relationship with God has weakened to a certain extent, it will take some time for us to renew it. At first the task might seem daunting. Rather than give up altogether, we should take gradual and realistic steps in renewing our relationship. At times the process will be difficult and costly in terms of what God leads us to do or stop doing. Regardless of the steps that are taken, we can rest assured that it will be well worth our time, effort, and sacrifice.

II. Josiah's Covenant: 2 Chronicles 34:29-33

A. The Covenant Read: vss. 29-30

Then the king called together all the elders of Judah and Jerusalem. He went up to the temple of the LORD with the men of Judah, the people of Jerusalem, the priests and the Levites—all the people from the least to the greatest. He read in their hearing all the words of the Book of the Covenant, which had been found in the temple of the LORD.

Hilkiah and some other court officials left right away and went to talk with Huldah the prophet. She lived in the northern part of Jerusalem (2 Chron. 34:22). The prophetess revealed that the Lord would punish Judah, its capital, and its people in accordance with what was written in His Word (vs. 24). God was indignant over the fact that His people had rejected Him by offering sacrifices to foreign gods and worshiping their idols (vs. 25).

Huldah declared that God was aware of Josiah's sorrow and humility over the disaster that awaited the people of Judah (vss. 26-27). Because the king was genuinely distressed by what he had heard, the Lord would not bring His promised judgment until after Josiah had died and was buried in peace (vs. 28).

Josiah immediately summoned the leaders of Judah and Jerusalem (vs. 29). Then the king—along with the priests, Levites, and all the people of Judah—went to the Lord's temple (vs. 30). Individuals from all walks of life came to hear what Josiah had to say. The common people stood with the politicians, nobles, and priests. Josiah knew that spiritual reform had to change everyone.

The king took the long-lost scroll and read to the people everything that had been read to him. His hope was that they would be stirred to confession and repentance. The people had to be instructed and awakened by the power of God's Word. They also had to be alerted to the coming dangers. Josiah knew they had to change course, if they were to avert disaster. The king, realizing that he alone could not change the heart of the nation, hoped the people would follow his example.

34:31 "covenant"—

This phrase signifies a sacred and binding agreement. A "covenant of the Lord" would appear to be a covenant that is ratified in his name through a solemn oath, in which Yahweh serves both as witness and guardian.

B.   The King's Pledge: vs. 31
The king stood by his pillar and renewed the covenant in the presence of the LORD—to follow the LORD and keep his commands, regulations and decrees with all his heart and all his soul, and to obey the words of the covenant written in this book.

The temple was the place where God had pledged to show His presence among His people. It was thus a fitting spot for the king and his subjects to meet and rededicate themselves in service to God. Josiah positioned himself by one of two bronze pillars in the portico of the temple and openly entered into a covenant before the Lord. This means the king made a binding agreement with God. By making his solemn promise to keep the law, Josiah sought to lead the nation in the paths of righteousness (2 Chron. 34:31).

C.   The People's Pledge: vs. 32
Then he had everyone in Jerusalem and Benjamin pledge themselves to it; the people of Jerusalem did this in accordance with the covenant of God, the God of their fathers.

Josiah had everyone make the same pledge he had made (2 Chron. 34:32). The Mosaic covenant reminded God's people that the Lord had chosen them to be a light to the nations. If they forsook this path, however, they would experience divine judgment.

In a huge gathering such as this there would be tremendous pressure to conform. No one could see into the hearts of others. No one can tell who was sincere and who was hypocritical. Promises would be easy to make in the heat of the moment, but hard to keep when the lure of idolatry beckoned.

Nevertheless, Josiah did all he could to bring God's laws to the awareness of the people. The portion of Scripture discovered in the temple was the spark that brought the king and his people to repentance, confession, and commitment to follow the Lord.

D. The King's Legacy: vs. 33

Josiah removed all the detestable idols from all the territory belonging to the Israelites, and he had all who were present in Israel serve the LORD their God. As long as he lived, they did not fail to follow the LORD, the God of their fathers.

In addition to renewing the covenant, Josiah also destroyed all the idols from the entire land of Israel, and he commanded that everyone worship only the Lord. For the rest of Josiah's rule as king, the people did not turn away from the God of their ancestors (2 Chron. 34:33).

Perhaps unlike any previous king in Judah's recent memory, Josiah personally supervised the destruction of idolatrous artifacts throughout the land. For instance, everywhere in the northern environs of Canaan Josiah tore down Asherah poles, crushed idols to dust, and smashed incense altars, before returning to Jerusalem (vs. 7). A serious decline in Assyria's power (brought about by the death of Ashurbanipal) gave Josiah the freedom to pursue such extensive spiritual reforms.

God may have used Josiah's commitment to Scripture to restore the devotion of His people to His Word. Undoubtedly this desire to follow the Hebrew sacred writings helped keep the hope of the nation alive during its long years of exile in Babylon. The truths of God's Word would also give the people encouragement and fortitude during the difficult time of restoration to follow.

Discussion Questions

1. What was the general character of Josiah's reign?
2. What did Josiah do during the eighth year of his reign?
3. What directive did Josiah give to his officials?
4. What specific steps did Josiah and the people take to renew the covenant?
5. What changes in our lives can we anticipate seeing as we draw closer to the Lord?

Ask Yourself . . .

Do I need a renewal in my walk with the Lord?

Are there things in my life that have become "idols" to me?

What specific steps do I need to take to clean these out my life?

What steps can I take to have a more willing heart before the Lord?

Are there times when I hear the Word of the Lord and it breaks my heart? When?

Illustrations

The reforms that Josiah undertook suggest that renewing our relationship with the Lord requires specific, sometimes costly steps. It is good for us to be aware of this truth before we begin the process of drawing closer to Him. Otherwise, we might become so discouraged or demoralized that we will quickly give up when the situation becomes tough.

As we seek to renew our relationship with the Lord, we should first examine our spiritual lives. For example, do we think about things that are pure and wholesome, or do we tend to dwell on matters that are immoral or offensive? How eager are we to pray to God, study His Word, and give Him praise? If we are honest with ourselves, we will probably discover at least one area of our inner lives that needs to be changed.

We should next examine the external aspects of our spiritual lives. For instance, which is more important to us—fellowshipping with God's people or doing questionable things with our unsaved acquaintances? What is our attitude toward worshiping with other believers? How enthusiastic are we to share the good news of Christ with our unsaved family members and friends? Do we go out of our way to encourage other believers who are struggling in their faith?

Self-evaluation will be painful at times. As part of the renewal process, the Lord will bring to mind areas of our lives He wants to change. It might be the way we think, the words we use, or the activities we do. Regardless of how God brings about change in our lives, His ultimate goal will be to draw us closer to Him.

Learning to Listen

DEVOTIONAL READING
Proverbs 4:20-27

DAILY BIBLE READINGS
Monday November 7
   *Acts 28:23-28 Gentiles Will
   Listen, Even If Others Don't*

Tuesday November 8
   *Jeremiah 25:1-7 The
   People Will Not Listen to
   God*

Wednesday November 9
   *Jeremiah 25:8-14 The
   People Will Pay the
   Consequences for Their
   Choices*

Thursday November 10
   *Jeremiah 26:1-6 Jeremiah
   Tells the People to Repent*

Friday November 11
   *Jeremiah 26:7-15
   Jeremiah's Life Is
   Threatened because of His
   Message*

Saturday November 12
   *Jeremiah 26:16-24 The
   People Realize Jeremiah's
   Words Are from God*

Sunday November 13
   *Romans 10:14-21 We Must
   Listen to God's Message*

Scripture

Background Scripture: *Jeremiah 25—26;
2 Chronicles 36*
Scripture Lesson: *Jeremiah 25:1-7; 26:12-13*
Key Verse: *"You did not listen to me," declares
the LORD, "and you have provoked me with what
your hands have made, and you have brought harm to
yourselves." Jeremiah 25:7.*

Lesson Aim

We must learn how to listen to God.

Lesson Setting

Time: 609–605 B.C.
Place: Judah and Jerusalem

Lesson Outline

Learning to Listen
   I.   Failure to Listen: Jeremiah 25:1-7
        A. *The Declaration of Jeremiah: vss. 1-3*
        B. *The Proclamation of Others: vss. 4-6*
        C. *The Judgment of the Lord: vs. 7*
   II. Call to Reform: Jeremiah 26:12-13

Introduction

Listen Carefully

Our ears are made so that sound vibrations can pass to the part of our brain that controls hearing. It starts with sound waves causing our eardrums to vibrate. Thousands of individual fibers make this possible. As a result, messages are sent through an auditory nerve to the center of hearing in our brain, which then classifies and interprets the sounds.

We are made to listen carefully, but when it comes to listening to God, something else comes into play—not our physical ears, but rather our spiritual hearts. This is why Scripture admonishes us to hear and heed God's Word. The focus isn't on our auditory nerves, but instead on our hearts.

To listen to God means to love, honor, worship, and obey Him. We can hear His truth with our ears but fail to respond with our hearts. In this case, we may hear but we do not love Him with the totality of our hearts, minds, and wills. We should avoid such faulty hearing at all costs.

Lesson Commentary

I. Failure to Listen: Jeremiah 25:1-7

A. The Declaration of Jeremiah: vss. 1-3

The word came to Jeremiah concerning all the people of Judah in the fourth year of Jehoiakim son of Josiah king of Judah, which was the first year of Nebuchadnezzar king of Babylon. So Jeremiah the prophet said to all the people of Judah and to all those living in Jerusalem: For twenty-three years—from the thirteenth year of Josiah son of Amon king of Judah until this very day—the word of the LORD has come to me and I have spoken to you again and again, but you have not listened.

When God called Jeremiah to be a prophet in 626 b.c., the tiny southern kingdom of Judah was under the control of the Assyrians, who had captured and destroyed the northern kingdom of Israel in 722 b.c. However, in 612 b.c., Nineveh fell to the Babylonians and this led to the quick demise of the Assyrian empire. The Egyptians tried to help the Assyrians. Tragically, Judah's King Josiah was killed when he foolishly intervened against the Egyptians (609 b.c.).

Nebuchadnezzar of Babylon defeated the Egyptians, and Judah passed under his control. Judah's remaining kings were weak vassals who sometimes sided with and at other times tried to rebel against the Chaldeans. They failed in their attempts, and in the end Nebuchadnezzar crushed Jerusalem in 586 b.c. In this tumultuous time, Jeremiah was deeply concerned about his country's political and religious affairs. His messages of repentance went unheeded, and he was carried off to Egypt by a rebellious remnant left behind by Nebuchadnezzar (Jer. 43:5-7).

Jeremiah 25:1-7 was delivered in the fourth year of King Jehoiakim's reign (605 b.c.). He succeeded Jehoahaz, who reigned only three months after Josiah's death (2 Kings 23:30-34; 2 Chron. 36:1-4). Both Jehoahaz and Jehoiakim owed their thrones to Pharaoh Necho of Egypt, who had defeated and killed Josiah in battle. Jehoiakim's name originally was Eliakim, but Necho changed it to show the vassal's subjection to him.

During Jehoiakim's reign, the Babylonians invaded the land, and Judah's king became his vassal. This arrangement lasted for three years, but then Jehoiakim rebelled. The Babylonians reacted swiftly to put down the rebellion and even made use of troops from other royal vassals in the region (2 Kings 24:1-2).

During Josiah's reign, he had enacted many sweeping religious reforms. Despite these, the tide of spiritual decay could not be stopped. In fact, during the reigns of subsequent kings such as Jehoiakim, it continued unabated. Such prophets as Jeremiah and Uriah consistently opposed Jehoiakim and his policies, and they incurred his wrath.

King Jehoiakim had Uriah murdered and he tried to suppress Jeremiah, even to the extent of burning his prophecies (Jer. 26:20-23; 36:20-26). Jehoiakim refused to listen to God's warnings about rebelling against Nebuchadnezzar. Though Jehoiakim died before arriving as a captive in Babylon (2 Chron. 36:6), his son Jehoiachin endured this terrible ordeal himself (vss. 9-10).

Jeremiah 25:1 indicates that the Lord's message to His prophet was intended for "all the people of Judah." This included the rich and the poor, the mighty and the weak, men and women, adults and children, and slaves and free persons. No one was exempt from what God declared through Jeremiah.

The prophet stated three facts about his career: (1) his sermons came from God; (2) he preached faithfully; and (3) the people refused to listen. This pattern had persisted for over 23 years among all God's people (vss. 2-3).

During Jeremiah's long career, God used him to bring powerful

---

25:3 "to obey"—

In a number of contexts, the verb "to hear" means to listen to, to heed by acting upon, or to put into practice something that was said. It can occur with several prepositions or with a preposition plus the noun for "voice" and carry the idea of obeying. This expression (the verb "to hear" followed by a preposition "in/with" and the noun "voice") frequently occurs with the idea of obedience. At the very least it means to give careful attention to someone's request and more often signifies obeying the person in the context.

object lessons to the attention of the rulers and the people. For instance, when God sent him to the potter's house (18:2), Jeremiah reminded the people, "Like clay in the hand of the potter, so you are in my hand" (vs. 6). Jeremiah then bought a jar and took it outside Jerusalem, where he smashed it in front of a crowd (19:1-10). He also announced, "This is what the LORD Almighty says: I will smash this nation and this city just as this potter's jar is smashed and cannot be repaired" (vs. 11).

On another occasion God instructed Jeremiah to buy and wear a linen belt and bury it in a cave. Many days later God told Jeremiah to go find the belt, which had rotted (13:1-6). The Lord explained, "In the same way I will ruin the pride of Judah and the great pride of Jerusalem" (vs. 9).

Jeremiah's decision never to marry was another of God's object lessons about His coming judgment on the nation (16:1-4). Additional vivid lessons were the baskets of spoiled figs (24:1-10), the yoke (27:1-22), and Jeremiah's buying a piece of land outside Jerusalem (32:1-15).

Jeremiah's career was marked not only by the nation's refusal to listen, but also by outright hostility. He was threatened with death if he did not stop his preaching (11:18-23). Priests and false prophets demanded that Jehoiakim execute Jeremiah (26:1-11). Thankfully, God allowed the prophet's life to be spared (vss. 12-24).

Later, King Zedekiah had Jeremiah beaten and imprisoned (37:11-15). Finally, after Jerusalem's fall, the rebellious remnant carted Jeremiah off to Egypt, where his words were also rejected (43:1-7).

All of this took a terrible emotional and spiritual toll on the prophet, and he paid a heavy price for his faithfulness. Jeremiah cried out to God against his wicked oppressors (18:19-20). He complained not only about the nation's spiritual hardness but also about the prosperity of the wicked (12:1-4). Jeremiah told God about his persecution, reproach, rejection, and loneliness. And in the prophet's distraught state, he charged that God's help seemed as uncertain as a seasonal brook that had dried up in hot weather (15:15-18).

On every occasion God met Jeremiah's needs, and the prophet responded with unwavering zeal and dedication. As conditions steadily worsened in Jerusalem, the prophet never wavered in speaking God's truth.

Of course, Jeremiah and God's other true prophets did not think up their messages on their own. They proclaimed truths that the Lord had revealed to them. The messages they delivered reflected their own personalities and life experiences. God worked through their distinctive human qualities to express His will. We know the result of this divine-human interaction was an inspired declaration of truth (2 Pet. 1:20-21).

We read in Jeremiah 1:10 that God dispatched Jeremiah to proclaim His somber message to the nations. As Jeremiah carried out his prophetic ministry, he would have the authority to declare the overthrow and destruction of many kingdoms, including Judah. The prophet would also announce the promise of God's future restoration of His people.

God had warned Jeremiah not to hold back any part of the messages given to him. He was to preach everything, even though his sermons were unpopular and unacceptable to kings, princes, priests, and people. At the time of Jeremiah's call, God had told him that many would fight against him (vss. 17-19). When Jeremiah grew weary of the pressure, opposition, and lack of response, God challenged him to renewed faith and endurance (12:1-13). Even when Jeremiah saw himself as a hopeless case, God called him to trust in Him and keep on preaching (15:15-21).

B.   The Proclamation of Others: vss. 4-6

And though the Lord has sent all his servants the prophets to you again and again, you have not listened or paid any attention. They said, "Turn now, each of you, from your evil ways and your evil practices, and you can stay in the land the Lord gave to you and your fathers for ever and ever. Do not follow other gods to serve and worship them; do not provoke me to anger with what your hands have made. Then I will not harm you."

Jeremiah 25:4-6 succinctly summarized the prophets' mission and their appeals to Judah and Jerusalem. The pattern was clear. God kept on sending Jeremiah and the other prophets to the people, but they kept on refusing to listen. The Lord's charge was unmistakable. If the people would repent from their evil deeds, God would spare them and they would keep living in the land promised to their ancestors.

25:6 "serve" or "worship"—

The verb "to bow down" always refers to an attitude or action directed toward an authority figure, whether human or divine. Since it is often used in conjunction with verbs of prostration, it denotes respect, submission, or worship for someone in a position of authority or honor.

85

The people's evil ways and practices were epitomized by their idolatry (vs. 6). In God's eyes, this was their worst offense. Idolatry meant that God's chosen people had rejected Him for false gods and goddesses.

Idolatry was rampant in Egypt and Canaan. That's why, when God called His people out of bondage in Egypt, He had warned them against worshiping the idols of the other nations (Exod. 20:4-5, 22-23). Sadly, though, the Israelites soon fell into idolatry by making and worshiping a gold calf (32:1-35). That rebellion persisted until the days of Jeremiah and the downfall of Judah.

C. The Judgment of the Lord: vs. 7

"But you did not listen to me," declares the LORD, "and you have provoked me with what your hands have made, and you have brought harm to yourselves."

As a result of the people's continued disobedience (Jer. 25:7), the Lord threatened Judah and the surrounding nations with complete destruction by the Babylonians (vss. 8-9). In the Bible the southern kingdom of Judah is regarded as usually more loyal to God than was the northern kingdom of Israel. Nevertheless, there were numerous kings in Judah who practiced idolatry and promoted injustice. Because of the disobedience of the nation and its people, Judah lost its independence in 586 b.c. when the Babylonians conquered it.

Jeremiah saw that even though God would use the Babylonians as His divine tool of judgment, they would themselves have to be judged one day (vss. 12-14). Nebuchadnezzar and Babylon were guilty of great cruelty and arrogance. The land of Babylon faced permanent desolation because of the guilt of its conquering armies. Jeremiah's prophecy of judgment on Babylon was fulfilled when it was conquered by the Medes and Persians (Dan. 5:30-31).

II. Call to Reform: Jeremiah 26:12-13

Then Jeremiah said to all the officials and all the people: "The LORD sent me to prophesy against this house and this city all the things you have heard. Now reform your ways and your actions

*and obey the LORD your God. Then the LORD will relent and not
bring the disaster he has pronounced against you."*

Jeremiah 26 provides the historical context for the prophecies of
chapters 7—10. Early in the reign of Jehoiakim, Jeremiah went to
the temple and declared that if the people would not listen to the
Lord, then He would destroy the sanctuary and Jerusalem. In fact,
the city would become "an object of cursing among all the nations
of the earth" (26:6).

This stern warning fell on antagonistic hearts, for the priests,
prophets, and all the people at the temple mobbed Jeremiah and
sought to have him executed. They were enraged by the idea that
God would destroy the temple (vss. 7-9). This firestorm of complaint prompted the officials of Judah to hold court at the New
Gate. (In ancient times, the city gates were the normal place for
court hearings.) They accused Jeremiah of being a traitor for
prophesying against Jerusalem and its sanctuary (vss. 10-11).

Jeremiah spoke in his own defense by reiterating a familiar
theme, namely, that God had commissioned him to proclaim dire
warnings of judgment against "this house and this city" (vs. 12).
Every word that Jeremiah received, he had declared. Thus, what he
said came with divine inspiration and authority.

The prophet's message was not all gloom and doom, however.
The possibility of mercy existed for the people of Judah. Jeremiah
declared that if they abandoned their idolatry, immorality, and
injustice, and began to obey the Lord, He would "relent and not
bring the disaster he has pronounced against you" (vs. 13). The
idea is that God preconditioned His judgment on the response of
the people. If they turned away from their sin, He would cancel the
disaster that He had pronounced would come against them.

Thankfully, they recognized that this prophet had faithfully dis-
charged his God-given responsibility and thus did not deserve to
die. Then some of the elders recalled that Micah had made similar
predictions without King Hezekiah ordering his death. Instead, the
people turned from their sins and worshiped the Lord, and God
decided not to destroy Jerusalem at that time (vss. 16-19).

The court was persuaded not to hand Jeremiah over to the mob
"to be put to death" (vs. 24). Though Jeremiah was spared, the
people did not spare themselves by repenting of their sins. They
continued headlong in their evil ways and eventually brought
disaster upon themselves and their nation.

Discussion Questions

1. To whom was Jeremiah's message directed?
2. What was the message that Jeremiah proclaimed?
3. How did the people respond to Jeremiah's message?
4. What defense for his actions did Jeremiah offer to the court?

Ask Yourself . . .

When are the times that I find myself not listening to the Lord's clear instruction?

What draws my heart away from obeying what He tells me in His Word?

How can I remain encouraged when facing stiff opposition to my faith?

How can I be quicker to repent when God brings me correction?

How does God respond to me when I repent of my sins and seek to obey Him?

Illustrations

You've probably heard sermons in which the speaker defined holiness as being set apart to God for His use. The underlying idea is that we belong to God and exist to do His will. Because we're His children, He disciplines us so that we might become more holy in our thinking, acting, and witness for Him.

The way we respond to God's discipline can shape our view of life. For instance, we become more worldly in our thinking if we respond to God's discipline with bitterness and anger. In contrast, we become more holy in our thinking when we respond to His discipline with humility and trust.

A holy response to God's discipline involves being realistic, not naïve, about life. Believers shouldn't minimize the pain and loss they are experiencing. Instead, Christians should remain confident that God will bring good out of evil and that He will not forsake them. Some people have said that God uses difficulties to force us out of our comfort zones and to cause us to grow more mature in our faith.

Our growth in holiness can enhance our witness to others. For instance, when a coworker tells you over a cup of coffee that she's unhappy with her marriage and asks for your advice, what you say will be shaped by how you have responded in the past to the discipline of God. You can share how God's Word has helped you deal with problems in relationships with others. You might even have an opportunity to give your testimony and ask the coworker to trust in Christ for salvation.

The Harvest of Sin

DEVOTIONAL READING

Joshua 24:14-28

DAILY BIBLE READINGS

Monday November 14
Jeremiah 19:1-9 The Lord
Tells Jeremiah to Warn the
Nation

Tuesday November 15
Jeremiah 19:10-15
Jeremiah Promises
Disaster

Wednesday November 16
Jeremiah 20:1-6 Jeremiah
Denounces Pashhur

Thursday November 17
Jeremiah 21:1-7 God
Rejects Zedekiah's Request

Friday November 18
Jeremiah 21:8-14 God Will
Judge the Evil of the City

Saturday November 19
Jeremiah 22:1-9 Forsake
God and Be Punished

Sunday November 20
Jeremiah 22:10-19 God
Tells What Will Happen to
Jehoiakim

Scripture

Background Scripture: *Jeremiah 19; 21:1-10*

Scripture Lesson: *Jeremiah 19:1-4, 10-11; 21:1-2, 8-10*

Key Verse: *This is what the L*ORD *says: See, I am setting before you the way of life and the way of death.* *Jeremiah 21:8.*

Lesson Aim

Sins of a nation have tragic consequences.

Lesson Setting

Time: About 590 B.C.

Place: Jerusalem.

Lesson Outline

The Harvest of Sin

   I. The Lesson of the Clay Jar: Jeremiah 19:1-4, 10-11

      A. *Buy the Jar: vss. 1-2*

      B. *Judgment Is Coming: vss. 3-4*

      C. *Break the Jar: vss. 10-11*

  II. The Prophecy to the King: Jeremiah 21:1-2, 8-10

      A. *The King's Request: vss. 1-2*

      B. *The People's Choice: vss. 8-9*

      C. *The Lord's Decree: vs. 10*

Introduction

False Hopes

Jerusalem fell almost 2,600 years ago. So what's the big deal? What does that have to do with us today? Much in every way, if we will take the trouble to think through the main issue: faithfulness or unfaithfulness to God.

Historical settings come and go, but God still speaks to His people about their professed faith in Him. Judgment fell on Jerusalem, on God's house. These were the good guys, so to speak, not the despised pagans. But the people of Judah and Jerusalem had in effect become pagans. Worst of all, they were blind to their spiritual corruption.

Perhaps we need to look at this story as an example of how people got lost, betrayed their vows, and were too proud to repent. We also must see in their story the faithful witness of a prophet who suffered grievously. Obedience to God never comes easily, especially when it goes against the grain of popular beliefs.

Lesson Commentary

I. The Lesson of the Clay Jar: Jeremiah 19:1-4, 10-11

A. Buy the Jar: vss. 1-2

This is what the LORD says: "Go and buy a clay jar from a potter. Take along some of the elders of the people and of the priests and go out to the Valley of Ben Hinnom, near the entrance of the Potsherd Gate. There proclaim the words I tell you, . . ."

Jeremiah's career as a prophet began during the promising days of spiritual revival under the godly King Josiah (640–609 b.c.). Sadly, the king was killed in battle with Pharaoh Necho, and from there on Josiah's four successors led Judah to her destruction. Only two of these kings, Jehoiakim and Zedekiah, are mentioned in Jeremiah 1:1-2, because the other two—Jehoahaz and Jehoiachin—reigned only three months each.

These were distressing, turbulent days for Judah and Jerusalem. Jeremiah's preaching for repentance and salvation was rejected. Nevertheless, the prophet stood like "a fortified city, an iron pillar and a bronze wall" against the kings, officials, priests and people (1:18).

The prophecy of Jeremiah was not written in strictly chronolog-ical order, but we find bits of history interspersed with long sermons. We also find poignant outcries of woe from the prophet, revealing his intense spiritual pain over the rejection of the Lord's message. At times he was threatened with death and imprisoned. On one occasion the scrolls on which his prophecy was written were burned. Jeremiah paid dearly for his faithfulness to God.

God called Jeremiah not only to preach, but also to use object lessons to show that judgment was coming. In this case, the Lord told him to visit a potter just outside the city of Jerusalem and buy a clay jar. This was the common clay waterpot large enough to hold several gallons of water.

The Lord directed Jeremiah to a specific place packed with vivid symbolism. The Valley of Ben Hinnom was southeast of the city. It was the dumping place for broken pots, garbage, and the bones of criminals. Rubbish constantly burned there. Children had been burned there on the altar of the pagan god Molech. It became a picture of Gehenna, or hell.

Jeremiah was to take a delegation of elders and priests with him. Of course, these leaders were solidly arrayed against Jeremiah. They had sold out the worship of the Lord. They hated Jeremiah because he exposed their sins and the sins of the people. For example, Jeremiah said, "The shepherds [elders] are senseless and do not inquire of the LORD; so they do not prosper and their flock is scattered" (10:21). Of the prophets and priests he said, "From the least to the greatest, all are greedy for gain . . . all practice deceit. They dress the wound of my people as though it were not serious. 'Peace, peace,' they say, when there is no peace" (8:10-11).

They considered Jeremiah a traitor because he said Jerusalem's only hope was to surrender and make peace with the invading Chaldeans from Babylon. Nevertheless, God told Jeremiah to take these men with him to the potter's house to buy a clay jar.

The jar, of course, was to be the object lesson for the sermon to follow. God told Jeremiah to "proclaim the words I tell you." This is a succinct picture of the prophet's role. Jeremiah and the other prophets did not act on their own. They were inspired by God the Holy Spirit that the Bible depicts them as preaching God's word.

The prophets were so in tune with God that their words were the words of God. Jeremiah had complained that he was not old enough to preach God's word, but the Lord said, "You must go to everyone I send you to and say whatever I command you" (1:6-7).

B. Judgment Is Coming: vss. 3-4

". . . and say, 'Hear the word of the LORD, O kings of Judah and people of Jerusalem. This is what the LORD Almighty, the God of Israel, says: Listen! I am going to bring a disaster on this place that will make the ears of everyone who hears of it tingle. For they have forsaken me and made this a place of foreign gods; they have burned sacrifices in it to gods that neither they nor their fathers nor the kings of Judah ever knew, and they have filled this place with the blood of the innocent.' "

This is the prophet's eighth message to the nation. When Jeremiah began to preach he reminded his audience that he was delivering a message from God Almighty, the God of Israel. This was the God who owned them by virtue of His redemption of them from Egypt. "The LORD Almighty" was a phrase that spoke to the people about God's awesome power, holiness, and greatness.

Jeremiah addressed the kings and the people. The kings represented political and spiritual authority. They exerted powerful influence on the religious habits of the people.

Jeremiah called them to listen to his very simple but tragic message: Disaster is coming. The disaster will be so terrible that when the news spreads, people's ears will tingle because of the horror of it. They will shudder in utter disbelief that such destruction could befall a city and nation.

Then Jeremiah explained why such awful judgment is coming. Again, it was not hard to understand his charge. The basic reason was that the people had forsaken the Lord. Having abandoned Him, they opened the door to all kinds of pagan obscenities.

Forsaking God was Jeremiah's constant indictment of the people (2:13; 5:7, 19; 9:13; 19:4; 22:9). He called this unfaithfulness spiritual adultery. It did not come about by official proclamation. In fact, no one ever formally said, "We want a divorce from God." Quite the contrary. The people leaned heavily on the temple of the Lord as their security and protection from foreign invaders. It was their lucky charm (7:4).

But into the temple they brought foreign gods. So the worship of the one true God was adulterated by pagan rites, festivities, and sacrifices. This religious syncretism was abominable to God, who had commanded, "You shall have no other gods before [or besides] me" (Deut. 5:7).

The temple that had been consecrated to God was polluted by sacrifices to idols. In addition, the people built shrines to Baal, the Canaanite deity who had been worshiped for centuries first in Israel and then in Judah and Jerusalem (Jer. 19:5). "The blood of the innocent" (vs. 4) refers to the hideous practice of child sacrifices (vs. 5). These pagan practices were at their worst under King Manasseh (2 Kings 21:1-7).

Therefore, Jerusalem's destruction would be so great that Ben Hinnom would be renamed the Valley of Slaughter (vs. 6). Jeremiah went on to preach violence of the worst kind. People would die by the sword. Famine would engulf the city during the siege and people would eat each other (vss. 7-9).

C. Break the Jar: vss. 10-11

"Then break the jar while those who go with you are watching, and say to them, 'This is what the LORD Almighty says: I will smash this nation and this city just as this potter's jar is smashed and cannot be repaired. They will bury the dead in Topheth until there is no more room.'"

God told Jeremiah to smash the waterpot in front of the elders and priests. While the potsherds crashed around them, Jeremiah declared, "That's the way God will smash this nation and city." The city's destruction will be irreparable. So many people will die that the burial ground in Topheth (another name for Ben Hinnom) will not be able to hold them.

II. The Prophecy to the King: Jeremiah 21:1-2, 8-10

A. The King's Request: vss. 1-2

The word came to Jeremiah from the LORD when King Zedekiah sent to him Pashhur son of Malkijah and the priest Zephaniah son of Maaseiah. They said: "Inquire now of the LORD for us because Nebuchadnezzar king of Babylon is attacking us. Perhaps the LORD will perform wonders for us as in times past so that he will withdraw from us."

For his scathing attack on Judah's sins, Jeremiah was beaten up and put in the stocks at the temple (20:1-2). He fell into a deep depression and cursed the day he was born (20:14-18). Imagine how hard it was for him to preach such terrible judgment for the people and country he loved.

Nevertheless, Jeremiah stood tall for the Lord and His word. He was put on the spot by King Zedekiah, the last king of Judah (597–587 b.c.). King Josiah had been succeeded by Jehoahaz, who was deposed and dragged off to Egypt. Pharaoh Necho put Jehoiakim on the throne of Judah.

However, Babylon's King Nebuchadnezzar drove off the Egyptians and Judah passed under his control. Judah's last three kings were weak, misguided rulers who tried to rebel against the Babylonians. Under Zedekiah, Jeremiah was imprisoned and beaten, then thrown into a cistern. However, God delivered him from his enemies.

On this occasion, the king sent emissaries to consult with Jeremiah because Nebuchadnezzar had returned to the attack. Zedekiah was looking for a miracle. He knew the history of his people. He knew that God had spared them in the past. Probably the greatest intervention he had in mind was the deliverance under King Hezekiah (2 Kings 19).

This request reveals the depths of the spiritual malady that afflicted the king and his advisers. They saw no connection between their idolatry and wickedness and God's judgment. They clung to the false hope that God would overlook their disobedience and come to their rescue.

B. The People's Choice: vss. 8-9

"Furthermore, tell the people, 'This is what the LORD says: See, I am setting before you the way of life and the way of death. Whoever stays in this city will die by the sword, famine or plague. But whoever goes out and surrenders to the Babylonians who are besieging you will live; he will escape with his life.' "

The Lord's answer through Jeremiah was not what Zedekiah and his men were hoping for. Instead of God doing a miracle for them, He was going to fight against them (vs. 5). The result would be the decimation of Jerusalem, the capture of the king and his

court, death by sword, famine, and plague, and deportation to
Babylon of the survivors (vs. 7). God through Nebuchadnezzar
would show them no mercy.

The Egyptians had been driven off. Nebuchadnezzar and his
forces surrounded the city. During the long siege people would die
from famine and disease. Once the walls were breached, they
would be killed by enemy soldiers.

Jeremiah's logic seemed impeccable, but the king, princes,
priests, false prophets, and people refused to believe him. To them
it was a matter of national pride to keep on fighting. Surrender is
for traitors. They blamed Jeremiah for undermining the morale of
the people and for weakening their will to keep on fighting. They
failed to grasp the underlying spiritual issues that had brought
them to this terrible dilemma.

C. The Lord's Decree: vs. 10

*" 'I have determined to do this city harm and not good,' declares
the LORD. 'It will be given into the hands of the king of Babylon,
and he will destroy it with fire.' "*

The word of the Lord promised no miraculous deliverance.
Quite the opposite. Jeremiah revealed that a divine decree had
determined the destruction of Jerusalem by fire. The king and the
nation must understand that God had already decided that
Jerusalem should be destroyed. It would be burned to the ground.

As we know, the king disobeyed the words that Jeremiah delivered from the Lord. God's messages never suited his purposes. He
and his people would go on fighting and die. If they had listened to
God, they would have been spared (22:4-5). Jeremiah consistently
preached repentance and faith as the only way of salvation.

What appeared to be a military and political issue was really a
matter of knowing and obeying God. The unrepentant Zedekiah,
determined to have his own way, brought down the kingdom. He
knew what was right to do, but lacked the courage to do it.

Discussion Questions

1. Why is God's judgment a hard message to believe?
2. What advantages are there in preaching by object lessons?
3. What pressures fell on Jeremiah? On Zedekiah?
4. How do you account for the deeply ingrained stubbornness on the part of the king and the people?
5. How can we protect ourselves from falling into such spiritual blindness and hardness?
6. How can we introduce Jesus and the Gospel as a life and death choice?

Ask Yourself . . .

How do I respond when I am confronted with a hard message?

How can I receive a hard message as something that is meant to bring life to me instead of rejecting it as just "gloom and doom?"

What can I do to keep from forsaking God's calling on my life?

In what ways does the Lord encourage me when I feel not up to a task He has called me to?

Illustrations

Jeremiah must have felt like a railroad flagman rushing down the tracks waving his lantern, frantically trying to stop a collision. We oftentimes appreciate people who warn us of danger, but we ridicule people who stand on street corners and preach, "Repent or perish!" Why is that?

"Repent or perish" makes us very uncomfortable, because we prefer not to acknowledge that we have broken our vows with the Lord and allowed other gods to take His rightful place. Deep down, we know we should trust Him, and that we should live by His laws, but sin has such a grip on us that we find it hard to listen to prophets of doom. However, we also need to realize that the call to repentance will actually bring us life. People prefer to listen to prophets who tell them to feel good about themselves. Don't worry about judgment day. Live for all the goodies you can get. But God's judgment decrees cannot be put off. We may try to put them out of our minds, but He keeps sending Jeremiahs to us to plead with us to surrender, to repent, and to live and receive salvation.

The church needs to lock in on the fact that judgment can be ignored only at our peril. The word of the Lord will be fulfilled, whether we like it or not. With love and with tears of compassion, we must issue the strong call for repentance and faith, lest people perish in their sins. Jesus Christ is our only hope.

Sliding down the Slippery Slope

DEVOTIONAL READING

Psalm 75

DAILY BIBLE READINGS

Monday November 21
2 Kings 17:1-6 Hoshea
Takes His People Away
from God

Tuesday November 22
2 Kings 17:7-13 God
Warns the People to Turn
from Their Evil Ways

Wednesday November 23
2 Kings 17:14-23 The
People Do Not Listen

Thursday November 24
Nahum 1:1-8 God Judges
the Sins of Nineveh

Friday November 25
Nahum 1:9-15 Judah's
Faithfulness Is Rewarded

Saturday November 26
2 Chronicles 36:11-14
Zedekiah Becomes King of
Judah

Sunday November 27
2 Chronicles 36:15-23
Jerusalem Falls to
Nebuchadnezzar

Scripture

Background Scripture: *2 Chronicles 36:9-21;
2 Kings 24:8-25; 26*

Scripture Lesson: *2 Chronicles 36:11-21*

Key Verses: *The LORD, the God of their fathers, sent word
to them through his messengers again and again,
because he had pity on his people and on his dwelling
place. But they mocked God's messengers, despised his
words and scoffed at his prophets until the wrath of the
LORD was aroused against his people and there was no
remedy. 2 Chronicles 36:15-16.*

Lesson Aim

Ignoring God is cumulative and contagious.

Lesson Setting

Time: 586 B.C.

Place: Judah and Jerusalem

Lesson Outline

Sliding down the Slippery Slope

  I. The Corrupt Rule of Zedekiah:
     2 Chronicles 36:11-16
     A. *Rebellion against God: vss. 11-12*
     B. *Rebellion against Nebuchadnezzar: vs. 13*
     C. *Adoption of Pagan Practices: vs. 14*
     D. *Mistreatment of God's Prophets: vss. 15-16*

 II. The Fall of Jerusalem: 2 Chronicles 36:17-21
     A. *The Slaughter of Many: vs. 17*
     B. *The Looting and Destruction of the Temple:
        vss. 18-19*
     C. *The Deportation of the Survivors: vs. 20*
     D. *The Fulfillment of the Lord's Word: vs. 21*

Introduction

Facing the End

"If I only had it all to do over again" is a statement adults some-times say, especially as they face the end of their lives. They usually mean that their focus and progress in life would have been radically different if they had an opportunity to repeat the past. From this we see that taking a retrospective look at one's life can be a humbling experience. It can also be instructive, especially if one can use the mistakes one has made to avoid making the same type of mistakes in the future.

When adults bemoan their oversights and wallow in their errors, little if any positive change in behavior occurs. However, if they allow their past failures to bring about wholesome and long-term change, their shortcomings can serve as opportunities for greater understanding. Adults also have a way of charting a different course for their life, hopefully one that is more godly and eternally meaningful.

Lesson Commentary

I. The Corrupt Rule of Zedekiah: 2 Chronicles 36:11-16

A. Rebellion against God: vss. 11-12

Zedekiah was twenty-one years old when he became king, and he reigned in Jerusalem eleven years. He did evil in the eyes of the Lord his God and did not humble himself before Jeremiah the prophet, who spoke the word of the Lord.

The ancient historian described the downfall of Judah and Jerusalem in terse terms. He moved quickly from Josiah's drama-tic reforms (2 Chron. 34—35) to the ill-fated reigns of Judah's last ungodly kings, Jehoahaz, Jehoiakim, Jehoiachin, and Zedekiah (36:1-16).

Jehoahaz and Jehoiachin reigned only three months each (vss. 2, 9); Jehoiakim and Zedekiah both reigned 11 years (vss. 5, 11). Zedekiah's record was particularly abysmal. He did what was evil in the Lord's sight. Instead of humbling himself when he heard God's warning through Jeremiah, Zedekiah rebelled against the Lord. And rather than turn to the Lord in repentance, Judah's king hardened his heart.

B. Rebellion against Nebuchadnezzar: vs. 13

He also rebelled against King Nebuchadnezzar, who had made him take an oath in God's name. He became stiff-necked and hardened his heart and would not turn to the LORD, the God of Israel.

In 597 b.c., Nebuchadnezzar made Mattaniah the king of Judah and changed his name to Zedekiah. This signified the Judahite ruler's submission to Babylon (2 Kings 24:17). For the first nine years of his reign, he honored his vow to regularly pay tribute to Nebuchadnezzar, but then Zedekiah refused to submit to the Babylonians any longer (25:1).

Second Chronicles 36:13 underscores how despicable Zedekiah's decision was to the Lord. We read that King Nebuchadnezzar of Babylonia had forced Zedekiah to promise "in God's name" that he would be loyal. But because he was stubborn, he refused to turn back to "the God of Israel." Such unfaithfulness greatly angered the Lord and that's why, in the end, "he thrust [his people] from his presence" (2 Kings 24:20).

It's clear that Zedekiah bore a great deal of responsibility for the destruction of Jerusalem. However, he is not the only one implicated in Scripture. Verse 3 says that God's pronouncement against Judah (to remove His people from His sight) was due in part to "the sins of Manasseh." He was perhaps the most wicked of Judah's kings. For instance, he was guilty of shedding innocent blood. His crimes were so great that God refused to forgive him (vs. 4). Even the impressive reforms enacted by Josiah could not turn God from "the heat of his fierce anger" (23:26). He decreed that Judah and Jerusalem would not escape His judgment (vs. 27).

Because God is both our Creator and Judge, He has the right to expect us to obey Him. Moreover, when we rebel against Him, He is fully just to punish us for our wrongdoing. Thankfully, the Lord does not deal with us as we deserve. He treats us with kindness and compassion even when we often should experience His wrath and condemnation.

36:13 "rebelled against"—

With the basic meaning of "be high," this verb can describe things or people that are high or exalted or delineate the process of making things higher or exalted. To raise the hand against someone is a term for rebellion (as in the present passage). This expression may have originally depicted someone lifting his hand to deliver a death-blow, but it came to mean taking the offensive against someone.

C. Adoption of Pagan Practices: vs. 14

Furthermore, all the leaders of the priests and the people became more and more unfaithful, following all the detestable practices of the nations and defiling the temple of the LORD, which he had consecrated in Jerusalem.

The apostasy in Judah and Jerusalem, led by Zedekiah, pervaded all levels of the country's leadership and swept most of the people along with it. The charge against them was clear: they had ceased following the Lord and had taken to the worship of idols, even in the "temple of the LORD" (2 Chron. 36:14).

The spiritual leaders should have taught the people the laws and ways of God, but instead they stood by silently when the worship of foreign gods was introduced in the temple. They followed superstitious practices and persecuted the prophets. Idolatry was the fundamental evil from which all others sprang. The people may not have formally abandoned the worship of Israel's one true God, but they combined it with the ceremonies of pagan cults.

In His unfailing love, God urged leaders and people of Judah to repent, but, regrettably, they continued to rebel against Him. Although the Lord was extremely patient with His people, He eventually judged them by allowing the king of Babylon to destroy Jerusalem.

D. Mistreatment of God's Prophets: vss. 15-16

The LORD, the God of their fathers, sent word to them through his messengers again and again, because he had pity on his people and on his dwelling place. But they mocked God's messengers, despised his words and scoffed at his prophets until the wrath of the LORD was aroused against his people and there was no remedy.

Into this dark, dismal spiritual morass God shined the beam of His love and pity for His people. God was true to His character. His love never changed, despite the sins of His people. While Judah and Jerusalem sank lower and lower, God continued to urge His people to repent.

God spoke to the people of Judah through His "messengers" (2 Chron. 36:15), the prophets. He appealed to the people on the basis of His ancient covenant. He was "the LORD," that is, the one true God. He was "the God of their fathers." He had revealed Himself to their most noteworthy ancestors, Abraham, Isaac, and Jacob. God was the one who had rescued His people from Egypt and given them a land of their own.

The Lord appealed to His people on the basis of His unfailing love for them and for Jerusalem, "his dwelling place." Jerusalem was where the people were supposed to assemble for worship. The city was the home of the temple, where God was supposed to meet with His people through their faithful worship of Him.

We know the message of warning that God had declared to His people, for it has been preserved for us in Scripture. It's important to understand that God spoke through such prophets as Isaiah, Jeremiah, and Ezekiel. Their messages were clearly intended to bring about repentance and obedience. These servants of God warned of judgment to come. They underscored that God was waiting for His people to respond to His love.

Verse 16 spares no words to stress how unresponsive the people were to God's messengers. When the prophets spoke, the people only laughed and shouted insults. They ignored what the Lord was trying to tell them. This continued until God became so angry that nothing could stop Him from punishing them.

God is patient with us when we fall into sin. He perseveres in the hope that we will turn away from our wrongdoing and return to Him in faith and devotion. He is willing to take the time to move us away from the road of destruction and guide us into the path of life. For instance, the Lord may forbear with us when we deliberately mislead family members and friends. He is patient when we waste time at work or when we read material that is immoral. The grace of God is apparent even when we gossip about others and tarnish their reputation.

There are times when the Lord might choose to discipline us for some sinful area of our lives. God corrects us for our good and wants us to be holy, as He is (Heb. 12:10). His intent is to help us learn what is right and to avoid doing what is wrong.

II. The Fall of Jerusalem: 2 Chronicles 36:17-21

A. The Slaughter of Many: vs. 17
He brought up against them the king of the Babylonians, who killed their young men with the sword in the sanctuary, and spared neither young man nor young woman, old man or aged. God handed all of them over to Nebuchadnezzar.

Unlike previous encounters, the Babylonians' reprisal against Judah and Jerusalem would be unsparing. As the invading army swept south through Judah, it destroyed one city after another.

Jeremiah 34:7 says that Lachish and Azekah were the last fortified cities to fall.

On January 15, 588 b.c., Nebuchadnezzar's army finally attacked Jerusalem. They encircled the city, established military camps, and constructed a siege wall around it. The campaign against Jerusalem lasted approximately two and one-half years. By July 18, 586 b.c., a severe famine spread throughout the city (2 Kings 25:1-3). The shortage of food was so great that some of Jerusalem's inhabitants resorted to cannibalism (Ezek. 5:10).

One of Nebuchadnezzar's objectives was to break through the walls and gates of Jerusalem. After erecting an earthen ramp, the attackers then wheeled a battering ram close to the wall so that it could be used to loosen material and dislodge bricks. The Babylonians eventually succeeded in their efforts, and this signaled the beginning of the end for the city and its inhabitants. It would not be long before enemy forces toppled the gates and began pouring into Jerusalem from all directions.

We learn from 2 Chronicles 36:17 that it was the Lord who "brought up against [His people] the king of the Babylonians." Once the invaders were inside Jerusalem, they killed the young men who sought refuge in the temple. Nebuchadnezzar's forces showed no mercy to anyone, whether man or woman, young or old. God allowed the Babylonians to slaughter everyone in the city.

B. The Looting and Destruction of the Temple: vss. 18-19

He carried to Babylon all the articles from the temple of God, both large and small, and the treasures of the LORD's temple and the treasures of the king and his officials. They set fire to God's temple and broke down the wall of Jerusalem; they burned all the palaces and destroyed everything of value there.

From the time Zedekiah made his failed escape attempt (2 Kings 25:4-7), almost a month passed before the Babylonians destroyed Jerusalem. The ominous moment came on August 14, 586 b.c. The invaders first removed everything that was left in the temple. They even robbed the treasury and the personal storerooms of the king and his officials (2 Chron. 36:18).

Once the sanctuary was gutted of its utensils and other valuable artifacts, Nebuchadnezzar's troops burned down the temple and destroyed every important building in Jerusalem. Nothing of value or importance was left standing or intact. The Babylonians even demolished the city wall (vs. 19).

Verses 18 and 19 suggest that the Babylonians were cruel in their treatment of those they conquered. They subdued their opponents like a ferocious animal. They evidently had no misgivings about destroying entire communities as they extended their sphere of control over others.

C. The Deportation of the Survivors: vs. 20

He carried into exile to Babylon the remnant, who escaped from the sword, and they became servants to him and his sons until the kingdom of Persia came to power.

Not everyone died in the siege and fall of Jerusalem. A number of people survived and remained in the city. There were also deserters who had defected to the king of Babylon, and large number of people who had not been involved in the fighting. The invaders deported all these people to Babylon (2 Kings 25:11).

The "remnant" (2 Chron. 36:20), or survivors, were sent to a foreign land as prisoners. There they became slaves of the king and his descendants "until the kingdom of Persia came to power." Cyrus conquered Babylon in 539 b.c., and allowed the Jews to return to Jerusalem the following year.

Not every last person was removed from Judah. The Babylonians left behind some of the poorest people of the land to cultivate vineyards and grow crops in the fields (2 Kings 25:12). The senior official in charge evidently decided they posed no immediate threat to the king, and thus allowed them to remain in the land.

D. The Fulfillment of the Lord's Word: vs. 21

The land enjoyed its sabbath rests; all the time of its desolation it rested, until the seventy years were completed in fulfillment of the word of the LORD spoken by Jeremiah.

Jeremiah 25:12 and 29:10 predict the length of the exile as being 70 years. According to the Mosaic law, the land was to lie fallow every seventh year (Lev. 25:4). This became known as the sabbatical year. Judah's exile in Babylon allowed the land to enjoy the Sabbaths it had missed (2 Chron. 36:21). Eventually God would remember His covenant and restore His people to their homeland (Lev. 26:45).

Discussion Questions

1. Why do you think Zedekiah refused to humble himself before the Lord?
2. In what ways did the leaders of Judah become more and more unfaithful to the Lord?
3. Why did the Lord allow the Babylonians to attack Jerusalem?
4. What happened to God's people as a result of the attack?
5. How does God deal with us when we interpret His patience with us as a license to sin?

Ask Yourself . . .

Do I ever find it hard to humble myself before the Lord?

Are there areas that I have taken God's patience as license to sin?

What things or circumstances do I wish I could do over again?

How does God's grace and patience give me opportunities to learn and grow?

What areas of my life have I seen God's redemption in spite of my own failings?

Illustrations

The people of Judah wrongly interpreted God's patience as a license to sin. This was a major miscalculation on their part, and it ultimately led to their downfall. We also run the risk of worsening our situation if we take His persevering spirit for granted. When God displays His tolerance to us, we should repent of our wrongdoing and return to Him in wholehearted devotion.

For example, Bob and Carol had been married for seven years when Bob began having an affair with another woman. God's patience was evident as He brought healing to the marriage through the help of a Christian counselor. Instead of being grateful, however, Bob eventually got involved in another adulterous relationship. The longer the affair lasted, the more he took God's patience for granted. Sadly, Bob's actions destroyed his marriage.

We abuse God's patience when we remain entrenched in sin. The more we persist in our wayward actions, the more we take His forbearance for granted. We make a mockery of His love by refusing to deal with our sinful tendencies. As genuine followers of Christ, we should make every effort to abandon ungodly ways and remain unwavering in our devotion to the Lord. If we refuse to do so, we eventually might experience God's severe displeasure (Heb. 10:26-27).

Our spiritual lives can be severely harmed when we interpret God's patience as a license to sin. For example, we will not be as close in our relationship with the Lord as we ought to be. Our sensitivity to His leading will be greatly diminished and our tendency will be toward sin.

Encouraging Others

DEVOTIONAL READING

Hebrews 10:19-25

DAILY BIBLE READINGS

Monday November 28
*Acts 2:42-47 All the
Disciples Share with Each
Other*

Tuesday November 29
*Acts 4:32-37 All Believers
Were of One Heart*

Wednesday November 30
*Acts 11:19-24 The Antioch
Church Grows in Number*

Thursday December 1
*Acts 11:25-30 Barnabas,
Saul, and Others Come
and Teach in Antioch*

Friday December 2
*Ephesians 4:25-32 Be Kind
to One Another*

Saturday December 3
*1 Thessalonians 5:1-11
Continue to Encourage
Each Other*

Sunday December 4
*Romans 1:8-15 Be
Mutually Encouraged by
Each Other*

Scripture

Background Scripture: *Acts 4:32-37; 9:26-27; 11:19-30;
15:36-41*

Scripture Lesson: *Acts 4:32-37; 9:26-27; 11:22-26;
15:36-41*

Key Verses: *When [Barnabas] arrived and saw the
evidence of the grace of God, he was glad and encouraged
them all to remain true to the Lord with all their hearts.
He was a good man, full of the Holy Spirit and faith.
Acts 11:23-24a.*

Lesson Aim

Building up others builds up Christ's church

Lesson Setting

Time: A.D. 35 to 50
Place: Jerusalem and Antioch

Lesson Outline

Encouraging Others

I. Barnabas's Generosity: Acts 4:36-37
II. Barnabas's Courage: Acts 9:26-27
III. Barnabas's Teaching: Acts 11:22-26a
    A. *A Ministry of Encouragement: vss. 22-23*
    B. *A Person of Character: vs. 24*
    C. *A Team Player: vss. 25-26a*
IV. Barnabas's Convictions: Acts 15:36-41
    A. *Difference of Opinion: vss. 36-38*
    B. *Separation in Ministry: vss. 39-41*

Introduction

Encouraging Others

When asked by the audience to pick the person who had most influenced his life, the missionary told about an older single woman who had opened her home to college students so they could get to meet veteran missionaries. She held a routine clerk's job, but her dedication to the spiritual growth and development of students was a prime factor in many of them going into Christian ministry. This woman was a behind-the-scenes encourager.

We never know how God can use us to encourage others in their Christian faith and walk with God. We need not be professional counselors to do this. We need only be open to God and to others. He will show us those whom we can help with kind words and deeds. This is a crucial role in building up one another in our faith.

Lesson Commentary

I. Barnabas's Generosity: Acts 4:36-37

Joseph, a Levite from Cyprus, whom the apostles called Barnabas (which means Son of Encouragement), sold a field he owned and brought the money and put it at the apostles' feet.

All those who trusted in Christ were united in spirit and focused on the same goals. They desired to glorify the Lord by proclaiming the Gospel and encouraging one another in the faith. To that end, nobody claimed that their possessions were their own. Instead, the disciples shared everything they had with each other (4:32).

We also learn that the apostles gave powerful witness to "the resurrection of the Lord Jesus" (vs. 33). On the day of Pentecost, Peter had proclaimed to a crowd of people that Jesus was risen from the dead, and the Lord used the apostle's testimony to bring many to a knowledge of the truth (2:14-41). That witness to the Resurrection continued in the weeks and months that followed. In fact, the truth of the Resurrection quickly became a central doctrine of the church (1 Cor. 15:3-8).

The grace and generosity of God was evident among this group of Jesus' followers. No one went in need of anything, for those who owned property—whether land or houses—would sell it and bring the money to the apostles. The leaders, in turn, would distribute the money to those who needed it (4:34-35).

"Joseph" (vs. 36), was especially known for his generosity. He was a Levite from Cyprus, a large island in the northeast corner of the Mediterranean. The apostles called him Barnabas, which means "Son of Encouragement." This man was a Jew of the Dispersion (those dispersed or scattered out of Israel's promised land). Barnabas undoubtedly knew Greek and was familiar with both Hellenistic Judaism (practiced by Jews who spoke Greek and observed Greek culture) and Gentile life. His heritage as a Levite also meant he knew the law.

Though Levites traditionally lived off the temple system, Barnabas had real estate. But on coming into the faith, he sold the property and donated the proceeds for the care of the poor (vs. 37). Later, Barnabas joined with Paul in refusing to make a living from the ministry of the Gospel (1 Cor. 9:6). Barnabas served as a good example of a Christian who freely gave to the needs of others.

Joseph, nicknamed Barnabas (Son of Encouragement), is first introduced at this point for several reasons. First, he was a generous giver and illustrated the very thing Dr. Luke was describing. Second, his noble act apparently filled Ananias and Sapphira with envy so they attempted to impress the church with their giving and ended up being killed. Third, Barnabas had a most important ministry in the church and is mentioned at least 25 times in the Book of Acts and another five times in the epistles. He was a spirit-filled man who was an encourager to the church.

II. Barnabas's Courage: Acts 9:26-27

When he came to Jerusalem, he tried to join the disciples, but they were all afraid of him, not believing that he really was a disciple. But Barnabas took him and brought him to the apostles. He told them how Saul on his journey had seen the Lord and that the Lord had spoken to him, and how in Damascus he had preached fearlessly in the name of Jesus.

As Jesus' followers proclaimed the Gospel, it continued to spread and also to arouse severe antagonism. This led to the martyrdom of Stephen (7:59-60). Saul (Paul) was one of the main persecutors of the church. He hounded and imprisoned Christians wherever he could find them (9:1-2). However, while Saul was journeying to Damascus, the risen Lord appeared to him and brought about his conversion (vss. 3-6). After this experience, Saul had to be led into the city by the hand because he was blind (vss. 7-9).

The Lord used a Christian of Damascus named Ananias to find Saul and restore his sight. Then, when Saul could see again, Ananias baptized him (vss. 10-19). Soon after his conversion, Saul began preaching about Jesus in the synagogues of Damascus.

Some Jews, who were unable to refute his teachings, conspired to murder him. But the believers foiled the plan by sneaking Saul out of the city at night (vss. 20-25).

Sometime after escaping from Damascus, Saul arrived in Jerusalem. At first he wasn't much better received there. The believers feared him and doubted his conversion (vs. 26). We shouldn't blame the believers for their suspicions. After all, Saul's reputation had been built on cruelty toward the Christian church. They could not easily dismiss what he had done. Caution, therefore, seemed the sensible course.

But in this case someone was needed who could show that caution should give way to acceptance. That someone was Barnabas. He encouraged Saul by staking his own reputation on the authenticity of Saul's conversion. Barnabas introduced Saul to the apostles and told them about his conversion and preaching in Damascus (vs. 27). The early church accepted Saul because Barnabas vouched for him (vs. 28).

III. Barnabas's Teaching: Acts 11:22-26

A. A Ministry of Encouragement: vss. 22-23
News of this reached the ears of the church at Jerusalem, and they sent Barnabas to Antioch. When he arrived and saw the evidence of the grace of God, he was glad and encouraged them all to remain true to the Lord with all their hearts.

The subsequent chapters in Acts narrate both the numerical and spiritual growth of the early church and the opposition they faced from various groups. Some Greek-speaking Jews began proclaiming the Gospel to Jews in Phoenicia (a coastal area north of Palestine), Cyprus, and the city of Antioch (the capital of the Roman province of Syria; 11:19). Some unnamed believers from Cyprus and Cyrene (a city in North Africa) also began preaching to the Greeks in Antioch (whether God-fearing Gentiles or pagans; vs. 20).

God blessed this evangelistic outreach, and a large number of people came to faith in Christ (vs. 21). The congregation at Antioch was the first primarily Gentile church. It was not only cross-cultural in its Jewish and non-Jewish flavor but also racially integrated.

The apostles in Jerusalem began to wonder about the authenticity of the new converts' religious fervor. They thus decided to send a representative to evaluate the situation. They wisely chose Barnabas for the assignment (vs. 22). Upon arriving in the city, Barnabas soon became convinced that the Gentile conversions were real. He was overjoyed to see the grace of God at work. Furthermore, he exhorted the believers to remain faithful to the Lord with all their hearts (vs. 23).

B. A Person of Character: vs. 24

He was a good man, full of the Holy Spirit and faith, and a great number of people were brought to the Lord.

Barnabas possessed exceptional spiritual qualities. The Spirit was in control of his life and he had an unshakable confidence in God. He had the understanding and affirming nature required for making an honest appraisal of the situation in Antioch (vs. 24).

C. A Team Player: vss. 25-26a

Then Barnabas went to Tarsus to look for Saul, and when he found him, he brought him to Antioch.

Barnabas sensed that now was the time to follow the Spirit's leading and strengthen this outpost of Christianity in the Gentile world. Barnabas apparently did not feel he was the person to lead the way, but he knew someone who was eminently qualified. Saul was the person (vs. 25). But Saul had not been heard of for about five years. During this time, he was operating out of Tarsus. He may have concentrated on personal growth and made a strong witness in the name of Christ among his family and friends.

Barnabas wasted little time. He went directly to Tarsus to find Saul. Barnabas expended much effort to find him. After locating Saul, Barnabas brought him back to Antioch, where they taught together for a whole year and encouraged the new believers (vs. 26). Here we find Barnabas not only sponsoring Saul when no one else apparently would identify with him, but he also encouraged Saul to become a missionary leader. Barnabas was even noble enough to step aside when it became evident to him that Saul was the best person to lead the church in its new mission to the Gentiles.

Antioch was the capital of Syria, 300 miles north of Jerusalem. With a population of half a million, Antioch ranked as the third largest city in the Roman Empire. A busy post and a center for luxury and culture, Antioch attracted all kinds of people. Antioch was a wicked city, perhaps second only to Corinth. Though all the Greek, Roman, and Syrian deities were honored, the local shrine was dedicated to Daphne, whose worship included immoral practices.

The decision of Barnabas to reach out to Saul set the stage for this talented believer to be used of God in amazing ways. Our knowledge of Saul's early years is sketchy. But what we know shows that God was quietly preparing a man with great insight into Jewish law and who felt at home in the Roman world.

Saul most likely was born during the first decade of the Christian era. His family lived in Tarsus, an important city of Cilicia in southeast Asia Minor (now Turkey; 21:39). Though Roman citizens, the members of Saul's family were devout Jews of the tribe of Benjamin (Phil. 3:5). While still a child or adolescent, Saul moved to Jerusalem, where he had relatives, for religious education. Saul studied under the leading teacher of the day, Gamaliel (Acts 22:3).

Saul eventually joined the Pharisees (Phil. 3:5). This religious sect emphasized strict obedience to Jewish law as well as to the teachings of their own leaders. More clearly than many other Jews, Saul recognized the threat Christianity posed to Judaism (Acts 22:4-5). At first, he spent some of his tremendous fund of energy in trying to shut down the new movement. Then he met Jesus (9:1-19), and his life was forever changed.

Acts 11:26 notes that Jesus' followers were first called Christians at Antioch. Some think opponents of the church sarcastically referred to believers as Christians. Others think the disciples adopted the name to underscore their allegiance to Christ. Either way, the name distinguished Jesus' followers from other groups.

IV. Barnabas's Convictions: Acts 15:36-41

A. Difference of Opinion: vss. 36-38

Some time later Paul said to Barnabas, "Let us go back and visit the brothers in all the towns where we preached the word of the Lord and see how they are doing." Barnabas wanted to take John, also called Mark, with them, but Paul did not think it wise to take him, because he had deserted them in Pamphylia and had not continued with them in the work.

During worship, the Christians at Antioch heard the Spirit tell them to set apart Barnabas and Saul for a special task. This they did, sending the two men out on a journey to Gentile lands (A. D. 46–48; Acts 13:1-3). After being sent out by the church and the Holy Spirit, Saul and Barnabas, along with John Mark their helper, sailed from the port of Seleucia to the island of Cyprus (vss. 4-12). The group then traveled to the coast of Asia Minor, where they ventured inland eight miles to the city of Perga (vs. 13).

At this point Mark decided to turn back to Jerusalem. The reason for this return is not indicated. One fact is clear, though. Saul (now called Paul) looked on Mark's departure dimly. In fact, in A. D. 49 the issue became a point of contention for Paul and Barnabas. The former suggested to the latter that they return to each city where they had previously proclaimed the Gospel. Paul's goal was to see how the new believers were getting along (15:36).

Barnabas liked the idea and wanted to take along John Mark (vs. 37). But Paul disagreed strongly with this recommendation because John Mark had deserted the team on the previous missionary journey (vs. 38). Initially the apostle did not intend this venture to be a new outreach. But God would use the unfolding circumstances to bring about an entirely unique missionary journey, one that was different in focus and scope from the first endeavor.

B. Separation in Ministry: vss. 39-41

They had such a sharp disagreement that they parted company. Barnabas took Mark and sailed for Cyprus, but Paul chose Silas and left, commended by the brothers to the grace of the Lord. He went through Syria and Cilicia, strengthening the churches.

Acts 15:39 suggests that there was a heated argument between Paul and Barnabas over John Mark's usefulness to them. Since neither individual could come to an agreement, Paul and Barnabas decided to part company. Barnabas left with John Mark for Cyprus. Meanwhile, Paul chose a believer named Silas to accompany him on his return visit to the churches he had visited on the previous missionary journey (vs. 40). The two set out with the blessing of the Antioch congregation and traveled throughout Syria and Cilicia to strengthen "the churches" (vs. 41).

Discussion Questions

1. Why do you think Luke chose Barnabas as an example of generosity?
2. How was Barnabas an encourager for Saul (Paul)?
3. What specific characteristics of Barnabas can you identify in Acts 11:24?
4. What brought about the sharp disagreement between Barnabas and Paul?
5. How can we encourage believers to use their skills in service for Christ?

Now Ask Yourself . . .

Who do I know that is an encourager to the body of Christ? How does that person encourage others in their growth?

What are some characteristics of someone who is an encourager?

Am I am encourager to others in their growth in the Lord?

What can I do to be more of an encourager?

Sometimes there are disagreements between believers. How do I handle these when they come up in my life?

Illustrations

There are many different ways we can be encouragers. We can reach out to others by helping them in times of need. You might consider donating food and clothing to a food pantry or opening up your home to an international student who needs a place to stay during the holidays. Another way we can encourage others is by giving them our personal recommendation. You might choose to give a fellow Christian a character reference for a job for which he or she has applied.

We can encourage others by commending them for their faithfulness to Christ. Perhaps you know about a young believer who is trying hard to live for Jesus. Why not express your appreciation for her or his dedication to the Lord? Finally, we can encourage others through simple acts of kindness. If someone seems discouraged, why not greet her with a smile and a warm hug? If a personal friend is recovering in the hospital from surgery, you might consider visiting him or sending him a get-well card. Regardless of what you do, it will undoubtedly be appreciated.

One simple thing to remember is that sincerity and listening to the Holy Spirit will ensure that our encouragement will be what's needed. Our displays of encouragement should be more than a one-time act of kindness. The Lord is pleased when He sees us developing a lifestyle of encouraging others. As we get into the habit of encouraging others, they will see that God, like His people, truly loves and cares for them .

Say 'Yes' to God

DEVOTIONAL READING

Psalm 103:15-18

DAILY BIBLE READINGS

Monday December 5
*Deuteronomy 30:11-20
God Lets Us Choose Life or
Death*

Tuesday December 6
*Joshua 24:14-18 Joshua
Tells the People to Choose
Whom They Will Serve*

Wednesday December 7
*Acts 4:12-20 Judge for
Yourself Whom You Will
Obey*

Thursday December 8
*Acts 5:12-20 The High
Priests Jail the Apostles,
but God Releases Them*

Friday December 9
*Acts 5:21-26 The Apostles
Are Found Teaching in the
Temple*

Saturday December 10
*Acts 5:27-32 The High
Priests Question the
Apostles*

Sunday December 11
*Acts 5:33-42 Gamaliel
Persuades the High Priests*

Scripture

Background Scripture: *Acts 5:12-42*

Scripture Lesson: *Acts 5:27-36, 38-42*

Key Verse: *Peter and the other apostles replied: "We must obey God rather than men!" Acts 5:29.*

Lesson Aim

If you must choose between God and men, choose God.

Lesson Setting

Time: A.D. 30

Place: Jerusalem

Lesson Outline

Say 'Yes' to God

  I. The Apostles Defend Themselves: Acts 5:27-32
    A. *The Accusation: vss. 27-28*
    B. *The Proclamation of the Resurrection:
       vss. 29-32*

 II. The Apostles Are Freed: Acts 5:33-36, 38-42
    A. *The Fury of the Sanhedrin: vs. 33*
    B. *The Advice of Gamaliel: vss. 34-36, 38-39*
    C. *The Punishment of the Apostles: vs. 40*
    D. *The Continued Joy and Devotion of
       the Apostles: vss. 41-42*

Introduction

Adults in your class probably consider themselves law-abiding citizens. It would be extremely difficult for them not to conform to the laws and regulations of society. They may fudge here and there, such as driving five miles over the speed limit, but they wouldn't flagrantly disregard the laws of the land, such as driving through red lights.

At times, however, your students are faced with situations in which they must obey God or submit to an authority that challenges their commitment to Christ. When that occurs, they need to understand that they should set aside their desire to be "good" citizens, "good" employees, "good" adult children, or even "good" spouses if they are to be obedient children of God. This is neither easy nor pleasant, but with God's help it can be done.

Lesson Commentary

I. The Apostles Defend Themselves: Acts 5:27-32

A. The Accusation: vss. 27-28

Having brought the apostles, they made them appear before the Sanhedrin to be questioned by the high priest. "We gave you strict orders not to teach in this name," he said. "Yet you have filled Jerusalem with your teaching and are determined to make us guilty of this man's blood."

More and more people were joining the Christian movement, and crowds were flocking to the apostles for healing (5:14-16). All this popularity filled the religious leaders with jealousy (vs. 17). Consequently, the high priest and his associates—all of them members of the Sadducean party—jailed the apostles again (vs. 18). At this time the Sadducees were the major opposition to the Christians within the Sanhedrin. The Sadducees had been instrumental in plotting Jesus' crucifixion and the earlier arrest of Peter and John.

During the night, God sent an angel to set the apostles free (vs. 19). The angel liberated them by opening the jail doors and leading them outside the prison. God sent the apostles back to the same task that had already infuriated the religious council. They were liberated for further ministry to proclaim in the temple all that Jesus had taught them about the Christian life (vs. 20).

The apostles could easily have found reasons not to continue preaching about Jesus. They had been told by their nation's religious leaders not to preach. Should they continue their witness concerning Jesus, they would surely be punished with beatings, further imprisonment, or even death. And the more they continued to proclaim Jesus as the Messiah, the more dangerous their situation would become.

Despite all this, Jesus' disciples wasted no time in returning to the temple and resuming their teaching. They chose to obey God's command to preach, which was renewed by the angel, rather than obey the national authorities (vs. 21).

As the apostles continued their preaching, the high priest convened the religious council and sent for the apostles from prison. The officers were astonished to discover that the apostles were not there, though no indication of a disturbance was present (vs. 22). After the officers reported this alarming news to the high priest and other religious leaders, someone notified them that the apostles were again teaching in the temple (vss. 23-25).

The captain of the temple was second in rank to the high priest among the Jewish people. Consequently, he wielded tremendous power among the Jews. Nevertheless, he did not have the apostles harmed, for he and his officers were afraid that the people might become hostile (vs. 26).

Meanwhile, the apostles did not resist arrest, though they might have had the support of the people. They peaceably accompanied the captain and his officers to the Sanhedrin (vs. 27).

The Sanhedrin was made up of the acting high priest, former high priests, relatives of the high priests, scribes, elders (tribal and family heads), Sadducees, and Pharisees. The Sadducees were dominant, though the Pharisees had a strong minority voice. The two parties often squabbled over theological issues, especially the resurrection of the body.

During the first century, the Sanhedrin was accountable to the Roman governor. The Roman Empire had stripped the council of most of its executive power. Their domain was formally restricted to Judea. They were given a great deal of freedom, however, over the religious affairs of the Jews. In fact, Rome expected this body to settle disputes over matters of Jewish law and not hand them over to the district governor.

The high priest and his associates had three reasons for arresting the apostles. To begin with, Peter and John had not obeyed the official orders to stop preaching in the name of Jesus Christ. Second, the witness of the church was refuting the doctrines held by the Sadducees, giving every evidence that Jesus Christ was alive. Third, the religious leaders were filled with envy at the great success of these untrained and unauthorized men (See Matt. 27:18; Acts 13:45)

As head of the Jewish council, the high priest addressed the apostles. He reminded them of the prohibition the Sanhedrin had placed on their preaching. But instead of honoring the restriction, the apostles had spread their teaching throughout Jerusalem. A part of their teaching had been pinning the guilt for the death of Jesus on the Sanhedrin. These things infuriated the high priest (vs. 28).

B. The Proclamation of the Resurrection: vss. 29-32

Peter and the other apostles replied: "We must obey God rather than men! The God of our fathers raised Jesus from the dead—whom you had killed by hanging him on a tree. God exalted him to his own right hand as Prince and Savior that he might give repentance and forgiveness of sins to Israel. We are witnesses of these things, and so is the Holy Spirit, whom God has given to those who obey him."

In response to the high priest, the apostles—with Peter as their spokesperson—did not hesitate to announce, "We must obey God rather than men!" (vs. 29). Perhaps by our modern standards such a response may seem unnecessarily reckless and tactless. But in order to appreciate the courage of the apostles, we have to consider the situation they were in.

God's servants stood before a hostile, self-serving court that was hardly concerned about justice. The apostles knew what was at stake. The Sanhedrin could demand that they be executed, just as they had with Jesus. But the apostles also knew something even greater was at stake. They had been entrusted with the message that God through Jesus was reconciling the world to Himself. They considered their lives secondary in importance to their message.

The council's order to stop proclaiming Jesus had directly challenged the apostles' loyalty to Christ. The Sanhedrin may have had great influence and authority, but the one who had commissioned the apostles had even greater authority. For them, this was an either/or matter—either obedience to human authorities, or faithfulness to God.

Peter and the others recognized the council's orders as part of a pattern of opposition. Peter boldly accused the religious leaders of slaying Jesus on a tree. By "tree" (vs. 30), the apostle was referring to the cross.

Peter declared that Jesus not only died but also that God raised Him up, exalted Him as Prince and Savior, and offered forgiveness of sins through faith in Him (vs. 31). Peter furthermore announced that he and the other apostles testified to Jesus' resurrection. Moreover, the Holy Spirit affirmed their witness. He is the one whom God "has given to those who obey him" (vs. 32). The implication couldn't be clearer. Peter and the rest of the apostles were obeying God, whereas the religious leaders (despite their assertions to the contrary) were disobeying God.

How were the apostles able to withstand the council's challenge to their commitment? Their victory flowed from genuine discipleship. They personally believed in Jesus and had committed themselves to His service. Our ability to overcome begins at the same point—with a personal trust in Christ that expresses itself in determination to serve Him. Moreover, our commitment to serve our Lord has to draw upon the strength that only the Spirit provides to those who are united with Christ by faith.

II. The Apostles Are Freed: Acts 5:33-36, 38-42

A. The Fury of the Sanhedrin: vs. 33

When they heard this, they were furious and wanted to put them to death.

The members of the council didn't attempt to refute the witness of the apostles. Instead, they fell into a rage. The Greek word rendered "furious" (vs. 33) originally meant "sawn through." This suggests that the effect of the apostles' accusation was like a chain saw on a pole of wood. It's no wonder the Sanhedrin demanded the apostles be executed, undoubtedly to silence this powerful threat to their authority.

B. The Advice of Gamaliel: vss. 34-36, 38-39

But a Pharisee named Gamaliel, a teacher of the law, who was honored by all the people, stood up in the Sanhedrin and ordered that the men be put outside for a little while. Then he addressed them: "Men of Israel, consider carefully what you intend to do to these men. Some time ago Theudas appeared, claiming to be somebody, and about four hundred men rallied to him. He was killed, all his followers were dispersed, and it all came to nothing. . . . Therefore, in the present case I advise you: Leave these men alone! Let them go! For if their purpose or activity is of human origin, it will fail. But if it is from God, you will not be able to stop these men; you will only find yourselves fighting against God."

The apostles probably would have been executed had it not been for the moderating voice of Gamaliel [guh-MAY-lih-uhl] (vs. 34). He was a Pharisee whom the general population liked. Though the majority of the Sanhedrin were Sadducees and opponents of the Pharisees, Gamaliel was much respected.

Gamaliel is reported to have been the grandson of the great Jewish rabbi Hillel, who was the founder of a liberal school of interpretation. From a theological standpoint, Gamaliel followed in his grandfather's footsteps. History's record of his cautious, tolerant character fits perfectly with Luke's description of him in Acts. In 22:3, Paul noted that he studied under Gamaliel. Though Paul later rejected Gamaliel's belief in salvation through works, the apostle benefited from Gamaliel's teaching all his life.

Gamaliel advised the Sanhedrin to wait and see. He also reminded his fellow council members that on other occasions, insurrections had fizzled out after the death of the leader. The first example he gave, the uprising of Theudas, probably occurred about 4 B.C. The second example, the revolt of Judas, occurred in A.D. 6. Gamaliel implied that, like those movements, the Christian movement would probably soon die out too, since its leader—Jesus—had died (vss. 35-37).

On the other hand, Gamaliel continued, there was a remote possibility that this movement was ordained by God. If that were the case, then nothing could stop it. Either way, Gamaliel's counsel was for restraint (vss. 38-39).

C. The Punishment of the Apostles: vs. 40

His speech persuaded them. They called the apostles in and had them flogged. Then they ordered them not to speak in the name of Jesus, and let them go.

Gamaliel's appeal curbed the rage of the Sanhedrin. But the council members refused to dismiss the apostles without some kind of punishment and warning. Out of sight of the crowds in the streets, they had the apostles flogged.

The flog was a whip made of leather strips embedded with chips of bone or metal. When captives were beaten across the back with a flog, their flesh would be left in shreds. Sometimes even their bones or internal organs would lie exposed.

Once again the Sanhedrin handed down a stern warning to the apostles against preaching in the name of Jesus. The council members had tried this once before without success, but now there really wasn't much more they could do. They knew the popularity of the apostles was increasing. Apart from executing them, the Sanhedrin could only warn them to stop.

D. The Continued Joy and Devotion of the Apostles: vss. 41-42

The apostles left the Sanhedrin, rejoicing because they had been counted worthy of suffering disgrace for the Name. Day after day, in the temple courts and from house to house, they never stopped teaching and proclaiming the good news that Jesus is the Christ.

The apostles went away glad for the honor of being disgraced (vs. 41). They had suffered for Christ in the same way that Jesus had suffered (Mark 15:15). Difficult circumstances could not conquer them, for they belonged to the Lord.

It seems a paradox to say someone is "worthy" of disgrace; it's a paradox to find joy in pain. Yet the disciples were living paradoxes.

The apostles may have been beaten and threatened, but they refused to be frightened off. Every day in the temple and in their homes, they continued to teach and preach the Gospel. They wanted everyone to know that "Jesus is the Christ" (vs. 42).

There is no way that difficult situations can naturally create positive results, and no way that rejoicing can naturally exist in suffering. It's only when we know Jesus as the apostles did that our perspective can be changed to make the paradox possible. When we have the same purpose and power that the apostles had, we will be better at rejoicing in our troubles. And when the Spirit gives us courage as He did the apostles, we can face hardships with a positive attitude.

The early Christians not only witnessed in the temple, but "from house to house." Unlike congregations today, these people had no buildings that were set aside for worship and fellowship. Believers would meet in different homes, worshiping the Lord, listening to teaching, and seeking to win the lost (see Acts 2:46). Their ministry was taken right into their homes and went on without ceasing.

Discussion Questions

1. Why do you think the apostles were brought again before the Sanhedrin?
2. Why was it hard for the members of the council to accept their responsibility in having Jesus executed?
3. Why did Peter and the rest of the apostles sense the need to repeatedly talk about Jesus' resurrection?
4. Why did the apostles rejoice when they were flogged by the authorities?

Now Ask Yourself . . .

How can I distinguish between a real challenge to my faith in Christ and a restriction that I just don't like?

Do I think subtle challenges to the Christian faith are more dangerous or less dangerous than overt attacks? Why?

As my commitment to Christ is challenged, what things might I lose when I decide to obey God? What might I gain?

Illustrations

The apostles' bold stand can serve as a model for us when we are opposed by evil. There can be no compromise. If following certain people prevents us from serving the Lord, we must obey Him rather than those people.

The issue goes far beyond mere legal matters. Many "laws" are unwritten—cultural expectations, prevailing attitudes in society, pressure from peers, the influence of traditions, and so on. All these weigh heavily upon believers, who must choose between the ways of people and the ways of God. When the ways of people are morally neutral, there's no problem. But when they violate God's principles, a choice is required.

To choose for God in the face of popular opinion requires great courage. That is why we, like the apostles, need the indwelling power of the Spirit. That is why we, like they, need to be absolutely convinced of the reality of the Resurrection—that Jesus is alive and lives in us!

We may never stand before a legal body like the Sanhedrin. But every day we face other kinds of challenges to our faith. And every day we need the same courage and conviction that motivated the apostles.

Overcoming challenges to our faith is a two-stage process. It begins with a clear understanding of God's will as revealed in Scripture and exemplified in Jesus. This understanding clarifies our purpose in this world so that we can recognize our God-given task in any situation. And we experience victory by drawing upon the Holy Spirit's enabling power to fulfill God's purpose for us regardless of the opposition.

Not Without Opposition

DEVOTIONAL READING

Micah 4:1-7

DAILY BIBLE READINGS

Monday December 12
*Acts 6:1-8 Stephen Does
Great Wonders and Signs*

Tuesday December 13
*Acts 6:9-15 Many Lie
about Stephen and His
Works*

Wednesday December 14
*Acts 7:1-16 The Sanhedrin
Listens to Stephen*

Thursday December 15
*Acts 7:17-29 The
Sanhedrin Hears the Facts*

Friday December 16
*Acts 7:30-43 Stephen
Shows How the People
Refused to Listen*

Saturday December 17
*Acts 7:44-43 The
Sanhedrin Are Like Their
Ancestors*

Sunday December 18
*Acts 7:54—8:1 The
Stoning of Stephen*

Scripture

Background Scripture: *Acts 6:1—8:3*

Scripture Lesson: *Acts 6:1-8; 7:55—8:1*

Key Verse: *But Stephen, full of the Holy Spirit, looked up to heaven and saw the glory of God, and Jesus standing at the right hand of God. Acts 7:55.*

Lesson Aim

Spirit-filled people will face opposition.

Lesson Setting

Time: About A.D. 32

Place: Jerusalem

Lesson Outline

Not Without Opposition

I. Service in the Church: Acts 6:1-8
   A. *The Complaint: vs. 1*
   B. *The Solution: vss. 2-4*
   C. *The Response: vss. 5-6*
   D. *The Growth: vss. 7-8*

II. Martyrdom in the Church: Acts 7:55—8:1
   A. *Stephen's Heavenly Vision: vss. 55-56*
   B. *Stephen's Stoning: vss. 57-58*
   C. *Stephen's Forgiving Heart: vss. 59-60*
   D. *Saul's Approval: vs. 8:1*

Introduction

Called to Serve and Forgive

God wants us to serve one another in the church. But many believers shy away from this because they don't want to put their reputation on the line. They're afraid to take a hit if something is perceived as a failure.

Self-appointed critics are often the first to complain. They seem to focus on minor matters and cause unnecessary squabbles within the church. This leads to conflict and division, both of which sidetrack believers from witnessing for Christ. Who wants to invite unbelievers to a squabbling church?

The early church found that having a forgiving heart was the key to effective service and witness. They knew they didn't have to be perfect before they could accept service responsibilities. Let your students know that if they humbly rely on God and have a forgiving heart, God will help them fulfill their duties in the church.

Lesson Commentary

I. Service in the Church: Acts 6:1-8

A. The Complaint: vs. 1

In those days when the number of disciples was increasing, the Grecian Jews among them complained against the Hebraic Jews because their widows were being overlooked in the daily distribution of food.

After Christ ascended, the church experienced explosive growth. People were entering God's kingdom by the thousands, far more than the 12 apostles could possibly minister to. Thus there was a need for additional Christians who were willing to wait on tables so that the apostles could devote themselves to praying and preaching the Word of God.

There is some debate over the identity of the "Grecian Jews" (vs. 1). Most likely they were Greek-speaking Jews who had become Christians. When Israel and Judah fell (in 722 and 586 B.C., respectively), the Jews were scattered throughout the Assyrian and Babylonian empires. This was known as the Diaspora [die-ASS-poh-ruh], or the dispersion. The Hellenistic Jews were descendants of the scattered Jews, who had returned to Jerusalem for religious reasons. This explains the presence of Greek-speaking synagogues in the city.

The Jewish community had many food pantries for the poor, especially for widows who had lost their means of support when their husbands died. In addition, many of the older Jews of the Diaspora came to Jerusalem to be buried there. Since many of these older widows had left family behind them, the burden for support fell on the community. Those who had become Christians might have been disqualified from regular Jewish aid. Thus the early Christian church had to make provisions for them.

The Hellenistic Jews, however, felt like second-class citizens in the church. Apparently their widows were being ignored when it came to the distribution of food and supplies for the poor. Since the apostles acknowledged the dilemma, the problem must have been real and not just a matter of perception. The situation possibly was a symptom of a much deeper problem—prejudice because of strong difference of opinion. It's also quite possible that a language barrier existed between the two groups, which increased the tensions between them.

B. The Solution: vss. 2-4

So the Twelve gathered all the disciples together and said, "It would not be right for us to neglect the ministry of the word of God in order to wait on tables. Brothers, choose seven men from among you who are known to be full of the Spirit and wisdom. We will turn this responsibility over to them and will give our attention to prayer and the ministry of the word."

The Twelve responded by calling a meeting of all the believers. The apostles could have assumed responsibility for overseeing the relief work. But they correctly saw this as a diversion from their main tasks of praying and preaching and teaching the Gospel. They thus decided to delegate to others the important job of administering the charitable distribution of food to the poor (vs. 2).

The apostles were not interested in just filling a vacancy with willing bodies. Every duty needing attention in the Body of Christ (the Church) was important. If any of these tasks were done by

Christians who were not Spirit-filled, the entire church suffered. Consequently, the first church leaders made it clear that those to be appointed had to be well respected and "full of the Spirit and wisdom" (vs. 3). The Twelve then would put these believers in charge of the food relief program.

More than one problem was solved in this way. Not only did the Greek widows receive needed supplies, but also the appointment of Hellenistic believers to positions of leadership helped wipe away the stigma of being second-class Christians among these people. In addition, the apostles would have greater freedom to pray and minister God's Word (vs. 4).

We commonly call these seven men of Acts 6 "deacons" because the Greek noun, "diakonos," used in Acts 6:1 means "ministration," and the verb, "diakoneo" used in verse 2 means "serve." However, this title of deacon is not given to them in this chapter. These seven men were humble servants of the church, men whose work made it possible for the apostles to carry on their important ministries among the people.

C. The Response: vss. 5-6

This proposal pleased the whole group. They chose Stephen, a man full of faith and of the Holy Spirit; also Philip, Procorus, Nicanor, Timon, Parmenas, and Nicolas from Antioch, a convert to Judaism. They presented these men to the apostles, who prayed and laid their hands on them.

The apostles' solution to the Greek-speaking Jews' complaint resolved a problem that could have become major. The Twelve allowed the Hellenistic Jews to choose their own representatives (vs. 5). All seven Christians had Greek names, which suggests that they were probably Hellenists. Only one of the seven was described as a proselyte—a Greek Gentile who had become a Jew before becoming a Christian.

Stephen is described as a believer full of faith and the Holy Spirit. We can assume that the other believers chosen also met these qualifications. In fact, Stephen and Philip would later demonstrate other spiritual gifts.

The primary responsibility of these seven believers, however, was one of service to the Hellenistic Jews. In fact, we get the word "deacon" from the Greek word for service. The first recorded evidence that Paul recognized the role of deacon as an official position of leadership in the church was when he wrote his letter to the Philippians (Phil. 1:1; see also 1 Tim. 3:8-13). The duties of deacons, however, were performed long before the role of deacons became an actual office within the church.

Luke also highlighted two things that the apostles did after the seven believers were chosen. First, the apostles prayed and laid hands on the seven, thus setting them apart for their church duties. In the same way the apostles delegated some of their church authority to Stephen and the other six believers (Acts 6:6).

D. The Growth: vss. 7-8

So the word of God spread. The number of disciples in Jerusalem increased rapidly, and a large number of priests became obedient to the faith. Now Stephen, a man full of God's grace and power, did great wonders and miraculous signs among the people.

The ministry of the seven believers had immediate results. The church rapidly grew in Jerusalem. Even a large number of Jewish priests became followers of Christ. Instead of a few people trying to do everything, other believers contributed to the well-being of the community of faith (vs. 7).

Though Stephen was responsible for waiting on tables, he performed many miraculous signs through the power of the Holy Spirit (vs. 8). Stephen also proclaimed the Gospel, which disturbed the Jews who had come from different parts of the Roman Empire. One group, the "Freedmen" (vs. 9), were possibly Hellenistic Jews who had been liberated from slavery. Both the Cyrenians and the Alexandrians had come from major cities in North Africa. Cilicia was located in the southeast corner of Asia Minor, and "Asia" (in today's Turkey) was a Roman province in the western part of Asia Minor.

Since Stephen's opponents could not defeat his message by debating with him, they secretly persuaded others to testify that Stephen had blasphemed against Moses and God. Naturally, what the false witnesses claimed alarmed the Jewish people and their rulers in Jerusalem. What may have incensed them the most was the charge that Stephen had said Jesus would destroy the temple and change Mosaic customs—charges similar to those that had been brought against Jesus at His trial (vss. 10-14). Consequently, the Sanhedrin ordered that Stephen be apprehended and brought before the council (vs. 15).

II. Martyrdom in the Church: Acts 7:55—8:1

What were the results of Stephen's death? For Stephen, it meant coronation (Rev. 2:10). He saw the glory of God and the Son of God standing to receive him. For Israel, Stephen's death meant condemnation. This was their third murder: they had permitted John the Baptist to be killed; they asked for Jesus to be killed; and now they were killing Stephen themselves. For the church in Jerusalem, the death of Stephen meant liberation. They had been witnessing in Jerusalem, but now they would be directed to take the message out of Jerusalem to the Samaritans (Acts 8) and even to the Gentiles (Acts 11). Finally, for Saul, Stephen's death would eventually mean salvation.

A. Stephen's Heavenly Vision: vss. 55-56

But Stephen, full of the Holy Spirit, looked up to heaven and saw the glory of God, and Jesus standing at the right hand of God. "Look," he said, "I see heaven open and the Son of Man standing at the right hand of God."

Stephen's opponents had accused him of slandering Moses, the law, the temple, and God. In response, Stephen argued that throughout Israel's history, the people of God had opposed Moses and the prophets. The people had also lived contrary to the letter and spirit of the law that Moses had received at Mount Sinai. Instead of worshiping God in the tabernacle and temple, they offered pagan sacrifices and venerated foreign deities. Rather than give their allegiance to the Messiah, about whom Moses and the rest of the Old Testament prophets spoke, the people were guilty of betraying and murdering Jesus (vss. 1-53).

While under the control of the Spirit, Stephen gazed steadily upward toward heaven and saw the glory of God. Stephen also saw Jesus standing in the place of honor at God's right hand (vss. 55-56). Despite the terrifying prospect of death, Stephen remained calm and hopeful. Unlike his detractors, he had the assurance that God the Son—his Savior and Lord—would receive him into His glorious presence.

B. Stephen's Stoning: vss. 57-58

At this they covered their ears and, yelling at the top of their voices, they all rushed at him, dragged him out of the city and began to stone him. Meanwhile, the witnesses laid their clothes at the feet of a young man named Saul.

Stephen's words were so blasphemous to the religious leaders that they put their hands over their ears and drowned out his voice with their shouts. Perhaps with the fury of an uncontrollable mob, the council rushed at Stephen, dragged him out of the city, and began to stone him (vss. 57-58).

The members of the Sanhedrin, not Stephen, were guilty of rebelling against God. Though he faced imminent death, Stephen demonstrated before his antagonists what it truly meant to honor the Lord. Stephen's desire was not to perpetuate a dead institution and its lifeless traditions; rather, he sought to please God, regardless of the circumstances or the cost to himself.

While these things were taking place, the official witnesses took off their outer garments and laid them at the feet of a young man named Saul. (He is later called Paul in 13:9). He was a Pharisee and associated with the Sanhedrin (Phil. 3:5). Possibly Saul was an instigator of Stephen's trial (Acts 8:3; 9:1-2).

C. Stephen's Forgiving Heart: vss. 59-60

While they were stoning him, Stephen prayed, "Lord Jesus, receive my spirit." Then he fell on his knees and cried out, "Lord, do not hold this sin against them." When he had said this, he fell asleep.

As he was being murdered, Stephen neither begged for mercy nor renounced Christ. Rather, Stephen committed himself to the Lord and asked Him to forgive the religious leaders (vss. 59-60). His words were similar to those spoken by Jesus at His crucifixion (Luke 23:34).

Stephen was the church's first martyr, though not its last. The early believers were glad to suffer as Jesus had suffered, for it meant they were counted worthy (Acts 5:41). Perhaps like Stephen, these unnamed martyrs also had a forgiving heart toward their foes. Such a response comes only from the Spirit.

D. Saul's Approval: vs. 8:1

And Saul was there, giving approval to his death.

Paul's (Saul's) statement about himself in Acts 22:20 agrees with 8:1. The hatred he had of all believers before his conversion was manifested in his attitude toward Stephen. God would eventually use Paul's disdain for Jesus to lead him to eternal life.

Paul realized he had been the worst of sinners. Because the devil had blinded his mind to the truth, only the Spirit could enlighten his understanding and convince him of his need for Christ. God in His mercy allowed this to happen so that Paul, the foremost of sinners, might be a trophy of His grace. The former persecutor of the church thus became an ideal display of Christ's unlimited patience. Paul would serve as an example to others who in the future would put their trust in Christ and receive eternal life (1 Tim. 1:16).

Discussion Questions

1. Why do you think the apostles delegated to others the task of choosing seven believers to oversee the daily distribution of food?
2. Why did the apostles want the seven believers to be full of the Spirit?
3. How do you think the people who knew Stephen best would have described him?
4. Why did Stephen's opponents incite the false witnesses to make the particular claims they did?

Now Ask Yourself . . .

When I perform Christian duties, what risks bother me the most? Why?

What do I believe God has called me to do in my church? How have I responded?

What areas of service do I see myself stepping out into? How can I be filled more with the Spirit as I begin to do so?

What hinders me the most from serving in the church?

Illustrations

In some churches, pastors attempt to do everything. They preach, keep the books, lead the youth group, and even do the janitorial work. Granted, in some cases, these leaders seem to have no choice. In many cases, however, there is the problem of church members' unwillingness to serve. Why are they unwilling? Perhaps risk is a factor.

Responsibility entails many risks, including the risk of opposition, failure, and stress. When believers accept responsibilities in the church, they are vulnerable to all these risks. Opposition can come not only from non-Christians but also from other believers. Though opposition from believers should cause us to check how we're handling our responsibilities, we should not let it discourage us.

Just because God has called us to a task and empowered us with the Spirit, it doesn't mean that feelings of failure won't occur. The same thing could also be said of stress. Rather than denying the presence of these risk factors, we can use them to keep us alert to our areas of weakness and prompt us to seek support from other believers.

If we are to bear fruit for the Lord, we must take risks. But we can have peace about those risks, knowing and trusting that Jesus will always be with us to help us overcome them.

Share the News

DEVOTIONAL READING

Isaiah 9:1-7

DAILY BIBLE READINGS

Monday December 19
*Luke 1:26-38 An Angel
Visits Mary*

Tuesday December 20
*Luke 1:39-45 Mary Visits
Elizabeth*

Wednesday December 21
*Luke 1:46-56 Mary Praises
God for Blessing His
People*

Thursday December 22
*Luke 2:1-7 Jesus Is Born
in Bethlehem*

Friday December 23
*Luke 2:8-14 An Angel
Appears to the Shepherds*

Saturday December 24
*Luke 2:15-20 The
Shepherds Hurry to
Bethlehem to See Jesus*

Sunday December 25
*Mark 16:15-20 The Good
News Is for Everybody*

Scripture

Background Scripture: *Luke 2:1-20*
Scripture Lesson: *Luke 2:1, 4-20*
Key Verse: *But the angel said unto them, "Do not be
afraid. I bring you good news of great joy that will be for
all the people. Today in the town of David a Savior has
been born to you; he is Christ the Lord." Luke 2:10-11.*

Lesson Aim

God's message is good news for everybody.

Lesson Setting

Time: About 6–5 B.C.
Place: Nazareth and Bethlehem

Lesson Outline

Share the News

   I. The Savior's Birth: Luke 2:1, 4-7
      A. At Bethlehem: vss. 1, 4-5
      B. In the Manger: vss. 6-7
  II. The Angel's Announcement: Luke 2:8-14
      A. The Angel of the Lord: vss. 8-12
      B. The Heavenly Host: vss. 13-14
 III. The Shepherds' Visit: Luke 2:15-20
      A. To Bethlehem: vss. 15-16
      B. To Spread the Word: vss. 17-18
      C. Mary's Response: vs. 19
      D. To Praise God: vs. 20

Introduction

A Wondrous Birth

Charles Schultz's Peanuts characters frequently give insight into human nature. As a bewildered Charlie Brown thinks about Christmas, Lucy comments, "Who else but you, Charlie Brown, could turn a wonderful season like Christmas into a problem?"

For many, Christmas is a problem to be endured rather than a holiday to be celebrated. Exhaustion from too much activity exaggerates family tensions. The parents are tired and the children are anxious. A demoralizing Christmas also may result from feelings of loss or incompleteness. Living with memories of happier holidays past, an elderly person may long for those who have died or are far away. The single person may feel miserably alone at Christmas, when everyone else seems to have someone. Even the weather can contribute to the Christmas blues.

Although your students may not put their feelings into words, they will bring some of these thoughts to your class. Use this lesson to focus on the good news of Jesus' wondrous birth. Giving Christ the central focus can turn a blue holiday into a joy-filled occasion.

Lesson Commentary

I. The Savior's Birth: Luke 2:1, 4-7

A. At Bethlehem: vss. 1, 4-5

In those days Caesar Augustus issued a decree that a census should be taken of the entire Roman world. . . . So Joseph also went up from the town of Nazareth in Galilee to Judea, to Bethlehem the town of David, because he belonged to the house and line of David. He went there to register with Mary, who was pledged to be married to him and was expecting a child.

Luke introduced Jesus' birth by setting it in its historical context. He mentioned two officials—the emperor of Rome, Caesar Augustus, and the governor of Syria, Publius Sulpicius Quirinius. Luke also mentioned a political event: the Roman census that drew Mary and Joseph to Bethlehem (vss. 1-2). This historical approach underscores the fact that at Christ's birth the eternal God invaded temporal human affairs. Not only that, but also God used secular rulers and events to accomplish His purposes.

The Roman census was not so much to count people as to determine who owed taxes and who could serve in the Roman army (though Jews were not subject to military conscription). To comply with the census, Joseph had to travel about 70 miles—at least a three-day journey—from Nazareth to Bethlehem, the town of his ancestors (vss. 3-4). Mary was almost ready to give birth, so it was not the best time for her to make a trip. But there was no way Joseph could delay the journey. So they decided Mary should go with him (vs. 5).

Bethlehem means "house of bread," the ideal birthplace for the Bread of Life (John 6:35). Its rich historic heritage included the death of Rachel and the birth of Benjamin, the marriage of Ruth and Boaz, and the exploits of David. It is worth noting that Benjamin means "son of my right hand," and David means "beloved." Both of these names apply to our Lord, for He is the Beloved Son (Luke 3:22) at God's right hand (Ps. 110:1).

B. In the Manger: vss. 6-7

While they were there, the time came for the baby to be born, and she gave birth to her firstborn, a son. She wrapped him in cloths and placed him in a manger, because there was no room for them in the inn.

Bethlehem at this time likely was overflowing with travelers who sought to register in the census, so suitable accommodations were difficult to find. The "inn" (vs. 7) could have been a reception room in a private home or a space at a public outdoor shelter, but it was probably not a large building with several individual rooms.

According to tradition, Mary gave birth to her firstborn in a cave that had been made into a stable (vs. 6). Others, however, think Joseph and Mary stayed in the open courtyard of a crowded home, where there would have been a series of stalls along the walls. Travelers used the stalls as stables and lean-to shelters. Quite possibly, Mary gave birth surrounded by the activity of the courtyard.

Like many peasant children, Mary's son would have been washed in a mixture of water and olive oil, rubbed with salt, and then wrapped in strips of linen. These would be placed around the arms and legs of the infant to keep the limbs protected. (The custom of wrapping infants this way is still practiced in many Middle Eastern countries.) Mary then laid the child in a trough used for feeding animals.

Being born in a stable was a humble beginning for one supposed to be the Savior of the world. Mary must have wondered how the angel's words about Jesus (1:32-33) could come true. We can be thankful, however, that Luke told this side of the account. He showed us how God stooped to lift fallen humanity. Jesus came as a poor, humble, and homeless baby. Because He identified with the lowest, He gives hope today to those who have no other source of hope.

II. The Angel's Announcement: Luke 2:8-14

A. The Angel of the Lord: vss. 8-12

And there were shepherds living out in the fields nearby, keeping watch over their flocks at night. An angel of the Lord appeared to them, and the glory of the Lord shone around them, and they were terrified. But the angel said to them, "Do not be afraid. I bring you good news of great joy that will be for all the people. Today in the town of David a Savior has been born to you; he is Christ the Lord. This will be a sign to you: You will find a baby wrapped in cloths and lying in a manger."

An angel announced the Messiah's birth to ordinary shepherds, not the powerful rulers or religious leaders (vs. 8). Since shepherds in Bible times lived out in the open and were unable to maintain strict obedience to the law of Moses, they generally were considered to be ceremonially unclean. As a result, they were despised by religious legalists and were typically excluded from temple worship. Custom didn't allow shepherds to serve as witnesses in legal cases.

Why did God single out these Bethlehem shepherds? Perhaps He wanted to make a point. It's not normally the influential or the elite who catch God's attention, but those who call for help and place their trust in the Lord.

Interestingly, these shepherds may have been watching over flocks reserved for temple sacrifices in Jerusalem. Suddenly, an angel of the Lord appeared and the radiance of God's glory surrounded them. The word "glory" (vs. 9), when applied to God in Scripture, refers to the luminous manifestation of His being. In other words, it is the brilliant revelation of Himself to humanity. It's no wonder the shepherds were terrified by the sight.

The angel reassured the shepherds with good news of a joyous event, namely, the birth of the Savior (vs. 10). Israel's Messiah and Lord had been born that night in Bethlehem, and He would make redemption available to all people, including the weak and oppressed—even society's outcasts (vs. 11). Military and political leaders during those times were frequently called "saviors." But Jesus was unique, being the Anointed One of God. The angel encouraged the shepherds to find the Christ child lying in a manger, wrapped snugly in strips of cloth (vs. 12).

It's worth mentioning that Christ is a word borrowed from Greek. It means "Anointed One," signifying divine commissioning for a specific task. In Old Testament times, kings and priests were anointed with oil as a sign of their divine appointment. The Hebrew word for the Anointed One is translated Messiah. It was used of the promised one who would deliver Israel from oppression. Most Jews thought He would be a political leader. They did not consider that His mission might be to free them from sin.

B. The Heavenly Host: vss. 13-14

Suddenly a great company of the heavenly host appeared with the angel, praising God and saying, "Glory to God in the highest, and on earth peace to men on whom his favor rests."

We can imagine the shepherds staring in amazement, trembling and trying to grasp the significance of the angel's announcement. Suddenly the night sky exploded with the sounds of angels praising God (vs. 13). They gave glory to God and announced peace for all who receive God's favor (vs. 14). People long for peace, but true peace cannot be achieved until individuals experience inner peace, which is possible only through faith in Jesus Christ.

III. The Shepherds' Visit: Luke 2:15-20

A. To Bethlehem: vss. 15-16

When the angels had left them and gone into heaven, the shepherds said to one another, "Let's go to Bethlehem and see this thing that has happened, which the Lord has told us about." So they hurried off and found Mary and Joseph, and the baby, who was lying in the manger.

As we have seen, the shepherds' initial response to the unusual sights and sounds was fear. But following the words about the birth of the baby, and following the praise of the angelic host, the shepherds moved from fear to curiosity (vs. 15). The angel had told the shepherds the location and specific situation of the holy birth. Now they decided to travel to Bethlehem and see for themselves what the Lord had told them about it.

It's not easy to convey in English the urgency of the shepherds' words. We might paraphrase it by saying, "Come on, let's quickly go and see Him without delay!" Thus, the shepherds hurried off and successfully found Mary and Joseph (vs. 16). The shepherds also saw the baby lying on the bed of hay. These most common of all people had the privilege of being the first on record to see the holy child.

At the time of Jesus' birth, there was a heavy messianic expectation among the Jews. Many believed the Messiah was coming. Old Testament prophecy inspired this hope among them, and Roman domination made them long for the Messiah as well. With respect to the former point, Micah had foretold that a ruler of Israel would come out of Bethlehem (Mic. 5:2). The prophet had also declared that this king would bring lasting security to Israel and would extend His influence to the ends of the earth. The birth of Jesus in Bethlehem fulfilled this prophecy. Also, God chose Bethlehem to indicate Jesus' royal status.

For some reason, shepherds were not allowed to testify in court, but God used some humble shepherds to be the first human witnesses that prophecy had been fulfilled and the Messiah had been born. The shepherds took the place of the angels in spreading the Good News. They received by faith the message God sent them and then responded with immediate obedience.

B. To Spread the Word: vss. 17-18

When they had seen him, they spread the word concerning what had been told them about this child, and all who heard it were amazed at what the shepherds said to them.

After the shepherds had seen Jesus, they became instant evangelists. Being in His presence must have convinced them that what the angel had said to them was true. Indeed the shepherds felt compelled to tell every person they met that they had seen the Messiah (vs. 17). The shepherds could have responded differently to the wonderful things they had seen and heard. They could have been so paralyzed by fear that they told no one about the wonders. The shepherds could have remained quiet. Thankfully, they spread the good news about the Messiah's birth.

Those who heard the news were astonished. The word translated "amazed" (vs. 18) conveys the idea that when the people heard the testimony of the shepherds, chills ran down their spines. This was neither immediate belief nor disbelief; it was simply attention. The shepherds' message captured the attention of all who heard, but we are not told whether they actually believed the reports.

C. Mary's Response: vs. 19

But Mary treasured up all these things and pondered them in her heart.

At first Mary, too, must have been astonished by what the shepherds said concerning her firstborn. But Luke 2:19 suggests that she did more than just remember what took place. She also treasured the incident and sought to fathom its significance. This remained true even though she did not fully understand all the ramifications of the events that were happening around her. Like Mary, we do not have to understand everything God is doing before we can appreciate His work in our lives. We can ponder God's ways and at the same time treasure what He is doing.

Mary's contemplation probably involved the thought that of all the women of Israel, she—a poor and seemingly insignificant countrywoman—had been favored by God to give birth to the Messiah. It is also probable that Mary told the details of this event to Luke, the writer of this Gospel. After all, Luke was familiar with many of the key people in the life of Christ.

D. To Praise God: vs. 20

The shepherds returned, glorifying and praising God for all the things they had heard and seen, which were just as they had been told.

The shepherds returned to their fields, but they were changed. How could they help but praise God for what they had seen (vs. 20)? Joy in heaven and on earth was the suitable reaction to the birth of the Savior.

Magazines, newspapers, and news broadcasts seem to highlight accounts of catastrophes, deprivations, and distress. Much "news" is the same old story that has been told by people for centuries. Human sin has made a mess of God's perfect creation. That's why all of us should reflect on God's gift to humanity—Jesus Christ. He came to earth to offer salvation to all people, regardless of their gender, race, or social status. Jesus is the Lord's gift to all who realize their need for Him to deliver them from bondage to sin.

Discussion Questions

1. What circumstances forced Joseph and Mary to travel to Bethlehem?
2. What sign did the angel give to the shepherds to confirm what he had declared?
3. How did the shepherds react to the angel's announcement concerning the baby Jesus?
4. How did Mary's response to the shepherds' story contrast with that of others?

Now Ask Yourself . . .

Are there places that I need to make room in my heart for the Savior?
What ways can I glorify God for the gift of His Son?
How can I spread the good news of what Christmas is really about?
Have I fully received the gift of Jesus in my life?

Illustrations

The announcement of Jesus' birth was good news to the shepherds and anyone who believed Jesus was the promised Savior. The birth of Christ should have the same impact on us. Our needs are just as great as the shepherds'. We may possess more than they; we may enjoy the pleasures of the world much more than they; but our need for the Savior is just as great. That is why we should value God's gift to humanity more than anything else in the world.

Although we need Christ and the salvation He offers, are we too preoccupied with the things of the world to care? The shepherds watched their flocks in the quietness of night. When the angel appeared, he had their undivided attention. In what ways can we quiet our spirits to give our attention to the greatest of divine gifts, the Savior?

The Lord not only wants us to receive His gift to humanity, but also to glorify Him for His gift. One way this can be done is by sharing with others the Good News about Christ. This can take place while walking with a friend in a park, while taking a midmorning break with a co-worker, while talking casually across the fence with a neighbor, or while spending a quiet evening with a family member.

We can also use times of private prayer to glorify the Father for sending His Son. Moreover, we can give praise to God in group worship. One possibility is getting together with a handful of other Christians to sing hymns and offer praise to the Lord for the gift of His Son. This activity not only honors God but can also be mutually encouraging to all who participate.

A Commitment to Change

DEVOTIONAL READING

Philippians 3

DAILY BIBLE READINGS

Monday December 26
Acts 9:1-9 Paul on the Damascus Road

Tuesday December 27
Acts 9:10-19 Ananias Gives Paul a Message

Wednesday December 28
Acts 9:20-25 Paul Escapes from Damascus

Thursday December 29
Acts 9:26-31 Barnabas Helps Paul in Jerusalem

Friday December 30
Galatians 1:11-24 How Paul Became a Disciple

Saturday December 31
Acts 22:2-11 Paul Gives His Testimony to the Crowd

Sunday January 1
Acts 22:12-21 Called to Preach to the Gentiles

Scripture

Background Scripture: *Acts 9; 22; 26*

Scripture Lesson: *Acts 9:1-6, 10-20*

Key Verse: *"This man is my chosen instrument to carry my name before the Gentiles and their kings and before the people of Israel." Acts 9:15b*

Lesson Aim

Understanding who Jesus really is will change a person's life.

Lesson Setting

Time: About A.D. 35.

Place: Road to Damascus

Lesson Outline

A Commitment to Change

  I.   The Conviction of Saul: Acts 9:1-6
       A. Saul's Pursuit of Believers: vss. 1-2
       B. The Lord's Confrontation with Saul: vss. 3-6

 II.   Saul's Commission: Acts 9:10-16
       A. Ananias Called to Go to Saul: vss. 10-12
       B. Ananias' Response: vss. 13-14
       C. The Lord's Reply and Commission of Saul: vss. 15-16

III.   Saul's Convalescence: Acts 9:17-20
       A. Ananias' Prayer: vs. 17
       B. Saul's Healing: vss. 18-19
       C. Saul's Declaration of Christ: vs. 20

Introduction

A Dramatic Conversion

Is it enough to believe in Jesus Christ if we wish to please God? Most adults you ask on the street would state that they believe in Jesus. That sounds pretty impressive until you realize that all the demons believe the same thing (Jas. 2:19). What makes a disciple is the thing that most adults resist: commitment. Interestingly, the word *disciple* has its root in the concept of discipline, and spiritual discipline is what we need if we are to be truly committed to Christ.

Most, if not all, adults in church would probably say without hesitation that they believe in Christ. But to what extent have they committed their lives to Christ? Certainly they may be committed enough to go to church, but how much further does their discipleship go? How often do they pray? How much time is spent studying God's Word? How frequently do they share the Gospel with others?

Some have said the true disciple is one who not only acknowledges Jesus as Savior, but they have truly made Him Lord of all of their life. In any case, the Holy Spirit can use this lesson to make a difference in all of our lives.

Lesson Commentary

I. The Conviction of Saul: Acts 9:1-6

A. Saul's Pursuit of Believers: vss. 1-2

Meanwhile, Saul was still breathing out murderous threats against the Lord's disciples. He went to the high priest and asked him for letters to the synagogues in Damascus, so that if he found any there who belonged to the Way, whether men or women, he might take them as prisoners to Jerusalem.

Having already been an accomplice in the stoning of Stephen, the first named Christian martyr (7:55-8:1a), Saul was like a vigilante. His very attitude was like a caged and angry animal. He thought he was doing the will of God in persecuting the church. Not surprisingly, he sought an audience with the Jewish high priest in order to secure written permission, equivalent to extradition papers, to arrest Jewish Christians in Damascus.

Damascus was about 175 miles northeast of Jerusalem, and it is known that at least 10,000 Jews lived there at that time. Some of them had become adherents of the "Way" (vs. 2)—an early name for Christianity.

Because of its location, Damascus was a major trade center during the first century A.D. As with the capital of Syria, the city had close economic ties with Israel. The city was considered an oasis in the middle of the desert because of its abundant water supplies.

Damascus eventually became an important city in the history of the Christian church. Later, in 636 A.D., Arabs conquered the town and made it a capital city for the Muslim world.

Damascus was not under the control of Judea, Galilee, or the Decapolis. What jurisdiction would the high priest have over the synagogues in Damascus? Usually Rome recognized the right of extradition when the high priest in Jerusalem demanded it. Another explanation is that Damascus may have been under the rule of the Nabatean king, Aretas IV. In order to gain favor with the anti-Roman Jews, he may have conceded this favor to the high priest.

The mention of "synagogues in Damascus" indicates that Christianity was still closely associated with Judaism. Mentioning the location, Damascus, shows that Christianity had spread rapidly. Some of these believers may have fled the persecution in Jerusalem.

On the road to Damascus, something occurred that altered world history. The pursuer was himself stopped in his tracks. Some say that Saul's conversion is the most important event in the church since Pentecost.

B. The Lord's Confrontation with Saul: vss. 3-6

As he neared Damascus on his journey, suddenly a light from heaven flashed around him. He fell to the ground and heard a voice say to him, "Saul, Saul, why do you persecute me?" "Who are you, Lord?" Saul asked. "I am Jesus, whom you are persecuting," he replied. "Now get up and go into the city, and you will be told what you must do."

Light is the symbol of God's perfect holiness (1 John 1:5). No wonder, then, that at critical points in history God has manifested

Himself through light. Here, at Saul's conversion, God shows Himself to Saul in light. The bright light was also seen by those with Saul on the road.

Now mighty Saul found himself face down on the ground. This is similar to what is found in accounts in Ezekiel (1:28) and Daniel (8:17).

After he fell to the ground, he heard a voice calling to him by name. The others with Saul also fell to the ground (Acts 26:14) and heard a sound, but could not understand the words spoken.

The voice asked Saul why he persecuted the speaker. This question is filled with significance for it shows the union of Christ with His church. This must have confused Saul. He must have figured that only God would speak from heaven, and yet Saul thought he was serving God, not persecuting Him. So Saul asked for clarification. "Who are you, Lord?" (vs. 5).

Saul referred to the speaker as "Lord." While it is true that the Greek word for *Lord* may be translated *Sir* (Matt. 13:27), in this context—with the voice from heaven—such an assumption would be inappropriate. *Lord* was the most sacred name the Jews had for God. To say Jesus is *Lord* is to declare that He is nothing less than divine. Until a person comprehends who Jesus is, he or she is not ready to receive God's revelation and become a believer.

After Saul asked his question, the speaker identifies Himself as Jesus. To Saul's consternation, he discovers that Jesus is alive! Now that Saul was confronted with the living Lord, he had to repent. Something that was probably difficult for the proud Pharisee to do! All of his good works and legalistic self-righteousness were nothing. He was a sinner who needed a Savior.

The phrase, "it is hard for you to kick against the goads," while not found here in most manuscripts, is found in Acts 26:14. It is a Greek proverb meaning useless resistance, one who only hurts himself.

There are some practical lessons to be learned from Ananias, whose name means "the Lord is gracious." First, God can use even the most obscure saint. Second, the experience of Ananias should be a reminder to never be afraid to obey God's will. Third, God's works are always balanced: a public miracle with a quiet meeting in a house. Finally, never underestimate the value of one person brought to Christ.

II. Saul's Commission: Acts 9:10-16

A. Ananias Called to Go to Saul: vss. 10-12

In Damascus there was a disciple named Ananias. The Lord called to him in a vision, "Ananias!" "Yes, Lord," he answered. The Lord told him, "Go to the house of Judas on Straight Street and ask for a man from Tarsus named Saul, for he is praying. In a vision he has seen a man named Ananias come and place his hands on him to restore his sight."

Saul was struck blind by his vision, but his companions helped him complete the journey into Damascus. There Saul stayed in a house and went on a total fast for three days, no doubt praying and wondering as he waited for instructions (vss. 7-9).

God then used a vision to communicate with Ananias, one of the faithful Christians in Damascus. In order to get clear instructions to Saul, God commissioned Ananias to go to Straight Street, where Saul was lodging with Judas. This was a mile long street from one end of Damascus to the other. It still exists today and is about as wide as an alley.

B. Ananias' Response: vss. 13-14

"Lord," Ananias answered, "I have heard many reports about this man and all the harm he has done to your saints in Jerusalem. And he has come here with authority from the chief priests to arrest all who call on your name."

All we really know about Ananias (not to be confused with the Ananias in chapter 5) comes from this account. In Acts 22:12 we learn that Ananias was "a devout observer of the law and highly respected by all the Jews living there."

God also revealed to Ananias that Saul had had a vision. Saul had seen Ananias restoring his eyesight through the laying on of hands.

Naturally, Ananias feared Saul, since Christians were well aware that Saul was one of their most merciless enemies. Ananias knew all about the young fanatic's mission to arrest Christians in Damascus. But the Lord assured Ananias that He had great plans for Saul.

Ananias can teach us two important lessons. First, God can use even an obscure person to do a great work. Secondly, we never know how our obedience to touch one life for Christ can impact the world.

Acts 9:15 is a good summary of Paul's life and ministry. It was all of grace, for he did not choose God; it was God who chose him (1 Tim. 1:14). He was God's vessel (2 Tim. 2:20-21), and God would work in and through him to accomplish His purposes (Eph. 2:10; Phil. 2:12-13). God's name would be glorified as His servant would take the Gospel to Jews and Gentiles, kings and commoners, and as he would suffer for Christ's sake.

C. The Lord's Reply and Commission of Saul: vss. 15-16

But the Lord said to Ananias, "Go! This man is my chosen instrument to carry my name before the Gentiles and their kings and before the people of Israel. I will show him how much he must suffer for my name."

How amazing that one who had persecuted the church so violently would now become one of its greatest witnesses. Saul's commission was to spread Christ's message to both Gentiles and Jews. This was a high calling, but it would involve considerable suffering.

Suffering is a strong theme that runs through the life and letters of Paul. Most of the incidents of the suffering recorded in 2 Corinthians 11:23-28 are not recorded in the Book of Acts, showing us that Acts is not a comprehensive account of all that Paul said and did. Ironically, the very man who had inflicted suffering on Christians, would now suffer greatly.

Notice that the references to the Lord's name appear three times in Acts 9:14-16. Saul's mission was to spread the name of the Lord, including that name's identity—Jesus Christ.

III. Saul's Convalescence: Acts 9:17-20

A. Ananias' Prayer: vs. 17

Then Ananias went to the house and entered it. Placing his hands on Saul, he said, "Brother Saul, the Lord—Jesus, who appeared to you on the road as you were coming here—has sent me so that you may see again and be filled with the Holy Spirit."

Here we see Saul in a recovery room so to speak. The Lord had encountered Saul on the road through a light and voice from heaven. Now He was going to communicate through Ananias. Here for the first time, Saul heard himself addressed as "brother." Ananias' apprehension of Saul was turned to love by the Lord.

Appropriately, Ananias made the same identification of Jesus that the Lord had made Himself on the road to Damascus. He identified Jesus as worthy of the same divine title as the God of the Hebrew Scriptures.

Saul's filling with the Holy Spirit clearly signified the completeness of his conversion, both to himself and Ananias. The physical healing and the spiritual healing both happened at this time, with the Holy Spirit being the pledge of Saul now being a disciple of Jesus Christ.

B. Saul's Healing: vs. 18-19

Immediately, something like scales fell from Saul's eyes, and he could see again. He got up and was baptized, and after taking some food, he regained his strength. Saul spent several days with the disciples in Damascus.

A medical doctor, Luke, narrated this account in Acts. Our physician-doctor informs us that something similar to "scales" fell from Saul's eyes (vs. 18). Hippocrates had used this term for any eye disease. The Greek word for scales is found only here in the New Testament, but is used outside of the Bible for the scales of crocodiles or fish.

Saul received not only renewed physical sight, but also insight. He received the Spirit in fullness and was baptized in water. He also ate after his fast. God tended to Saul's physical and spiritual needs.

C. Saul's Declaration of Christ: vs. 20

At once he began to preach in the synagogues that Jesus is the Son of God.

Saul spent several days with Christians at Damascus. His mission was launched when he began preaching in the synagogues about Jesus.

Preaching to the Jews in the synagogues was Saul's strategy throughout his missionary journeys. He immediately began to proclaim the Christ that he had persecuted, declaring boldly that Jesus is the Son of God. This is the only place in Acts that this title is used, but Paul used it in his epistles at least 15 times. It was a major emphasis in his ministry.

The dramatic change in Saul was a source of wonder to the Jews at Damascus. Every new convert's witness for Christ ought to begin right where he is at that time.

Discussion Questions

1. Why did Saul zealously persecute Christians before he encountered the Lord on his way to Damascus?
2. What do Saul's words and reaction to the Lord indicate about Saul's character?
3. Why do you think the Lord chose Ananias to meet with Saul?
4. If you were Ananias, how would you have reacted to God's instructions?
5. How is Saul's mission akin to the mission of every Christian?
6. How do you think Saul's preaching in the synagogues affected his listeners?

Now Ask Yourself . . .

Do I ever ask myself, who is Jesus?

What ideas about Christ are essential for me to understand if I am to accept Jesus as my Savior?

What are some false ideas I have heard about Jesus? How do these make it more difficult for me to receive Jesus as Lord?

What does it mean to commit to Christ as Savior and Lord?

Illustrations

Jesus said, "Where your treasure is, there your heart will be" (Matt. 6:21). Most of us commit ourselves to a great many things. Now is a good time to stop and take a look at our commitments and our motivation behind them. Do we begin to see a pattern? This pattern will show us where our commitment, or treasure, truly lies.

When you stop and think about it, the most valuable treasure a person can seek is Christ. He is Lord of all creation, and He loves us so much that He died in our place to bring us back into fellowship with God the Father.

When this life is over and eternity begins, only the things we did in His honor, in His name, will have any lasting value.

In Philippians 3, consider what Paul writes: "I consider everything a loss compared to the surpassing greatness of knowing Christ Jesus my Lord, for whose sake I have lost all things. I consider them rubbish, that I may gain Christ and be found in him" (vss. 8-9a).

We need to ask ourselves if we have truly gained that revelation of the Lord, that all else in our lives is considered as trash for the garbage pile. If we do not know Jesus in such a way, we can pray and ask the Holy Spirit to reveal Him to us. Then we can be equipped to go out and truly share because people around us will see a transformed life in front of their eyes.

Overcoming Rejection

DEVOTIONAL READING

Psalm 96

DAILY BIBLE READINGS

Monday January 2
Acts 13:1-12 Paul and Barnabas Are Sent to Do God's Work

Tuesday January 3
Acts 13:13-22 Paul Speaks in the Synagogue

Wednesday January 4
Acts 13:23-31 The Message of Salvation Is for All

Thursday January 5
Acts 13:32-39 Through Jesus, All Believers Are Forgiven for Their Sins

Friday January 6
Acts 13:40-46 More People Gather to Hear the Word of God

Saturday January 7
Acts 13:47-52 The Word of God Continues to Spread

Sunday January 8
Luke 10:5-17 Don't Let Rejection Stop You

Scripture

Background Scripture: *Acts 13:4—14:28*
Scripture Lesson: *Acts 13:14-15, 42-52*
Key Verse: *"For this is what the Lord has commanded us: 'I have made you a light for the Gentiles, that you may bring salvation to the ends of the earth.' " Acts 13:47.*

Lesson Aim

Don't let rejection stop your ministry.

Lesson Setting

Time: About A.D. 45
Place: Pisidian Antioch

Lesson Outline

Overcoming Rejection

I. Preaching in Pisidian Antioch: Acts 13:14-15
II. Going to the Gentiles: Acts 13:42-52
  A. *An Invitation to Speak Further: vs. 42*
  B. *An Exhortation to Remain Faithful to God: vs. 43*
  C. *Jealously among the Jewish Leaders: vss. 44-45*
  D. *Turning to the Gentiles: vss. 46-47*
  E. *Joy among the Gentiles: vs. 48*
  F. *Persecution of Paul and Barnabas: vss. 49-50*
  G. *Going On to Iconium: vss. 51-52*

Introduction

Opening New Doors

God opened new doors for the Gospel and Paul and Barnabas took it westward. The Ethiopian eunuch took it southward. And other believers took it eastward.

New doors are not always geographical, however. In our day new doors of evangelistic opportunity might be in our own backyard. That's because of immigration. People cross national boundaries to find freedom, education, and economic security. Out of some horrific tragedies, such as wars and famines, people move on. Wherever they go, Christians can welcome and help them in Christ's name.

Here are three ways we can participate in missions: by giving financially; by going on short-term missionary trips; and by joining the missions committee or the group of individuals that establishes the missions strategy in our church.

Lesson Commentary

I. Preaching in Pisidian Antioch: Acts 13:14-15

From Perga they went on to Pisidian Antioch. On the Sabbath they entered the synagogue and sat down. After the reading from the Law and the Prophets, the synagogue rulers sent word to them, saying, "Brothers, if you have a message of encouragement for the people, please speak."

This week's lesson concerns the joint missionary journey of Barnabas and Paul. Luke noted that the two, accompanied by John (their helper), sailed to Cyprus and proclaimed the Gospel in the Jewish synagogues (vss. 4-5).

While in Paphos, the group encountered a Jewish sorcerer and false prophet name Bar-Jesus (surnamed Elymas [L-ih-muss]) who was an attendant of the proconsul, Sergius [SIR-jih-us] Paulus. When Elymas opposed the missionaries, Paul declared that he would become blind. This actually happened, and God used it to bring the proconsul to faith (vss. 6-12).

Luke made a subtle shift in his writing as he followed the

travels of Barnabas and Paul to Pamphylia [pam-FILL-ih-ah]. Until now it had always been "Barnabas and Saul," apparently indicating that Barnabas took the lead role in their cooperative work. Now, however, Luke spoke of "Paul and his companions" (vs. 13), and afterward of "Paul and Barnabas" (vss. 42-43, 46, 50). This may indicate that at this point Paul and Barnabas came to an agreement that from then on Paul would be the leader. If so, this means Barnabas was a model, not only of encouragement, but also of humility and a servant attitude.

The missionaries left Cyprus and sailed for Perga [PURR-guh], the capital of Pamphilia, which was a coastal province in Asia Minor. At this time John left them to return to Jerusalem (vs. 13). Though Scripture doesn't say why, some think John Mark was displeased that Paul took over leadership from Barnabas, John's cousin. Or perhaps John was reluctant to shift the mission focus toward the Gentiles—something Paul was eager to do. Another possibility is that John's courage simply failed him when he faced a difficult journey into the interior of Asia Minor. Regardless of the reason, Paul later took a dim view of John's departure (15:36-40).

Apparently Paul and Barnabas didn't minister in Perga at this time, though they did on their return (14:25). Instead, they set out for Pisidian Antioch, traveling inland about 110 miles through rugged, robber-infested mountain roads. The city sat high on the Anatolian plateau at 3,500 feet. It had a mixed population of local Phrygians and colonized Jews, Romans, and Greeks. Not much is left of Pisidian Antioch today. The Turkish town of Yalvac is nearby.

In Pisidian Antioch, the evangelism method used by Paul and Barnabas was simple. They spoke in the synagogue on the Sabbath (vs. 14). It was customary for the synagogue rulers to invite visiting teachers to speak after Scripture had been read. In this case those in charge asked whether the missionaries had any word of encouragement to bring (vs. 15). Paul used this opportunity to proclaim the Gospel to the attendees.

II. Going to the Gentiles: Acts 13:42-52

A. An Invitation to Speak Further: vs. 42

Since Paul was addressing a synagogue congregation, he used Old Testament scriptures to support his argument. In Acts 13:33, Psalm 2:7 is quoted; and note that it refers to the resurrection of Christ, not His birth. Then he quoted Isaiah 55:3, referring to the covenant that God made with David. Jesus had to be raised from the dead or the covenant would be false.

His third quotation was from Psalm 16:10, the same passage Peter quoted from in his message at Pentecost. The Jews considered Psalm 16 to be a messianic psalm which, since David was dead, it could only apply to Jesus Christ.

As Paul and Barnabas were leaving the synagogue, the people invited them to speak further about these things on the next Sabbath.

Paul addressed Jews as well as "Gentiles who worship God" (vs. 16). We don't know all the Scripture texts the apostle used. But we do know that he summarized Israel's history to the time of Jesus (vss. 17-23). Paul told the audience about John the Baptist's ministry. Then Paul testified to the death and resurrection of Jesus, declaring that His resurrection fulfilled ancient prophecies (vss. 24-37). The apostle called on his listeners to believe the good news and receive the forgiveness of their sins through faith in Christ (vss. 38-41).

This is Paul's first recorded missionary address. It follows the same approach as Peter's sermons recorded earlier in Acts. The focus was on the messiahship of Jesus and His resurrection from the dead. Paul had good reason for doing this. Apart from the Resurrection, the Gospel was meaningless (1 Cor. 15:12-18). The apostle would later say to the Corinthian believers, "I resolved to know nothing while I was with you except Jesus Christ and him crucified" (2:2).

The people of Pisidian Antioch had never before heard the Gospel. They were so intrigued by the good news that they invited Paul and Barnabas to return the following Sabbath and tell them more about Jesus (Acts 13:42).

B. An Exhortation to Remain Faithful to God: vs. 43

When the congregation was dismissed, many of the Jews and devout converts to Judaism followed Paul and Barnabas, who talked with them and urged them to continue in the grace of God.

It's unclear whether any in the congregation had yet begun to believe in Jesus. But after the service, many flocked around Paul and Barnabas. As the discussion about the Lord continued outside the synagogue, the missionaries urged them "to continue in the grace of God" (vs. 43). By this they must have meant to go beyond a mere intellectual curiosity of Jesus to embrace Him fully by faith. Paul and Barnabas wanted to see their listeners wholeheartedly follow the Savior, depending upon Christ's merits apart from works.

C. Jealously among the Jewish Leaders: vss. 44-45

On the next Sabbath almost the whole city gathered to hear the word of the Lord. When the Jews saw the crowds, they were filled with jealousy and talked abusively against what Paul was saying.

In the week that followed, word about the evangelists and their message spread everywhere. On the sabbath it seemed as if the entire city came to hear Paul and Barnabas (vs. 44). Assuredly most of the citizens of Pisidian Antioch had not been in the synagogue before, much less rushed to hear a religious speaker. But Paul had presented the Gospel in a persuasive manner, and God used this to make a big impact among the residents of the city.

The Gospel had a double effect on the population. While some of the residents believed, others became hostile. For instance, the Jewish leaders became jealous of Paul and Barnabas, and spoke harshly about them and their message (vs. 45). The antagonists were trying to turn the crowds against the missionaries.

Undoubtedly the Jewish leaders had been living in Pisidian Antioch for years. Yet they had managed to attract only a modest number of Gentiles to their synagogue and religion. And now two outsiders—who had been in town only about a week—had created a great deal of excitement throughout the city. The arousal of jealousy seemed inevitable.

Many of us know just how the Jewish leaders of Pisidian Antioch felt. Perhaps someone in our church seems to have more success in ministry. Or we might be laboring faithfully in the shadows while someone else gets heaped with praise. Or perhaps while our church has empty pews week after week, the congregation down the road is building a larger sanctuary. In each of these situations, resentment can develop.

When we see others succeeding where we haven't or receiving the affirmation we crave, it's hard for us to rejoice with them. Our natural reaction is to be jealous and try to undermine what God is doing. However, the more desirable response is to sincerely congratulate the successful ministry of others and praise God for working so mightily through them.

D. Turning to the Gentiles: vss. 46-47

Then Paul and Barnabas answered them boldly: "We had to speak the word of God to you first. Since you reject it and do not consider yourselves worthy of eternal life, we now turn to the Gentiles. For this is what the Lord has commanded us: 'I have made you a light for the Gentiles, that you may bring salvation to the ends of the earth.' "

Sadly, the religious leaders remained entrenched in their jealously. This prompted Paul and Barnabas to declare that they would have to abandon their practice of taking the Gospel only to the Jews. Instead, the missionaries would also go to the Gentiles. This was a pattern that Paul repeated in city after city throughout his missionary journeys (vs. 46).

Why was it necessary for the Gospel to go first to the Jews? God planned that through the Jewish nation all the world would be blessed with the knowledge of the truth (Gen. 12:3). In addition, Paul, a Jew, loved his people and wanted to give them every opportunity to join him in proclaiming the good news of salvation (Rom. 9:1-5). Regrettably, many spurned Jesus as the Messiah, and they didn't understand that God was offering salvation to anyone—whether Jew or Gentile—through faith in Christ.

The decision of Paul and Barnabas to focus their efforts on the Gentiles was scriptural. For instance, Isaiah 49:6 (which is quoted in Acts 13:47) says that the people of Israel were to be a "light for the Gentiles." In other words, the Jews were to carry news about the one true God to others. Sadly, they largely failed in this mission.

Nevertheless, through Israel came Jesus, the light of the nations (Luke 2:32). And Jewish missionaries such as Paul and Barnabas were prepared to shine the light of Christ's salvation on unsaved Jews and Gentiles in the hope that many would be saved.

E. Joy among the Gentiles: vs. 48

When the Gentiles heard this, they were glad and honored the word of the Lord; and all who were appointed for eternal life believed.

The Gentiles of Pisidian Antioch were glad to hear that there was good news for them. They "honored the word of the Lord" (vs. 48) by believing in Christ and obeying His will. Thus, despite strong opposition from religious antagonists, the proclamation of the Gospel bore fruit.

F. Persecution of Paul and Barnabas: vss. 49-50

The word of the Lord spread through the whole region. But the Jews incited the God-fearing women of high standing and the leading men of the city. They stirred up persecution against Paul and Barnabas, and expelled them from their region.

"The word of the Lord" (vs. 49) refers to the Gospel. New converts from Pisidian Antioch carried the good news to others. "The whole region" probably included more than Pisidia, which was mountainous territory. Roman roads and the Greek language made the rapid spread of the Gospel possible.

Regrettably, matters in Pisidian Antioch took a nasty turn. The religious leaders persuaded some of the female converts to Judaism as well as some leading men of the city to drive Paul and Barnabas out of the area. (Some think the women were wives of the men.) Christian evangelism had been stirring up excitement, so perhaps the excuse for expelling the missionaries was disturbing the peace (vs. 50).

G. Going On to Iconium: vss. 51-52

So they shook the dust from their feet in protest against them and went to Iconium. And the disciples were filled with joy and with the Holy Spirit.

Upon leaving the area, Paul and Barnabas shook the dust off their feet in protest (vs. 51). This was a Jewish gesture of scorn and disassociation. The missionaries implied that because the religious leaders had rejected the Gospel, they bore full responsibility for the consequences of their actions.

Despite the persecution Paul and Barnabas encountered, the joy of the new converts in Pisidian Antioch was undiminished (vs. 52). Also, the Lord enabled the missionaries to proclaim the good news to such places as Iconium, Lystra, and Derbe. In each location, people responded to the message of salvation, which was confirmed by demonstrations of God's power. But opposition surfaced again in Iconium and Lystra. In Lystra, Paul was stoned by an angry mob and left for dead. He survived, and left the next day to continue preaching the Gospel (14:1-20).

Before returning to their home church of Syrian Antioch, Paul and Barnabas retraced their steps through Asia Minor and encouraged the new believers in each place (vss. 21-28).

The unbelieving Jews were not going to sit back and let Paul and Barnabas take over. First, they disputed with them, and then brought legal action against them and expelled them from their borders. The missionaries were not discouraged, however, and left behind a group of joyful disciples.

151

Discussion Questions

1. What opportunity did Paul and Barnabas take advantage of while in Pisidian Antioch?
2. How did Paul and Barnabas handle the attacks of their opponents?
4. How did the Jewish leaders react as the message of the Lord continued to spread?
4. What shift in focus occurred as a result of the opposition the missionaries encountered?

Now Ask Yourself . . .

Why is it important for me to be involved in taking the Gospel to others?

How has God helped me to deal with opposition I've encountered to the proclamation of the Gospel?

What opportunities do I have in my life right now to proclaim the Gospel?

Is my life filled with joy and the Holy Spirit even when I am facing persecution? If not, how can I make that change?

In what ways can I support missions and missionaries?

Illustrations

"Mission" is not a popular word. To some people it smacks of religious imperialism. To others it signifies leaving home and living in some depraved culture. Some other believers may ask, "Why bother when there's enough to do at home?"

This week's lesson, however, makes it clear that participation in missions is not something God left as an option for His church. He wants all believers to support the work of missions, whether directly or indirectly.

Since the days of the early church, God has continued to select certain believers for missionary service, and many of them stay on the field for life. But numerous opportunities are also available for short-term service that may include only a summer or an extended vacation. And we don't have to travel to a foreign country to discover opportunities to reach the lost and help the hurting.

Find out what your church's mission statement is and seek the Lord on how you can be a part of supporting it. While it may involve going and doing something, it might also include giving, hosting missionaries when they are in town, and certainly praying for the work.

Changed Hearts, Changed Homes

DEVOTIONAL READING

Philippians 1:3-11

DAILY BIBLE READINGS

Monday January 9
Acts 16:1-10 Paul, Silas, and Timothy Travel Together

Tuesday January 10
Acts 16:11-15 Lydia and Her Household Accept Christ

Wednesday January 11
Acts 16:16-24 Paul and Silas Land in Prison

Thursday January 12
Acts 16:25-34 The Jailer and His Household Accept Christ

Friday January 13
Acts 16:35-40 Paul's Roman Citizenship Helps His Case

Saturday January 14
Luke 19:1-10 Salvation Comes to Zacchaeus's House

Sunday January 15
Acts 10:1-10 God Uses Faithful Households

Scripture

Background Scripture: *Acts 16:6-40*

Scripture Lesson: *Acts 16:9-15, 27-33*

Key Verse: *"Believe in the Lord Jesus, and you will be saved—you and your whole household." Acts 16:31b.*

Lesson Aim

Your belief in Jesus will impact your entire household.

Lesson Setting

Time: A.D. 50

Place: Philippi

Lesson Outline

Changed Hearts, Changed Homes

   I. Overcoming Geographic Boundaries: Acts 16:9-12
      A. The Vision Experienced by Paul: vs. 9
      B. The Decision to Go to Macedonia: vss. 10-12

  II. Overcoming Gender Barriers: Acts 16:13-15
      A. Meeting Some Women: vs. 13
      B. Responding to Paul's Message: vs. 14
      C. Enjoying Lydia's Hospitality: vs. 15

III. Overcoming Confining Circumstances: Acts 16:27-33
      A. The Jailer's Alarm: vss. 27-28
      B. The Jailer's Question: vss. 29-30
      C. The Salvation of the Jailer and His Family: vss. 31-33

Introduction

Responding to Need

Many times the very people we think most need Christ are the least interested in Him. For instance, after an elderly man lost his home in a flood, he suffered a heart attack and was hospitalized. He was not a Christian, and his daughter thought he would now be open to the Gospel. But he wasn't.

The account of Paul and Silas in Philippi shows that they were eager to proclaim the Gospel to those who were seeking the Lord (such as Lydia and her friends) as well as to those who were not (such as the jailer and his family). Both Lydia and the jailer had the same spiritual need, namely, to repent and trust in Christ, and God used the testimony of Paul and his colleagues to lead them to faith.

No one knows when the door to someone's heart will open to the Gospel. Thus, we must be faithful to explore the evangelistic opportunities whenever, however, and wherever they arise.

Lesson Commentary

I. Overcoming Geographic Boundaries: Acts 16:9-12

A. The Vision Experienced by Paul: vs. 9

During the night Paul had a vision of a man of Macedonia standing and begging him, "Come over to Macedonia and help us."

Some time after the Jerusalem council, Paul and Barnabas discussed the possibility about going on another missionary journey. But they sharply disagreed over whether they should take John Mark, who had deserted them on their previous missionary journey. Because the issue could not be resolved, Barnabas took John Mark with him to Cyprus, while Paul took Silas with him on his journeys through Syria and Cilicia (15:36-41).

When the missionaries came to Derbe and Lystra, Paul had a young disciple named Timothy circumcised. Then, as the group visited congregations in various cities, they delivered the decisions that the apostles and elders in Jerusalem had reached. Meanwhile, God blessed the disciples with both spiritual and numerical growth (16:1-5).

The events in this week's lesson took place about A.D. 50. Paul, Silas, and Timothy traveled through the area of Phrygia [FRIDGE-ih-uh] and Galatia [guh-LAY-shuh], for the Spirit had prevented them from preaching the Gospel in a Roman province in the western part of Asia Minor (vss. 6-7). After traveling through Mysia [MISH-ih-uh] (a region west of Bithynia [bih-THIN-ih-uh]), the missionary team reached the large port city of Troas [TROW-az] (vs. 8). Because of its location on the Aegean [uh-JEE-uhn] coast, Troas was considered the gateway from Asia Minor to Greece.

While Paul was in Troas, he had a vision of "a man of Macedonia" (vs. 9), who summoned him to come and help him and others in this European region of the Roman Empire. Macedonia [mass-uh-DOE-nee-uh] was on the northwestern sector of what is now Greece. The terrain of the region is mountainous and cut by wide rivers and fertile valleys.

B. The Decision to Go to Macedonia: vss. 10-12

After Paul had seen the vision, we got ready at once to leave for Macedonia, concluding that God had called us to preach the gospel to them. From Troas we put out to sea and sailed straight for Samothrace, and the next day on to Neapolis. From there we traveled to Philippi, a Roman colony and the leading city of that district of Macedonia. And we stayed there several days.

For the first time in Acts, we find the word "we" (vs. 10), rather than words like "they" (vs. 7) or "him" (vs. 9), referring to Paul and his traveling companions. The change in pronouns probably means that the author (Luke) at this point began to accompany the apostle and his associates on their travels.

Some have suggested that Luke, after joining Paul at Troas, spoke to the apostle about the spiritual need in Macedonia. If so, God may have used this conversation to prepare Paul for the vision of the Macedonian man.

Paul and his companions took the vision seriously. After concluding that God wanted them to preach the Gospel in Macedonia, the missionaries made preparations to do so (vs. 10). What might have been out-of-bounds before (Europe) for Paul was now in bounds. Geographic barriers could not confine his proclamation of the Gospel.

From Troas to Neapolis, the port of Philippi was a distance of about 150 miles, and it took Paul and his companions two days to make the journey. Later, the trip in the opposite direction would take five days, apparently because of contrary winds (Acts 20:6). Philippi lay 10 miles inland from Neapolis, and was a Roman colony.

Luke briefly described their trip to Macedonia first by sea and then by Roman highway. Their voyage took them first to Samothrace [SAM-oh-thrace], a major landmark because of its mountainous location. Then they sailed to Neapolis (one of the two best ports of Macedonia) directly serving Philippi [FILL-ih-pie] (vs. 11).

Philippi lay about 10 miles northwest of Neapolis [nee-APP-uh-liss]. Philippi was the eastern terminus of the major Roman trade route across Greece to the Adriatic Sea. It had been a Roman colony since 42 B.C. It was more of an agricultural than a commercial center. Luke called it a "leading city" (vs. 12) of one of the four districts of Macedonia.

II. Overcoming Gender Barriers: Acts 16:13-15

A. Meeting Some Women: vs. 13

On the Sabbath we went outside the city gate to the river, where we expected to find a place of prayer. We sat down and began to speak to the women who had gathered there.

After arriving in a new city, it was Paul's practice to visit the local synagogue on the Sabbath. Jewish tradition required that there be at least 10 men before a synagogue could be established. Apparently the Jewish population of Philippi was too small to form a synagogue. Consequently, the missionaries searched for a place of prayer, which usually would have been outdoors near a river. Nonrabbinic sources attest the ancient habit of the Jews to recite prayers near rivers or the seashore.

Paul and his associates found some women meeting along the banks of the Gangites River (vs. 13). This was a deep and rapid stream about 10 miles from the sea. The women undoubtedly welcomed any visiting Jewish teacher who could help them in their reading and studying of Scripture.

B. Responding to Paul's Message: vs. 14

One of those listening was a woman named Lydia, a dealer in purple cloth from the city of Thyatira, who was a worshiper of God. The Lord opened her heart to respond to Paul's message.

Though a man had summoned Paul into Europe, the first recorded person to receive the Gospel in Europe was a woman. Her name was Lydia [LIDD-ee-yuh], and she was a worshiper of God (vs. 14). This means she was a Gentile who venerated the Lord of Israel and heeded the moral teachings of the law. However, she had not become a full proselyte to Judaism.

Lydia was also a businesswoman who sold purple cloth. Her native home was 600 miles away in Thyatira [thigh-uh-TIE-ruh]. This city was located in the district of Lydia, a region in western Asia Minor. The city had long been a center for the production of expensive purple dyes.

As Paul made clear elsewhere, gender is no barrier to the spread of the Gospel (Gal. 3:28). While Lydia listened, the Lord enabled her to understand and believe what the apostle was saying. Lydia is an outstanding example of the fact that God "had opened the door of faith to the Gentiles" (14:27). Jesus revealed to Paul that he would be His instrument "to open [Gentile] eyes and turn them from darkness to light" (26:18). Lydia's conversion was a magnificent fulfillment of Christ's promise.

C. Enjoying Lydia's Hospitality: vs. 15

When she and the members of her household were baptized, she invited us to her home. "If you consider me a believer in the Lord," she said, "come and stay at my house." And she persuaded us.

After Lydia confessed her faith in Christ, she and the members of her household were baptized. Then she placed herself and her house at the disposal of Paul and his associates (vs. 15). Lydia's success in sales is indicated by her sizable house in Philippi, which could accommodate not only her household but also four traveling missionaries. Lydia's newfound faith expressed itself in generous hospitality toward Paul and his party.

III. Overcoming Confining Circumstances: Acts 16:27-33

A. The Jailer's Alarm: vss. 27-28

The jailer woke up, and when he saw the prison doors open, he drew his sword and was about to kill himself because he thought the prisoners had escaped. But Paul shouted, "Don't harm your-self! We are all here!"

While in Philippi, the missionaries met a demon-possessed slave girl who had made a considerable amount of money for her owners by fortune-telling. God enabled Paul to expel the demon from the slave girl. This greatly upset her owners, for it meant they were no longer able to make money off of her. When the owners protested to the local magistrates, they in turn had Paul and Silas severely beaten. The two then were placed deep inside the city jail with their feet chained to large blocks of wood called stocks (vss. 16-24).

Paul and Silas did not let the confining circumstances demoralize them. Instead, they overcame the situation by praying and singing hymns to God (vs. 25). It was around midnight, and we can only imagine how the other prisoners must have felt as they heard the two missionaries worship the Lord.

Suddenly, there was a severe earthquake that shook the prison to its foundations. All the doors flew open, and the chains of every prisoner fell off. Assuming that all the prisoners had escaped, the jailer unsheathed his sword so that he could kill himself (vss. 26-27). For allowing a jailbreak, the warden would normally have been put to death, just as Peter's guards had been executed (12:19). However, in this case Paul and Silas remained in their cells. In fact, Paul shouted to the jailer that none of the prisoners had escaped (16:28). The apostle's intervention staved off the jailer's suicide.

B. The Jailer's Question: vss. 29-30

The jailer called for lights, rushed in and fell trembling before Paul and Silas. He then brought them out and asked, "Sirs, what must I do to be saved?"

After telling someone to light a torch, the anxious jailer rushed into the cell of Paul and Silas and then fell trembling before them (vs. 29). At this point the jailer asked one of the most famous questions recorded in the Bible: "Sirs, what must I do to be saved?" (vs. 30).

Some have suggested that all the jailer meant was "What on earth do I do to get myself out of this mess?" While "saved" certainly can mean "spared," and while we can't say infallibly what was on the jailer's mind, there is no question about what Paul meant by his answer. The apostle focused on the jailer's need for eternal life, not deliverance from physical danger.

C.   The Salvation of the Jailer and His Family: vss. 31-33

They replied, "Believe in the Lord Jesus, and you will be saved— you and your household." Then they spoke the word of the Lord to him and to all the others in his house. At that hour of the night the jailer took them and washed their wounds; then immediately he and all his family were baptized.

Crystallized into less than a dozen words is the answer to the quest and question of the centuries: "Believe in the Lord Jesus, and you will be saved" (vs. 31). John 3:16 contains a similar message of hope for sinners.

Paul's response is interesting in light of the matters that had been discussed at the Jerusalem conference. Not once did the apostle insist that the jailer had to be circumcised or become a convert to Judaism. Paul also didn't offer the jailer a cheap assurance that things weren't really as bad as he thought. Moreover, the apostle didn't tell him to look at the bright side of things, or to go home and sleep off his worries.

The aftershocks of this spiritual earthquake extended beyond the jailer to his household (vs. 32). Not only did the jailer trust in Jesus, but also his family followed the Lord.

Water was applied in two ways. Less than an hour after the conversions had taken place, the jailer washed the wounds of Paul and Silas, and the jailer and his household were baptized (signifying a spiritual cleansing from sin; vs. 33). Though the jailer and his family were spiritually exuberant, they did not forget the physical needs of the two missionaries. After bringing Paul and Silas into his home, the jailer set a meal before them. The result of all this was rejoicing (vs. 34).

The phrase "and your household" does not mean that the faith of the jailer would automatically bring salvation to his family. Each sinner must trust Christ personally in order to be born again. The phrase's true meaning is "and your household will be saved if they will believe also."

Discussion Questions

1. What kind of help do you think the man in Paul's vision wanted?
2. Why would Lydia want Paul and his companions to stay in her home?
3. How did Paul and Silas reflect the character of Christ while they were shackled in the Philippian prison?
4. What reasons did Paul and Silas have for rejoicing while in the jailer's home?
5. What are some current obstacles that Christians may face when presenting the Gospel in our society?

Now Ask Yourself . . .

What are some effective ways I've found to overcome obstacles to evangelism?

Are there times that circumstances demoralize me when I'm trying to share the Gospel with others?

How can I know better who might be responsive to receiving the Gospel?

How can I learn to discern better in every opportunity presented to me?

Illustrations

As this week's lesson makes clear, there are numerous obstacles to evangelism we can encounter. For instance, we can experience rejection from our peers, harassment from local authorities, and even public protests. We might face ridicule from those who consider the Gospel to be a myth or fable. We might encounter jealousy, antipathy, or power struggles within our church. Finally, we might face racial, social, or economic barriers when presenting the Gospel in our society.

One way to overcome these kinds of obstacles is by remaining calm and levelheaded. Another approach is to deal with problems we encounter by being direct and bold-spirited in our presentation of the Gospel. In some situations we might find ongoing dialogue and the sharing of ideas an effective way of surmounting barriers to witnessing.

The ministry of Paul and his associates reminds us of how pleased God is when we remain determined in our efforts to evangelize the lost. Despite the obstacles we encounter as we share the Gospel, the Lord can enable us to prevail. At first our options may not seem evident. In time, however, God can help us discern what course of action we should take.

January 22, 2006
The Job Christ Gives

Turn Right toward God

DEVOTIONAL READING
Psalm 96:1-13

DAILY BIBLE READINGS
Monday January 16
*Acts 17:1-9 In
Thessalonica, the Jews
Become Jealous of Paul*

Tuesday January 17
*Acts 17:10-15 Berea
Receives Paul's Message
with Eagerness*

Wednesday January 18
*Acts 17:16-21 Paul Is
Saddened by the Many
Idols in Athens*

Thursday January 19
*Acts 17:22-28 Paul
Condemns the Altar to the
Unknown God*

Friday January 20
*Acts 17:29-32 As God's
Children, He Commands
Us to Repent*

Saturday January 21
*Mark 1:1-8 John the
Baptist Preaches
Repentance*

Sunday January 22
*Revelation 2:2-7 Listen to
the Spirit and Repent*

Scripture

Background Scripture: *Acts 17:16-34*
Scripture Lesson: *Acts 17:22-34*
Key Verse: *"[God] commands all people everywhere to
repent. For he has set a day when he will judge the world
with justice by the man he has appointed. He has given
proof of this to all men by raising him from the dead."*
Acts 17:30-31.

Lesson Aim

God's revelation demands our repentance.

Lesson Setting

Time: A.D. 50
Place: Athens

Lesson Outline

Turn Right toward God
I.   The Idolatrous Athenians: Acts 17:22-23
     A. *They Were Very Religious: vs. 22*
     B. *They Were Spiritually Ignorant: vs. 23*
II. The God Who Made Everything: Acts 17:24-28
     A. *He Does Not Live in Temples: vs. 24*
     B. *He Is Self-Sufficient: vs. 25*
     C. *He Settled the Nations: vs. 26*
     D. *He Desires Worship: vss. 27-28*
III. The God Who Will Judge the World: Acts 17:29-31
     A. *He Is Not Represented by Idols: vs. 29*
     B. *He Commands Repentance: vs. 30*
     C. *Jesus Will Be His Instrument of Judgment: vs. 31*
IV. The Crucial Issue: Acts 17:32-34
     A. *The Resurrection Divided Them: vs. 32*
     B. *Some Believed: vss. 33-34*

Introduction

Good News for Everyone

In a conversation between a Christian and an unbelieving scientist, many issues pertaining to Christianity were discussed. The scientist was a thoughtful man and the discussion was not argumentative. The scientist listened carefully to what the Christian had to say, but did not seem particularly interested in believing the Gospel. Then the Christian asked him, "What do you make of the resurrection of Christ?"

"I don't know," he said. "I've never thought about it."

Perhaps in a way he was like the people Paul spoke to in Athens. Certainly he was like many people today—too busy or too preoccupied with other things to think about the meaning of Christ's death and resurrection. Therefore, we need to be prepared for honest, thoughtful questions.

Lesson Commentary

I. The Idolatrous Athenians: Acts 17:22-23

A. They Were Very Religious: vs. 22

Paul then stood up in the meeting of the Areopagus and said: "Men of Athens! I see that in every way you are very religious."

On the apostle Paul's second missionary journey, he took the Gospel from Asia to Europe for the first time (Acts 16). Paul and Silas were jailed in Philippi, but some people were converted, and the church was established in northeastern Greece. Then he and his team moved southward along the coast to Thessalonica, Berea, and Athens (17:1-15).

While waiting for Silas and Timothy to join him, Paul surveyed the city and "was greatly distressed to see that the city was full of idols" (vs. 16). Eager with zeal to proclaim the Gospel, Paul first engaged the Jews and the God-fearing Greeks in the synagogue. He also preached in the marketplace every day.

There he encountered Epicurean and Stoic philosophers, who argued with him "because Paul was preaching the good news about Jesus and the resurrection" (vs. 18). However, they were intrigued by "this new teaching" and his "strange ideas," so they invited him to a meeting of the Areopagus [air-ee-OPP-uh-guss], where both Athenians and foreigners loved to talk about "the latest ideas" (vs. 21).

The Areopagus was the council of scholars and philosophers. In any case, they did serve some official purpose as they gathered in the marketplace to hear Paul's case (vs. 17). The council retained great prestige and was looked upon as the arbiter in matters of morals and religion. That is why Paul's sermon before them was so important.

Paul began by acknowledging the religious fervor in Athens. Although Athenians in general may have been very religious, neither the Stoics nor the Epicureans (vs. 18) were known for their religious zeal. The Epicureans were influential among the upper classes. They said pleasure was the highest goal in life. The Stoics were more popular and opposed the Epicureans. Both accepted the existence of gods, but philosophical discussions centered more on ethics than religion.

B. They Were Spiritually Ignorant: vs. 23

"For as I walked around and looked carefully at your objects of worship, I even found an altar with this inscription: TO AN UNKNOWN GOD. *Now what you worship as something unknown I am going to proclaim to you."*

Paul had taken the time to observe the idols of Athens. The streets were lined with statues. Pillars mounted with heads of the god Hermes predominated in Athens.

However, because of a long-ago plague that had hit the city, Athenians had erected a number of altars to an unknown god. Since none of the regular or known gods had stopped the plague, the Athenians had offered sacrifices to an unknown god, and the plague had subsided. These altars were still around when Paul visited the city.

This fact of history gave him an excellent starting point for his speech. God in heaven is not an unknown God, but a knowable God. This God Paul knew personally through Jesus Christ. He would proclaim God to this august assembly of the wise men of Athens. He assumed that as worshipers they would be interested in hearing about the one true God.

II. The God Who Made Everything: Acts 17:24-28

A. He Does Not Live in Temples: vs. 24

"The God who made the world and everything in it is the Lord of heaven and earth and does not live in temples built by hands."

Paul first pointed to God as the Creator of everything. Therefore, He is the Lord of everything. God's supremacy had to be recognized. He is not one among many gods, because He created the universe. He owns it and controls it. "Lord" means sovereign ruler. His sovereignty extends to every human being as well, not just to nature.

The gods of the Greeks were distant beings who had no concern for the problems and needs of men. But the God of Creation is also the God of history and geography. He created mankind "from one man" (Acts 17:26) so that all nations are made of the same stuff and have the same blood. The Greeks felt they were a special race, different from other nations; but Paul affirmed otherwise. God is not a distant deity; "He [is] not far from each one of us" (Acts 17:27). This led to Paul's logical conclusion: God made us in His image, so it is foolish for us to make gods in our own image. Greek religion was nothing but the manufacture and worship of gods who were patterned after men and who acted like men.

Therefore, nothing that human beings create—not even the magnificent temples of Athens—could contain God. Although the glory of ancient Athens had receded considerably by the time Paul arrived, the city was still rightfully proud of its heritage, its philosophy, its architecture, and its temples. Perhaps Paul even turned his head or pointed toward the Parthenon when he declared that God does not live in temples.

This was a highly critical point to make, because the Greeks and the Romans firmly believed that their gods really lived in their temples. Their power, pride, and security rested in their temples. Nevertheless, God did not live there.

B. He Is Self-Sufficient: vs. 25

"And he is not served by human hands, as if he needed anything, because he himself gives all men life and breath and every thing else."

The God who made everything is totally self-sufficient. He does not live in temples built by hands, and His needs are not met by anything human beings can do.

God lacks nothing that anyone can do for Him. He gives life, breath, and everything to His creatures because He is self-sufficient and all-powerful. This fact cuts the heart out of the pagan worship that predominated in Athens.

C. He Settled the Nations: vs. 26

"From one man he made every nation of men, that they should inhabit the whole earth; and he determined the times set for them and the exact places where they should live."

Paul continued to build his case for the existence of one supreme deity. God made everything in the physical world. He also created one human, Adam, from whom all nations sprang. This was Paul's synopsis of the record in Genesis. It contradicted the prevailing belief that the Athenians had sprung from the soil of Attica.

God also set the boundaries and times for the nations He created. In other words, it was no accident that the Athenians came to be what they were and where they lived. The Athenians, of course, loved to discourse on their past philosophical, political, military, and cultural achievements. However great Athens was, it all came from God's hand. They could not give the credit and the glory to their hierarchy of gods, not to Athena, not to Hermes, not to Zeus.

D. He Desires Worship: vss. 27-28

"God did this so that men would seek him and perhaps reach out for him and find him, though he is not far from each one of us. 'For in him we live and move and have our being.' As some of your own poets have said, 'We are his offspring.' "

For all of His creative gifts, God expected only one thing in return—honest worship. He created men and women for personal fellowship. They were supposed to seek Him and find Him. He is not the unknown God ("he is not far from each one of us"), but the God who desires praise, thanksgiving, and loyalty.

In fact, Paul said, all of life finds meaning and purpose within the circle of God's creative love and power. Of course, the members of the Areopagus should have known this, because a famous Greek poet, Epimenides, made the same point. Paul quoted him directly (vs. 28). Whether they agreed with Epimenides or not, at least Paul used one of their own to substantiate his basic point. Paul's declaration was especially aimed at the Stoics, who pursued self-sufficiency as the highest good.

III. The God Who Will Judge the World: Acts 17:29-31

A. He Is Not Represented by Idols: vs. 29

"Therefore since we are God's offspring, we should not think that the divine being is like gold or silver or stone—an image made by man's design and skill."

Paul then directly confronted the Athenians' appetite for idols.

165

He argued that since humans are God's offspring, and because He created everything, it is ridiculous to think that He could be represented by an idol made of gold, silver, or stone.

B. He Commands Repentance: vs. 30

"In the past God overlooked such ignorance, but now he commands all people everywhere to repent."

Not only was it an unworthy idea to try to represent God by idols, but idols also demonstrated mankind's spiritual darkness, or ignorance. As the Old Testament prophets repeatedly warned, idolatry—although real to the worshiper—was foolishness.

Having permitted people to suffer the ignorance of worshiping idols for countless centuries, God intervened and revealed the truth about Himself. He did not excuse the sin of idolatry, but He did disclose how idolaters can be forgiven. The way to salvation is to repent. Repentance is necessary because of sin, including the sin of idolatry.

Therefore, Paul's announcement was something completely new to the Greeks. Repentance was not something they taught, because they had no concept of breaking the laws of a personal, holy, righteous God in heaven. God commanded repentance from His creatures because of who He is. As Creator, He established the rules of righteousness. It was no longer a matter of debating whose philosophy was best. It was time to listen to God speak from heaven.

C. Jesus Will Be His Instrument of Judgment: vs. 31

"For he has set a day when he will judge the world with justice by the man he has appointed. He has given proof of this to all men by raising him from the dead."

Why is it necessary to repent? Because judgment day is coming. He is not capricious and arbitrary, like the gods of the Greeks. Judgment implies that God's creatures have broken His laws. Justice must be served.

God's instrument of judgment will be the Lord Jesus Christ, the one whom He raised from the dead. Paul did not mention Jesus by name here, but they knew who he was talking about because Paul had already been preaching the Good News to them (vs. 18). He wanted to affirm the principle that judgment is coming. God's proof that this would happen was sealed by Christ's resurrection.

It proved that God had spoken in history, and that He will speak again when it is time to judge the world. The great goddess Athena has not raised anyone from the dead.

IV. The Crucial Issue: Acts 17:32-34

A. The Resurrection Divided Them: vs. 32

When they heard about the resurrection of the dead, some of them sneered, but others said, "We want to hear you again on this subject."

Paul touched a raw nerve in Athens when he spoke of the resurrection of the dead. Some of the philosophers admitted that the human soul might live on in endless cycles, or that it might somehow be absorbed into the universe. But none of them expected a bodily resurrection to life. Although they loved to debate new ideas, this was too much for some of them to stomach. Their intellectual sensibilities were offended.

On the other hand, some of Paul's listeners were more open-minded. They wanted to talk more about the resurrection of the dead. They had followed Paul's logic to a point, but he had also created some vast questions that they could not settle on the spot. So they asked for more time to discuss these things.

B. Some Believed: vss. 33-34

At that, Paul left the Council. A few men became followers of Paul and believed. Among them was Dionysius, a member of the Areopagus, also a woman named Damaris, and a number of others.

Some scholars think Paul failed in Athens because he did not preach a sermon full of Christian doctrine. However some of the men and women obviously came back to hear Paul explain the Gospel more fully. As a result, they believed. That is, they repented of their sins and committed themselves to Christ.

Also, a beachhead for the Gospel was established in this center of Greek civilization. One of the council members of some influence, Dionysius, was converted. Also, Damaris, undoubtedly a woman of significance, believed.

It was the doctrine of the Resurrection that most of the members of the Council could not accept. This kind of teaching was definitely incompatible with Greek philosophy. They believed in immortality, but not in resurrection. There were three different responses to the message. Some laughed and mocked and did not take Paul's message seriously. Others were interested but wanted to hear more. A small group accepted what Paul preached, believed on Jesus Christ, and were saved.

Discussion Questions

1. How does the flourishing of false religions affect Christians?
2. How was Paul prepared for his encounter in Athens?
3. Do you think Paul took the right approach in Athens?
4. Why is it important to declare that God will judge the world by the Lord Jesus Christ?
5. Why is the resurrection of Christ crucial to the church's witness to the world?

Now Ask Yourself . . .

How can I learn to engage people of other religions—or no religion—about the Gospel?

Am I distressed when I see people worshiping things other than God?

Do I acknowledge other peoples' beliefs before I present the Gospel to them?

When I am confronted with God's righteous judgement, am I led to repentance?

Am I afraid to discuss the Gospel with those around me that seem to be more intellectual and therefore, perhaps more resistant to the truth about Jesus?

Illustrations

At the World's Parliament of Religions in Chicago some years ago it was apparent to the thousands who attended that other non-Christian religions were aggressively pursuing their agendas of converting people to their views. The parliament was like trying to play a football game with 30 teams on the field at the same time.

Nevertheless, in spite of calls for tolerance and acceptance of all faiths as equally true, the church cannot back down. Christians must be bold in asserting, as Paul did, that God commands all people to repent. Judgment is coming. This is not a matter of intolerance, but of dread certainty.

God the Creator has not made all religions equally valid. Paul did not tell the Greek philosophers that their views were as good as his. He risked the sneers of the philosophers, but he did not back down from declaring that Jesus was God's appointed instrument of His righteous judgment. Christians today need the same kind of holy boldness to declare their faith in a pluralistic society. We can respect the individual but still speak the truth of God's Word courageously.

January 29, 2006

The Job Christ Gives

A Whole-Life Plan

DEVOTIONAL READING

1 Corinthians 15:1-11

DAILY BIBLE READINGS

Monday January 23
*Acts 20:1-12 Paul Raises
Eutychus from the Dead*

Tuesday January 24
*Acts 20:13-24 Paul
Reminds the Ephesian
Church of His Example*

Wednesday January 25
*Acts 20:25-38 Paul Urges
Church Leaders to Watch
Over the Flock*

Thursday January 26
*Acts 21:17-26 Paul Arrives
in Jerusalem*

Friday January 27
*Acts 21:27-36 Paul Is
Arrested*

Saturday January 28
*Acts 25:1-12 Paul Appeals
to Caesar*

Sunday January 29
*Acts 26:19-32 Agrippa and
Festus Want to Set Paul
Free*

Scripture

Background Scripture: *Acts 20:13-38*
Scripture Lesson: *Acts 20:18-32*
Key Verse: *"I consider my life worth nothing to me, if only I may finish the race and complete the task the Lord Jesus has given me—the task of testifying to the gospel of God's grace." Acts 20:24.*

Lesson Aim

The task of living for Jesus never stops.

Lesson Setting

Time: A.D. 57–58
Place: Ephesus

Lesson Outline

A Whole-Life Plan

I. Paul's Faithfulness: Acts 20:18-21
   A. *Enduring Many Trials: vss. 18-19*
   B. *Boldly Declaring the Truth: vss. 20-21*
II. Paul's Determination: Acts 20:22-27
   A. *The Certainty of Imprisonment and Hardship: vss. 22-23*
   B. *The Importance of Declaring the Gospel: vs. 24*
   C. *The Assurance of a Clear Conscience: vss. 25-27*
III. Paul's Exhortation: Acts 20:28-32
   A. *Feeding and Leading the Flock: vs. 28*
   B. *Guarding against Spiritual Wolves: vss. 29-31*
   C. *Being Entrusted to God's Care: vs. 32*

Introduction

Serving with Faith and Confidence

When Pastor Mike left his congregation to go to another church, the parting was both sweet and bitter. The people of his former congregation had deeply appreciated his ministry, but some of them felt a touch of guilt. Was there something wrong with them? Is that why the pastor was leaving? Understandably, Mike felt unprepared to handle the grief of separating from his former congregation.

Paul's decision to part company from the leaders of the Ephesian congregation was also a sweet and bitter experience. When he finished speaking to them, they wept, embraced, and kissed him (Acts 20:37). This reminds us that service for Christ in His church transcends what we say and do. Authentic ministry builds strong bonds of love, trust, and respect. It also builds ties that last over many years and miles.

Lesson Commentary

I. Paul's Faithfulness: Acts 20:18-21

A. Enduring Many Trials: vss. 18-19

When they arrived, he said to them: "You know how I lived the whole time I was with you, from the first day I came into the province of Asia. I served the Lord with great humility and with tears, although I was severely tested by the plots of the Jews."

Last week's lesson ended with Paul in the midst of his second missionary journey, which may have lasted from A.D. 49–52. After leaving Philippi, he ministered in Thessalonica, Berea, Athens, and Corinth (17:1—18:22). Then, after spending some time in Syrian Antioch, Paul began his third missionary journey, which lasted from A.D. 53–57 (18:23).

After traveling through Galatia and Phrygia, the apostle ministered in Ephesus for two years and three months (19:8, 10; 20:31). During Paul's stay there, a silversmith named Demetrius caused a riot over the apostle's evangelistic activities. However, the city clerk was able to calm the crowd and get them to disperse (19:23-41).

After the riot, Paul left Ephesus and traveled through Macedonia and Achaia. Then, doubling back, he arrived in Troas, where a young man named Eutychus took a fatal fall but was restored to life. Paul eventually made his way to Miletus, which was 30 miles south of Ephesus (20:1-15).

While Paul was in Corinth (the capital of Achaia), he planned to "sail for Syria" (vs. 3). But when he learned that his enemies intended to murder him (perhaps during the voyage to Palestine), he changed his travel plans. The apostle decided to go north into Macedonia, cross the Aegean Sea to Asia Minor, and catch another ship from there.

That delay prevented Paul from reaching Jerusalem in time for Passover. The apostle wanted to avoid visiting Ephesus because he was hurrying to reach Jerusalem by the day of Pentecost. Thus, while in Miletus, Paul requested that the Ephesian elders come to him (20:16-17).

In Paul's address to the church leaders, he stressed that during his time of ministry in their city, he remained honest and upright in all he said and did (vs. 18). The apostle recalled what he had suffered to bring the Gospel to them. Paul also noted that he served them with "humility and with tears" (vs. 19). The apostle's reference to "the plots of the Jews" reminds us that religious legalists had opposed him throughout much of his ministry.

Because serving the Lord was the foundation of Paul's life, opposition and hardship could not deter him from his divinely appointed mission. The apostle refused to give up, for he considered himself a "servant of Christ Jesus" (Rom. 1:1). As such, Paul completely belonged to the Savior. The apostle did not serve grudgingly. Rather, he ministered willingly and eagerly.

B. Boldly Declaring the Truth: vss. 20-21

"You know that I have not hesitated to preach anything that would be helpful to you but have taught you publicly and from house to house. I have declared to both Jews and Greeks that they must turn to God in repentance and have faith in our Lord Jesus."

Under such intense physical, emotional, and spiritual pressures, Paul undoubtedly was tempted to quit. He affirmed, however, that he would never do so. And rather than change his message to gain relief, the apostle boldly declared the truth of the Gospel.

Throughout his ministry in Ephesus, Paul remained consistent in what he said, whether publicly or in the homes of believers

Paul used six graphic pictures of his ministry to explain why he would not quit but would go to Jerusalem to die for Jesus Christ if necessary. Paul saw himself as an accountant (Acts 20:24) who had examined his assets and liabilities. He also saw himself as a runner who wanted to finish his course in joyful victory (Phil. 3:12-14; 2 Tim. 4:7b-8). Paul's third picture is that of the steward, for he would give account for what he had received from the Lord (1 Cor. 4:2). The next picture is that of witness, "testifying to the gospel of God's grace" (Acts 20:24). The word means to solemnly give witness. Picture five is the herald (Acts 20:27) who tells what the king tells him to declare. The final picture is that of watchman (Acts 20:28). He had to stay awake and alert, ready to sound the alarm if he saw danger.

(vs. 20). The apostle's teaching was not shaped by the dangers he faced but rather by the needs of the congregation. He left no stone unturned in his desire to impart the message of salvation. His own concerns were secondary to building up the Body of Christ and equipping the saints for faithful service.

Paul reached out to both Jews and Greeks with the same message. He told them that they needed to repent and place their faith in Christ (vs. 21). Regardless of the audience, the apostle never wavered from proclaiming this simple truth. In a day when immorality and lawlessness seem on the rise, it's good for us to remember the importance of turning away from sin and turning to God in faith. This is the only way to enjoy His forgiveness through Christ.

II. Paul's Determination: Acts 20:22-27

A. The Certainty of Imprisonment and Hardship: vss. 22-23

"And now, compelled by the Spirit, I am going to Jerusalem, not knowing what will happen to me there. I only know that in every city the Holy Spirit warns me that prison and hardships are facing me."

Paul was a man under divine compulsion. He was driven by the Spirit, and he never flinched from his duty, even though he knew he faced danger in Jerusalem. Despite the ominous prospects, he was determined to go to the holy city (vss. 21-22).

Some say that Paul was out of God's will in going to Jerusalem after the warnings of imprisonment and affliction. But there is no evidence that Paul was rebelling against God. On the contrary, the Lord Jesus Himself confirmed that the trip was part of His will (23:11). There was no condemnation, but rather affirmation, that Paul bore witness to Christ in Jerusalem.

B. The Importance of Declaring the Gospel: vs. 24

"However, I consider my life worth nothing to me, if only I may finish the race and complete the task the Lord Jesus has given me—the task of testifying to the gospel of God's grace."

Many believers today would find it hard to accept Paul's statement that he considered his life "worth nothing" (Acts 20:24). But we shouldn't be too surprised. After all, he later wrote that he considered everything "a loss compared to the surpassing greatness of knowing Christ" (Phil. 3:8).

Paul no longer desired to hold on to his life (1:21). He sought only the furtherance of God's kingdom and the honor of Christ, no matter what the earthly cost might be. For Paul, what he put into life was far more important than what he got out of it. That's why such things as achieving recognition, having fun, or being successful were not as important.

Early on, Paul had preached in Jerusalem, but then he had to flee for his life (Acts 9:29-30). The apostle was not about to flee again. He knew that he faced persecution in Jerusalem, though he would not learn the details until he heard the prophecy made by Agabus (21:10-11). Paul's deep sense of duty toward Christ drove him on despite the threat of danger.

Paul's supreme desire was to accomplish the task Jesus had given him to do (Acts 26:15-18). After Paul was arrested in Jerusalem, he had three opportunities to give his testimony. Despite horrible treatment and imprisonment, he kept affirming how he had experienced God's grace through faith in Christ, and how his life had been irrevocably changed.

C. The Assurance of a Clear Conscience: vss. 25-27

"Now I know that none of you among whom I have gone about preaching the kingdom will ever see me again. Therefore, I declare to you today that I am innocent of the blood of all men. For I have not hesitated to proclaim to you the whole will of God."

Paul said to the Ephesian elders, "none of you . . . will ever see me again" (Acts 20:25). Being aware that he faced severe opposition in Jerusalem, the apostle did not anticipate ever returning to Asia Minor. Though Paul may have done so after his release from his first Roman imprisonment, he could not at this time have foreseen that possibility.

Throughout his ministry, Paul had been a singleminded person, and the most important goal of his life was to tell others about Christ. No one could say that potential converts failed to hear the good news because of laziness on Paul's part. Though the apostle

The word "elder" is presbutos in the Greek and refers to a mature person who has been selected to serve in office (Acts 14:23). These same people are called "overseers" in Acts 20:28, which is episkopos or "bishop." They were chosen to shepherd the flock so they were also pastors.

used tact and discernment, he never tried to conceal any of the truths associated with the Gospel (Acts 20:26-27).

III. Paul's Exhortation: Acts 20:28-32

A. Feeding and Leading the Flock: vs. 28

"Keep watch over yourselves and all the flock of which the Holy Spirit has made you overseers. Be shepherds of the church of God, which he bought with his own blood."

Paul used a shepherding metaphor to describe the nature of the Ephesian elders' work. In Bible times, shepherds were keepers of sheep. These animals are curious but dumb, and often failed to find their way home. Shepherds, being aware of this, never took their eyes off their wandering flocks (Ps. 32:8). When the animals strayed into a briar patch or fell over a precipice in the rugged hills of Palestine, the shepherds would search for them and carry them to safety (Luke 15:6).

In the arid climate of Palestine, shepherds had to search diligently and constantly for sources of water. They might find a quiet stream for the sheep (Ps. 23:2), or they might spot an old well with a quiet pool or trough close by (Gen. 29:2; 30:38; Exod. 2:16). Often the shepherd carried a small container to scoop up liquid for thirsty sheep who could not reach the available water any other way.

Perhaps with these thoughts in mind, Paul urged the Ephesian elders to feed and shepherd God's spiritual flock, the church. In referring to his listeners as "overseers" (Acts 20:28), Paul was stressing their responsibility as leaders to watch over and protect their congregation. They were to take this responsibility seriously, for God had purchased the church "with his own blood." Paul believed so strongly in the unity of God the Son and God the Father that he could speak of Christ's death as the shedding of the blood of God.

B. Guarding against Spiritual Wolves: vss. 29-31

"I know that after I leave, savage wolves will come in among you and will not spare the flock. Even from your own number men

will arise and distort the truth in order to draw away disciples after them. So be on your guard! Remember that for three years I never stopped warning each of you night and day with tears."

Paul warned the Ephesian elders of two dangers threatening their church. One would come from the outside. The apostle said that after he left, false teachers, like savage wolves, would infiltrate the congregation and spiritually attack unsuspecting believers. The other threat would come from within the congregation. Paul was referring to arrogant and self-serving individuals who would distort the truth in order to draw a following (vss. 29-30).

It's no wonder that Paul admonished the Ephesian elders to "be on your guard!" (vs. 31). The threat to them and their fellow believers could not be more real. Paul's ministry among them exemplified what he taught. During his several years of work in Ephesus, he constantly watched over and cared for the believers in the church. He even cried over their needs.

C. Being Entrusted to God's Care: vs. 32

"Now I commit you to God and to the word of his grace, which can build you up and give you an inheritance among all those who are sanctified."

Paul knew that God would watch over the congregation in Ephesus. Thus the apostle entrusted the believers to the Lord's care (vs. 32). Paul reminded the elders that during his ministry among them, he was never greedy, but rather supported himself. The apostle was a sterling testimony of Christ's teaching regarding the blessing of giving to others, especially the weak (vss. 33-35).

We can only imagine how moved everyone was at Paul's words. When he had finished speaking, the entire group knelt down and prayed. Everyone wept freely as they embraced the apostle. The elders were most saddened by the possibility of never seeing Paul again. Despite this sobering possibility, they had the inner fortitude to walk with him to the ship on which he would sail (vss. 36-38).

Discussion Questions

1. What did Paul say characterized his ministry among the believers in Ephesus?
2. Why was the proclamation of the Gospel so important to Paul?
3. In what sense was Paul "innocent of the blood of all men" (Acts 20:26)?
4. How could the Ephesian elders deal successfully with the dangers that Paul said would threaten their congregation?
5. How can we, as Christians, display the same kind of love and care that Paul had shown to the believers in Ephesus?
6. How can we help our church leaders in the task of feeding and leading Jesus' followers?

Now Ask Yourself . . .

How can I serve the Lord with humility?

Am I eager to serve the Lord even when it costs me personally?

Do I consider my life "worth nothing" as I serve the Lord?

Have I, at times, hesitated in speaking the Gospel freely?

Am I on guard against the things both inside and outside of the church which might pull me away from the Lord?

Illustrations

There are two facts about Paul that rise to the surface in this week's lesson. First, he always saw himself as a servant of the church, not its boss. Second, he resolutely taught the necessity of turning from sin and turning to God in faith. In Paul's mind experiencing God's grace was the only way for Christians to survive and grow spiritually.

Paul's warning to the Ephesian elders is a sobering reminder that the church faces attacks from those inside and outside the fellowship. This should not shock us. After all, spiritual wolves love sin, hate God, and reject Christ. They will do anything to destroy the work of God among His people.

Years later Paul told the Christians in Philippi that he could do all things through Christ, who strengthened him (Phil. 4:13). This included living with difficult situations (as described in vs. 12).

This reminds us that God alone has the power to rescue us from dire circumstances, uphold us in our darkest moments, strengthen us to live in a godly manner, and enable us to be fruitful in our ministries. It's no wonder that Paul could say with confidence, "Therefore, my dear brothers, stand firm. Let nothing move you. Always give yourselves fully to the work of the Lord, because you know that your labor in the Lord is not in vain" (1 Cor. 15:58).

Power-full Living

DEVOTIONAL READING

Psalm 34:1-8

DAILY BIBLE READINGS

Monday January 30
*Romans 1:1-7 Paul Is
Called to Be an Apostle*

Tuesday January 31
*Romans 1:8-17 Do Not Be
Ashamed of the Gospel*

Wednesday February 1
*Romans 1:18-25 God's
Wrath Is Being Revealed*

Thursday February 2
*Romans 1:26-32 Many Are
Filled with Wickedness*

Friday February 3
*Romans 2:1-11 God Does
Not Show Favoritism*

Saturday February 4
*Romans 2:12-24
Obedience Leads to
Righteousness*

Sunday February 5
*Romans 2:25-29 It's a
Matter of the Heart*

Scripture

Background Scripture: *Romans 1*
Scripture Lesson: *Romans 1:1-13, 16-17*
Key Verse: *I am not ashamed of the gospel, because
it is the power of God for the salvation of everyone
who believes: first for the Jew, then for the Gentile.
Romans 1:16.*

Lesson Aim

The power of God to save lives comes through the
Gospel.

Lesson Setting

Time: A.D. 57
Place: From Corinth to the church in Rome

Lesson Outline

Power-full Living

   I. Paul's Identity and Calling: Romans 1:1-7
     A. *Set Apart for the Gospel: vss. 1-4*
     B. *Called to the Gentiles: vss. 5-6*
     C. *Called to the Romans: vs. 7*
  II. Paul's Desire: Romans 1:8-13
     A. *Paul's Prayer: vss. 8-10*
     B. *Paul's Purposes: vss. 11-13*
 III. Paul's Confidence: Romans 1:16-17
     A. *In the Gospel's Power: vs. 16*
     B. *In God's Righteousness: vs. 17*

Introduction

Getting Right with God

Paul declared that the good news about Christ did not embarrass him, for the Gospel represented the power of God at work in saving everyone who believes (Rom. 1:16). Sadly, we find many people in our culture who reject the importance of getting right with God by embracing the Gospel. It's true that, according to the polls, a lot of people claim to be "religious." Nevertheless, many in the West take little account of God. Perhaps there is little fear of facing a holy God because the idea of sin has virtually been abolished.

The Gospel, which Paul proclaimed, won't make the evening news on television. It won't even make newspaper headlines. It's thus the responsibility of believers to carry the Good News far and wide so that all may hear it and have the opportunity to be saved. Perhaps God in His grace might use our proclamation of the Gospel to prompt some who hear it to get right with Him.

Lesson Commentary

I. Paul's Identity and Calling: Romans 1:1-7

A. Set Apart for the Gospel: vss. 1-4

Paul, a servant of Christ Jesus, called to be an apostle and set apart for the gospel of God—the gospel he promised beforehand through his prophets in the Holy Scriptures regarding his Son, who as to his human nature was a descendant of David, and who through the Spirit of holiness was declared with power to be the Son of God by his resurrection from the dead: Jesus Christ our Lord.

The word Paul used for "servant" would be meaningful to the Romans, because it is the word "slave." There were an estimated 60 million slaves in the Roman Empire; and a slave was looked on as a piece of property, not a person. In loving devotion, Paul had enslaved himself to Christ, to be His servant and obey His will.

"All roads lead to Rome." This common proverb seemed almost true during Paul's lifetime. This booming metropolis was connected to other parts of the ancient world by an intricate system of highways. Its communications system was unsurpassed at the time. During the first century A.D., Rome was at the hub of trade and commerce. Because of its location and prestige, Rome was a strategic city for the spread of the Gospel, which is the focus of this quarter's lessons.

It's not surprising that we begin our study with the Book of Romans, for it presents a comprehensive and systematic doctrine

178

of salvation in Christ. This letter has singularly fired great people of the faith, such as Augustine, Martin Luther, John Bunyan, and John Wesley. Romans is Paul's theological masterpiece.

Paul called himself a servant, or slave, of Jesus Christ (vs. 1). In other words, Paul belonged to and obeyed the Savior. As a bond-slave of the Lord, Paul had been bought with a price and then set free so that he could serve Jesus in love for the rest of his life.

Paul said he was a "called" apostle. In other words, he did not enter his ministry as the result of personal choice; rather, he had received a divine summons, which put him into that position. Paul traced his appointment to a divine decision in the counsel of eternity. God had marked Paul off for the work of proclaiming the Gospel even before he was born (Gal. 1:15).

The Good News that Paul heralded had its origin in the Hebrew Scriptures and had been the subject of the prophets' interest (Rom. 1:2). In fact, the message of truth had even been proclaimed to Abraham (Gal. 3:8). Thus the truth Paul heralded was not something novel or deviant, but rather grounded in the revelation of the Old Testament.

The person of the Gospel is God's Son, "Jesus Christ our Lord" (Rom. 1:4). The message emphasizes Jesus' real humanity; according to the flesh—that is, His human nature in its entirety—He descended from King David through Mary (vs. 3). The Gospel also stresses Christ's absolute deity. He is the eternal Son in union with the Father (vs. 4).

The good news includes the fact that Jesus' resurrection from the dead transferred Him from His state of humility to a new phase of lordship and glory. His entrance into post-resurrection glory was perfectly compatible with the essential sinlessness of His humanity and the direct result of the Holy Spirit's limitless power.

B. Called to the Gentiles: vss. 5-6

Through him and for his name's sake, we received grace and apostleship to call people from among all the Gentiles to the obedience that comes from faith. And you also are among those who are called to belong to Jesus Christ.

Paul attributed his ability to carry out the functions of his office to the grace of God (vs. 5). In fact, Paul's apostleship was God's gracious gift to him. The purpose for which the Lord saved and called Paul was that he might bring the Gentiles to obedience through faith in Christ.

The good news that Paul proclaimed announces that God's kingdom is at hand and that forgiveness is available through faith in Christ. It is the duty of everyone who hears the truth to obey its first demand—trust in Christ. The moment we believe in Him, we are obeying the Gospel. Oppositely, to reject the Good News is to disobey it.

Paul's readers had already heard and believed the Good News (vs. 6). And by their obedient faith they had joined God's family. They thus belonged to Jesus Christ, and He was their Savior and Lord.

C. Called to the Romans: vs. 7

To all in Rome who are loved by God and called to be saints: Grace and peace to you from God our Father and from the Lord Jesus Christ.

God had commissioned Paul to carry Jesus' name "before the Gentiles" (Acts 9:15). This included the people in Rome. As the apostle wrote to the Roman believers, he called them "saints" (Rom. 1:7). By this Paul meant God's holy people. Like other Christians, they had renounced their sin and devoted their lives in service to the Lord.

Paul's standard greeting of grace and peace is included in the letter he wrote to the Romans. Through their faith in Christ, they became the recipients of the Father's unmerited favor and unending peace. Ephesians 2:7 reminds us that God has shown "the incomparable riches of his grace, expressed in his kindness to us in Christ Jesus." Such is a magnificent display of the Lord's great love for us (Rom. 1:4).

II. Paul's Desire: Romans 1:8-13

A. Paul's Prayer: vss. 8-10

First, I thank my God through Jesus Christ for all of you, because your faith is being reported all over the world. God, whom I serve with my whole heart in preaching the gospel of his Son, is my witness how constantly I remember you in my prayers at all times; and I pray that now at last by God's will the way may be opened for me to come to you.

As in other letters Paul wrote, this one contained his expression of gratitude to the believers in Rome. He was especially thankful that their faith in God was becoming known "all over the world" (vs. 8). Rome was the center of the empire and the inhabited world. Thus whatever happened in the capital city became known throughout the realm. The testimony of the church in Rome was so strong that in A.D. 49 Claudius the emperor expelled all the Jews because of the influence of someone named "Chrestus," which most likely is a reference to Christ (Acts 18:2).

Paul's concern for the Roman Christians was real and concrete. The apostle related that God knew how often Paul had prayed for his fellow believers in the capital. This wasn't an occasional occurrence. Rather, Paul lifted them up in prayer "constantly" (Rom. 1:9). And this wasn't an idle claim, for the apostle called on God as his witness, the same God whom he served with his whole heart in the proclamation of the Gospel.

Paul had wanted to visit Rome numerous times, but up until then had not been able to do so (vs. 13). During those intervening years, the apostle had done his evangelistic preaching and church planting in Greece and Asia Minor. Now he saw his way clear to make a possible visit to the capital of the empire. Paul thus asked that God would give him a prosperous journey to Rome (vs. 10). Paul, of course, knew that God would decide how and when his prayer request would be fulfilled. Later on the Lord did open the way for Paul to visit Rome, but as a prisoner.

B. Paul's Purposes: vss. 11-13

I long to see you so that I may impart to you some spiritual gift to make you strong—that is, that you and I may be mutually encouraged by each other's faith. I do not want you to be unaware, brothers, that I planned many times to come to you (but have been prevented from doing so until now) in order that I might have a harvest among you, just as I have had among the other Gentiles.

Paul noted two compelling reasons to visit Rome. First, he wanted to work with the Roman Christians in seeing a vast multitude of new converts to the faith. Second, the apostle wanted to partner with his fellow believers in Rome in seeing the church spiritually strengthened (vs. 11).

Paul saw himself as a strengthener and encourager of others. And these were the spiritual gifts he wanted to utilize in Rome. Paul's building plan was people, not structures. He sensed he could encourage other Christians by his biblical teaching and godly example.

It's important to note that Paul didn't want his relationship with the Roman Christians to be one-sided. In other words, the apostle wanted both to minister to them and be ministered to by them (vs. 12). And that's why Paul sought mutual encouragement from them. This fits his description of how spiritual gifts are to be used in the church (Eph. 4:11-13).

Paul anticipated a bountiful spiritual "harvest" (Rom. 1:13) of Gentile converts resulting from his ministry with the other believers in Rome. By the end of the apostle's third missionary journey, he had traveled through Syria, Galatia, Macedonia, and Achaia. He now sensed that the time had come to redirect his ministry efforts to the eastern part of the empire.

The word "salvation" carried tremendous meaning in Paul's day. Its basic meaning is "deliverance," and it was applied to personal and national deliverance.

III. Paul's Confidence: Romans 1:16-17

A. In the Gospel's Power: vs. 16

I am not ashamed of the gospel, because it is the power of God for the salvation of everyone who believes: first for the Jew, then for the Gentile.

Paul's ambition to herald the Gospel in Rome arose from his sense of indebtedness to all people (vs. 14). He was under assignment to preach to the civilized and the uncivilized, to the cultured and the uncultured. Paul felt it was his duty to reach all regardless of their race, social status, or mental ability. The capital was the great prize to be won, and Paul anticipated his visit with eagerness. He was ready to go (vs. 15).

Paul had no reason to be ashamed of the Gospel he proclaimed. To be sure, it had no special appeal to the intellectuals. And the Good News could not boast of a great antiquity in that city, like the pagan religions of Rome. Nevertheless, the preaching of the Gospel unleashed the power of God (vs. 16). When the Lord exercised His power through the heralding of the Good News, He delivered the lost from eternal ruin. God rescued people from the tyranny of the devil, the mastery of the sin-principle, and the state of spiritual death.

Salvation is the experience of all who trust in Christ. In fact, salvation never occurs apart from faith. Salvation covers everything God does for us in Christ. God forgives our sins and grants us eternal life. We face the prospect of enjoying His presence forever.

Salvation is the possession equally of Jews and Gentiles. Neither has any priority on the claims of the Gospel. Of course, since Jews were the heirs of the promises of Abraham and the people from whom the Messiah came, it was appropriate that the Gospel should have been preached first to them. Paul followed this order on several occasions. In general, the Jews rejected the message of salvation through a crucified Messiah, and Paul then turned to the Gentiles.

B. In God's Righteousness: vs. 17

For in the gospel a righteousness from God is revealed, a righteousness that is by faith from first to last, just as it is written: "The righteous will live by faith."

Paul noted that the Gospel message included God's gift of righteousness by faith. The Good News revealed a God of righteousness, holiness, and justice who both judged people righteously and then declared them righteous by means of their faith in Christ (vs. 17).

In this verse Paul was not talking about a divine attribute, namely, God's justice. Rather, the apostle was referring to a righteousness of which the Lord is the author and which provides an answer to the sinful condition of people. People must appropriate this righteousness by faith. It is the experience of all who trust in Christ.

A right standing with God comes by faith and appeals to faith— "from first to last"(vs. 17). "The righteous will live by faith" is a quotation from Habakkuk 2:4. Paul took pains to connect the Gospel of Jesus Christ to the Old Testament. The prophet Habakkuk's words confirm Paul's point that righteousness comes through faith.

Discussion Questions

1. How had Christ and His Gospel radically changed Paul's life?
2. Why do you think Paul made the preaching of the Gospel such an important part of his ministry?
3. Why did Paul stress both the true humanity and absolute deity of Christ?
4. Why did Paul call on God as his witness concerning his claim regarding his prayers for the Romans?
5. Under what circumstances might some believers today be ashamed of the Gospel?

Now Ask Yourself . . .

What would I say to someone who remarks, "I think the Gospel of Christ is ridiculous"?

What calling does God have on my life? Do I see it as a divine calling?

Have I known God's grace and peace? How can I extend God's grace and peace to those around me?

Do I know what it means to "pray at all times"?

Have I ever been ashamed of the Gospel? If so, what misconception has led me to that?

Illustrations

Powerful ideas have spawned a chain of events that have affected the world. For instance, some historians say that the American Revolution was one of those episodes that left a permanent imprint on the history of humankind. In our time we could point to political and economic ideas that have impacted humankind both positively and negatively. In the end, though, none of these philosophies can match the Gospel of Christ, for none of them deals with our basic need to find forgiveness and righteousness from God.

Paul knew a lot about religion in his time, and he debated with some of the best Greek and Jewish minds of his day. The apostle never flinched when it came to staking out the claim that the Gospel was God's power to change people and give them eternal life. Paul made it clear that he was not just offering a new idea. In fact, he preached a person, Jesus of Nazareth, whom the authorities had executed and whom God had raised from the dead. Only this message can offer the lost eternal hope and peace. When they believe in Jesus, God declares them righteous.

The truth is that Jesus Christ, God's anointed Son, is alive and in heaven. We thus need not make any apologies for believing in Him. Rather, like Paul, we should be eager to tell the Good News with confidence.

Right in His Sight

DEVOTIONAL READING

Psalm 33:13-22

DAILY BIBLE READINGS

Monday February 6
   Exodus 32:25-35 God Will Punish Sin

Tuesday February 7
   Numbers 32:14-24 God Knows Your Sin

Wednesday February 8
   Romans 3:1-8 God Is Faithful

Thursday February 9
   Romans 3:9-18 No One Is Righteous

Friday February 10
   Romans 3:19-26 All Have Sinned

Saturday February 11
   Romans 3:27-31 We Are Justified by Faith

Sunday February 12
   Mark 9:42-49 Do Not Cause Others to Sin

Scripture

Background Scripture: *Romans 3*

Scripture Lesson: *Romans 3:1-4, 19-31*

Key Verse: *For all have sinned and fall short of the glory of God, and are justified freely by his grace through the redemption that came by Christ Jesus. Romans 3:23-24.*

Lesson Aim

Any sin is an affront to God.

Lesson Setting

Time: A.D. 57

Place: From Corinth to the church in Rome

Lesson Outline

Right in His Sight

I. Jewish Advantages: Romans 3:1-4
   A. *The Revelation of God: vss. 1-2*
   B. *The Faithfulness of God: vss. 3-4*

II. Forgiveness through Christ: Romans 3:19-31
   A. *The Purpose of the Law: vss. 19-20*
   B. *The Way to Be Saved: vss. 21-23*
   C. *The Basis for Justification: vss. 24-26*
   D. *The Elimination of Pride: vss. 27-28*
   E. *The Impartial Love of God: vss. 29-31*

Introduction

Admitting Need

Grandpa tried to help his grandson put together a new toy. "I know how to do this," the boy said, rejecting his grandfather's assistance. Perhaps initially we might think such a attitude represents childish pride. But then it's sobering to realize that this way of thinking is evident in many of us as adults.

"I don't need your help" means we feel self-sufficient. When we have such an attitude, it's humiliating to admit that we need help. Perhaps this is the greatest stumbling block that keeps many people from coming to faith in Christ. After all, who wants to admit sin and guilt? And who wants to say that God's judgment is fair and well deserved?

The Gospel cuts to the heart of the issue—our stubborn pride and willful independence from God. Until we understand and accept the consequences of our sins, we will not be prepared to come to Him on His terms. It's only when we admit our need that we will be ready to receive His gift of salvation through faith in Christ.

Lesson Commentary

I. Jewish Advantages: Romans 3:1-4

A. The Revelation of God: vss. 1-2

What advantage, then, is there in being a Jew, or what value is there in circumcision? Much in every way! First of all, they have been entrusted with the very words of God.

From Romans 1 we learned that Paul described the power of the Gospel in terms of God declaring believing sinners righteous. From 1:18 to 3:20 the apostle discussed why all people need God's righteousness. Because of sin, every human being stands condemned before the Lord, who is holy.

Paul advanced his argument by first expounding the failure of the Gentiles to worship and obey God (1:18-32). Then the apostle focused on the fairness of God's judgment of humankind (2:1-16). Paul followed this discussion with a description of the failure of the Jews to live up to God's perfect moral standard (2:17—3:8). The apostle concluded that the entire world is guilty of disobeying the Lord (3:9-20).

Paul anticipated how the Jews would react to his explanation in 2:25-29. They were likely to reply in this way: "If being a true Jew depends on the inward condition of the heart rather than on racial and ritual distinctions, what advantage then is it to be a Jew? How is a Jew better off to have circumcision when, in the final analysis, circumcision does not really count?" (3:1).

Paul declared that there was a decided advantage in being a Jew. The principal benefit was that God had made the Jews the special custodians of His written revelation to humanity (vs. 2). Jewish birth gave them a unique exposure to God's Word. The oracles of God promised the Jews a permanent redemption through the Messiah, preserved them from the grosser immoralities of pagans, and prepared them for receiving the Gospel.

B. The Faithfulness of God: vss. 3-4

What if some did not have faith? Will their lack of faith nullify God's faithfulness? Not at all! Let God be true, and every man a liar. As it is written: "So that you may be proved right when you speak and prevail when you judge."

The spiritual benefits God had bestowed on the Jewish people were undeniable. But with such privileges came great responsibilities. Sadly, many Jews were not faithful in their responsibility. Indeed, they failed to live up to God's holy standards.

The fact that the Jews were the recipients of God's Word raised the important issue of faith in God's Word (vs. 3). More specifically, Paul addressed the issue as to whether the lack of faith on the part of the Jews nullified God's faithfulness. The apostle immediately answered, "Not at all!" (vs. 4). God is always portrayed in Scripture as being utterly faithful to His Word (Deut. 7:9; 1 Cor. 1:9; Heb. 10:23). Paul expanded upon this theme of God's faithfulness in the face of Israel's unfaithfulness in Romans 9 through 11.

Paul made a puzzling statement when he declared, "Let God be true, and every man a liar" (Rom. 3:4). The apostle was emphasizing God's faithfulness in the face of the Jews' unfaithfulness. In other words, in light of God's spotless integrity, all people do appear like liars.

In support of Paul's argument, he quoted from Psalm 51:4. From this we learn that God's judgment against sin displays His faithfulness to His righteous character. God's faithfulness means He will never ignore sin, and when He judges, His judgment is perfect.

All of Paul's witnesses agreed: the Jews were guilty before God. In Romans 3:1-8, Paul summed up the argument and refuted those Jews who tried to debate him. They raised three questions. (1) "What advantage is it to be a Jew?" Reply: Every advantage, especially possessing the Word of God. (2) "Will Jewish unbelief cancel God's faithfulness?" Reply: Absolutely not—it establishes it. (3) "If our sin commends His righteousness, how can He judge us?" Reply: We do not do evil that good may come of it.

God's faithfulness is both comforting and challenging for us as Christians. It is a comfort to know that God will always fulfill the promises He has made. It is a challenge in that we can count on God's discipline when we sin.

II. Forgiveness through Christ: Romans 3:19-31

A. The Purpose of the Law: vss. 19-20

Now we know that whatever the law says, it says to those who are under the law, so that every mouth may be silenced and the whole world held accountable to God. Therefore no one will be declared righteous in his sight by observing the law; rather, through the law we become conscious of sin.

Throughout the first three chapters of Romans, Paul argued that at the bar of divine justice three witnesses testified against humanity. The creation pressed charges against the pagan for having rejected the light of nature. The conscience accused the moralist for having broken the moral law that God has written on the tablet of the human heart. And Scripture witnessed against the Jew for having violated the law of Moses. As 3:5-18 makes clear, the evidence was undeniable and condemning.

Paul affirmed that the pronouncements of the law are for all those who are "under the law" (vs. 19). His readers were under the law in the sense that they were obligated to obey it. They were answerable to the law because of their accountability to God Himself.

The purpose of the law was to silence every mouth and hold the entire world accountable to God. The law effectively and inarguably points to God's righteous and holy standards, and points to our utter inability to measure up to it. No one is in a position to argue sin away or make excuses, for the law invalidates all rationalizations.

Paul closed this section by pointing out that the law was never provided as a means of attaining righteousness or of being pronounced righteous before God (vs. 20). Rather, the law was given to make people aware of their sin. It is through the law that human beings become conscious of sin and see their need for a solution to the problem. In this light the law is an instrument of condemnation, not justification. The law, written on the hearts of all, shines the spotlight on our need for redemption. Admitting this is a crucial step toward being saved.

B. The Way to Be Saved: vss. 21-23

But now a righteousness from God, apart from law, has been made known, to which the Law and the Prophets testify. This righteousness from God comes through faith in Jesus Christ to all who believe. There is no difference, for all have sinned and fall short of the glory of God.

Paul had said that no one can be declared righteous by observing the law (vs. 20). Since the law cannot save, but only shine the spotlight on sin, God's provision for salvation must be made "apart from law" (vs. 21), that is, "through faith in Jesus Christ" (vs. 22).

Righteousness apart from the law was previously revealed in "the Law and the Prophets" (vs. 21)—namely, the Old Testament. The word "Law" here refers to the first five books in the Old Testament, while "Prophets" refers to the other Old Testament books. The means of receiving this righteousness is by trusting in Christ (vs. 22). It is not something that can be worked for or earned. Whether Jew or Gentile, faith is the sole requirement. Faith is not considered a work, but rather a response of the broken heart to the saving work of God.

Paul said that, no matter who we are or what we have done, we are all saved in the same way. This is because all human beings—both Jew and Gentile—are sinners before God (vs. 23). Even the Jewish people could not be exempted from God's condemnation, for they were as guilty as the Gentiles.

Paul had in mind two aspects of sin: overt transgression and failure to do what is right. We are all guilty on both counts. Regardless of what we do—no matter how noble it might be—we still fall short of God's glorious standard.

The term for "fall short" is a single word in the Greek and is in the present tense to indicate continuing action. The tragedy is that human beings perpetually fall short of God's glory. The word rendered "glory" refers not just to God's magnificent presence but also to the outward display of His attributes, including His goodness, righteousness, and holiness. Our sin has separated us from God and excludes us from enjoying these displays of His glory.

C. The Basis for Justification: vss. 24-26

And are justified freely by his grace through the redemption that came by Christ Jesus. God presented him as a sacrifice of atonement, through faith in his blood. He did this to demonstrate his justice, because in his forbearance he had left the sins committed beforehand unpunished—he did it to demonstrate his justice at the present time, so as to be just and the one who justifies those who have faith in Jesus.

Against the dark backdrop of our sin and guilt, Paul painted a brilliant picture of God's grace. God not only is just and holy but also kind, loving, and gracious. Without these there would be no hope for any of us.

We are justified (or declared righteous by God) "freely" (vs. 24). Because of God's grace, there is no charge. In fact, nothing we can do will ever earn God's righteousness. When we think we can do enough good to satisfy God's holiness, we insult His grace.

Paul used the Greek word translated "redemption" to describe what God has done for us in Christ. This word pictures God rescuing us out of the slave market of sin. In a sense, He has purchased our freedom out of the riches of His incomparable grace.

The person and work of the Christ is the overwhelming proof of God's grace. Because God's justice demanded a sacrifice for our sins, Jesus died on the cross. He took the punishment of our sins and satisfied God's anger against us. When we believe that Jesus shed His blood and sacrificed His life for us, God declares us to be righteous (vs. 25).

In God's "forbearance" (literally, "holding back"), He had suspended the full punishment for sins before Jesus' death. Such sins had been symbolically atoned for in the animal sacrifices of the temple. These sacrifices, however, were merely the shadow of Christ's saving work on the cross.

Paul noted that, because of what Jesus had done, God was entirely fair to not punish those who had sinned in former times. Likewise, the Lord was entirely just in this "present time" (vs. 26) to declare believing sinners to be right in His sight. Sinners cannot hurtle the legal barrier, but Christ can and did for them as

The theological term for the salvation Paul was declaring is "justification by faith." Justification is the act of God whereby He declares the believing sinner righteous in Christ on the basis of the finished work of Christ on the cross.

their representative. Consequently, God can legitimately welcome and pardon them when they trust in Christ.

D. The Elimination of Pride: vss. 27-28

Where, then, is boasting? It is excluded. On what principle? On that of observing the law? No, but on that of faith. For we maintain that a man is justified by faith apart from observing the law.

Paul next asked some hard-hitting questions. First, "Where, then, is boasting?" (vs. 27). He declared that boasting was "excluded" (or, "completely shut out"). Since human beings are justified by grace through faith, no works can be involved. Hence, no one can boast, for salvation is a free gift (Eph. 2:8-9).

This prompted a second question: "On what principle [is boasting excluded]? On that of observing the law?" (Rom. 3:27). Paul answered, "No" (or, "Not at all"). As the apostle stated earlier, God did not give the law to provide justification but rather to show people their state of sin and their need to be reconciled with God. Justification (or being "declared righteous") is available only through faith, "apart from observing the law" (vs. 28).

E. The Impartial Love of God: vss. 29-31

Is God the God of Jews only? Is he not the God of Gentiles too? Yes, of Gentiles too, since there is only one God, who will justify the circumcised by faith and the uncircumcised through that same faith. Do we, then, nullify the law by this faith? Not at all! Rather, we uphold the law.

Apparently some thought God was the exclusive property of Jews. Paul countered by noting that Gentiles do not have one God and the Jews another (vs. 29). Likewise, faith is not a national possession. God does not save Gentiles on the basis of a different principle from that by which He saves Jews. One God justifies both Jews and Gentiles by faith (vs. 30).

Paul then noted that God declares righteous those who come to Christ by faith. They thereby receive a perfect standing of uprightness before the Lord. Their new status in God's sight fulfills all the demands that any divine moral code could have ever required of them (vs. 31).

Discussion Questions

1. What spiritual advantages did Paul say there were to being a Jew?
2. How has God proven Himself to be just in His treatment of the Jews, despite the unfaithfulness of some to Him?
3. Why would God go to so much trouble to forgive those who have rebelled against Him?
4. What role does the law serve in bringing us to Christ?
5. Why do you think anyone would spurn God's gracious offer of salvation through faith in Christ?

Now Ask Yourself . . .

Have I, at times, spurned God's grace? If so, when and why?

Do I always find God to be just, or do I feel that He is unfair at times? What is the difference between fairness and justice?

Have I sometimes had a tendency toward boasting because I have forgotten that salvation is a free gift from God?

How can I show God's gracious gift to someone when that person only sees God as a judge handing down the law?

Illustrations

If God were only just, humanity would not have a prayer. Our situation is clear: we have sinned before a holy God. The only just response from God is death.

At the same time, if God were solely loving, we would all be swept up to His bosom without a glance at the sinfulness of our hearts.

Neither happens, however, because God is neither exclusively just nor exclusively loving; He's all both. He loves us and wants us to join Him in His eternal kingdom. But He first had to establish a way for our sin to be annulled. That was what God, the Father, accomplished through Jesus Christ.

In a metaphorical sense, God has sent us an invitation marked RSVP (Répondez s'il vous plaît)—French for "Please reply." Although our Lord waits patiently for our favorable response, He has set a limit on how long He will wait. At some point He must say, "Enough!" and the doors of heaven will swing shut. Before it's too late, we must say yes to His invitation and join His great banquet.

Promises to Live By

DEVOTIONAL READING
Psalm 32:6-11

DAILY BIBLE READINGS
Monday February 13
2 Chronicles 20:20-21 The Successful Have Faith

Tuesday February 14
Genesis 12:1-9 Abraham Does Whatever the Lord Asks

Wednesday February 15
Romans 4:1-8 We Are Justified by Our Faith

Thursday February 16
Romans 4:9-15 Faith Is More Important Than the Law

Friday February 17
Romans 4:16-25 Do Not Waver with Unbelief

Saturday February 18
Galatians 3:1-14 Receive the Spirit through Faith

Sunday February 19
Galatians 3:15-25 We Are Set Free by Our Faith

Scripture
Background Scripture: *Romans 4*
Scripture Lesson: *Romans 4:2-3, 13-25*
Key Verse: *Yet he did not waver through unbelief regarding the promise of God, but was strengthened in his faith and gave glory to God, being fully persuaded that God had power to do what he had promised.* Romans 4:20-21.

Lesson Aim
Faith can be absolutely sure that God will keep His promises.

Lesson Setting
Time: A.D. 57
Place: From Corinth to the church in Rome

Lesson Outline
Promises to Live By
I. Abraham's Justification—Not by Works: Romans 4:2-3
II. Abraham's Justification—Not by the Law: Romans 4:13-17a
III. Abraham's Justification—By Faith: Romans 4:17b-22
IV. Abraham's Faith and Ours: Romans 4:23-25

Introduction

Following an Example
of Faith

The young mother's husband died after a long illness. A year later she and her two children decided to hold a "Heaven Party" to focus on their loved one's perfect place of residence. More than 60 friends came to play games, talk about what heaven might be like, and to eat and sing together. Their faith encouraged many people.

The power of faith remains undiminished from Abraham's time to ours. Such faith compels us to hold strongly to Jesus, "the author and perfecter of our faith" (Heb. 12:2). When we consider Abraham's testimony, we see how he struggled when God's promise of a son through the patriarch's wife, Sarah, seemed humanly impossible to fulfill. But Abraham's faith in God kept him going. The same principle held true for the young widow and her children mentioned above.

We can help fellow believers in their struggles by being an example of faith. And we can bear testimony to those who were role models of faith to us. Such faith has the potential to make a profound difference!

Lesson Commentary

I. Abraham's Justification— Not by Works: Romans 4:2-3

If, in fact, Abraham was justified by works, he had something to boast about—but not before God. What does the Scripture say? "Abraham believed God, and it was credited to him as righteousness."

Paul built his case for faith—righteousness on Abraham and David—two of the most respected figures in the Old Testament. Abraham would be particularly important as an example, for the Jews thought they had a privileged relationship with God by virtue of their physical relationship with Abraham as his descendants. Paul knew that if he could show that Abraham was justified by faith and not by works, then their false presumptions would fall like a house of cards.

Paul began by asking, "What then shall we say?" (vs. 1). His concern was to address what Abraham discovered on the issue of justification by faith. Abraham, of course, was the ancestor of the Jews and the central person in their history. Did he become justified on the basis of obedience to some moral code?

The Jews of Paul's day believed that Abraham had so much righteousness in terms of good works that he had a surplus of merit. This merit was allegedly available to Abraham's descendants. Many Jews also believed that Abraham was a perfect example of a person justified by works. Paul fully agreed that Abraham was an upright person and that, as such, he had something to boast about before people—but not before God (vs. 2).

To underscore his point, Paul appealed to Genesis 15:6, which he quoted in Romans 4:3, "Abraham believed God, and it was credited to him as righteousness." Because Abraham believed the divine promise concerning a son, God credited (or "imputed") righteousness to the patriarch's account. (The Greek word for "credited" was an ancient accounting term.) Hence, Abraham's life was a perfect illustration of Paul's point, namely, that righteousness comes through faith and not through obedience to the law of Moses. Abraham, therefore, is the spiritual ancestor of all who believe (Gal. 3:7).

It's the perennial temptation to imagine we have to earn God's approval. We tend to think, "If only I try a little harder, He'll accept me because of my goodness." But in reality, there has always been only one way to feel the smile of God's favor upon us. That way is by putting our faith in Jesus Christ.

The experience of David illustrates the same truth from a different angle. Sinful David had to come to God by faith. His works could not earn him the Lord's favor, for his deeds were tainted by sin (Rom. 4:6). Those whom God blessed have not merited His good pleasure; rather, He graciously declares them to be righteous in His sight. On the basis of His unmerited favor, God cancels the debt of sin. Consequently, they are no longer guilty in His sight and are not under His wrath (vss. 7-8).

The Jews might ask what relationship circumcision had to the justification of Abraham. Paul declared that the patriarch was justified at least 14 years before he submitted to the rite of circumcision (vss. 9-10). Thus, circumcision had nothing at all to do with Abraham's right-standing before the Lord. Circumcision was the visible guarantee that the patriarch would become the father of many spiritual descendants among the Gentiles as well as the Jews. All who exercise the same kind of faith that Abraham displayed will participate in the spiritual blessings that God promised to the patriarch (vss. 11-12).

In the phrase "Abraham believed God" the word "believed" means "to say amen." The word "credited" is a Greek word which means "to put to one's account."

II. Abraham's Justification— Not by the Law: Romans 4:13-17a

It was not through law that Abraham and his offspring received the promise that he would be heir of the world, but through the righteousness that comes by faith. For if those who live by law are heirs, faith has no value and the promise is worthless, because law brings wrath. And where there is no law there is no transgression. Therefore, the promise comes by faith, so that it may be by grace and may be guaranteed to all Abraham's offspring—not only to those who are of the law but also to those who are of the faith of Abraham. He is the father of us all. As it is written: "I have made you a father of many nations."

The Jews gloried in circumcision and the Law. If a Jew was to become righteous before God, he would have to be circumcised and obey the Law. But Abraham was declared righteous before his circumcision and before the Law was given. The key word in verses 13-17 is "promise." Abraham was justified by believing God's promise, not by obeying God's Law.

Paul noted that it was not through the law that Abraham received the promise that "he would be heir of the world" (vs. 13). In point of fact, God's promise to the patriarch—contained in the Abrahamic covenant in Genesis 12:1-3—occurred several centuries before God gave the law through Moses (Gal. 3:17).

The Lord promised Abraham that he would have many descendants, and that through his seed the peoples of the earth would be blessed (Gen. 12:3). This is probably what Paul was referring to in saying that Abraham "would be heir of the world" (Rom. 4:13). This incredible promise was given several hundred years prior to the giving of the law.

Paul next pointed out that if the Jews could become Abraham's heirs by simply keeping the law, then "faith has no value" (vs. 14, or "has been made empty"). In such a situation the divine promise is made invalid. To assert that God's blessing goes to the law keepers also amounts to saying that His promises to those who have faith (which would include Abraham and David) are meaningless and useless.

As Paul stressed in verse 15, when we try to keep the law, we always end up being under God's wrath. Keeping the law in order to gain God's favor (and salvation) only produces spiritual arrogance, for the purpose of the law was to reveal sin, not to bring justification.

Paul affirmed that where there is no law, there is no transgression. If people don't know right from wrong, then in one sense they cannot be held accountable for their actions. Of course, as Paul pointed out in 2:14-15, even those who do not have the Mosaic law have God's moral law written on their hearts. Thus all people intuitively know right from wrong, and therefore all are responsible and are without excuse for disobeying God.

Paul declared that all of Abraham's offspring—both the Jews ("those who are of the law," 4:16) and believing Gentiles ("those who are of the faith of Abraham")—receive the promise of righteousness (or justification) by faith and according to God's grace. If it were received by keeping the works of the law, then no one could receive it, for all are guilty of breaking the law.

Paul added the significant point that God's promise of salvation is extended to all who believe, whether Jews and Gentiles. Through faith in Christ, all can receive God's righteousness and call Abraham their spiritual ancestor. It's no wonder that God called the patriarch "a father of many nations" (Gen. 17:5; Rom. 4:17).

III. Abraham's Justification— By Faith: Romans 4:17b-22

He is our father in the sight of God, in whom he believed—the God who gives life to the dead and calls things that are not as though they were. Against all hope, Abraham in hope believed and so became the father of many nations, just as it had been said to him, "So shall your offspring be." Without weakening in his faith, he faced the fact that his body was as good as dead—since he was about a hundred years old—and that Sarah's womb was also dead. Yet he did not waver through unbelief regarding the promise of God, but was strengthened in his faith and gave glory to God, being fully persuaded that God had power to do what he had promised. This is why "it was credited to him as righteousness."

Our faith in God is the one factor that relates us all (whether Jew or Gentile) to Abraham, for the patriarch himself was one who had faith in God. Indeed, Abraham believed in the God "who gives life to the dead and calls things that are not as though they were" (vs. 17). Paul was referring here to the birth of Isaac to Abraham and Sarah, both of whom were so old that, from a physical standpoint, it was impossible for them to have children (Gen. 18:11). But because of God's miraculous work, they gave birth to Isaac in their old age. We must not forget that God has the miraculous power to create out of nothing, to make possible what seems impossible—even our salvation.

While from a human perspective there was no hope that Abraham and Sarah could give birth to a child, Abraham still believed in God and His ability to fulfill His promise (Rom. 4:18). In so doing, Abraham became the spiritual ancestor of many people, as God had promised in Genesis 15:5.

If Abraham walked merely by sight and not by faith, things would have seemed bleak. After all, "his body was as good as dead" (Rom. 4:19), meaning that he was advanced in age—about 100 years old. To make matters worse, Sarah's womb was infertile. Even in earlier years, she had been unable to conceive a child (Gen. 16:1-2; 18:11). But now that she was 90 years old, there was virtually no likelihood (at least from outward appearances) that she would be able to give birth to a child. Despite this, Abraham's faith remained steadfast.

Romans 4:19 says Abraham "faced the fact" of his aged body and his elderly wife. Faith in God does not involve a refusal to deal with reality. Likewise, it doesn't involve an ignorance of the true state of affairs around us. Rather, faith looks beyond earthly realities to the God who can supernaturally change things.

The testimony of Abraham is that he never wavered in believing the promise of God. In fact, the patriarch's faith grew stronger, and in that "gave glory to God" (vs. 20). Despite the apparent odds against him, Abraham was absolutely convinced that the Lord was able to do anything He promised—including the birth of a son through Sarah (vs. 21). Because of Abraham's faith, God declared him to be righteous (vs. 22).

God is glorified when we trust in His promises. Our assurance that God will keep His word gives us strength to face our problems. With the kind of faith that Abraham had at our side, we will be less doubtful about the Lord and His intentions. We will be more at ease with ourselves and our circumstances.

IV. Abraham's Faith and Ours: Romans 4:23-25

The words "it was credited to him" were written not for him alone, but also for us, to whom God will credit righteousness—for us who believe in him who raised Jesus our Lord from the dead. He was delivered over to death for our sins and was raised to life for our justification.

The historical facts in Abraham's case are not isolated and irrelevant data. Rather, they have consequences for believers today. For instance, Paul noted that the wonderful truth of God declaring Abraham to be righteous wasn't just for his benefit (vs. 23). What was true for the patriarch thousands of years ago remains applicable for believers today (vs. 24).

We have the assurance of Scripture that when we believe in the Lord, He will "credit righteousness" to us. This is the same God who not only enabled Sarah to conceive and bear a son in her old age but also brought Jesus our Lord back "from the dead." Perhaps at first, His crucifixion seemed like a needless tragedy. But in the Father's eternal plan He allowed His Son to die on the cross because of our sins. And then God raised Jesus from the dead so that we could be made right with Him (vs. 25).

It's helpful to note that, throughout the history of the church, Jesus' "sacrifice of atonement" (3:25) has been understood in different ways: 1) Jesus' death paid a ransom to Satan for souls held captive in the devil's domain; 2) Jesus' death reversed the effects of sin begun by Adam; 3) Jesus' death was the supreme act of victory that won the release of people held in bondage; 4) Jesus mysteriously took on sinful human nature while on the cross and triumphed over it; 5) Jesus' death provided an example of obedience for all Christians to follow; 6) Jesus' death softens the hearts of people so that they will repent; 7) God rewarded Jesus for His obedience, and Jesus passed this reward (salvation) along to believing people; and 8) Jesus died in the place of sinful people and paid the penalty of their sin.

Regardless of which view is preferred, it is nonetheless clear that we can enjoy fellowship with God thanks to the work of Christ. We give Him our sins, and He forgives us and makes us right with the Lord (2 Cor. 5:21). What incredibly good news this is that we can share with the world!

Discussion Questions

1. What was the basis for God declaring Abraham to be righteous?
2. In addition to Abraham and David, can you think of any other Old Testament characters who were justified by faith?
3. What was the basis of God's promise to Abraham that he would be "heir of the world" (Rom. 4:13)?
4. What prevented Abraham from doubting God's promise?
5. How can the example of Abraham encourage us in our times of doubt?

Now Ask Yourself . . .

How is it possible for my faith to grow in the face of seeming impossibilities?

Do I know for sure that God has declared me righteous based on what Jesus has done?

What can I do to encourage my faith to grow when facing difficult circumstances? How can I encourage others in similar places?

Is there anything in my life that I feel is too difficult for God to do? How can I get beyond that to faith?

Illustrations

How do we develop an abiding faith in the Lord? We must take God at His word and apply the teachings of Scripture to our lives. As we step out in faith and obey God, He demonstrates His reliability to us time after time. Our faith in God increases as we live for Him and serve Him in new and different ways. The more we trust Him, the more assured we become that He'll uphold us regardless of the circumstances.

We might continue to struggle with doubts even after we're seasoned in our faith. Instead of allowing uncertainty to control us, we should examine it in the light of what Scripture teaches. The truth of God's Word can calm us when we're feeling anxious about something, as it says in Psalm 94:19: "When anxiety was great within me, your consolation brought joy to my soul." We can also see Jesus, Himself, speaking this to us in John 14:1: "Do not let your hearts be troubled. Trust in God, trust also in me."

Our faith in God can also be strengthened by reflecting on our past experiences and those of other believers (for instance, Abraham). God's faithfulness to us and others in the past can encourage us when we're going through difficult times. When we consistently trust in the Lord, we become increasingly convinced that He knows what's best for us. We also become more willing to wait for His timing when it comes to enjoying the blessings of faith. Some of these come in this life, but some are received in eternity, and we find, as the old hymn says, "Great is Thy Faithfulness."

Hope to Hold On

DEVOTIONAL READING
Psalm 32:1-5

DAILY BIBLE READINGS
Monday February 20
*2 Timothy 1:8-14 Be
Courageous, Not Ashamed*

Tuesday February 21
*James 5:7-11 Have
Patience in Suffering*

Wednesday February 22
*1 Peter 4:12-19 Do Not Be
Surprised by Painful Trials*

Thursday February 23
*Romans 5:1-11 Through
Suffering, We Find Hope*

Friday February 24
*Romans 5:12-17 We Have
Life through Christ*

Saturday February 25
*Romans 5:18-21 God's
Grace Is Greater Than Our
Sin*

Sunday February 26
*1 Thessalonians 3:6-13
Our Faith Encourages
Others*

Scripture

Background Scripture: *Romans 5*
Scripture Lesson: *Romans 5:1-11, 18-21*
Key Verse: *Hope does not disappoint us, because
God has poured out his love into our hearts by the
Holy Spirit whom he has given us. Romans 5:5.*

Lesson Aim

Hope in Christ provides courage to endure present
problems.

Lesson Setting

Time: A.D. 57
Place: From Corinth to the church in Rome

Lesson Outline

Hope to Hold On
   I. A New Relationship with God: Romans 5:1-11
       A. *Partaking of God's Grace: vss. 1-2*
       B. *Rejoicing in Life's Trials: vss. 3-5*
       C. *Reflecting on God's Love: vss. 6-8*
       D. *Accepting God's Reconciliation: vss. 9-11*
   II. Justification for All Who Believe: Romans 5:18-21
       A. *Righteousness through Christ: vss. 18-19*
       B. *Grace through Christ: vss. 20-21*

Introduction

Reaping the Benefits

The first rule of advertising is to describe the benefits of the goods being sold. This is based on the awareness that, before making a purchase, people want to know how their life will be better for using certain products and services. Perhaps that's why, when we watch those 30-second dramas being enacted on television commercials, we're told that using the right item will make us successful.

We know, of course, that such promises are inflated. This is far different than God's pledges to us. For instance, the Lord has promised that when we trust in Christ, we reap the eternal benefits of divine righteousness and grace. We don't have to make any purchases or perform a noble deed. In fact, there is nothing we can do on our own to enjoy the riches of God's love. We must simply put our faith in Jesus for salvation and forgiveness.

Lesson Commentary

I. A New Relationship with God: Romans 5:1-11

A. Partaking of God's Grace: vss. 1-2

Therefore, since we have been justified through faith, we have peace with God through our Lord Jesus Christ, through whom we have gained access by faith into this grace in which we now stand. And we rejoice in the hope of the glory of God.

In Romans 3:21—4:25, Paul defined what it meant to be justified. Then in chapter 5, he focused on the benefits of justification. For Paul, justification was not only an event that put believers in a right position with God. Being declared righteous also had practical, lifelong implications for Christians.

First among these benefits is the peace we have with God through Jesus Christ (vs. 1). Because of sin, we were separated from God and faced eternal condemnation (1:18—3:20). But because of Christ, not only do we avoid receiving the wrath we deserve, we also enjoy a state of peace with God. We deserve fury and instead receive grace.

Paul was not talking about peace as simply a restful feeling. More importantly, he was talking about a state of harmony between the believer and God. All this is possible because of what Jesus did on the cross (Eph. 2:14). Formerly we were God's enemies; now we are His friends (Col. 1:21-22).

A second benefit that results from justification is direct access to God (Rom. 5:2). Formerly we were prevented from coming into the presence of God because of sin. Now we have full and unrestricted access. The Greek word translated "access" means the "privilege of approach." This is now available through faith in Jesus Christ.

A third key blessing we enjoy is "this grace in which we now stand." Because believers have been justified—that is, declared righteous—they live in the sphere of God's grace. And it is here that they enjoy every spiritual blessing in Christ. The gift of grace gives them the hope of experiencing God's glory—the glory from which they previously fell short (3:23). Grace may be viewed as a foot in the door of God's glory, which will one day swing wide open and grant believers unhindered access to the immediate presence of God.

As Paul reflected on these themes, he called his readers to rejoice in the hope of sharing God's glory (5:2). This wasn't wishful thinking but rather a firm assurance based on the unchanging promises of God. Believers look with confidence to all that the Lord has in store for them in Christ.

Why should we rejoice? We do so because we are acquitted of our sins and counted as righteous before God by means of our faith. We also rejoice because we have peace with God. Whereas once we were fearful, now we are joyful. Though we were previously doubtful, we now are certain about our future in union with Christ. We look to the time when we will enter into the fullness of God's majesty and splendor, rid forever of the stain and stigma of sin.

In listing the blessings in the first few verses of chapter 5 of Romans, Paul accomplished two purposes. First, he told how wonderful it is to be a Christian. Our justification is not simply a guarantee of heaven, but it is also the source of tremendous blessings that we can enjoy here and now. His second purpose was to assure his readers that justification is a lasting thing.

B. Rejoicing in Life's Trials: vss. 3-5

Not only so, but we also rejoice in our sufferings, because we know that suffering produces perseverance; perseverance, character; and character, hope. And hope does not disappoint us, because God has poured out his love into our hearts by the Holy Spirit, whom he has given us.

It would be incorrect to assume that peace with God brings

peaceful circumstances in the course of daily living. All of us go through times of suffering when our circumstances may seem anything but peaceful. Therefore, in Romans 5:3-5 Paul turned his attention to the believer's attitude toward suffering.

Notice that Paul said we were to rejoice "in" our sufferings, not "because of" them (vs. 3). This is an important distinction. Paul was not telling us that we should be joyful since things go wrong in our lives; rather, he was telling us that we can be joyful in the midst of troubling situations.

The word rendered "sufferings" could also be translated "afflictions," "distresses," or "pressures." These are broad words that encompass all kinds of things that can go wrong. Some people have financial pressures; some have health afflictions; some have job-related distresses; others struggle with broken relationships. Whatever the difficult situation, Paul said, we can have joy in the midst of it. In Christ we have the power to choose how we will respond to our circumstances, no matter how burdensome they may become.

Notice the steady progression in verses 3 and 4: suffering produces perseverance (or steadfast endurance); perseverance strengthens our character; and character leads to hope. Believers can have a joyful attitude in the midst of suffering for they know that enduring such trials is not meaningless. The pain God allows them to experience can bear Christlike fruit, namely, perseverance, character, and hope.

Paul affirmed that hope does not disappoint us, for God has lavished us with His love (vs. 5). The verb translated "poured out" speaks of the inexhaustible supply of God's compassion given to believers through the Spirit. He is the agent who expresses God's love in and through the hearts of believers. Such love enhances our hope because it does not hinge on circumstances. Even when life throws us a punch, God's love continues to flow through our hearts.

False offers of hope arise from many quarters, but the only lasting assurance comes when we discover and trust in God's love. Human feelings tend to vacillate from hot to cold, but God's compassion endures and touches us where and when we need it. We no longer need to paper over life's problems, for we can face them realistically in the light of God's love.

C. Reflecting on God's Love: vss. 6-8

You see, at just the right time, when we were still powerless, Christ died for the ungodly. Very rarely will anyone die for a righteous man, though for a good man someone might possibly dare to die. But God demonstrates his own love for us in this: While we were still sinners, Christ died for us.

To illustrate the love of God he had just described, Paul stated that "at just the right time, when we were still powerless, Christ died for the ungodly" (vs. 6). For centuries the Mosaic law had been in operation—provoking and exposing sin, and showing people their need to be reconciled with God. But now the time had come for the Messiah to be born, at just the right time in God's eternal plan of redemption (Gal. 4:4).

Christ came when we were "powerless" (Rom. 5:6). The original word means "weak," "without strength," "feeble," and "sickly." In the present context, it points to those who are weak in terms of their ability to create any righteousness for themselves. Though they couldn't, God did by having Jesus take our place on the cross and dying on our behalf.

What an amazing thing Jesus did for us! People rarely give up their lives for others. Occasionally we might find someone who is willing to die for a good person (vs. 7), but we were neither upright nor good—not in the sense that God reflects these qualities. The profound truth is that Christ died for sinners—even while we were alienated from the Lord (vs. 8).

The contrast is stark between the one who laid down His life and those for whom He died. Such an act of devotion can only be motivated by boundless love. And indeed, this love was demonstrated when Christ laid down His life on our behalf. Jesus' death on the cross illustrates the relentless and amazing pursuit of God for us.

When God declared us righteous in Jesus Christ, He gave to us seven spiritual blessings that assure us that we are not lost. They are (1) peace with God (vs. 1); (2) access to God (vs. 2a); (3) glorious hope (vs. 2b); (4) Christian character (vss. 3-4); (5) God's love within (vss. 5-8); (6) salvation from future wrath (vss. 9-10); and (7) reconciliation with God (vs. 11).

D. Accepting God's Reconciliation: vss. 9-11

Since we have now been justified by his blood, how much more shall we be saved from God's wrath through him! For if, when we were God's enemies, we were reconciled to him through the death of his Son, how much more, having been reconciled, shall we be saved through his life! Not only is this so, but we also rejoice in God through our Lord Jesus Christ, through whom we have now received reconciliation.

The good news is that the sacrifice of Christ enables us to be made right in God's sight (vs. 9). This being the case, Jesus will certainly rescue us "from God's wrath." "Wrath" in this verse refers to God's final judgment of humankind (1 Thess. 1:10). Since we are forgiven in Christ, the Lord will not subject us to His eternal condemnation of the wicked (John 5:24).

Paul reasoned that if we, as God's enemies, were restored to friendship with Him through Jesus' death, we will certainly be delivered from eternal punishment because of the Savior's life. "Reconciliation" (Rom. 5:10) refers to removal of the ill-will that previously stood between us and God. At one time we were God's enemies because of our disobedience. But because of Jesus' death, we have been restored in our relationship with God.

Paul's point, then, is that since God no longer looks on us as His enemies, the basis of our salvation is complete. Furthermore, Jesus ministers to us "through his life." This refers to His post-resurrection life. In what ways does Jesus presently meet our spiritual needs? As our great High Priest, Christ makes intercession for us from heaven (Heb. 7:25). He prays for us continuously (1 John 2:1).

Our being reconciled to the Father through the Son is not just a biblical truth we affirm. It is also a present reality that fills us with joy. After all, we who were once God's enemies are now His friends (Rom. 5:11). And as the Lord's ambassadors, we should share this wonderful news with others.

II. Justification for All Who Believe: Romans 5:18-21

A. Righteousness through Christ: vss. 18-19

Consequently, just as the result of one trespass was condemnation for all men, so also the result of one act of righteousness was justification that brings life for all men. For just as through the disobedience of the one man the many were made sinners, so also through the obedience of the one man the many will be made righteous.

Paul noted that when Adam sinned, his offense brought the entire world under the reign of death, and humanity became enslaved to sin (vs. 12). In contrast, all who receive God's wonderful and gracious gift of righteousness experience new life in Christ and triumph over sin (vs. 17). It's true that Adam's one sin brought condemnation to the entire human race. Nevertheless, Jesus' "one act of righteousness" (vs. 18, namely, His death on the cross) makes all believers right in God's sight and gives them eternal life.

The meaning of the phrase "brings life for all men" is debated. Some think Paul was teaching that all human beings in the end will be saved—a view known as universalism. But such a view would contradict Paul's teaching that all human beings are lost because of sin (2:12). The truth is that only those who trust in Christ are declared righteous, while those who reject Him remain lost in their sins.

The joy of the Gospel is that Jesus enables us to trade judgment for forgiveness. Paul explained that, because of Adam's single act of disobedience, the entire human race was plunged into sin. In contrast, Jesus' work on the cross enables all who believe to "be made righteous" (5:19).

B. Grace through Christ: vss. 20-21

The law was added so that the trespass might increase. But where sin increased, grace increased all the more, so that, just as sin reigned in death, so also grace might reign through righteousness to bring eternal life through Jesus Christ our Lord.

Paul's Jewish readers might have wondered where the Mosaic law fit into the discussion. The apostle noted that God added the law so that the people could be more aware of how sinful they are. But instead of turning from their evil ways, people sinned more and more. The entire human race would have surely perished had it not been for the abundant kindness that God provided in Christ (vs. 20).

Throughout history sin has ruled over all people and brought them to death. But the good news is that the grace of God rules. His kindness in Christ gives us a right standing in His presence and forgiveness of sins (vs. 21). Clearly, the grace of God is more than a doctrine. It is a life principle that affects us on a daily basis. Paul assured us that, because we have trusted in Christ, we will live eternally in Him.

Discussion Questions

1. What is the basis for our access into God's heavenly presence?
2. How is it possible to rejoice in sufferings?
3. Why would the Father allow His Son to die for the ungodly?
4. What is the basis for our reconciliation with God?
5. What would our lives be like if God had not made the effort to reconcile us to Himself?

Now Ask Yourself . . .

What is the difference between happiness and joy? Why would that make a difference to me when I am going through hard things?

Do I rejoice when going through sufferings? How do I do so?

What kind of testimony of God does the world see when I rejoice in sufferings?

How do I stand in the grace God has given me by faith in Jesus Christ?

Have I allowed God to work the fruit of perseverance, character and hope in me during my trials?

Illustrations

When sin entered the world, it seemed as if all was lost. But that was not the end of the story. To match the terrible consequences of sin, God intervened with His powerful, sustaining grace. Grace prevailed in the person of Christ. Grace prevailed on the cross. Grace prevailed in the empty tomb. And God's amazing grace still prevails today in the life of believers.

When we receive the truth of the Gospel, we have multiple reasons to rejoice. For instance, we have hope and the certainty of enjoying God's wonderful presence. We can know the peace that can only come from the comfort of the Holy Spirit. We also receive the overflowing power of God's love. We furthermore are reconciled to God. And because of Jesus' work on the cross, God declares us righteous and makes us fit for heaven.

What a relief it is to know that we have been transferred from the domain of sin and death to the kingdom of God's beloved Son! We are now free to obey—out of love, not necessity, and through God's power, not our own. Even if we occasionally stumble, Jesus will catch us and hold us in His loving arms.

Many places in the epistles, the writers open and close their letters with greetings of peace, grace and mercy. The Lord knows we need constant reminders of those three things as we walk through this life. Truly we can rejoice and rest in the promises of God who is able to make all grace abound to us in our times of difficulty.

March 5, 2006

A Time for Decision

God Moves Hearts

DEVOTIONAL READING

Isaiah 52:7-12

DAILY BIBLE READINGS

Monday March 6
  Jeremiah 31:31-34 God Writes His Will on Our Hearts

Tuesday March 7
  Ezekiel 16:24-32 God Gives Us New Hearts

Wednesday March 8
  Ezra 1:1-4 King Cyrus Makes a Declaration

Thursday March 9
  Ezra 1:5-11 God Moves His People's Hearts

Friday March 10
  Romans 12:1-2 Be a Living Sacrifice

Saturday March 11
  Ephesians 1:3-14 His Will Is Found in Christ

Sunday March 12
  Philippians 2:5-13 God Uses Us for His Purpose

Scripture

Background Scripture: *Ezra 1*
Scripture Lesson: *Ezra 1*
Key Verse: *In order to fulfill the word of the* LORD *spoken by Jeremiah, the* LORD *moved the heart of Cyrus king of Persia to make a proclamation throughout his realm and to put it in writing. Ezra 1:1b.*

Lesson Aim

God moves hearts to do His will.

Lesson Setting

Time: 538 B.C.
Place: Babylon

Lesson Outline

God Moves Hearts

  I. The Proclamation of Cyrus: Ezra 1:1-4
     A. *The Lord's Doing: vs. 1*
     B. *The Temple Goal: vs. 2*
     C. *The People Freed: vs. 3*
     D. *The Local Assistance: vs. 4*
  II. The Temple Provisions: Ezra 1:5-11
     A. *The People's Response: vs. 5*
     B. *The Neighbors' Assistance: vs. 6*
     C. *The Temple Utensils: vss. 7-11*

Introduction

Facing a God-given Opportunity

Some time ago a church in Austria decided to do something to demonstrate Christian compassion for the Jews in their city who had been driven out during World War II. The parishoners worked assiduously to track down people all over the world. Then the congregation invited them to return to the city for a visit with all expenses paid by the parishoners.

At first the invitees were hesitant, but in the end more than 50 of them accepted the offer. They returned and shared a powerful emotional reunion that satisfied their long pent-up desires. Since then, the church has hosted several similar get-togethers, making a strong impact on the rest of the city, including its officials.

God opens doors for us to show His love. When He moves hearts to respond to Christian love, He is praised and our churches and communities are strengthened.

Lesson Commentary

I. The Proclamation of Cyrus: Ezra 1:1-4

A. The Lord's Doing: vs. 1

The first half of Ezra narrates the initial return of Jewish exiles from Babylon and their struggles to establish their homes and rebuild the temple. The second half of Ezra deals with the spiritual reforms that the scribe himself initiated throughout the land of Judah. The book, as a whole, emphasizes the importance of the Word of God and genuine worship while living in a hostile world.

In the first year of Cyrus king of Persia, in order to fulfill the word of the LORD spoken by Jeremiah, the LORD moved the heart of Cyrus king of Persia to make a proclamation throughout his realm and to put it in writing.

The books of Ezra and Nehemiah present the history of God's people during the years following the destruction of Jerusalem and the temple (586 B.C.). They, together with the prophecies of Haggai and Zechariah (both dated about 520 B.C.) and Malachi (about 432 B.C.), comprise the main Hebrew records of those years. Because of the similarities in style, many scholars believe the book of Ezra may have been written by the same person who wrote 1 and 2 Chronicles—probably Ezra himself. If so, Ezra could be considered a "3 Chronicles."

The return to Palestine from Babylonian captivity came in three separate stages. Zerubbabel's group went first (537 B.C.) to restore the temple (Ezra 1—3). The work then begun was interrupted for some years (4:5-7, 23), to be resumed at the encouragement of the prophets Haggai and Zechariah (5:1-2) and completed about 515 B.C. The second return took place about 458 B.C. under Ezra, who called for reform and a return to covenant obligations (Ezra 7—10). Nehemiah led the third group of returnees (445 B.C.), and spearheaded the rebuilding of Jerusalem's walls (Neh. 1—13).

The destruction of Jerusalem in 586 B.C. forms the backdrop for Ezra 1:1. The Babylonians had overrun Jerusalem. When the invaders destroyed the city, they leveled the temple in the process. They then took many survivors captive, settling them in colonies throughout Babylonia.

A generation after Jerusalem fell, the Jews were still in exile. By this time they had grown accustomed to their new homes and way of life. All but the aged had been born in exile and knew Judah only through stories. It was not God's plan for the situation to remain that way. He wanted to repopulate Judah, rebuild Jerusalem, and restore the temple.

God knew it would take a little prodding to get the Jews to leave their new land and return to Judah. He decided to use one man to get things rolling. That man was Cyrus, king of Persia, the empire that had replaced the Babylonian Empire.

Years earlier the Lord had sent Jeremiah the prophet a message. In it the Lord promised to return His people to their homeland from captivity. The fulfillment of God's Word concerns bringing to an end the 70 years of captivity that had been prophesied by Jeremiah before the fall of Jerusalem (Jer. 25:11-12; 29:10). In the first year that Cyrus was king of Persia, God fulfilled His pledge by having Cyrus send an official message to all parts of his kingdom (Ezra 1:1).

Jerusalem had suffered minor deportations in 605 and 597 B.C. before Nebuchadnezzar destroyed the city and temple and carried away all the leading families in 586 B.C. Then in 539 B.C. Cyrus the Persian conquered Babylon, and the Lord began the gracious work of restoring His chosen people to the land of promise.

B. The Temple Goal: vs. 2

"This is what Cyrus king of Persia says: 'The LORD, the God of heaven, has given me all the kingdoms of the earth and he has appointed me to build a temple for him at Jerusalem in Judah.' "

Somehow Cyrus had realized that he owed his kingdom to "the God of heaven" (Ezra 1:2). This was an astonishing admission. Pagan kings were not prone to acknowledge anyone else's superiority, even though their kingdoms were filled with idols of all sorts. In fact, kings proved the superiority of their religions and idols by virtue of their conquests.

By that logic, Israel's God was supposedly weaker than the deities of Babylon and Persia. He was inferior because He had been defeated and His temple plundered in Jerusalem. But when God stirred the heart of Cyrus, He made it clear to the ruler that He had given him his kingdoms. To be God's genuine servant, Cyrus had to make this admission throughout his entire realm. Such a public announcement undoubtedly shocked some people.

In his official letter, Cyrus also proclaimed that God had appointed him to build a temple for Him in Jerusalem. This was equally incredible, for once an invading king destroyed the local places of worship, they typically were never restored. Of course, Nebuchadnezzar of Babylon had destroyed the temple of the Jews in Jerusalem, but still it was not common for succeeding monarchs to undo the destruction of a predecessor. This was especially true of religious sites, for they fermented rebellions.

Imagine how the edict of Cyrus electrified the Jewish community in Babylon. Seven decades had passed and suddenly God was about to restore His people to their homeland. The Lord was fulfilling the pledge He had previously made.

The emperor sent heralds to shout his proclamations in the language of each major city of the Persian Empire, which stretched from Egypt and Asia Minor to India. Printed versions followed later, worded in Aramaic, the language of international affairs, to be posted and stored in archives. The version in Ezra 1:2-4 is worded in Hebrew; the version quoted in 6:3-5 is written in Aramaic.

C.   The People Freed: vs. 3

" 'Anyone of his people among you—may his God be with him, and let him go up to Jerusalem in Judah and build the temple of the LORD, the God of Israel, the God who is in Jerusalem.' "

Moses had pleaded with Pharaoh to free God's people, but for a while Pharaoh stubbornly resisted. Here we have no record of a leader of the Jews pleading for their release. Perhaps Cyrus made the announcement of his own accord, as a result of God's work in his heart.

The king's offer was not stingy. Any Jew who wanted to leave Babylon was free to do so (Ezra 1:3). Cyrus even added a prayer for God's protection as the exiles returned. Cyrus also gave them a specific commission to build the temple. The intent of their departure was not just to make a better living for themselves, but more importantly to worship their ancestral God. Worship of the Lord stood at the center of Cyrus's generous offer.

In this verse, the Lord is portrayed not just as the God of the universe but also as the God of Israel, who was to be worshiped in Jerusalem. Cyrus called Him "LORD" and "God" so there would be no doubt about the king's recognition of His sovereignty. Such a God as this had to be worshiped and His people had to work to that end.

There are other factors worth noting here. By urging his Jewish subjects to return to their homeland and rebuild their temple, Cyrus promoted goodwill throughout his empire. Such goodwill helped to foster stability and peace.

D. The Local Assistance: vs. 4

" 'And the people of any place where survivors may now be living are to provide him with silver and gold, with goods and livestock, and with freewill offerings for the temple of God in Jerusalem.' "

Cyrus further dictated that local people should help the Jews on their mission to Jerusalem. "The people of any place" (Ezra 1:4) were the native inhabitants throughout the empire. The "survivors" were the exiled Jews who lived among them.

Cyrus ordered that the Jews were to be given everything they needed for their return to their homeland and for the rebuilding of their temple. The exiles needed money (gold and silver). They also needed basic necessities and livestock for food. They moreover needed freewill offerings for the temple.

We can imagine that the king's edict may have rankled some local people. After all, they would not have been accustomed to helping out foreigners in this way. Cyrus, of course, realized that he could not resettle the exiled Jews without giving them the resources they needed to be successful in their venture.

When God stirred the heart of Cyrus, the Lord made sure that His people got more than a certificate of release and a safe conduct passage. He provided for all their needs and for the resumption of true (as opposed to idolatrous) worship in His name in Jerusalem.

Cyrus's proclamation invited all his subjects throughout his realm to participate in the rebuilding of the Jerusalem temple by giving those who would return contributions of money, goods, and livestock (Ezra 1:4). When the emperor called those who were returning "survivors," he introduced the prophets' term for a "remnant" into his decree (see Isa. 10:20-22; Zeph. 3:13).

II. The Temple Provisions: Ezra 1:5-11

A. The People's Response: vs. 5

Then the family heads of Judah and Benjamin, and the priests and Levites—everyone whose heart God had moved—prepared to go up and build the house of the LORD in Jerusalem.

God had stirred the heart of Cyrus to restore the exiled Jews to their homeland. The Lord also stirred the hearts of His people to respond to this wonderful opportunity (Ezra 1:5). They were

Ancient Jewish and the oldest Christian traditions assigned the authorship of Ezra and Nehemiah to Ezra. Many contemporary scholars continue to support the view that Ezra also wrote the books of Chronicles. Included in the evidence that supports this view is the fact that the last two verses of 2 Chronicles and the first two verses of Ezra are virtually identical. Ezra may have done this to make a smooth chronological flow between the two books. Some scholars have suggested that a "Chronicler," perhaps a disciple of Ezra, brought together the memoirs of Judah's kings, Ezra, and Nehemiah to compose 1 and 2 Chronicles, Ezra, and Nehemiah.

Only the eyes and ears of faith can detect the Lord at work, stirring the hearts of believers and unbelievers alike. Sometimes He moves the hearts of Christians to risk their security and comfort. Sometimes He motivates them to support others with prayers and gifts.

moved by more than just a desire to be released from captivity. They responded to God's call to build a house of worship for Him. They had had enough of pagan idolatry in Babylon. They longed for the pure worship of God in Jerusalem.

Several groups are mentioned here—the tribes of Judah and Benjamin, priests, and Levites. Judah and Benjamin were the surviving two tribes of the original 12 tribes of Israel. The other 10 tribes had been deported by the Assyrians in 722 B.C. and subsequently lost their identity through intermarriage.

The family heads, priests, and Levites are listed in Ezra 2, together with an inventory of people and their possessions. It was important to reestablish the ministries of the priests, Levites, temple singers, and gatekeepers, for all of them had preserved the ancient laws about the true worship of God.

There were some Jews, however, who had made a good life for themselves under the rule of the Babylonians. They thus were not interested in going back to Jerusalem and scratching out a hand-to-mouth existence there. They had become wealthy in exile and were in no mood to abandon what they now had.

B. The Neighbors' Assistance: vs. 6

All their neighbors assisted them with articles of silver and gold, with goods and livestock, and with valuable gifts, in addition to all the freewill offerings.

The local citizens responded to Cyrus's order with promptness and generosity. Amazingly, they dug into their own pockets (in a manner of speaking) for silver, gold, goods, and livestock. They also gave "valuable gifts" (Ezra 1:6) and money for temple offerings.

Ezra did not write that God put it into the hearts of the people to do this, but there is no possible way to account for this outpouring other than the work of God. Sadly, people ordinarily do not do such things, especially for those of different nationalities, races, and religions.

Perhaps the Jewish exiles did not count for much in the Persian Empire, but under God's good hand they received enough for their journey back to Jerusalem, and then some. We can imagine how thanksgiving to God poured from their hearts for His generous and gracious providence in their lives.

C. The Temple Utensils: vss. 7-11

Moreover, King Cyrus brought out the articles belonging to the temple of the LORD, which Nebuchadnezzar had carried away from Jerusalem and had placed in the temple of his god. Cyrus king of Persia had them brought by Mithredath the treasurer, who counted them out to Sheshbazzar the prince of Judah. This was the inventory:

gold dishes	*30*
silver dishes	*1,000*
silver pans	*29*
gold bowls	*30*
matching silver bowls	*410*
other articles	*1,000*

In all, there were 5,400 articles of gold and of silver. Sheshbazzar brought all these along when the exiles came up from Babylon to Jerusalem.

Cyrus gave back to the Jews all their Jerusalem temple articles that had been taken by Nebuchadnezzar (Ezra 1:7). Cyrus also ordered his treasurer to make a strict inventory and give it to the Jews (vs. 8). In all, 5,400 articles of gold and silver were returned to the exiles, who (in turn) took them back to Jerusalem.

When God stirred the heart of Cyrus, He did a thorough job. Through the king of Persia, the Lord made sure that His people had enough not just to live on, but also to rebuild the temple and restore His worship. Such a powerful God is still at work today in the lives of His people.

Sheshbazzar is called "the prince of Judah" (Ezra 1:8). This particular title "prince" does not necessarily imply descent from royalty. Sheshbazzar probably was a Jewish deputy of the governor of the Persian province of Samaria, from which a new province, Judah, was being carved to accommodate the returning exiles.

The partial inventory of verses 9-10 likely lists the most significant temple items restored to the exiles. The number of special items adds up to 2,499 out of the total of 5,400 returned temple articles (vs. 11). Sheshbazzar personally took responsibility for delivering the temple treasures to Jerusalem.

Discussion Questions

1. What prophecy was God fulfilling in the lives of His people?
2. How did God bring about the fulfillment of this prophecy?
3. What was the basic thrust of the edict Cyrus had made?
4. How did the Jewish and non-Jewish people respond to the king's decree?
5. In what ways has God recently shown Himself to be faithful to you?

Now Ask Yourself . . .

When I face seemingly impossible situations, how can I draw upon God's power to help me?

How might God want to use me to help others who are feeling overwhelmed by life circumstances?

What are some ways I can work with other members of my church to accomplish God's will for the congregation?

How open and humble am I to the way God is moving in my life? What sometimes prevents me from following Him more wholeheartedly?

Illustrations

What does it mean to acknowledge God's supremacy in all we do? What can we learn from King Cyrus in this regard? How do we see God's hand in the big movements among nations in our time and in the little movements that make up our lives?

These are compelling questions because they focus on the issue of control. Every day we face this matter. Who is really in charge? Presidents, dictators, corporate CEOs, my boss, university presidents, prestigious scientists and researchers, or the multimedia magnates?

All of us can use reminders about who is really in control of life. The truth is that when we try to usurp God's control over us, things go awry. We think we can choose the right and the best, but sin and human frailties seriously skew our choices. We think we know all the facts, but our awareness is limited.

How liberating and comforting it is to turn control of our lives over to God! He is good, wise, and all-powerful. He makes His will known to us in His Son, Jesus Christ, and through the Bible by His Holy Spirit. Therefore, we have hope and joy. After all, we have the assurance of Romans 8:28—"And we know that in all things God works for the good of those who love him, who have been called according to his purpose."

Living in God's Present

DEVOTIONAL READING

Psalm 100:1-5

DAILY BIBLE READINGS

Monday March 6
Deuteronomy 32:4-9
Remember the Past and
Learn from It

Tuesday March 7
Isaiah 58:11-14
Take Delight in God;
Remember Your Heritage

Wednesday March 8
Joshua 4:1-8
Joshua Has the People
Make a Reminder

Thursday March 9
Ezra 3:1-6
The People Rebuild the
Altar

Friday March 10
Ezra 3:7-13
Rebuilding of the Temple
Begins

Saturday March 11
Ezra 4:1-10
Many Try to Discourage
the Builders

Sunday March 12
Ezra 4:11-24
The Rebuilding Stops

Scripture

Background Scripture: *Ezra 3*

Scripture Lesson: *Ezra 3:1-3, 6-7, 10-13*

Key Verse: *All the people gave a great shout of praise to the LORD, because the foundation of the house of the LORD was laid. Ezra 3:11b.*

Lesson Aim

Remember the past but enjoy God's present.

Lesson Setting

Time: 537–536 B.C.

Place: Jerusalem

Lesson Outline

Living in God's Present

I. Rebuilding the Altar: Ezra 3:1-3
   A. *The Assembly: vs. 1*
   B. *The Priests: vs. 2*
   C. *The Sacrifices: vs. 3*

II. Rebuilding the Temple: Ezra 3:6-7, 10-13
   A. *The Building Materials: vss. 6-7*
   B. *The Foundation: vs. 10*
   C. *The Worship: vs. 11*
   D. *The Mixed Sounds: vss. 12-13*

Introduction

Laying Foundations

God calls us to lay many foundations in our lives. Some of them are for houses, churches, schools, office buildings, and new factories. Others are for the long-term security of our lives—spiritual foundations that begin with our commitment to Christ.

Secure foundations are built with faith, prayer, worship, Bible study, witness, and service. Whatever happens in our homes, churches, and communities, we can find stability and hope in Christ, for He is the anchor of our souls.

Sometimes we neglect our spiritual foundations. Erosion sets in because we have not kept Jesus first in our hearts. This calls for renewal and recommitment. We should take the lead in spiritual renewal in our homes and churches. Then our strong faith will be a witness and encouragement to others.

Lesson Commentary

This list appears again in Nehemiah 7:6-65 with some variations in the names and slight differences in the numbers. The party of exiles who returned to Jerusalem from Babylon consisted of leaders, ordinary people, and temple personnel. Among the ordinary people, some could trace their genealogy back to a particular clan, while others could prove their connection to a hometown. Some people and priests could not verify their genealogies.

I. Rebuilding the Altar: Ezra 3:1-3

A. The Assembly: vs. 1

When the seventh month came and the Israelites had settled in their towns, the people assembled as one man in Jerusalem.

Ezra 2 contains a detailed list of the groups of exiles who returned to Jerusalem and rebuilt the temple. Under the initiative of Jeshua (the high priest or representative religious leader) and Zerubbabel (the governor or representative political leader), the first cluster progressively journeyed to their homeland from 536–516 B.C.

This chapter is significant because it serves as a tangible reminder of God's dependability. It demonstrates that the Lord was faithful in bringing back a committed remnant from captivity to Jerusalem. It is a sterling testimony to God's watchful care over His people despite seven decades of their living in exile.

The census may be divided as follows: leaders and families (vss. 1-35); priests and Levites (verses 36-42); temple laborers (vss. 43-58); individuals who had inadequate proof of their family history (vss. 59-63); servants and animals (vss. 64-67). Incidentally, the names Nehemiah and Mordecai (vs. 2) were common among the exiled Jews and thus should not be identified with the later historical figures by the same names.

Key family leaders voluntarily gave a variety of items that would be essential to the restoration of the temple in Jerusalem (Ezra 2:68-69; Neh.7:70-72). The pioneers then eventually resettled in the places where their ancestors once had lived (Ezra 2:70). The memory of these places had not been dimmed despite the tragedy of extended exile in a foreign land.

In last week's lesson we learned about the Jews in exile preparing to return to Judah. When we first encounter them in this week's lesson, it is autumn of 537 B.C. They had been in their homeland for about three months. During that time, they settled in the cities surrounding Jerusalem. Before any more time passed, however, the Jews wanted to reestablish the proper worship of God. The pioneers thus assembled as a group in Jerusalem (3:1).

The "seventh month" marked the beginning of the civil year for the exiles. This lunar month Tishri falls during parts of September-October. Its first day was Rosh Hashanah (New Year's Day), the tenth was Yom Kippur (the day of Atonement), and the fifteenth to the twenty-second was the Feast of Tabernacles (see Lev. 23:23-43). It was only natural that the newly settled exiles would gather in the holy city to celebrate these holy days on the site of Solomon's temple.

B. The Priests: vs. 2

Then Jeshua son of Jozadak and his fellow priests and Zerubbabel son of Shealtiel and his associates began to build the altar of the God of Israel to sacrifice burnt offerings on it, in accordance with what is written in the Law of Moses the man of God.

Under the initiative of Jeshua and Zerubbabel as well as their associates, the people gradually built an altar for worshiping the Lord (Ezra 3:2). (Jeshua was mentioned first because this was primarily a religious matter.) Sheshbazzar, who was the governor of Judah at this time in the eyes of the Persians (see 1:8, 11), did not act as the popular leader of the exiles. Zerubbabel regularly filled that role until, at some point, he replaced Sheshbazzar as the official governor (see Hag. 1:1; 2:2).

In the law, Moses had directed Israel to build its altar of burnt

Like wise believers of every age, the returned exiles gave top priority to worship. Before launching the temple project that Cyrus had commissioned them to undertake, they built the altar of burnt offering on its historic site amid the ruins of Solomon's temple. Even as Abraham and Joshua before them, the exiles marked their entrance into the promised land with the construction of an altar to the Lord (see Gen. 12:7; Josh. 8:30-31).

offering of earth or uncut stones at the place God would designate (see Exod. 20:24-25; Deut. 27:5). Since this was a formal altar, the exiles probably built it of native stones (Ezra 3:2). And on it an animal sacrifice was offered, incense was burned, and religious ceremonies were carried out as an expression of worship.

Everything the group did was in accordance with the Mosaic law. They remembered Moses as God's official representative and messenger (vs. 2). The burnt offerings served several purposes: a voluntary act of worship; atonement for unintentional sin in general; and an expression of devotion, commitment, and complete surrender to God. All of the activities associated with the altar reminded God's people that it was necessary to approach the Lord through the provision of an acceptable atoning sacrifice.

C. The Sacrifices: vs. 3

Despite their fear of the peoples around them, they built the altar on its foundation and sacrificed burnt offerings on it to the LORD, both the morning and evening sacrifices.

The group succeeded in setting the altar on its base (Ezra 3:3). They did this despite a lingering fear over the presence of non-Jews in the area. Once the altar was finished, God's people sacrificed burnt offerings on it at sunrise and sunset (Exod. 29:38-42; Num. 28:3-8). This stands as a tribute to the Jews' wholehearted trust in the Lord (Ps. 62:6-8).

The Jews performed every aspect of their worship in strict accordance with God's Word (Ezra 3:4). Perhaps they wanted to avoid bringing the Lord's displeasure through some violation of the law.

God's people observed the Feast of Tabernacles (or Booths, Ingathering). This was typically done between September and October five days after the Day of Atonement. Tabernacles involved a week of celebration for the harvest as well as living in booths and offering of sacrifices. It was intended to commemorate the journey from Egypt to Canaan and to give thanks for the productivity of Canaan. The feast must have had great significance to the exiles who had just experienced a second exodus from a second bondage to carve out a home amid hostile neighbors.

God's people offered the right number of sacrifices for each day of the festival. Through this celebration, the Jews memorialized their successful journey from Mesopotamia to Palestine. They

Even though the Jews had no temple yet, they worshiped the God of heaven, whom even Solomon had declared at his temple dedication cannot be contained in a building made with hands (see 1 Kings 8:27).

Though we don't offer morning and evening animal sacrifices to the Lord on a stone altar, our heavenly Father expects many "spiritual sacrifices" from us (1 Pet. 2:5). These include sacrifices of praise, or "the fruit of lips that confess his name" (Heb. 13:15). The greatest sacrifice we give Him is our lives, "living sacrifices, holy and pleasing to God" (Rom. 12:1).

gave thanks for God's abundant provision and protection, and they expressed their gratitude for experiencing a safe return.

The Jews also reestablished all the other various sacrifices, sacred seasons, and feasts associated with the temple (vs. 5). This included the new moon festival. This religious holiday occurred at the beginning of each new month. Through the offering of special sacrifices and the blowing of trumpets, the Jews set apart this time of observance. During the festival, all forms of work and activity were discontinued.

II. Rebuilding the Temple: Ezra 3:6-7, 10-13

A. The Building Materials: vss. 6-7

On the first day of the seventh month they began to offer burnt offerings to the LORD, though the foundation of the LORD's temple had not yet been laid. Then they gave money to the masons and carpenters, and gave food and drink and oil to the people of Sidon and Tyre, so that they would bring cedar logs by sea from Lebanon to Joppa, as authorized by Cyrus king of Persia.

Ezra noted that, while the sacrifices and festive seasons of Israel had been restored, the foundation of the Lord's temple had not yet been laid (Ezra 3:6). This was an important matter, for God wanted His people to rebuild the temple. This house of worship would enable them to properly focus their minds and hearts on the Lord. Thus, the Jews allocated funds to purchase building materials and to hire laborers to construct the temple.

This was in accordance with Cyrus's decree (vs. 7). This king had inherited the throne of Anshan, a region in eastern Elam, from his father in 559 B.C. It was evident from the beginning of Cyrus's reign that the king was ambitious. One of his first actions was to increase his territory by unifying the Persian people. And then, in 550 B.C., he attacked and conquered the region of Astyages.

Even with a vast area already under his control, Cyrus was still determined to expand his power by conquering other kingdoms. So he made an alliance with Babylon against Media, a large but weakly ruled kingdom north of Babylon. He succeeded in subjugating Media and then turned his attention west, to Lydia. In 546 B.C. this, too, came under his control. And in the east, Cyrus extended his kingdom to the borders of India.

The preparations for building by the exiles parallel Solomon's preparations for the first temple. For example, the finest wood in the ancient world was secured from Lebanon through the mediation of Phoenician merchants from Tyre and Sidon and paid for with agricultural products (Ezra 3:7; compare 2 Chron. 2). Also, the cedar logs were bound into ocean-going rafts and floated down the Mediterranean coast from Byblos in Lebanon to Joppa, which served as port for Jerusalem.

The plan for rebuilding the temple was highly organized in advance, and its individual parts were entrusted to the supervision of Levites over the age of 20. In earlier situations 30 and 25 had been the minimum ages for Levitical activity (see Num. 4:3; 8:24). The exilic band did not include an abundance of Levites. The supervising Levites fell into three groups. The clans of Jeshua and Kadmiel were mentioned in the roster of exiles (see Ezra 2:40). The descendants of Henadad are also included among the Levites in Nehemiah's time who built the wall of Jerusalem and sealed the covenant (3:9; see Neh. 3:18, 24; 10:9).

By 539 B.C. Cyrus was ready to deal with the fertile plains of Babylon. His takeover there was relatively peaceful because the Babylonian people were dissatisfied with their own ruler. They welcomed Cyrus as a liberator.

Returning now to our main discussion, under the initiative of Zerubbabel and Jeshua as well as their associates and fellow Jews, construction on the temple began. This was probably the spring of 536 B.C. (Zerubbabel is mentioned first because this was initially a civil matter with religious significance.)

The leaders gave Levites the responsibility to oversee the rebuilding of the temple (vs. 8). Jeshua and all of his priestly associates joined together as a group to supervise the rebuilding operation (vs. 9).

B. The Foundation: vs. 10
When the builders laid the foundation of the temple of the Lord, the priests in their vestments and with trumpets, and the Levites (the sons of Asaph) with cymbals, took their places to praise the Lord, as prescribed by David king of Israel.

The Jews eventually succeeded in laying the temple foundation. They commemorated this momentous occasion by blowing trumpets and sounding cymbals. The Jews praised and thanked God for His abundant provision. Every action was done in strict accordance with the historic traditions of Israel (Ezra 3:10).

C. The Worship: vs. 11
With praise and thanksgiving they sang to the Lord: "He is good; his love to Israel endures forever." And all the people gave a great shout of praise to the Lord, because the foundation of the house of the Lord was laid.

The people worshiped God for who He is (namely, His personal attributes and characteristics) and thanked Him for what He does (namely, His presence, power, provisions, and preservation). These emphases are seen in the responsive chorus. The returnees praised God for His kindness and His unfailing love to them even after 70 years of captivity. The entire assembly was united in applauding God for enabling them to lay the temple foundation (Ezra 3:11).

D. The Mixed Sounds: vss. 12-13

But many of the older priests and Levites and family heads, who had seen the former temple, wept aloud when they saw the foundation of this temple being laid, while many others shouted for joy. No one could distinguish the sound of the shouts of joy from the sound of weeping, because the people made so much noise. And the sound was heard far away.

The size and grandeur of the rebuilt temple foundation paled in comparison to the glorious one Solomon had built. Many of those who were alive prior to the exile were sad and disappointed at the sight of the smaller, less impressive scene (Ezra 3:12). The combined sounds of joy and weeping were so loud that they could not be distinguished. Ezra noted that the noise was heard for a considerable distance (vs. 13).

As older adults move on in years, it is easy for them to spend lots of time thinking about days gone by. The work of the Lord, however, cannot move forward on the ruined glories of the past. Those who have witnessed God's work in former years should be able to discern His hand in the present.

This underscores how important it is for us to recognize and support new methods and media God may be using. With every new manifestation that the Lord is still with His people and that His work is still being done, it is fitting for us to join in the chorus of thanksgiving.

Both Haggai (Hag. 2:3) and Zechariah would find themselves addressing a segment of the population discouraged by "the day of small things" (Zech. 4:10). But in the second month of 536 B.C., the dominant mood among the returned exiles still was great joy (Ezra 3:13). Even people at a great distance could hear the resounding noise of a community of people who dared take the Lord at His word and risk everything they had to go to ruined towns and farms and trust Him to take a remnant, plant them, and grow a nation.

Discussion Questions

1. Why did God's people decide to assemble?
2. What was the basis for the people's fear and how did they respond to it?
3. Why was it important for the people to lay the foundation for the Lord's temple in Jerusalem?
4. How did the people respond once the temple foundation had been laid?
5. How should we respond when God does new and different things in our lives?

Now Ask Yourself . . .

How can I maintain a balance between remembering the past and enjoying God's present?

What sacrifice can I offer to the Lord this week?

Does the Lord want me to attempt a new beginning in some area of my life?

As I worship the Lord, how can I use His Word to make sure I'm doing things that are pleasing to Him?

As I serve the Lord, how can I do so in His strength and for His glory?

Illustrations

Whatever fears the returnees might have had, they courageously overcame them. This in turn enabled them to offer sacrifices to God. Doing so must have been a powerful witness to their pagan neighbors, who possibly resented the worship of the Lord but moreover disliked the idea of sharing the land of Judah and Jerusalem with God's people.

Once the returnees had brought their offerings to God, they sought help from people living in Lebanon. After getting some construction materials, the Jews started the difficult task that lay before them. The temple foundation was completed to the tune of great rejoicing mixed with sorrow.

In the minds of many adults, worship has its time and place, and work has its time and place. They are distinct and separate. The imaginary wall between the two is practically unclimbable.

This week's lesson, however, underscores to us that work and worship are interconnected. The Jews were busy constructing the temple in order to worship God properly; and they worshiped God as a result of their building. These observations stress why we should not separate our worship from our work. As we serve the Lord, our work should be an act of worship that brings glory to God.

Let's Celebrate

DEVOTIONAL READING

Psalm 96:1-13

DAILY BIBLE READINGS

Monday March 13
Ezra 5:1-5
God Watches Over
the Jews

Tuesday March 14
Ezra 5:6-17
King Darius Receives a
Letter

Wednesday March 15
Ezra 6:1-12
Darius Decrees the Temple
Is to Be Rebuilt

Thursday March 16
Ezra 6:13-18
The Temple Is Dedicated

Friday March 17
Ezra 6:19-22
The People Celebrate
with Joy

Saturday March 18
Psalm 33:1-11
Rejoice in the Lord

Sunday March 19
Psalm 33:12-22
Happy Is the Nation
Focused on God

Scripture

Background Scripture: *Ezra 6*

Scripture Lesson: *Ezra 6:14-22*

Key Verse: *The people of Israel—the priests, the Levites and the rest of the exiles—celebrated the dedication of the house of God with joy. Ezra 6:16.*

Lesson Aim

It is good for us to celebrate God's great acts.

Lesson Setting

Time: 516 B.C.

Place: Jerusalem

Lesson Outline

Let's Celebrate

   I. The Temple Completed: Ezra 6:14-15

  II. The Temple Dedicated: Ezra 6:16-18

     A. *The Celebration: vs. 16*

     B. *The Sacrifices: vs. 17*

     C. *The Priests: vs. 18*

  III. The Passover Observed: Ezra 6:19-22

     A. *The Preparations: vss. 19-20*

     B. *The Hunger for God: vs. 21*

     C. *The Feast: vs. 22*

Introduction

Celebrating Victories

During their town's annual Fourth of July parade, two or three churches made magnificent floats—so good that often one of them took home first prize. It was their way of informing the public that the worship of God was still a viable option for many people.

Then, as time went on, the floats these congregations made gradually disappeared. Why? It's because they required too much work to build and there were not enough people who volunteered to make them.

Making floats, of course, is just one way we can share with others the victory we have in Christ. Sometimes we can celebrate with music that has a special Christian emphasis. On other occasions we can give praise to the Lord through the performance of skits. Regardless of what we do, our focus should remain on God and not ourselves.

Lesson Commentary

I. The Temple Completed: Ezra 6:14-15

So the elders of the Jews continued to build and prosper under the preaching of Haggai the prophet and Zechariah, a descendant of Iddo. They finished building the temple according to the command of the God of Israel and the decrees of Cyrus, Darius and Artaxerxes, kings of Persia. The temple was completed on the third day of the month Adar, in the sixth year of the reign of King Darius.

The ultimate goal of God's people was to build a sanctuary (that is, a unique dwelling place specifically set apart for Him) in which the Lord could demonstrate His visible presence among His people. Every detail of its exterior construction and interior contents were to correspond exactly with God's definitive instructions. The temple reminded the people that the Lord desired to regularly meet with them.

The prophets Haggai and Zechariah had been urging God's people to resume their restoration work on the temple. The prophets directed their message to the resettled Jews living in Jerusalem and the region of Judah (Ezra 5:1). As a result of this ministry of encouragement and exhortation, Zerubbabel and Jeshua restarted the work on the sanctuary (vs. 2).

Haggai's identity is not supplemented with genealogical data in the Scriptures, but Zechariah is always connected with his ancestor Iddo (see Zech 1:1). Nehemiah 12:16 refers to another Zechariah who had been the head of the priestly clan of Iddo. The prophet Zechariah, who ministered for several years beginning in 520 B.C., may have been the grandson of that earlier Zechariah. If this is the case, then Zechariah the prophet was also a priest.

It did not take long for Persian officials in the nearby Trans-Euphrates region to question the legitimacy of these restoration efforts (Ezra 5:3). The authorities asked and received the names of the individuals involved in the work on the temple (vs. 4). Despite these intimidation tactics, God watched over His people and prospered their efforts. The Persian officials did not stop the Jews in their work. They allowed them to proceed until a reply from the monarch was received concerning the matter (vs. 5).

Ezra included a copy of the letter that was sent to King Darius. The Persian officials said that the Jews were busy rebuilding their temple at Jerusalem. Part of the letter contains a summary of what the Jewish leaders reported to their interrogators. Most important is the claim that during the first year of King Cyrus, he authorized the Jews to rebuild their temple in Jerusalem. The Persian officials asked Darius to verify these claims and make a decision concerning the matter (vss. 6-17).

A search for the decree of Cyrus was made, but evidently the records were not found in Babylon. Instead, an important scroll was found in Ecbatana, the former capital of Media and then the summer residence of the Persian kings. The official communication verified Cyrus's original command authorizing the rebuilding of the temple and the restoration of its foundation (6:1-2).

Verses 3-12 reveal the content of Darius's letter. The king specified the size of the temple and ordered that stolen articles were to be returned. His officials were to permit the Jews to complete their work. In fact, funds from the royal treasury were to be used to pay for building materials and sacrificial animals. Those who opposed the king's edict would be severely punished. He directed that his orders be implemented with care, thoroughness, and diligence.

In verse 13 we learn that Tattenai (who was the governor of the province west of the Euphrates River), Shethar-Bozenai (another official of the Persian government), and their colleagues complied at once with the command of King Darius. Clearly, the prophecies the Lord had made through Haggai and Zechariah were coming to pass. God was giving the Jews success in rebuilding and dedicating their temple.

The people needed encouragement from the word of God delivered by Haggai and Zechariah (vs. 14). During years of delay, the people had fallen into deep discouragement. They now needed

The governor of Trans-Euphrates and his allies must have been surprised to find out Darius expected them to become the facilitators of the temple project they had opposed. Because they feared the king, they diligently supported the Jews. Meanwhile, the exiles were responding with renewed spiritual vigor to the practical challenges of Haggai and the visionary exhortations of Zechariah (Ezra 6:13-14a).

Ezra's report of the completion of the temple takes into account all of the layers of responsibility for it (Ezra 6:14b). The elders of the Jews were responsible for the laborers at the job site. Haggai and Zechariah provided the spiritual motivation that produced success. The decrees of three Persian emperors—Cyrus, Darius I, and Artaxerxes I—authorized the project at the level of world politics. However, it was "the God of Israel" whose word of command encompassed everyone and everything else involved.

reminders of God's love.

The people needed consistent exhortation because their work was hindered by more than just their enemies. It was also hindered by their selfishness and fear. When they decided to trust and obey the Lord, they prospered and God took care of their enemies.

Ezra noted that the work on the sanctuary was done at the Lord's command and under the direction of the kings of Persia. This was an unlikely coalition, but God is the prime mover of earthly rulers. In this case, He worked through pagan kings to bring about the restoration of His people and their worship of Him in Jerusalem.

"The sixth year of the reign of King Darius" (vs. 15) occurred long before the time of Artaxerxes, the third emperor credited with the temple's erection. Artaxerxes is the one who commissioned Ezra to enhance temple worship and teach the law of Moses (see 7:19-20, 25-26). The lunar month Adar corresponds roughly with February-March in our solar calendar. In 516 B.C., the third of Adar would have been March 12. The destruction of Solomon's temple by Nebuchadnezzar had begun on August 14, 586 B.C. (see 2 Kings 25:8). About 70 years had elapsed between the destruction of the first temple and the construction of the second.

When God makes a promise, it shows two aspects of His character. First, we see that He is the Lord of all. What He declares will come true and nothing can thwart His will. Second, we see that God does not change His mind, rethink His strategy, or apologize for not doing something according to our timetable. He is faithful to His Word and will surely bring it to pass.

Ultimately, God's promises are encouragements to faith, for they demonstrate the resolve of the Lord's character. His promises give us the courage to face and deal with difficult circumstances.

II. The Temple Dedicated: Ezra 6:16-18

A. The Celebration: vs. 16

Then the people of Israel—the priests, the Levites and the rest of the exiles—celebrated the dedication of the house of God with joy.

Having completed their work, the people and their leaders broke into celebration. This was a significant milestone in the nation's history. After all, "the house of God" (Ezra 6:16) was not just another building to His people. It was the place where the Lord manifested His presence.

The key to understanding this celebration is the contrast between living in exile in a land saturated with pagan idolatry and being able to worship the one true God in His sanctuary. God's people were overcome with joy because they now had the latter opportunity.

The upright remnant had learned the painful lesson of their past idolatries for which God had judged them. While in exile in Babylon, they missed so much the opportunity for worship afforded by the Jerusalem temple that they established what later became the synagogue service. This included prayers, Scripture readings, and moral instruction.

The completion of the second temple ensured that the worship of the one true God remained a vital part of Jewish national life. His people resumed their daily temple services, their annual feasts and fasts, and their worship.

B. The Sacrifices: vs. 17

For the dedication of this house of God they offered a hundred bulls, two hundred rams, four hundred male lambs and, as a sin offering for all Israel, twelve male goats, one for each of the tribes of Israel.

Having returned from Babylon without much money, the people's sacrifice of 100 bulls, 200 rams, 400 lambs, and 12 goats represented a costly commitment to God (Ezra 6:17). Although the 10 northern tribes of Israel had long since disappeared, they were remembered by the 12 goats, one for each tribe.

The dedication of God's house required significant sacrifices for two reasons. First, sacrifices proved the people's commitment to the Lord. Second, sacrifices reminded them of their sin and God's holiness.

From this we see that true worship is costly. In the New Testament, Christians are called on to give of themselves to God because Christ died for them (Rom. 12:1-2; 1 Cor. 6:19-20). After all, the new covenant ratified by the blood of Jesus supersedes the old covenant of animal sacrifices (Heb. 9:12-14; 10:11-13).

Everyone celebrated the dedication of the new temple with great joy as they offered hundreds of animal sacrifices as whole burnt offerings and sin offerings (Ezra 6:16-17). However, this marvelously joyous celebration was tiny compared to the dedicatory service during the reign of Solomon (see 1 Kings 8:5, 63).

The divisions of priests and Levites had been ready for activation as soon as the temple was built and dedicated (Ezra 6:18). The Aramaic passage that began at Ezra 4:8 ends with Ezra 6:18. The description of the first Passover celebrated at the new temple is fittingly reported in Hebrew.

Adar had been the last month of the lunar calendar, so "the fourteenth day of the first month" (Ezra 6:19) was about five weeks after the temple was completed. The newly rededicated priests and Levites ritually cleansed themselves and slaughtered the Passover lambs the worshiping families brough them (vs. 20; see Deut. 16:5-6).

C. The Priests: vs. 18

And they installed the priests in their divisions and the Levites in their groups for the service of God at Jerusalem, according to what is written in the Book of Moses.

After offering sacrifices, the people divided the priests and Levites into their various divisions. They were to serve at the temple of God in Jerusalem in accordance with the instructions "written in the Book of Moses" (Ezra 6:18).

III. The Passover Observed: Ezra 6:19-22

A. The Preparations: vss. 19-20

On the fourteenth day of the first month, the exiles celebrated the Passover. The priests and Levites had purified themselves and were all ceremonially clean. The Levites slaughtered the Passover lamb for all the exiles, for their brothers the priests and for themselves.

The highlight of the temple's completion came with the Passover observance. It is difficult for us to imagine how much the renewal of this ancient ritual meant to the Jews in Bible times. They had not kept it for several generations. With the rebuilding and rededication of the temple in Jerusalem they now had the opportunity.

It was on April 21, 516 B.C. that the returned exiles observed Passover (Ezra 6:19), a holy day that originally was intended to commemorate Israel's deliverance from Egypt. The priests and Levites had gone through the purification ritual and thus were ceremonially clean. In accordance with the Mosaic law, they slaughtered the Passover lamb for all the returned exiles, for the other priests, and for themselves (vs. 20).

The early church connected the Messiah with the Passover lamb. For instance, Paul referred to Christ as "our Passover lamb" (1 Cor. 5:7). Likewise, Peter equated the "precious blood of Christ" (1 Pet. 1:19) to that of a "lamb without blemish or defect" (see Exod. 12:5; Lev. 22:17-25). The apostle also noted that believers have been healed by the Messiah's "wounds" (1 Pet. 2:24).

B. The Hunger for God: vs. 21

So the Israelites who had returned from the exile ate it, together with all who had separated themselves from the unclean practices of their Gentile neighbors in order to seek the LORD, the God of Israel.

Keeping the Passover underscored the Jews' hunger to know and worship God. They ate the lamb as a sign that they had repented of their sins and wanted to seek the Lord. They were joined by other Jews who had renounced pagan worship (Ezra 6:21).

In this way the upright remnant publicly declared their faith in the one true God. This faith set them apart from the ungodly inhabitants of the land. The Jews' observance underscored the reality of their walk with God.

By keeping the Passover, the people acknowledged their total dependence on the Lord. They wanted to learn more about Him and demonstrate that He was not just another local tribal deity. Out of the fires of suffering emerged within the remnant a new level of interest in the things of God.

The exiles included in their Passover celebration the Jewish inhabitants of the land who had neither experienced the captivity in Babylon nor immigrated to Egypt (Ezra 6:21; see 2 Kings 25:22-26). These nonremnant Jews had to separate themselves from the practices of their Gentile neighbors and rededicated themselves to observing the law of God.

C. The Feast: vs. 22

For seven days they celebrated with joy the Feast of Unleavened Bread, because the LORD had filled them with joy by changing the attitude of the king of Assyria, so that he assisted them in the work on the house of God, the God of Israel.

Ezra 6:22 notes that the people celebrated the Feast of Unleavened Bread for seven days. This is one of the Old Testament festivals that God established for the Israelites. It involved eating bread made without yeast, holding several assemblies, and making designated offerings. It was designed to commemorate how the Lord rescued His people out of Egypt with rapid speed.

This was a joyous time of celebration based on what God had done through the Persian monarchs. These kings had conquered territory formerly controlled by the Assyrian Empire, which was one of the kingdoms that had exiled God's people (Neh. 9:32). Because of the Lord's intervention through the Persian monarchs, the Jews were strengthened and encouraged to restore the temple in Jerusalem.

The Persian emperor Darius I is called "the king of Assyria" in Ezra 6:22 for the same reason Cyrus was called "the king of Babylon" in 5:13. These rulers took over the titles as well as the empires of those they conquered. When God directed the Persians to restore the temple of the Lord, He reversed a policy of deportation and destruction that reached back to the Assyrians whose realm the Persians had absorbed.

Discussion Questions

1. What prompted the Persian officials to allow the Jews to complete the rebuilding of the temple?
2. What role did Haggai and Zechariah serve in this endeavor?
3. In what way did the people of Israel celebrate the dedication of the temple?
4. Who participated in the Passover celebration?
5. What are some ways we can celebrate God's goodness in our lives?

Now Ask Yourself . . .

Under what circumstances am I most likely to give up on a difficult task?

What promises in Scripture can God use to change my attitude when I'm feeling discouraged?

How can I depend on God's presence and love to help me overcome opposition from others to His work?

How has God used unbelievers in my life to bring about His will for me?

Am I just as comfortable worshiping God as I am at doing work for Him?

Illustrations

A psychologist once said that in a month he could change the outlook, personality, and behavior of anyone to a model he had selected. He supposedly could manipulate circumstances in such a way that only the desired set of responses would seem possible. This is the nature of temptation and doubt. We are thrust into circumstances that seem either impossible or irresistible.

The account recorded in Ezra 6:14-22 reminds us that God is ready to do the impossible—to bless His people in their weakness and to call them to rely on Him. When we look at the impossible, God is ready to make it possible. We can have confidence, through Christ, that we will receive the spiritual blessings God has promised us.

Of course, opposition to God's work is not a thing of the past. Like the Jews who were trying to complete the reconstruction of the temple, Christians face opposition on many fronts. As believers attempt to carry out some task for the Lord, they may even encounter people who will actively seek to stop their work.

As much as we may dislike conflict, the Bible describes the Christian way of life as one that entails conflict with the forces of evil. We can learn from the Book of Ezra how to persevere in our witness despite the opposition of those who resist things that are good and deserving of praise—that is, things that are true, noble, right, pure, lovely, and honorable (Phil. 4:8). We are also reminded of the value of celebrating God's great acts in our life. Let us not hesitate to do the latter!

March 26, 2006

A Time for Decision

Radical Change Required

DEVOTIONAL READING

Deuteronomy 6:1-9

DAILY BIBLE READINGS

Monday March 20
  Jeremiah 7:1-8
  Jeremiah Tells the People
  to Change

Tuesday March 21
  Hosea 11:1-11
  A Heart Can Be Changed

Wednesday March 22
  Ezra 9:1-6
  Ezra Deals with the Exiles'
  Unfaithfulness

Thursday March 23
  Ezra 9:7-15
  Ezra Voices a Prayer to
  God

Friday March 24
  Ezra 10:1-8
  The People Acknowledge
  Their Sin

Saturday March 25
  Ezra 10:9-17
  Those Who Sinned Are
  Punished

Sunday March 26
  Matthew 18:1-9
  Change to Enter the
  Kingdom of God

Scripture

Background Scripture: *Ezra 9—10*

Scripture Lesson: *Ezra 9:1-3; 10:9-14*

Key Verse: *"Now make confession to the LORD, the God of your fathers, and do his will." Ezra 10:11.*

Lesson Aim

Doing what God wants may require radical changes in our lifestyles.

Lesson Setting

Time: 458 B.C.

Place: Jerusalem

Lesson Outline

Radical Change Required

I. The People's Sin: Ezra 9:1-3
  A. *Intermarriage with Pagans: vss. 1-2*
  B. *Ezra's Response: vs. 3*

II. Ezra's Challenge: Ezra 10:9-11
  A. *The People Gathered: vs. 9*
  B. *The Unfaithfulness of the People: vs. 10*
  C. *The Need of the People to Confess: vs. 11*

III. The People's Response: Ezra 10:12-14
  A. *Acknowledgement of Ezra's Charge: vs. 12*
  B. *Agreement to Act: vss. 13-14*

Introduction

Steps to Spiritual Wholeness

Ezra's encounter with sin in his faith community finds many parallels today. He discovered many, including civic and religious leaders, who had violated God's will. On a more positive note, Ezra discovered the power of remorse, confession, and repentance at work among God's people. The scribe found members of the faith community who were willing to acknowledge and renounce their sins. Beyond that, they accepted considerable hardship in order to make things right.

Sin, confession, restoration—these are the steps to spiritual wholeness. No one is exempt, for everyone has sinned. Perhaps it has not been openly and flagrantly, but we all have broken God's laws and we have all fallen far short of His glory. That's why we need spiritual leaders of courage who are willing to identify with people in their sin. The Holy Spirit honors these leaders, especially when they confront people with the requirements of God's holiness.

Lesson Commentary

I. The People's Sin: Ezra 9:1-3

A. Intermarriage with Pagans: vss. 1-2

After these things had been done, the leaders came to me and said, "The people of Israel, including the priests and the Levites, have not kept themselves separate from the neighboring peoples with their detestable practices, like those of the Canaanites, Hittites, Perizzites, Jebusites, Ammonites, Moabites, Egyptians and Amorites. They have taken some of their daughters as wives for themselves and their sons, and have mingled the holy race with the peoples around them. And the leaders and officials have led the way in this unfaithfulness."

Ezra and Nehemiah go together, but they make an odd couple. Both books narrate events in Jerusalem after a remnant of Judah returned from the Babylonian captivity. Ezra was a meditative scribe who led reforms by means of teaching and holiness of character. Nehemiah was an official in the Persian government who led reforms by means of bold plans and force of character.

Some leaders spark reform with skilled rhetoric that sweeps followers along on a wave of emotion. Others prevail because of flawless organization that mobilizes resources and personnel efficiently and effectively. A few carry the field on the strength of their charismatic personalities alone. Ezra approached the task of inspiring the returned exiles in Judah and Jerusalem with none of those qualities. He was an exceedingly rare leader whom God equipped to guide by the power of a godly example.

Ezra arrived in Jerusalem on August 4, 458 B.C. (see Ezra 7:8-9). While he was tying up the loose ends of delivering the gifts and goods he brought and settling his fellow travelers, a delegation of Jewish leaders came to Ezra with a problem they felt needed urgent attention. It was the ninth month (see 10:9), which corresponds roughly to December. Ezra had been in Jerusalem about four months.

All the people of Israel were involved in this problem, but it was the participation of the priests and Levites that posed the greatest danger (9:1). These men had intermarried with some of the idolatrous women of the land. This moral compromise threatened the spiritual purity of Israel. Those who brought the problem to Ezra spun out a list of names of nations reminiscent of the peoples in the land when Joshua conquered it (see Josh. 9:1; 24:11).

Only the Ammonites, Moabites, and Egyptians still existed in Ezra's day. The archaic names reminded everyone that the threat of intermarriage with idolaters was an ancient one that had gotten Israel into serious spiritual trouble since the days of the conquest under Joshua (Ezra 9:2; see Exod. 34:11-16; Deut. 7:1-4). The complaining leaders admitted that the leadership class had led the way in this abomination. Evidently they wanted Ezra to use his imperial mandate to enforce a prohibition against such intermarriages.

The prophet Malachi preached against returned exiles who divorced Jewish wives to marry foreign women instead (see Mal. 2:10-16). Ancient rabbis took this to mean that many Jewish wives had aged prematurely from the rigors of the return and the rebuilding and their husbands preferred more attractive local women. It may also be that many unmarried men had accepted the challenge of returning to Jerusalem and later could find only local brides. Still others may have married idolaters for economic advantage.

The prohibitions against intermarriage with surrounding nations are expressed not in racial terms but in religious ones. Converts to faith in Israel's God from among the nations were not stigmatized. Spiritual purity was the issue. Ezra did not respond to the report by exercising his imperial power. Instead, he went into mourning.

B. Ezra's Response: vs. 3
When I heard this, I tore my tunic and cloak, pulled hair from my head and beard and sat down appalled.

Evidently Ezra received the news and responded in grief to it in the temple. Everyone else who felt the same dread about the future gathered around the priest-scholar to mourn with him (Ezra 9:4). The sense of the passage is that Ezra sat appalled for some time before the evening sacrifice at 3:00 P.M. Ezra was no showman, staging a tantrum to create a superficial effect. His was a genuine grief observed, and its effect was authentic and enduring.

235

Ancient Hebrews expressed their sorrow visibly and audibly. Wearing sackcloth of dark goat or camel hair (Jer. 6:26; Isa. 32:11), lying in dirt or ashes and putting them in one's hair (Job 2:12; Ezek. 27:30), tearing one's own clothing (2 Sam. 1:11; 3:31), wailing and weeping aloud (Ezek. 27:30-32), even lacerating one's body (Jer. 16:6; 41:5) in violation of the law of God (Lev. 19:28) marked occasions of deep distress. Men typically shaved their hair or beards to symbolize loss (2 Sam. 10:4; Isa. 15:2; Ezek. 7:18). In contrast, full hair and beard represented vigor and prosperity.

A Phoenician carving on a sarcophagus older than the time of Ezra shows professional female mourners tearing at their hair. Ezra is the only man whom the Bible tells us spontaneously tore at his hair because his sorrow was so intense he could not wait for a razor. By contrast, when Nehemiah was later confronted with similar sin (Neh. 13:25), he tore out the offenders' hair!

Tearing garments was a typical Jewish method of displaying grief (Ezra 9:3; see Gen. 37:29, 34; Esth. 4:1). Ezra's pulling out his hair and beard is unparalleled in the Bible, though others shaved their head in grief (see Job 1:20; Amos 8:10). Ezra's grief exceeded normal bounds, and he sat where he was, immobilized with appalling sorrow, anger, and dread (Ezra 9:4). The Hebrew word rendered "appalled" vividly suggests trembling, paleness, and stunned senses.

II. Ezra's Challenge: Ezra 10:9-11

A. The People Gathered: vs. 9

Within the three days, all the men of Judah and Benjamin had gathered in Jerusalem. And on the twentieth day of the ninth month, all the people were sitting in the square before the house of God, greatly distressed by the occasion and because of the rain.

In Jesus' day, the priests presented the evening sacrifice between 2:30 and 3:30 P.M., and it's likely this was when Ezra got down on his knees and spread out his hands to the Lord in prayer (Ezra 9:5). In his petition (vss. 6-15), he confessed that God's people had violated His law and thus experienced His judgment. Ezra also acknowledged the Lord's grace in disciplining His people far less than they deserved.

The priest-scholar recognized that if the crisis of intermarriage was not averted, the returnees risked losing Jerusalem, Judah, and the right to worship in the temple. The people responded favorably to Ezra. They wept bitterly (10:1), confessed their sin through Shecaniah, one of their leaders (vs. 2), and vowed to keep the stipulation in the Mosaic covenant regarding intermarriage (vss. 3-8).

The Hebrew expression for making a covenant was "to cut a covenant." Ancient covenant ceremonies required the contracting parties to divide sacrificial animals and walk between the halves of the carcasses (Gen. 15:9-17). Implicit in this ritual was the threat that violating the covenant would lead to the death and dismemberment of the violator. The bloody ritual had fallen out of use, but the terminology "to cut a covenant" was still employed (see Ezra 10:3).

The faith community would expel the foreign wives and the children born to them. Ezra in turn required the leadership to take an oath to act in accordance with the law. The scribe then fasted and mourned over the transgressions of the returnees.

Verse 7 notes that a proclamation was made throughout Judah and Jerusalem requiring all the returned exiles to assemble at Jerusalem. If any failed to show up within three days, the civil and religious leaders could decree that the violaters have all their property confiscated. Also, they would be expelled from the faith community (vs. 8). To lose the legal right to own land meant to be disinherited. And expulsion from the land meant one could not worship at the temple.

All the people of Judah and Benjamin gathered within the designated time to deal with the intermarriage issue (vs. 9). In 458 B.C., the twentieth day of the ninth month (Kislev) was well into December. The rainy season had begun in October; its heaviest rains would fall in December and January. The highest temperature might have reached 50°. The crowd gathered in the open square suffered as much from physical discomfort as spiritual turmoil.

B.   The Unfaithfulness of the People: vs. 10

Then Ezra the priest stood up and said to them, "You have been unfaithful; you have married foreign women, adding to Israel's guilt."

In his function as a priest, Ezra confronted the people's infidelity in the matter of marrying foreign women (Ezra 10:10. The prophets had written over and over about the moral pollution of the land of Canaan (9:10-11; see Deut. 9:4; 18:9-13; 1 Kings 14:22-24). Because of the corruption of the Canaanite people at the time of the Conquest, Israel had been forbidden to intermarry with them or form other intimate alliances (Ezra 9:12; see Deut. 7:1-3). Prosperity in the promised land had always depended in part on not being entangled with foreign people and their gods. The Assyrian and Babylonian conquests in 722 and 586 B.C. had occurred because Israel had wantonly and persistently rebelled against the law of God (Ezra 9:13).

C.   The Need of the People to Confess: vs. 11

"Now make confession to the LORD, the God of your fathers, and do his will. Separate yourselves from the peoples around you and from your foreign wives."

Ezra ordered the faith community to take two actions: inwardly they were to confess their rebellion against God's ways;

The law of Moses forbade intermarriage between Israelites and the various nations inhabiting Canaan at the time of the Conquest (Deut. 7:1-3). Further, the law forbade the presence of Ammonites, Moabites, and their descendants in the sanctuary of God (23:3). Yet Rahab the Canaanite and Ruth the Moabite both married into the tribe of Judah and the lineage of David and Jesus (Matt. 1:5).

The prohibition seems to have been against marriage with foreign women committed to idolatry, not foreign women who had identified with the God of Israel. The concern of the law was that idolatrous wives "will turn your sons away from following me to serve other gods, and the LORD's anger will burn against you" (Deut. 7:4). Marriage with converts to faith in the Lord was not unlawful and may explain the lengthy interview process preceding the divorces reported in Ezra 10.

237

Ezra's solution to the problem of marriage to foreign wives was different from Pau's approach. The reason is that in Ezra's day, his fellow Jews were abandoning the Lord by intermarrying with pagans. In contrast, the believers about whom Paul wrote were already married when they trusted in Christ. The apostle advised these believers to do everything they could to preserve their marriages, even though their spouses remained unbelieving (see 1 Cor. 7:10-15).

outwardly they were to separate themselves from idolatry, especially their foreign wives (Ezra 10:11). The larger issue was doing God's will in terms of being a holy people. Clearly, then, the separation was not racially motivated. The issue was intermarriage with worshipers of other gods, which would result in abandoning the true worship of the living God.

III. The People's Response: Ezra 10:12-14

A. Acknowledgement of Ezra's Charge: vs. 12
The whole assembly responded with a loud voice: "You are right! We must do as you say."

The men not only assembled in Jerusalem within the stipulated period of time and expressed their grief (Ezra 10:9), but they also acknowledged to Ezra their sin and guilt (vs. 12). Such a positive response is evidence of the Lord's grace working through the godly leadership of Ezra.

Church leadership profits from men and women with superior administrative skills and gifts in understanding problems and formulating responses to them. Ezra reminds us that our churches also need men and women whose hearts hunger and thirst to know God and heed His will. Such folk are not impractical; they are invaluable.

In Ezra 10:9, the Hebrew word rendered "rain" is plural, suggesting that it was a heavy rain (possibly torrential). Moreover, the statement in verse 13 that it was the rainy season was not a subtle ploy on the part of the leadership to evade the necessity to repent. Rather, it was an expression of sincere intent for the repentance to be carried out in a deep and lasting fashion.

B. Agreement to Act: vss. 13-14
"But there are many people here and it is the rainy season; so we cannot stand outside. Besides, this matter cannot be taken care of in a day or two, because we have sinned greatly in this thing. Let our officials act for the whole assembly. Then let everyone in our towns who has married a foreign woman come at a set time, along with the elders and judges of each town, until the fierce anger of our God in this matter is turned away from us."

The assembly that shivered in the rain voiced their united agreement with Ezra's assessment of the situation and the solution he proposed. They recognized that they deserved the wrath of God as long as this situation continued. This response was probably a summary of the opinions of the delegates who gathered after the crowd dispersed to find shelter. Everyone realized that implementing Ezra's solution would be painful and difficult in individual cases. Unraveling this tangled web of faithless marriages would be hard and bitter work (Ezra 10:13-14).

The committee proposed that a task force made up of elders and respected mediators examine each case of intermarriage and work out the details of the separations. The elders were older men of the various Jewish villages who had formed a council to make decisions for governing the faith community. When they gathered from all the towns, they represented God's people as a whole.

Four men of note, including one Levite, opposed the system (vs. 15). Their reasons are not given. Perhaps they had intermarried. Perhaps they thought the remedy too drastic. Despite the dissent, the plan was adopted.

In Ezra 10:13, the Hebrew word rendered "sinned" carries with it the idea of rebellion. The same word is used in 1 Kings 12:19 to describe the revolt of the northern tribes against Rehoboam, the son of King Solomon.

Ezra appointed the panel to assess each offensive marriage. Every clan was represented. The interviews with those whose marriages had to be reviewed started 10 days after the mass assembly in the rain and lasted for three months, that is, until March 27, 457 B.C. (vss. 16-17). In all, 110 men were found guilty of marrying foreign wives and were required to separate from them (see vss. 18-44).

The priests, Levites, and temple personnel head the list of 110 men who had offended God by marrying foreign wives. The pledge and the sin offering they made probably was the same response required of the others on the list. Nine of the original 33 families that returned from Babylon were involved in this offense. But that means no one from 24 of the original remnant families intermarried with idolaters.

The guilty ones tended to group within certain families that had strayed from the Lord. The most touching cases were the ones that involved children who were taken away from their fathers. Presumably, these foreign women and their children returned to their families and became dependent on parents, brothers, or uncles.

Discussion Questions

1. How much courage did the leaders display by coming to Ezra and reporting the incident of intermarriage with pagans?
2. Why was the issue of marriage to foreigners such a grave concern to Ezra?
3. Why did Ezra react so strongly to the news?
4. Why did Ezra demand that the transgressors separate themselves from their foreign wives?
5. Why did the entire assembly respond favorably to Ezra's demands?

Now Ask Yourself . . .

What is usually my first reaction to an awareness of sin in my heart?

Is there any sin in my heart that I need to acknowledge before God?

Is there anyone whom I consider like Ezra to be a prayer warrior? How can his or her example encourage me to be more genuine and heartfelt in my times of prayer?

How does God want me to express His holiness?

How can I encourage other believers to pursue moral purity in their lives?

Illustrations

Spiritual leadership does not necessarily arise from popularity, votes, power, or prestige. That's how the world counts leadership, but it's quite different in the Lord's way of doing things. Godly leaders have a strong moral fiber that prompts them to do what is right, even if others view it as unpopular.

Ezra was not a popular public figure when God chose him for leadership. But he was God's servant when the future of Israel as a nation was at stake. Ezra was neither a military commander nor a politician. But because he had grown up faithfully studying, teaching, and obeying God's Word, he was the one to call the community of faith to account and to demand a return to an upright way of life.

God's hand was on Ezra, but he didn't brag about it. He gave God the glory, so when the crunch came he knew God well enough to realize what had to be done. Courageously, he confessed and then called for an end to the law-breaking. He led the nation, not by denying, dodging, or covering up sin, but by exposing it.

In our churches, confession and repentance are the proper responses to such leadership. Moreover, genuine repentance does not end with statements of confession, for such would imply nothing more than lip service. Conscientious believers go further by striving for a radical change in their lifestyles. Their gratitude for God's forgiveness and mercy is expressed by making needed changes to improper attitudes and inappropriate behaviors.

Taking the Lead

DEVOTIONAL READING

Isaiah 26:1-9

DAILY BIBLE READINGS

Monday March 27
Psalm 138
Boldness Comes from the
Lord

Tuesday March 28
Nehemiah 1:1-11
Nehemiah Prays

Wednesday March 29
Nehemiah 2:1-5
Nehemiah Asks to Go to
Jerusalem

Thursday March 30
Nehemiah 2:6-10
The King Grants
Nehemiah Permission

Friday March 31
Nehemiah 2:11-20
Nehemiah Finds the Walls
in Ruins

Saturday April 1
Proverbs 28:1-10
The Righteous Are as Bold
as Lions

Sunday April 2
Acts 4:23-31
Speak with Boldness

Scripture

Background Scripture: *Nehemiah 1—2*
Scripture Lesson: *Nehemiah 2:4-8, 15-18*
Key Verse: *"Come, let us rebuild the wall of Jerusalem,
and we will no longer be in disgrace." Nehemiah 2:17b.*

Lesson Aim

If God's work is to get done, sometimes we must be bold
and take the lead.

Lesson Setting

Time: 446–445 B.C.
Place: Susa and Jerusalem

Lesson Outline

Taking the Lead

  I. Nehemiah's Request before the King:
    Nehemiah 2:4-8
    A. *The First Question and Response: vss. 4-5*
    B. *The Second Question and Response: vss. 6-8*
 II. Nehemiah's Inspection of the Wall:
    Nehemiah 2:15-18
    A. *The Secret Inspection: vss. 15-16*
    B. *The Summons to Rebuild the Wall: vss. 17-18*

241

Introduction

Accepting the Challenge

Challenging tasks come in many forms. We meet them early in our school years, then in college, then in our jobs, and finally in our families and churches. Often it seems easier to accept new challenges when we are younger than when we are older. But we're never too old to take on hard tasks.

A veteran of many years in the U.S. Navy chaplains' corps retired. Instead of looking for a comfortable place where he could relax and take it easy, he chose a run-down church in a tough urban neighborhood. When his friends asked him why, he said, "It was the toughest thing I could find to do."

That's the attitude with which we must always be open to God's leading. We need the Holy Spirit's guidance, as well as courage and faith, to follow the Lord, regardless of our ages and circumstances. The thrill of living for God is always there when we offer ourselves for His service.

Lesson Commentary

I. Nehemiah's Request before the King: Nehemiah 2:4-8

A. The First Question and Response: vss. 4-5

The king said to me, "What is it you want?" Then I prayed to the God of heaven, and I answered the king, "If it pleases the king and if your servant has found favor in his sight, let him send me to the city in Judah where my fathers are buried so that I can rebuild it."

Jerusalem probably means "a foundation of peace." Not until David rose to power did the covenant people actually claim Jerusalem as their sacred city. But when God gave David His approval to enshrine the ark there, the people believed God had chosen Jerusalem for His habitation (Ps. 132:13).

The Book of Nehemiah begins by relating what happened in the city of Susa, the winter capital of Persia and the resort center of its kings. It was November-December, 446 B.C. Nehemiah's blood brother Hanani (Neh. 7:2) and representatives from the territory of Judah came to Susa to see him. The Jewish patriot asked about the situation for the resettled Jews in their homeland (1:1-2).

The situation at this time was gloomy for the Jews living in the region of Judah, for the wall surrounding Jerusalem was completely destroyed. This was sad, for it represented the protection of the Lord and also illustrated His fidelity in reestablishing His people. During the time of Ezra, attempts to rebuild the wall may have been started and then were stopped by orders from the king (Ezra

4:21-23; 9:9). Perhaps any progress that had been made in restoring the city wall had been reversed.

Jerusalem's wall was one of the city's most distinctive features during the kingdom years. The wall encircling the city provided its best defense against attack. When the Babylonians demolished the wall, Jerusalem became defenseless against any invading army. Is it any wonder, then, that a devout Jew like Nehemiah would want to rebuild the wall of his beloved city?

Nehemiah was so overwhelmed with grief by what he had heard that he sat down and wept (Neh. 1:4). He also expressed his concern for days, through fasting and praying before the Lord, whose dwelling is heaven. In the address recorded in verses 5-11, Nehemiah affirmed both God's surpassing greatness and His involvement in the lives of His people. Nehemiah acknowledged that the Lord kept His covenant with those who loved and obeyed Him.

Based on the assurance of God's unfailing love, Nehemiah petitioned the Lord to listen to His servant's prayer. Nehemiah confessed his sins, that of his family, and that of his fellow Jews. Though they had not kept the Mosaic law, Nehemiah asked God to be gracious to His people. In particular, Nehemiah petitioned the Lord to grant him success as he went before the king of Persia with his request.

Nehemiah 2 brings us to the following spring, namely, April and May of 445 B.C. It was the twentieth year of Artaxerxes' reign, and Nehemiah was serving as the king's cupbearer (vs. 1). In this capacity, Nehemiah tasted all the wine before it was served to the king. Nehemiah certified that none of it was poisoned or contaminated. The position of cupbearer often included advisory responsibilities. As a trusted and loyal servant, Nehemiah had a considerable amount of influence in the imperial court.

On previous occasions, Nehemiah's appearance was pleasant, not depressed. (Regardless of their personal problems, the servants of the king were expected to keep their feelings concealed and to appear cheerful in his presence.) In this situation, however, Artaxerxes noticed a change in Nehemiah's countenance and asked why he seemed sad. The king surmised that Nehemiah was distressed about something. Nehemiah became even more concerned, for it was uncertain what the emotionally volatile ruler might do (vs. 2).

Nehemiah wished the king a long and prosperous rule. He indi-

The city of Jerusalem was set on a hill some 2,500 feet above sea level. It was located 33 miles east of the Mediterranean Sea and 14 miles west of the Dead Sea. Because access was difficult and the city lacked natural resources, it at one time enjoyed a relatively protected location. But when a major regional trade route developed through the city, Jerusalem became commercially and strategically desirable to every subsequent political force that arose to power.

Both Jewish and Christian traditions recognize Ezra as the author of the Book of Nemehiah. This is based on the external evidence that Ezra and Nehemiah were originally one book. It is also evident in the similar theological orientation and emphases of the two books. Ezra wrote probably Nehemiah sometime during or after the governor's second term in office (prior to 400 B.C.).

243

cated that his gloomy appearance was due to the distressing situation of his homeland. The city of his ancestors was still in a devastated condition. Without the protection of walls, it would be too difficult to rebuild Jerusalem, for such efforts were subject to attack and vandalism (vs. 3)

The king next asked Nehemiah what he would request to solve the problem (vs. 4). At this point Nehemiah turned to the Lord in silent prayer. Perhaps he asked for wisdom about what to say and that God would grant him favor in his earthly master's sight (vss. 3-4). Nehemiah asked for permission to go back to Judah and to his ancestral city. He also asked for permission to rebuild the city, including its walls (vs. 5).

In the exchange between Artaxerxes and Nehemiah (Neh. 2:2-8), the emperor was always brusque and demanding, while the courtier was formal and deferential. Nehemiah never mentioned Jerusalem by name but always tied the city to himself and his family. He did not waste the emperor's time with wishful generalities; God had helped him formulate a specific plan during those months of fasting and prayer.

B. The Second Question and Response: vss. 6-8

Then the king, with the queen sitting beside him, asked me, "How long will your journey take, and when will you get back?" It pleased the king to send me; so I set a time. I also said to him, "If it pleases the king, may I have letters to the governors of Trans-Euphrates, so that they will provide me safe-conduct until I arrive in Judah? And may I have a letter to Asaph, keeper of the king's forest, so he will give me timber to make beams for the gates of the citadel by the temple and for the city wall and for the residence I will occupy?" And because the gracious hand of my God was upon me, the king granted my requests.

At this point in his narrative, Nehemiah mentioned the presence of one of Artaxerxes' wives. Perhaps she played a role in the emperor's decision in Nehemiah's favor. Artaxerxes gave permission by asking how long it would take Nehemiah to get to Judah and when he would be back (Neh. 2:6). Although Nehemiah may have anticipated a brief leave of absence from service in the imperial court, his actual stay in Jerusalem lasted 12 years (5:14; 13:6).

Nehemiah next asked the king for official documents to present to the governors assigned in the Trans-Euphrates region of the empire (2:7). These papers would authorize whatever Nehemiah's rebuilding efforts required. In this situation, he would need permission to freely travel through various territories without any complications.

Nehemiah also needed an escort to safeguard his journey. He requested a letter to the appropriate official giving him access to the required building supplies he needed to restore Jerusalem. The king granted these requests because God showed His kindness to His servant (vs. 8).

II. Nehemiah's Inspection of the Wall: Nehemiah 2:15-18

A. The Secret Inspection: vss. 15-16
So I went up the valley by night, examining the wall. Finally, I turned back and reentered through the Valley Gate. The officials did not know where I had gone or what I was doing, because as yet I had said nothing to the Jews or the priests or nobles or officials or any others who would be doing the work.

Nehemiah knew that Artaxerxes granted his requests because the hand of God graciously moved him to do so. He didn't bother to describe his journey, although it should have been quicker than Zerubbabel's and Ezra's since he was unencumbered by children, livestock, and household possessions. Nehemiah presented his documents authorizing his mission to the authorities in Trans-Euphrates (Neh. 2:9). His status was enhanced by the presence of his armed imperial escort.

Ominously, Nehemiah introduced into his narrative two characters who were upset that he had arrived to promote the welfare of the Jews (vs. 10). Sanballat's name was Babylonian; he was likely named after Sin, the moon god. He was probably from Upper or Lower Beth Horon, two villages about 12 miles northwest of Jerusalem on the main road to the Mediterranean coast. He was a leader of the Samarian opposition. Tobiah was a Jewish name meaning "The Lord Is Good." He probably was a worldly Jew living in and controlling the territory associated with Ammon east of the Jordan River (vs. 10). These two men would be Nehemiah's bitter enemies for years to come.

After contacting the officials of the satrapy of Trans-Euphrates, Nehemiah went on to Jerusalem (vs. 11). As Ezra had done before him, Nehemiah rested three days before initiating any activity (see Ezra 8:32). Before telling anyone in Jerusalem what he had come to do, Nehemiah surveyed the most damaged portion on the city walls. As an outsider he wanted to be able to give the leaders of Jerusalem an informed account of what needed to be done when he revealed his mission.

Nehemiah requested Artaxerxes' permission to use timber from "the king's forest" (Neh. 2:8). The best-known source of fine timber in the Persian Empire was in Lebanon, where Zerubbabel secured materials for the temple (Ezra 3:7). However, it is improbable that these costly, imported cedar logs were used to rebuild the gates of Jerusalem. A likely location of the king's forest is Solomon's garden (2 Kings 25:4; Eccl. 2:5), which the early historian Josephus located at Etham, roughly six miles south of Jerusalem. Native oak, poplar, or terebinth in this area would have made good construction timbers for gates.

God had enabled Nehemiah to win the approval of the emperor of Persia for rebuilding the walls of Jerusalem. He secured the cooperation of the officials of Trans-Euphrates with an imperial edict. That left just one thing: securing the commitment of the residents of Jerusalem and Judah to do the work. It's often easier to get permission to lead a project than it is to motivate the people involved to carry it out.

Perhaps the greatest challenge Nehemiah faced was transmitting his conviction that rebuilding Jerusalem's walls at this time was God's idea—not the fantasy of a government official who would go home in a while and leave the locals to live with the trouble he had stirred up. Nehemiah took a few trusted associates—probably men who had accompanied him from Susa—and set out to inspect the walls (Neh. 2:12-13). Nehemiah rode a donkey; the others walked. The inspection party went out through the ruins of the Valley Gate on the west side of the southern point of Jerusalem and turned to the left toward the Jackal Well near the city's southern extremity. They passed the Dung Gate before reaching the well.

After rounding the bottom of Jerusalem, Nehemiah turned north up the Kidron Valley along the eastern wall (vs. 14). Here the Fountain Gate exited to the King's Pool (the Pool of Siloam; see 3:15). The hillside from Jerusalem into the Kidron Valley is steep. The old wall of Jerusalem had been far down the hill and a system of terraces that supported buildings had been anchored against that wall. When the old wall was destroyed, the terraces had crumbled too. Nehemiah had to dismount and continue on foot because the slope along the east side of Jerusalem was choked with rubble that even a donkey could not negotiate in the moonlight.

Nehemiah's inspectors picked their way an unspecified distance farther along the ruins of the eastern wall (2:15). This side would be the most daunting section to rebuild. Much of the rest stood on relatively level ground. Finally they turned back, retraced their steps over the rocks, rounded the southern point of Jerusalem, and reentered the Valley Gate to the southwest.

Neither Persian officials nor Jewish leaders were previously informed about Nehemiah's investigation before it occurred (vs. 16). Here we see that Nehemiah was characterized by practicality and prudence. He recognized that adversaries had previously hindered the rebuilding efforts in Jerusalem. With insight, he decided to examine the condition of the ancient city and its physical defenses without any fanfare. He used this information to formulate a precise plan for rebuilding the walls and restoring the city of Jerusalem.

B. The Summons to Rebuild the Wall: vss. 17-18

Then I said to them, "You see the trouble we are in: Jerusalem lies in ruins, and its gates have been burned with fire. Come, let us rebuild the wall of Jerusalem, and we will no longer be in disgrace." I also told them about the gracious hand of my God upon me and what the king had said to me. They replied, "Let us start rebuilding." So they began this good work.

When the time was right, Nehemiah gathered everyone and surprised them all. He reviewed their disgrace and defenselessness. He challenged them to join him in rebuilding the defenses and removing their humiliation. And as his clincher, Nehemiah shared the amazing story of God's intervention with Artaxerxes to secure official sanction for this task (Neh. 2:17-18).

The response of the priests, nobles, officials, and ordinary people was profoundly united: "Let us start rebuilding." In the books of Ezra and Nehemiah, the concept of "the hand of the Lord my God" (see Ezra 7:6, 28; 8:31) or "the gracious hand of my God" (see 7:9; 8:18, 22; Neh. 2:8, 18) explains the influencing force behind everything that happens. Emperors, nations, and the people of God are all tools in that gracious hand.

Opposed to the gracious hand of God were three potent human enemies (Neh. 2:19). The company of Sanballat and Tobiah was joined by Geshem the Arab. Together they launched a campaign of ridicule and mockery against the small Jewish community. Their initial charge was the old standby: rebellion against the emperor (see Ezra 4:11-16).

Nehemiah shrugged off Sanballat, Tobiah, and Geshem as though they were minor annoyances (Neh. 2:20). He could do so because he looked at the situation in Jerusalem through a theological lens. The God of heaven wanted the walls built. He and the Jews were the servants of the God of heaven by terms of a covenant. Sanballat, Tobiah, and Geshem had no covenant status. Jerusalem belonged to God and His people. The blustering nations around them had no part in God's plan for Jerusalem.

Nehemiah probably would not have been the great leader he was without Sanballat's and Tobiah's opposition. The presence of difficult people in our own lives may be the Lord's way of stretching our capacity to love the unlovable, and thus become more like Christ.

Ancient sources reveal that Geshem led an assortment of Arab tribes that controlled the deserts south of Judah from Egypt to the Arabian peninsula. He was more powerful than Sanballat and Tobiah combined, but his hostility to the Jews appears to have been less intense. Sanballat to the north, Tobiah to the east, and Geshem to the south forged a hostile boundary around Judah.

Discussion Questions

1. When Hanani visited Nehemiah, what did they discuss?
2. How did Nehemiah respond to the news he received?
3. Why was King Artaxerxes willing to grant Nehemiah's request?
4. How was Nehemiah able to convince his fellow Jews to join him in rebuilding the Jerusalem wall?
5. What leadership principles do you think can be gleaned from Nehemiah's life?

Now Ask Yourself . . .

What sorts of things tend to hinder my service for the Lord?

What spiritual resources has God made available to help me overcome these obstacles?

What great tasks for God has the Spirit put on my heart to do?

What fears might I have to undertake such a venture?

How might God use me to encourage other believers to overcome their fears of serving Him?

Illustrations

Nehemiah was a man who had a burden—a God-sent desire—to restore the walls of Jerusalem. The circumstances, however, did not seem to warrant any hope of success. But Nehemiah overcame the obstacles with God's help—just as your students can if they will depend on Him.

Consider, for example, Henry Stenhouse, an ophthalmologist from Goldsboro, North Carolina. When he was 100 years old, he decided to run for the United States Congress. He was prompted to take such a bold step by his concern for the young children who attended his party. Stenhouse said he was distressed about the quality of life in the country, and he wanted to do something to make life better for the children.

Some of the adults in your class may think their options are closed when they reach a certain age; or they may feel closed in by confining circumstances. Yet here is the story of a man who proved that constructive action begins with a person who has a strong desire and a concern. If your students are willing to act on their ministry desires, God will give them the courage and ability they need to start new ventures despite what may appear to be overwhelming obstacles.

Of course, we cannot do the Lord's work unless we trust in Him and obey His Word. Consider Nehemiah. He did not start his building project without first going to God in prayer. Nehemiah knew God's promises, and he knew about the presence of sin in his life. Nehemiah also knew the importance of God's name and honor. Only then was he ready to start doing a great work for the Lord. The same also holds true for us.

Setting Up Our Defenses

DEVOTIONAL READING

Nehemiah 9:6-15

DAILY BIBLE READINGS

Monday April 3
Nehemiah 4:1-6
Sanballat Ridicules
Rebuilding the Wall

Tuesday April 4
Nehemiah 4:7-15
Many Enemies Plot
against Jerusalem

Wednesday April 5
Nehemiah 4:15-23
Work Continues, with
Preparations to Fight

Thursday April 6
Nehemiah 5:1-5
The People Petition
Nehemiah

Friday April 7
Nehemiah 5:6-11
Nehemiah Demands
Justice

Saturday April 8
Nehemiah 5:12-19
Nehemiah Serves Well

Sunday April 9
Luke 10:1-12
We Are Like Lambs among
Wolves

Scripture

Background Scripture: *Nehemiah 4*
Scripture Lesson: *Nehemiah 4:6-8, 15-23*
Key Verse: *"Our God will fight for us!" Nehemiah 4:20.*

Lesson Aim

As we are doing God's work, we need to prepare for opposition.

Lesson Setting

Time: 445–443 B.C.
Place: Jerusalem

Lesson Outline

Setting Up Our Defenses

  I. The Rebuilding Opposed: Nehemiah 4:6-8
     A. *A Partially Rebuilt Wall: vs. 6*
     B. *A Plot against God's People: vss. 7-8*
  II. The Rebuilding Continues: Nehemiah 4:15-23
     A. *The Frustration of Enemy Plans: vs. 15*
     B. *The Bearing of Arms while Rebuilding: vss. 16-18*
     C. *The Assurance of God's Presence: vss. 19-20*
     D. *The Maintaining of Vigilance: vss. 21-23*

Introduction

Refusing to Give Up

The third verse of "Amazing Grace" says: "Through many dangers, toils, and snares I have already come." That verse is particularly appropriate for the hostility that Nehemiah and his colleagues encountered. And it is likewise true when we are doing God's work.

If we're content to let things go on in a routine sort of way, nobody bothers us. But when we dare to throw down the challenge of a great opportunity for God's glory, opposition suddenly appears. For example, if a church wants to buy property for a new sanctuary, suddenly people start to protest about the traffic, noise, pollution, and so forth.

Nehemiah knew what John Newton wrote about in "Amazing Grace." In this week's Scripture passage, we discover that the nature and intensity of the opposition were quite different than before. Nehemiah was not looking for trouble. He wanted to do God's will—build the wall. But Nehemiah's enemies would not let his project go uncontested. Thankfully, he refused to give up.

Lesson Commentary

I. The Rebuilding Opposed: Nehemiah 4:6-8

Here is one way of outlining Nehemiah 3:
- *The reconstruction team for the northern section is listed (vss 1-5).*
- *The reconstruction team for the western section is listed (vss 6-12).*
- *The reconstruction team for the southern section is listed (vss 13-15).*
- *The reconstruction team for the southeastern section is listed (vss 15-27).*
- *The reconstruction team for the northeastern section is listed (vss 28-32).*

A. A Partially Rebuilt Wall: vs. 6
So we rebuilt the wall till all of it reached half its height, for the people worked with all their heart.

Nehemiah 3 contains a roster of the work crews that labored on the walls and gates of Jerusalem under Nehemiah's leadership. The locations of the work crews are noted, starting with the high priest in the northeast corner of Jerusalem next to the temple and moving counterclockwise around the city to the last group, made up of goldsmiths and merchants.

The 10 gates received the most attention from the builders. A city gate was not just a set of doors in a stone wall, but a small fortress protecting its entryway. Along the western wall, workers repaired long sections, suggesting it was not totally destroyed. The eastern wall required most of the manpower because of the steepness of the terrain and the devastation of the original wall. It's likely Nehemiah moved his wall farther up the slope and left the worst debris outside the new wall.

Nehemiah 4:1 picks up where 2:20 left off. Sanballat, the Samarian leader, assembled his army in his capital city to agitate Nehemiah and his workers. Along with all the petty bureaucrats, Tobiah joined Sanballat on the speakers' platform as a visiting dignitary. The intensity of Sanballat's anger at the Jews exposed the lie behind his ridicule. Under the veneer of his propaganda, Sanballat was worried about what Nehemiah was doing. This tenacious exile threatened his power over Judah.

In a rapid series of five questions, Sanballat made Nehemiah and the Jews seem ridiculous in the eyes of the army of Samaria (4:2). He implied the Jews were powerless to do anything. He scoffed at the idea that such a bunch could fortify a city. He suggested they were religious fanatics trusting God to raise the walls in response to sacrifices. He claimed they had barely strength for one day, so they had better work fast. He mocked the wall as a fortress made of charcoal briquettes. The native limestone, when subjected to fire, turned brittle and crumbly. In time Sanballat would find that the Jews had no trouble finding sound building stones.

The Samarian army must have responded favorably to Sanballat's taunts, because Tobiah followed them up with the kind of joke that assumed his audience was ready to hear it (vs. 3). If a stray fox jumped up on that ridiculous wall, the whole thing would totter and collapse from the shock. Imagine the clash of swords on shields and battle yells from the assembled army as they responded to the jibes and jeers of their leaders.

At this point in his memoir, Nehemiah inserted a prayer. He had no time to bother with the empty words of posturing opponents. He committed these hecklers to God, who alone has the right to take vengeance on those who oppose His purposes (see Deut. 32:35; Rom. 12:19). Nehemiah asked God to take note of the abuse hurled at His servants and to deflect that spite back on those who initiated it.

Nehemiah prayed that the enemies of God's people might know the horrors of the kind of captivity the Jews had survived. Nehemiah prayed that their offense might never be forgiven, because they had opposed the purposes of God to protect His people (Neh. 4:4-5).

Nehemiah prayed as Jeremiah and certain of the psalmists had when they asked God to bring calamity on their enemies (see Ps.

A papyrus document dated about 40 years after the time of Nehemiah identifies Sanballat as the governor of Samaria. The letter concerns Sanballat's adult sons, suggesting that he was elderly at the time. Other archaeological finds pertaining to Samaria in the time between the Old and New Testaments connect the name Sanballat (perhaps a grandson) with the movement that produced the Samaritan religion and temple.

Tobiah's ancestors may have been powerful landowners in the vicinity of Ammon with influence at Jerusalem as early as the eighth century B.C. Benjamin Mazar of the Hebrew University in Jerusalem has produced a genealogy containing nine generations of Tobiads. Their influence was felt as late as the second century B.C.

251

In the 1960s noted archaeologist Kathleen Kenyon excavated a short section of what she concluded was Nehemiah's wall along the eastern side of ancient Jerusalem. Her report described the wall as more than nine feet thick and roughly finished as though it had been thrown up in haste.

137:7-9; Jer. 18:23). Centuries later Jesus said, "You have heard that it was said, 'Love your neighbor and hate your enemy.' But I tell you: Love your enemies and pray for those who persecute you" (Matt. 5:43-44). While this may be an apparent point of tension between the Old and New Testaments, it's important to note that Nehemiah and these other Old Testament saints prayed not about their personal enemies but about the foes of God.

While Sanballat and Tobiah waged a war of words, the Jewish laborers from Jerusalem and the surrounding towns were mounting stone on stone all around the two-mile perimeter of Jerusalem. Before the opponents knew what was happening, the wall had reached half its planned height all the way around (Neh. 4:6). The wall went up quickly because the exilic community toiled hard. The last phrase of verse 6 could be rendered as "they had a heart to work."

B. A Plot against God's People: vss. 7-8

But when Sanballat, Tobiah, the Arabs, the Ammonites and the men of Ashdod heard that the repairs to Jerusalem's walls had gone ahead and that the gaps were being closed, they were very angry. They all plotted together to come and fight against Jerusalem and stir up trouble against it.

Jerusalem was surrounded by adversaries. The Ashdodites were west of the city. From the north the Jews had to contend with Sanballat and the Samaritans. The Ammonites, led by Tobiah, could come at them from the northeast, while Geshem and the Arabians could strike from the southeast.

Sanballat and Tobiah had to change their strategy since their saber-rattling mockery clearly had discouraged no one. First, they recruited more allies. Sanballat and his Samarians to the north, Tobiah and his Ammonites to the east, and Geshem and his Arabs to the south were joined in angry opposition to Jerusalem's walls by the Ashdodites, people of the strongest Phoenician city on the Mediterranean coast to the west of Judah (Neh. 4:7).

Second, the alliance that ringed Judah and Jerusalem started planning attacks on Jerusalem. Nehemiah heard rumors about the impending raids; perhaps this was something Sanballat and Tobiah wanted him to hear. Their biggest problem was that Nehemiah had Artaxerxes' permission to rebuild the walls of Jerusalem. An actual attack would risk bringing Persian wrath on their heads. A threatened attack might do what taunts had not—demoralize the Jews (vs. 8).

In response the Jews started praying. It's clear that Nehemiah organized the prayer vigil, because it was accompanied by around-the-clock sentries to detect any raiders. Even as they prayed and watched, the builders were feeling the cumulative effect of the pressure of the task and the opposition. They were exhausted from the toil and discouraged by the rubble they had to work in. In response the opponents engaged in psychological warfare by claiming they could use the cover of the rubble to send terrorists in among the builders to kill them before they knew the attackers were at hand (vss. 9-11).

When Sanballat and Tobiah sensed that rumors of war were affecting the morale of the builders, they planted more rumors in Jewish villages that bordered enemy lands. Soon Nehemiah had repeated intelligence reports that together indicated attacks from every point of the compass. In response Nehemiah stopped the construction and posted heavy guards inside Jerusalem wherever the wall was still low or where there were open spaces (vss. 12-13).

Nehemiah's "army" was his corps of builders, grouped by family units. Their armaments consisted of the weapons that were their personal property. After he mustered the troops, Nehemiah gave the officers and the fighters three-part battle instructions. First, don't fear the enemy. Second, keep your mind fixed on God's greatness. Third, fight for your families and your homes (vs. 14).

II. The Rebuilding Continues: Nehemiah 4:15-23

A. The Frustration of Enemy Plans: vs. 15
When our enemies heard that we were aware of their plot and that God had frustrated it, we all returned to the wall, each to his own work.

Nehemiah showed great organizational skill when he devised the initial scheme for portioning out the work on the walls and gates among the work crews. He revealed flexibility in the face of daunting opposition as he anticipated and headed off the various schemes of the encircling foes. There came a time, however, when he needed to put in place a plan that could handle a variety of threats. Otherwise, the walls and gates weren't going to get done.

After waiting an unspecified number of days for a surprise attack, Nehemiah somehow heard the news that Sanballat, Tobiah, Geshem, and the Ashdodites had given up on ambushing the workers. Nehemiah took no credit for the failure of the numerically

Nehemiah never prayed without working nor worked without praying. Like him, we should approach opposition with confidence in God. But we should not stop there. We also should use every ounce of our courage and ability to overcome that opposition in God's name.

It was through God's providence that the rebuilders discovered the enemies' plot. For example, the opposition soon realized that the Jews knew about their plans and that God had thwarted any attack. This motivated God's people once again to faithfully return to their work on the wall (Neh. 4:15).

overwhelming enemies. He knew only God could have frustrated their plans to attack (Neh. 4:15).

B. The Bearing of Arms while Rebuilding: vss. 16-18

From that day on, half of my men did the work, while the other half were equipped with spears, shields, bows and armor. The officers posted themselves behind all the people of Judah who were building the wall. Those who carried materials did their work with one hand and held a weapon in the other, and each of the builders wore his sword at his side as he worked. But the man who sounded the trumpet stayed with me.

Nehemiah's enthusiasm and confidence in the Lord kept the people working hard. Despite the mocking, their hearts were in the work. Furthermore, God used the readiness of His people to frustrate the enemy alliance.

After receiving the good news, Nehemiah encouraged everybody to get back to work. From this point on, until the walls and gates were finished, half the people worked while the other half served as armed sentries (Neh. 4:16). Officers ready to take charge in the event of a military emergency waited at intervals behind the workers and guards. The carriers who transported materials to the various work stations around the walls kept one hand free to carry their weapons. The builders wore swords on their belts (vss. 17-18).

A trumpeter stayed with Nehemiah at all times so that he could signal everyone to gather at any point on the walls where trouble developed. The trumpet was a ram's horn (*shofar*) and was the standard signal for assemblies or attacks (see Exod. 19:16-17; Josh. 6:20; Judg. 6:34).

C. The Assurance of God's Presence: vss. 19-20

Then I said to the nobles, the officials and the rest of the people, "The work is extensive and spread out, and we are widely separated from each other along the wall. Wherever you hear the sound of the trumpet, join us there. Our God will fight for us!"

The ram's horn would also remind the workers by its association with Sinai, Jericho, and Gideon that God would fight with them against their opponents.

Nehemiah realized that his workers (both officers and common people) were thinly spread out over the expanse of the wall. There also was a significant amount of repair work left to be done at various sections of the wall. To maximize his defensive capabilities, Nehemiah said that wherever his people heard the sound of the trumpet, they were to assemble immediately at that location. He encouraged the rebuilders not to be afraid to take decisive action, for the Lord would fight for them (Neh. 4:19-20).

D. The Maintaining of Vigilance: vss. 21-23

So we continued the work with half the men holding spears, from the first light of dawn till the stars came out. At that time I also said to the people, "Have every man and his helper stay inside Jerusalem at night, so they can serve us as guards by night and workmen by day." Neither I nor my brothers nor my men nor the guards with me took off our clothes; each had his weapon, even when he went for water.

Solomon wrote, "Unless the LORD builds the house, its builders labor in vain. Unless the LORD watches over the city, the watchmen stand guard in vain" (Ps. 127:1). Nehemiah understood this truth and experienced it during the time the people watched and worked from first light until after the sun went down (Neh. 4:21).

Nehemiah felt compelled by the gravity of the security issue to have workers from neighboring towns remain in Jerusalem at night rather than return to their homes (vs. 22). Jerusalem and its temple were the twin focal points of the faith and history of the Jews, but most of the exiles lived in other towns. The sparseness of Jerusalem's population would continue to be a problem for Nehemiah throughout his governorship (see 7:4; 11:1-2).

Nehemiah and his closest associates endured great hardships as they set the pace for all the workers on the wall project (4:23). When they could catch some sleep, they slept in their clothes. They kept their weapons with them at all times so they could be in the front lines if an attack materialized at any point.

We sometimes wrongly assume that God will automatically solve our problems without our involvement. But part of our maturity as believers comes from seeing how God works through our prayers and efforts. With power steering on a car, the power kicks in when we turn the wheel. In the Christian life, we find that God acts when we step forward in faith. While we may be waiting for God to do something, He may be waiting for us to take the first step.

It is clear that God's people took the threats of harm seriously. Despite the peril of danger, they remained devoted to their work. What a picture this is of dedication to God and loyalty to one another. Everyone worked together as a team to accomplish the task. Nehemiah reminded them of God's presence, power, provisions, and protection, and this strengthened them to continue.

Discussion Questions

1. What pressures did the news of the enemies' planned attack place upon the builders?
2. What do you think kept the Lord's people going despite the harassment they experienced?
3. Why was it necessary for Nehemiah to maintain a balance between prayer and action?
4. What does Nehemiah's thorough plan reveal about his leadership abilities?
5. What principles of spiritual warfare can we draw from Nehemiah's response to his enemies' threats?

Now Ask Yourself . . .

How do I usually pray for my enemies, especially when they opposed my work for God?
How can I achieve a better balance between prayer and work?
What insights from Nehemiah's praying can I put into practice in my own life?
What spiritual lessons did I learn the last time I experienced a serious hardship?
How does God use opposition from others to strengthen my trust in Him?

Illustrations

The Lord's work in any era advances against opposition. Jesus made this clear when He said hell itself would attack, but not prevail against His church (Matt. 16:18). Each generation needs wisdom to discern the enemy's strategy and to develop plans to resist.

Christian adults are often surprised by the opposition they encounter in striving to serve the Lord. They wrongly assume the path will be easy. But even though the sources of opposition may not be obvious when they begin their work, the opposition will appear. They may be as subtle as discouragement or as blatant as outward attempts to interfere with a believer's service for the Savior.

Sometimes the attacks are obviously physical, such as what Nehemiah and his people faced.

Other times the attacks are psychological and emotional. We have to be prepared for both. If the enemy cannot sidetrack us with suffering or persecution, for example, we may find ourselves being subverted by sinful attachments. The usual avenues of such attacks are immorality, money, and power.

Therefore, to be strong for God we need wisdom, courage, and faith. We need the kind of wise instructions Nehemiah gave. We need leaders who will call us to battle and show us how to protect ourselves. They will call us to prayer, obedience, and disciplined study of God's Word. Our greatest need in the face of hostility is to know how to put on and use the complete armor of God (Eph. 6:10-18).

All Fear Is Gone

DEVOTIONAL READING

John 20:11-18

DAILY BIBLE READINGS

Monday April 10
Mark 15:1-15
Jesus Goes Before Pilate

Tuesday April 11
Mark 15:16-20
The Soldiers Mock Jesus

Wednesday April 12
Mark 15:21-32
Many People Ridicule
Jesus

Thursday April 13
Mark 15:33-41
Jesus Dies on the Cross

Friday April 14
Mark 15:42-47
Jesus' Body Is Placed in
the Tomb

Saturday April 15
Mark 16:1-8
The Stone Is Rolled Away!

Sunday April 16
Mark 16:9-20
Jesus Appears to the
Eleven

Scripture

Background Scripture: *Mark 15–16*
Scripture Lesson: *Mark 15:21-24, 34-37; 16:1-8*
Key Verse: *"Don't be alarmed," he said. "You are looking for Jesus the Nazarene, who was crucified. He has risen! He is not here. See the place where they laid him."* *Mark 16:6.*

Lesson Aim

Jesus conquered death and its fears.

Lesson Setting

Time: A.D. 30
Place: Jerusalem

Lesson Outline

All Fear Is Gone

   I. Jesus' Crucifixion: Mark 15:21-24
      A. *Conscripting Simon: vs. 21*
      B. *Nailing Jesus to a Cross: vss. 22-24*
  II. Jesus' Death: Mark 15:34-37
      A. *Jesus' Cry of Anguish: vs. 34*
      B. *Confused Onlookers: vss. 35-36*
      C. *Jesus' Death: vs. 37*
 III. Jesus' Resurrection: Mark 16:1-8
      A. *The Deliberations of the Women: vss. 1-3*
      B. *The Announcement of the Angel: vss. 4-7*
      C. *The Reaction of the Women: vs. 8*

Introduction

Triumph over Adversity

The first time a death in the family confronts us, we realize as never before its terrible finality. This is the end. Until then, we think we are immortal. We fail to grasp the fact of our mortality. But, as the apostle Paul revealed, the mortal must be clothed with immortality (1 Cor. 15:53).

The account of Christ's death and resurrection reminds us that "death has been swallowed up in victory" (vs. 54). Jesus experienced death for all of us, so that our sins might be forgiven. He was raised for our justification. His resurrection proves His victory over sin and death.

Death is final only in the sense that it terminates our mortality. It is not the end, but the beginning. Christ's empty tomb guarantees that all who believe shall be saved and enjoy eternal life with the Father in heaven.

Lesson Commentary

I. Jesus' Crucifixion: Mark 15:21-24

A. Conscripting Simon: vs. 21

A certain man from Cyrene, Simon, the father of Alexander and Rufus, was passing by on his way in from the country, and they forced him to carry the cross.

According to Mark 15:15, part of Jesus' maltreatment included being flogged. The flog was a whip made of leather strips embedded with chips of bone or metal. When captives were beaten across the back with a flog, their flesh would be left in shreds. Sometimes even their bones or internal organs would be exposed. Many died from the horrible punishment.

After Jesus' flogging, the soldiers who were responsible for His execution took charge of Him. These men were non-Jewish residents of Palestine. They took Jesus into their headquarters and called out the entire battalion (Mark 15:16). Evidently the soldiers were aware of the charge against Jesus. They draped over Him a purple cloak and placed on His head a crown of thorns, thus creating for Him mock royal clothing (vs. 17). Then, after treating Jesus in a degrading manner, the soldiers led Him away to the place of crucifixion (vss. 18-20).

Crucifixion as a means of torture and execution was invented in the East and adopted by the Romans, who used it for slaves and lower class persons. It was one of the most cruel and dehumanizing methods of punishment ever contrived. Many victims of crucifixion lingered for two or three days before dying of exhaus-

258

tion, exposure, and their wounds. A victim of Roman crucifixion typically had to carry the crossbeam of his cross to the place of execution. Jesus, however, was weak because of flogging and the strain He had been under during the preceding days. He evidently made it as far as a gate of the city (vs. 21).

The Roman government authorized its soldiers to commandeer horses and people whenever needed. The soldiers escorting Jesus through the streets of Jerusalem made use of this authority when He faltered under the heavy load of the cross. There is uncertainty as to whether Jesus was carrying the whole cross or just the crossbeam. Some beams could have weighed as much as 40 pounds, which would have been heavy enough to make someone in Jesus' condition stagger. Thus the Roman soldiers ordered a man named Simon to carry the cross the rest of the way.

Simon was from Cyrene, a city in what is now Libya in North Africa. At the time of Jesus, a large Jewish population dwelt in Cyrene. Simon was possibly an ethnic Jew who had come to Jerusalem to celebrate the Passover, or he might have been a native African who had converted to Judaism. The Gospel of Mark makes reference to the sons of Simon as though they were known to the early church. This has led some to think that Simon eventually became a believer after witnessing the crucifixion of Christ.

Crucifixion was the form of execution adopted by the Romans for rebels and lesser criminals. First, the executioners used iron nails to pin the convict's wrists to the horizontal beam of the cross. Then they lifted this beam and attached it to another beam placed upright in the ground. Next, they nailed the convict's feet or ankles together to the vertical beam, with his knees bent to one side. Above his head they erected a sign stating the crime for which he was being executed.

B. Nailing Jesus to a Cross: vss. 22-24

They brought Jesus to the place called Golgotha (which means The Place of the Skull). Then they offered him wine mixed with myrrh, but he did not take it. And they crucified him. Dividing up his clothes, they cast lots to see what each would get.

The procession eventually left the confines of the city and arrived at a location "called Golgotha" (Mark 15:22). The name of the spot means "The Place of the Skull," and may have been given because the location was a skull-shaped mound or because it was used for executions.

Before crucifying Jesus, the soldiers offered Him "wine mixed with myrrh" (vs. 23). Myrrh was a fragrant gum derived from trees that grew in Arabia. Once Jesus tasted it, however, He refused to drink it, possibly because He wanted to be fully conscious until His death (Ps. 69:21). It may be that the soldiers offered this drink because it would help to deaden Jesus' senses to the pain He was about to experience; or giving Him a foul-tasting drink may have been just another cruel joke.

In any case, the soldiers next crucified Jesus (Mark 15:24). At the execution site, the soldiers attached the crossbeam perpendicularly to a longer beam (the stake) at or near its top while it was lying on the ground. Then they affixed Jesus' hands and feet to it by means of nails. Above His head they erected a sign stating the crime for which He was being executed (vs. 26). Finally, the soldiers lifted and dropped the cross into a hole.

As mentioned earlier, victims sometimes lasted for two or three days, finally succumbing to death due to poor blood circulation and heart failure. If the executioners wanted to make the victim last longer, they would have first outfitted the cross with a block of wood as a seat or a footrest, which would give the victim support and improve circulation. If the executioners wanted to shorten the victim's life, they would break his legs with a club to remove his ability to support himself with his legs.

On the cross Jesus was naked or at most wore a loincloth. The soldiers gambled to see which of them would keep Jesus' clothes (Luke 23:34; John 19:23-24). The clothing of the person crucified was traditionally a spoil for those who crucified him. In this case, the soldiers unwittingly fulfilled Psalm 22:18.

II. Jesus' Death: Mark 15:34-37

A. Jesus' Cry of Anguish: vs. 34

And at the ninth hour Jesus cried out in a loud voice, "Eloi, Eloi, lama sabachthani?"—which means, "My God, my God, why have you forsaken me?"

It was nine o'clock in the morning when the crucifixion took place (Mark 15:25). Mark records three negative reactions at Jesus' crucifixion. The first came from passersby, who mocked Him with His own prophecies of resurrection (vss. 29-30). The second negative reaction came from the religious leaders. They said nothing directly to Jesus, but they exchanged among themselves smug assurances that they had gotten the best of Him (vss. 31-32). The third instance of ridicule came from those who were crucified with Him (vss. 27, 32). These men at first insulted Jesus, though later on one of them had a change of heart (Luke 23:40-43).

Jesus' crucifixion is presented in all four Gospels with brevity and reserve and without sappiness. The predominant theme centers on the mockery of the Savior rather than on His physical suffering.

At noon, when the sun was at its highest, a mysterious darkness fell over the area for three hours (Mark 15:33). Much like the plague of darkness that came before the first Passover (Exod. 10:21-23), this darkness symbolized God's curse. Near the end of the period of darkness, Jesus cried out (Mark 15:34). He was experiencing the agony of separation from the Father. This was the torment He had anticipated in Gethsemane (14:32-36). Jesus' cry, which the Gospel of Mark recorded in its original Aramaic, quoted Psalm 22:1. This is a prophetic psalm that was fulfilled in many ways during that day.

B. Confused Onlookers: vss. 35-36

When some of those standing near heard this, they said, "Listen, he's calling Elijah." One man ran, filled a sponge with wine vinegar, put it on a stick, and offered it to Jesus to drink. "Now leave him alone. Let's see if Elijah comes to take him down," he said.

Because Jesus used the word "Eloi" (Mark 15:34), some of those who heard His words imagined He was calling Elijah to rescue Him from His deplorable situation (vs. 35). According to Jewish tradition, Elijah would one day return and deliver the upright from their suffering.

One of the bystanders immediately ran, obtained a sponge, and soaked it with wine vinegar, a popular beverage among infantry soldiers and poorer people in Palestine. Placing the sponge on a reed (the stalk of a hyssop plant), the bystander extended it to Jesus so that He might drink from it. However, others standing around told the one with the sponge to leave Jesus alone. They superstitiously thought that Elijah might indeed come to rescue the Savior (vs. 36).

C. Jesus' Death: vs. 37

With a loud cry, Jesus breathed his last.

After Jesus took a drink of the wine vinegar, the end finally came as He cried out once and died (Mark 15:37). From John 19:30 it would appear that what Jesus cried out was "It is finished"—a declaration of victory. Joseph of Arimathea, a member of the Sanhedrin, received permission to remove Jesus' lifeless body from the cross for burial. Joseph wrapped the body in linen and placed it in a rock-hewn tomb (Mark 15:42-47).

III. Jesus' Resurrection: Mark 16:1-8

A. The Deliberations of the Women: vss. 1-3

When the Sabbath was over, Mary Magdalene, Mary the mother of James, and Salome bought spices so that they might go to anoint

Despite the fact that Jesus led a life totally free from sin (see 1 Pet. 2:22), He was nonetheless made to be sin on people's behalf (2 Cor. 5:21). Of course, this does not mean that He became a sinner. But as an offering for human sins, He became the object of the Father's wrath and judgment for those sins. Jesus took the place of sinners on the cross as a substitute, bearing the punishment that they deserved. He willingly did this not only so that believers could have our sins forgiven, but also so that we could become the righteousness of God.

In His death, Christ gave us a perfect example of the type of dedication God desires of us; demonstrated the great extent of God's love; underscored the seriousness of sin and the severity of God's righteousness; liberated us from the power of sin and death; and rendered satisfaction to the Father for our sins.

Our Lord's resurrection had far-reaching consequences. With respect to His identity, it was His greatest confirming sign, for it bore witness to His messiahship (John 2:18-22). With reference to Jesus' followers, His resurrection made their salvation a reality (1 Cor. 15:14, 17). And concerning Jesus' enemies, His resurrection broke Satan's power over death (Heb. 2:14). Jesus' rising from the dead also ensured that the Lord would one day resurrect and judge His enemies (Acts 17:31).

Jesus' body. Very early on the first day of the week, just after sunrise, they were on their way to the tomb and they asked each other, "Who will roll the stone away from the entrance of the tomb?"

While Mark 15 records Jesus' sacrifice, chapter 16 shows God's acceptance of that sacrifice. The grand confirming act of the life and death of Jesus is His resurrection from the dead. The Savior was buried late on Friday afternoon. The Sabbath ended at sundown on Saturday. Jesus' followers were free to go to His tomb now, but of course they did not want to do so at night.

Thus, at first light on Sunday, three prominent women from Jesus' earthly ministry—Mary Magdalene, Salome, and Mary the mother of James—went to the burial site (vss. 1-2). Along the way the women had been discussing who would roll the stone away from the entrance to the tomb so that they could anoint Jesus' body (vs. 3). This was a customary practice to mask the odor brought on by decay. It was also an act of devotion.

According to Matthew 28:2, at some point before the women's arrival, an earthquake had occurred. An angel of the Lord had descended from heaven, rolled back the stone from the entrance, and sat upon it. The angel did not remove the stone to enable Jesus to leave the tomb; rather, the angel did it to permit others to enter the sepulcher and see for themselves that Jesus' body was gone.

B. The Announcement of the Angel: vss. 4-7

But when they looked up, they saw that the stone, which was very large, had been rolled away. As they entered the tomb, they saw a young man dressed in a white robe sitting on the right side, and they were alarmed. "Don't be alarmed," he said. "You are looking for Jesus the Nazarene, who was crucified. He has risen! He is not here. See the place where they laid him. But go, tell his disciples and Peter, 'He is going ahead of you into Galilee. There you will see him, just as he told you.' "

When the women arrived at the tomb, they saw the stone had already been rolled aside (Mark 16:4). Upon entering the tomb, the women saw an angel, whom verse 5 says was "a young man dressed in a white robe." It's understandable that the women would have been startled at the sight of this heavenly visitor and also at the realization that the body of their Savior was gone.

The angel had four facts he wanted the women to know. First, both he and the women were focused on the same person, "Jesus the Nazarene" (vs. 6). Second, Jesus had been crucified, and thus really had been dead. Third, He had risen and therefore was no longer dead. Fourth, Jesus was not at the tomb, for He had broken the grip of the grave.

The angel directed the women to relay a message to Jesus' disciples, including Peter (vs. 7). The celestial being wanted them to know about Jesus' resurrection and that He would be meeting them in Galilee, in accordance with His previous statement (14:28). The mention of Peter in 16:7 was a gesture of reassurance and forgiveness extended toward the man who had denied knowing the Lord (14:66-72). Peter probably felt as though he no longer could have a place among the other disciples. From this message he would understand that he was forgiven and accepted again.

The Resurrection is the central fact of human history. The church has persisted through the centuries despite persecution because it is built on the reality of Jesus rising from the dead. His resurrection provides us with proof that He is indeed who He claimed to be—the Son of God, the Savior, and our returning King.

C. The Reaction of the Women: vs. 8

Trembling and bewildered, the women went out and fled from the tomb. They said nothing to anyone, because they were afraid.

The women, being overcome by fear, ran away and initially did not tell anyone what had happened (Mark 16:8). Eventually, however, both they and the rest of Jesus' disciples were convinced that He truly had risen from the dead. Fear gave way to faith as they proclaimed the Gospel "into all the world" (vs. 15).

By comparing early manuscripts, most New Testament scholars have concluded that Mark 16:8 is the last verse in the second Synoptic Gospel that has survived. Perhaps the Gospel originally had another ending that has been lost. Or perhaps Mark intended for his Gospel to end abruptly on the note of surprise and amazement that greeted the fact of Jesus' resurrection. After all, the Resurrection not only ends one account but begins another. The history of the church, which includes us, proceeds directly from the victory over death won by Jesus Christ, the Son of God.

Discussion Questions

1. How detailed is Mark's Gospel concerning Jesus' crucifixion?
2. What was the significance of Jesus' words recorded in Mark 15:34?
3. What had the women planned to do when they reached the burial site of Jesus?
4. Why do you think the women were alarmed at the angel's announcement?
5. What do you consider the most convincing proof that Jesus rose from the dead?

Now Ask Yourself . . .

If tomorrow I had to choose between losing my life and denying my Lord, which would I choose—really?

What would best describe my reaction to Jesus' death?

When was the last time I thanked Jesus for dying for me?

How should I live my life differently now that I have studied Mark's record of Jesus' death and resurrection?

Is there some way in which I need to say *no* to my "crowd" in order to remain faithful to Jesus?

Illustrations

People today find it no easier to believe in Jesus' resurrection than did the disciples when they first heard the news. In our experience, people who are dead do not come back to life. So perhaps we should not be surprised when our non-Christian friends view the Resurrection message as interesting but not at all convincing.

As Christians we need to recognize the importance of affirming that Jesus' resurrection actually took place. But how do we do it? We do it by cultivating a personal relationship with the risen Lord in our daily life. When we pursue a personal relationship with our Savior, we show that we truly believe He is alive, having been raised from the dead.

Although we cannot see, hear, or touch Jesus physically now, we can draw near to Him spiritually and devotionally. Furthermore, those who want to know Christ intimately are wise to set aside a definite time each day to spend concentrating upon the risen Lord and His Word.

For some believers, Bible reading and meditation come easier. For other believers, prayer and silence in the Lord's presence come easier. Whatever we decide to do, we need to begin to do it, for when we do, we enlarge the scope and richness of our time with the risen Lord.

What naturally results from this is a desire on our part to express our faith, especially by sharing the Gospel message with others. In fact, the Gospel will burn in our hearts, and sharing the good news about Jesus' resurrection will not be a burdensome obligation but a joyful privilege to us. In whatever way we do it, we show our trust and hope in the resurrected Lord.

Be Confident in the Lord

DEVOTIONAL READING

Isaiah 49:13-18

DAILY BIBLE READINGS

Monday April 17
Psalm 71:1-8
Always Rely on God

Tuesday April 18
Proverbs 3:19-26
The Lord Will Be Your
Confidence

Wednesday April 19
Nehemiah 6:1-9
Many Scheme to Harm
Nehemiah

Thursday April 20
Nehemiah 6:10-14
Nehemiah Prays for
Strength

Friday April 21
Nehemiah 6:15-19
The Wall Is Finally
Completed

Saturday April 22
2 Corinthians 3:1-6
Confidence Comes from
Christ

Sunday April 23
Philippians 3:1-11
Confidence Is Not in the
Flesh

Scripture

Background Scripture: *Nehemiah 6*
Scripture Lesson: *Nehemiah 6:1-9, 15-16*
Key Verse: *When all our enemies heard about this, all the surrounding nations were afraid and lost their self-confidence, because they realized that this work had been done with the help of our God. Nehemiah 6:16.*

Lesson Aim

Self-confidence comes from relying on God.

Lesson Setting

Time: 445 B.C.
Place: Jerusalem

Lesson Outline

Be Confident in the Lord
  I. Continued Opposition to Rebuilding:
     Nehemiah 6:1-9
    A. *The Status Report: vs. 1*
    B. *The Refusal to Meet: vss. 2-4*
    C. *The Open Letter: vss. 5-7*
    D. *The Firm Resolve of Nehemiah: vss. 8-9*
  II. News of the Wall's Completion:
     Nehemiah 6:15-16

Introduction

Persevering with Faith

Jonathan took the leadership of a Christian education ministry that was floundering. With boldness, wisdom, and faith he energized the work and took it to new levels of effectiveness. Then Lou Gehrig's disease struck him. Rather than quit and spend his time complaining, Jonathan attacked his work with renewed vigor. His cheerfulness and courage inspired many.

Jonathan gave an inspiring address to the congregation, many of whom were moved to tears. He did not wallow in self-pity but rather challenged his fellow Christians to persevere in faith, regardless of what illnesses or other setbacks might come their way.

Jonathan knew God so deeply that he accepted his illness with graciousness. After several years, he succumbed to the ravages of the disease, but he left a powerful mark on his church, his family, and his ministry.

Lesson Commentary

I. Continued Opposition to Rebuilding: Nehemiah 6:1-9

A. The Status Report: vs. 1

When word came to Sanballat, Tobiah, Geshem the Arab and the rest of our enemies that I had rebuilt the wall and not a gap was left in it—though up to that time I had not set the doors in the gates.

Nehemiah 5 is a digression from the main theme of chapters 1:1—7:3. We learn that the returnees had to deal with internal problems as well as external opposition. The presence of discouragement among the Jewish settlers became despair when an economic crisis came to a head during the rebuilding of the wall. The problem was all the more serious because some Jews were exploiting other Jews (5:1).

Nehemiah and the Jewish settlers in Judah were up against plenty of obstacles. Ridicule by neighbors, an ongoing threat of attack, and the enormity of the wall-rebuilding task itself worked varying degrees of discouragement upon the Jews.

Large families, poor growing seasons, and heavy Persian taxes produced harsh economic circumstances for the Jews of Judah. Those settlers without land were in need of food, but lacked the money necessary to purchase food at the inflated prices. Those who owned land that had once fed others were forced to mortgage their property to feed themselves. Still others had borrowed money at excessive interest rates to pay the Persian taxes (vss. 2-4).

Following the custom in times of economic crisis, the Jews in this last group had offered their children as collateral against the loans and interest, their children could be—and had been—sold into slavery. Oddly enough, these Jews had been together as families while in exile; but now back in their homeland, they were forced apart. These people had lost not only their property but also their families (vs. 5).

Nehemiah was upset when he heard the complaints of his peers. He told the guilty Jewish aristocrats they were charging their own people too much interest. It was not necessarily wrong for them to make loans, but their excessive rates were leading to serious abuses of their fellow Jews. After rebuking the nobles and rulers, Nehemiah brought the lenders and the borrowers together in one place. It was not desirable to interrupt the wall reconstruction, but Nehemiah felt the economic crisis warranted it (vss. 6-7).

At this assembly Nehemiah described the offense of the lenders. They had forced Jewish debtors and their families into slavery. This offense was all the more glaring in contrast with the efforts of some Jews had been making to buy back Jewish slaves from Gentile owners. It might be the case, said Nehemiah, that one Jew would sell another Jew to a Gentile, only to have the enslaved Jew bought back from the Gentile by other Jews. This was ludicrous and evil. A Jew should never have been sold into slavery in the first place (vs. 8).

When Nehemiah confronted the lenders with their offenses, they had nothing to say in their defense. They were aware that their actions within the community had made all Jews—including themselves—more vulnerable to an outside attack. That vulnerability put the Jews and their rebuilding project at great risk.

Nehemiah gave one more reason why the financial practices of the Jewish aristocrats were wrong. By disobeying God's will in these matters, they were opening up the nation to sneering by their enemies. This was an especially serious danger while they were in the midst of reconstructing the city wall (vs. 9).

Nehemiah said that he and those in his circle had made loans of money and grain; but they did not charge excessive interest. He commanded the offenders to stop their wrongful practices. He also told them to restore confiscated property and the interest that had been paid on loans. The lenders, agreed, despite the financial loss this would entail. Nehemiah had them vow publicly that they

In Nehemiah's time, famine was particularly discouraging because it was often thought to be a sign of God's judgment. Also, frustration levels were rising as the workers suffered under what they suspected to be God's judgment—even as many were making every effort to be obedient to Him.

The king's tribute, or tax, was no light matter either. Persia collected taxes in silver and gold coins, but little of the coinage circulated back to the economies of the provinces. Most of it was melted into bullion. A depressed economy resulted as more and more coinage was taken out of circulation, and the people became further impoverished.

Those who could not pay the king's tax were forced to sell or forfeit their land. In turn, Persia usually removed requisitioned land from agricultural production, cutting down on the food supply in the provinces and inflating the price of food.

The collective purpose of the Jewish people—to restore Jerusalem and rebuild the wall—was nearly crushed by greed; but when the Jewish settlers turned away from selfishness and considered the needs of others, God's task for them went forward.

would make things right (vss. 10-12).

Nehemiah shook out the folds of his robe to signify that God would completely eliminate everything owned by those who violated their oath. The whole group affirmed their pledge, praised the Lord, and did what they had promised. During Nehemiah's first term as governor (445–443 B.C.), he exercised financial restraint (in contrast to former governors). Out of reverence for God, he did not tax his people to support his administration or entertain his guests. Instead of acquiring land for personal benefit, he channeled his energies into rebuilding the wall. Nehemiah prayed that God would remember his kindness (vss. 13-19).

The phrase "word came to Sanballat" (6:1) returns us to the main narrative of chapters 1:1—7:3. As the wall neared completion, external opposition from the antagonists of the Jews—Sanballat, Tobiah, and Geshem the Arab (among others)—reached a head. They made one last attempt to derail Nehemiah's rebuilding project. They learned that Nehemiah had rebuilt the wall and closed the breaches in it, though he had not yet set the doors on the gates (6:1). As we will see, Nehemiah remained dedicated to his God-given task.

B. The Refusal to Meet: vss. 2-4

Sanballat and Geshem sent me this message: "Come, let us meet together in one of the villages on the plain of Ono." But they were scheming to harm me; so I sent messengers to them with this reply: "I am carrying on a great project and cannot go down. Why should the work stop while I leave it and go down to you?" Four times they sent me the same message, and each time I gave them the same answer.

Nehemiah's enemies decided to ask if the governor would meet with them in one of the villages in the plain of Ono. (This was in the extreme northwest corner of the Judean territory.) Knowing the antagonists were planning to harm him, Nehemiah said he could not come, for he was doing a great work for God. This question and response happened four times (Neh. 6:1-4).

C. The Open Letter: vss. 5-7

Then, the fifth time, Sanballat sent his aide to me with the same message, and in his hand was an unsealed letter in which was written: "It is reported among the nations—and Geshem says it is true—that you and the Jews are plotting to revolt, and therefore you are building the wall. Moreover, according to these reports you are about to become their king and have even appointed prophets to make this proclamation about you in Jerusalem: 'There is a king in Judah!' Now this report will get back to the king; so come, let us confer together."

The fifth time Sanballat sent his servant to Nehemiah with an unsealed letter (Neh. 6:5). The official seal usually certified that the letter's contents had not been tampered with. An open letter, however, could be read by anyone without any threat of breaking that seal.

The document alleged that the Jews were planning to rebel against the king of Persia and this was the reason Nehemiah was rebuilding the wall of Jerusalem. Also, it was purported that the governor wanted to be the next Jewish king (vs. 6).

Supposedly Nehemiah had appointed prophets to make divinely inspired declarations in Jerusalem concerning him. The gist of these announcements was that Nehemiah would be Judah's new monarch (vs. 7).

Nehemiah's enemies stressed that these reports of subversive activity would get back to the king of Persia. Judah's governor, thus, was enjoined to meet with his accusers and talk the matter over with them.

There are times when others will challenge our motives and goals for ministry. It is beneficial for us to periodically take stock of our goals, methods, and resources; but we should not be so unsure of our purpose that we completely rethink our directives every time we are challenged. There is a time for consideration, and then there is a time to work to completion.

D.   The Firm Resolve of Nehemiah: vss. 8-9

I sent him this reply: "Nothing like what you are saying is happening; you are just making it up out of your head." They were all trying to frighten us, thinking, "Their hands will get too weak for the work, and it will not be completed." [But I prayed,] "Now strengthen my hands."

Sanballat was using a variety of accusations as a pretext for meeting. Nehemiah, however, said the charges were unfounded (Neh. 6:8). He realized his enemies were trying to frighten and demoralize the Jews (vs. 9). If the Jews could become paralyzed with fear, the rebuilding efforts would be discontinued. The governor prayed that God would make His people strong.

The Bible does not explain why Nehemiah so easily dismissed the accusations of his opponents and apparently took no steps to prevent their letters from reaching the king. However, it seems plausible that Nehemiah was relying on his years of trustworthy

One option for Nehemiah and the Jews was to give up and scatter in fear. But fleeing would contradict Nehemiah's trust in God and would violate the sanctity of the temple.

The Book of Nehemiah records Nehemiah's determination to rebuild the walls of Jerusalem and renew the commitment of its people to the Lord. This brisk, forceful book emphasizes the importance of faithfulness to God and perseverance in trials.

Nehemiah refused to give up. He motivated God's people to complete the important task of rebuilding the wall.

service as the king's cupbearer. He might have known that he had the full confidence of Artaxerxes, who would quickly see through the deception of anyone who accused Nehemiah of sedition. The governor of Judah also knew the process by which letters such as those Sanballat had written would be read and evaluated.

In short, Nehemiah had a clear conscience and an impeccable reputation. Thus, no amount of false accusations could cause him to lose heart. He knew that none of it would stick.

II. News of the Wall's Completion: Nehemiah 6:15-16

So the wall was completed on the twenty-fifth of Elul, in fifty-two days. When all our enemies heard about this, all the surrounding nations were afraid and lost their self-confidence, because they realized that this work had been done with the help of our God.

A supposed friend of Nehemiah named Shemaiah, who was confined to his home, invited the governor to retreat with him to the protective shelter of the temple. He informed Nehemiah that his enemies were plotting to murder him at night. The governor, however, did not think it was wise for him to go. He knew that his enemies had paid Shemaiah to trick him (Neh. 6:10-11).

All of the commotion reported in Nehemiah 4 through 6 occurred in the 52 days from the second of the month of Ab to the twenty-fifth of the month of Elul—approximately August 11 to October 2, 445 B.C. (vs. 15). Everyone in the coalition opposed to the construction of the walls were informed instantly by their intelligence network. They were awed because such an outcome was humanly impossible. In their hearts they knew the God of Israel had been at work. Tinges of terror colored their thoughts of the future, and they doubted whether good things lay ahead for them (vs. 16).

Interestingly, the account of the completion of Jerusalem's walls with the aid of God is not followed with a story about a celebration. Circumstances were still too insecure to justify a party. Tobiah operated a fifth column inside the Jewish community through his network of business associates and relatives. He was married to a daughter of one of the original families of the exiles and his son was married to a daughter of one of the most vigorous wall builders. Tobiah also had influence with the high priest (vss.

17-18, see Ezra 2:5; Neh. 3:4, 30; 13:4).

Since Tobiah had been unable to prevent the construction of the walls, he set out to exploit his base of influence within those walls. All his contacts repeatedly praised Tobiah to Nehemiah and reported Nehemiah's reactions back to him (6:19). Since Nehemiah's opinion of Tobiah never improved on the basis of these recommendations, Tobiah kept up a steady barrage of correspondence to wear down Nehemiah and weasel his way into the Jerusalem power structure.

All of this kept Nehemiah motivated to tend to the finishing details of the defenses of Jerusalem. He oversaw the mounting of the massive wooden doors in the 10 gate-fortresses of the city (7:1). He updated the organization of the temple gatekeepers, singers, and Levites and apparently expanded the gatekeepers' duties to include the city gates. Hanani, who started this whole sequence of events by visiting his brother in Persia, got the nod from Nehemiah to oversee the defenses of the whole city (vs. 2). He shared this responsibility with Hananiah, who commanded the troops garrisoned at the citadel just north of the temple courtyard. Integrity, rather than family connections or position, won these two their jobs.

Nehemiah was not convinced that the danger of attack from their many enemies was past. He directed Hanani and Hananiah to be cautious about opening the new city gates (vs. 3). Gatekeepers were not to open the gates at first light. They were to wait until the full light of morning showed the surrounding countryside was free of potential attackers. In the evening the gates were to be closed and barred before the fading light of dusk could conceal a foe. Finally, civilians still had to serve regularly as a defensive militia until the crisis passed.

Nehemiah knew that the final step to defending Jerusalem involved bolstering the population of the city to the point that it did not have to rely on the men from neighboring towns. The city had to be able to defend itself. To research how to get people to move into Jerusalem, Nehemiah familiarized himself with the record of the original party of exiles who accompanied the first wave of exiles from Babylon to Jerusalem nearly a century earlier (compare Neh. 7:6-73a with Ezra 2:1-70). Nehemiah 7:70-72 adds some detail to Ezra's account concerning the temple treasures brought back by the exiles.

Jerusalem had a lot of space compared with the small number of residents living in it. At this point the houses had not been rebuilt. Nehemiah had the leaders, officials, and common people assemble by families for registration. He found the genealogical record pertaining to those who first returned from captivity in Mesopotamia (Neh. 7:4-5). This list is reproduced in verses 6-73.

271

Discussion Questions

1. Who were the various enemies of the Jewish people mentioned in Nehemiah 6:1?
2. Why did these people oppose the rebuilding of Jerusalem's wall?
3. How did Nehemiah respond to the underhanded tactics of his antagonists?
4. What was the reason God's people were able to successfully complete their task?
5. Why is it important for us to rely on God when we are doing His work?

Now Ask Yourself . . .

When others learn about my service for the Lord, what do they typically hear?

When I face opposition from others for doing God's work, do I respond with courage or cowardice?

When others make repeated attempts to distract me from living for God, am I easily swayed or do I remain resolute in my commitment?

When the Lord does a good work in my life, do I take the credit or do I give Him the credit?

What are some noteworthy things God has done through me that He wants me to share with others?

Illustrations

The issues facing us in life are often complex. For instance, how should we respond to those in need? Also, what should we do when others challenge our motives and goals for ministry?

This week's lesson is instructive in both areas. God wants us to respond to those in need with compassion and understanding as well as our material assistance. The Lord also wants us to remain dedicated to our God-given tasks and bring them to completion despite the opposition of others.

Moreover, as we have seen from this week's lesson, Nehemiah's complete reliance on God became the underlying basis for the Jews being able to finish rebuilding the wall despite opposition. Similarly, regardless of the pressures we face, God can enable us to carry out His will.

The Lord will often work through our level-headed thinking and clear understanding of Scripture to discern what is morally proper and improper. As we turn to God in faith and commune with Him in prayer, He will give us great success in ministry.

Admittedly, it's easy for us to allow events and problems to distract us from the core issues of life. Just as Nehemiah had to put up with the ongoing distractions of his enemies' messages, we also have to stay on target in life and not allow ungodly influences to derail us. If we know where we are going, we have a better likelihood of getting there.

Hearing God Again

DEVOTIONAL READING

Psalm 119:33-40

DAILY BIBLE READINGS

Monday April 24
  James 5:13-20
  *Confess Your Sins to Each
  Other*

Tuesday April 25
  Nehemiah 7:73—8:6
  Ezra Reads the Law

Wednesday April 26
  Nehemiah 8:7-11
  *Nehemiah Tells the People
  to Rejoice*

Thursday April 27
  Nehemiah 8:12-18
  The Celebration Continues

Friday April 28
  Nehemiah 9:1-6
  *The Israelites Confess
  Their Sins*

Saturday April 29
  Luke 15:11-20
  *A Young Man Returns to
  His Father*

Sunday April 30
  Luke 15:21-32
  *A Homecoming
  Celebration*

Scripture

Background Scripture: *Nehemiah 8—9*
Scripture Lesson: *Nehemiah 8:13—9:3*
Key Verse: *They stood where they were and read from the Book of the Law of the* LORD *their God for a quarter of the day, and spent another quarter in confession and in worshiping the* LORD *their God. Nehemiah 9:3.*

Lesson Aim

Recommitment to God's Word produces confession and celebration.

Lesson Setting

Time: 445 B.C.
Place: Jerusalem

Lesson Outline

Hearing God Again

I. The Feast of Booths: Nehemiah 8:13-18
    A. *The Feast of Booths Commanded: vss. 13-15*
    B. *The Feast of Booths Observed: vss. 16-18*
II. The Confession of Sin: Nehemiah 9:1-3
    A. *Gathering Together: vs. 1*
    B. *Confessing and Worshiping: vss. 2-3*

Introduction

Responding to God's Law

We all accept the axiom that ignorance is no excuse when we break the law. Yet we tend to tolerate ignorance of God's decrees and wonder why our lives and our churches seem to lack spiritual authority and power.

A researcher in church growth has noted that preaching is pretty much useless unless people first confess their sins. But why should they confess when they have no standard by which to measure their behavior?

The stipulations in God's Word are that standard. Unless we know those decrees and respect them, there's not much likelihood for confession to occur. Our task is to make God's Word clear and applicable to all of life. Only then will we see spiritual growth and strong discipleship in our lives and in our churches.

Lesson Commentary

I. The Feast of Booths: Nehemiah 8:13-18

A. The Feast of Booths Commanded: vss. 13-15

On the second day of the month, the heads of all the families, along with the priests and the Levites, gathered around Ezra the scribe to give attention to the words of the Law. They found written in the Law, which the LORD had commanded through Moses, that the Israelites were to live in booths during the feast of the seventh month and that they should proclaim this word and spread it throughout their towns and in Jerusalem: "Go out into the hill country and bring back branches from olive and wild olive trees, and from myrtles, palms and shade trees, to make booths"—as it is written.

In Nehemiah 8—13 we read about the loyalty of God's people in their enforcement of the law. The first half of the book concentrated on the physical preservation of God's people. In the second half, the focus is on the spiritual preservation.

The Jews assembled in Jerusalem in the fall of 445 B.C. This was one of the most noteworthy seasons on Israel's religious calendar (Lev. 23:23-43). The people gathered in an open plaza in front of the Water Gate, which was located on the eastern side of Jerusalem slightly south of the wall's midsection. The leaders asked Ezra to read a copy of the law, which he did for five to six hours. Everyone paid close attention to the reading (Neh. 7:73—8:3).

Ezra and other important officials were standing on a wooden platform. When he opened the Hebrew Scriptures, God's people stood up out of respect. Everything that was done and the way it was reported points to the deep commitment and devotion of God's people.

Ezra praised the Lord and the audience affirmed their commitment to the law. Perhaps in unison they raised their hands and then prostrated themselves to the ground in worship. Various individuals, including Levites, translated the Scriptures and interpreted their meaning for the people. Their goal was to make it clear and understandable (vss. 4-8). They translated the Hebrew to Aramaic, the universal trade language of the day. The assistants gave the sense of the text so that the people could grasp what was being read.

Nehemiah, Ezra, and the Levites announced that the day was sacred to God. The reading and explanation of the law produced grief among the people, perhaps over their lack of commitment to its stipulations. Nehemiah directed the people not to mourn or weep, for it was a time for celebration, sharing, and feasting.

God had blessed His people, and their expression of gratitude was to be joyous and warmhearted. On such an occasion grieving was inappropriate. Nehemiah stated that the joy produced by the Lord was a source of strength for His people. The Levites calmed the group down by reminding the people of what Nehemiah had said. The audience then departed to do all that the leaders had said (vss. 9-12).

The next day the leaders of each family along with the priests and Levites assembled to meet with Ezra. These men were the most important religious leaders of the community. Their understanding of God's Word would help ensure that the rest of the people grasped and obey it.

Ezra helped the attendees to understand the law better. They discovered that the Feast of Booths was celebrated during the fall season five days after the Day of Atonement. The leaders announced in Jerusalem and Judah that the people were to observe the sacred day. They were to obtain a variety of branches to make temporary shelters for living outside. This was done in accordance with the law (vss. 13-15).

When Ezra stood to read the law, he was fulfilling Deuteronomy 31:11-12. The Jews did not possess personal copies of the law. The main way they were able to become familiar with it was by hearing it read and explained. This is what Ezra had returned to Jerusalem to do; but during the 52 days when the wall of Jerusalem was being built, there was little time for an assembly. After the wall's completion, the people expressed a desire to hear more instruction in the law.

The Levites were descendants of Levi (Gen. 29:34). They originally may have been regarded as priests (Deut. 18:6-8), but they eventually became subordinate to the priestly descendants of Aaron, a brother of Moses (Num. 3:9-10; 1 Chron. 16:4-42). Over the years, the Levites became butchers, doorkeepers, singers (1 Chron. 15:22; 16:4-7), scribes and teachers (2 Chron. 35:3; Neh. 8:7, 9), and even temple beggars (2 Chron. 24:5-11).

The Feast of Booths (Tabernacles, Ingathering) was characterized by a week of celebration for the harvest in which God's people lived in booths and offered sacrifices. This observance memorialized the Israelites' journey from Egypt to Canaan and gave them an opportunity to thank the Lord for the productivity of the land.

The purpose of the reading was not only to preserve the law but also to encourage every generation to revere and obey God's law. This public reading led the Jews to renew their commitment to God's covenant and to instruct their children to do the same.

Nehemiah 9 has twin themes: the people's sin and God's mercy. Despite the people's sin and disobedience, God dealt with them compassionately.

B. The Feast of Booths Observed: vss. 16-18

So the people went out and brought back branches and built themselves booths on their own roofs, in their courtyards, in the courts of the house of God and in the square by the Water Gate and the one by the Gate of Ephraim. The whole company that had returned from exile built booths and lived in them. From the days of Joshua son of Nun until that day, the Israelites had not celebrated it like this. And their joy was very great. Day after day, from the first day to the last, Ezra read from the Book of the Law of God. They celebrated the feast for seven days, and on the eighth day, in accordance with the regulation, there was an assembly.

The people complied with the directive. They made temporary shelters in every possible location of the city. The people living in the surrounding villages also built temporary shelters. This holiday had not been observed in quite this way and with this much joy since the time of Joshua. The people were once again giving thanks to God for His blessings with the same enthusiasm and zeal as the Israelites of Joshua's day had done.

Understanding of biblical truth is dry without the joy that God produces. Likewise, feasting and joy are meaningless without the firm foundation of God's Word. That is why Ezra read from the law each day throughout the entire seven-day period of celebration. On the eighth day, a solemn assembly took place in accordance with the law (Neh. 8:16-18).

II. The Confession of Sin: Nehemiah 9:1-3

A. Gathering Together: vs. 1

On the twenty-fourth day of the same month, the Israelites gathered together, fasting and wearing sackcloth and having dust on their heads.

The ninth chapters of Ezra, Nehemiah, and Daniel all contain prayers of confession dealing with the national sins that led to the Babylonian captivity and the loss of Israel's sovereignty over its own affairs. These confessions of the sins of people long dead were not requests that the original sinners be forgiven. They were statements of identification with the past. Through the prayer in Nehemiah 9, Ezra helped his contemporaries rehearse the sins of the past, recognize the present results of those sins, and prepare to move into a tomorrow marked by faithfulness and blessing. As Christians today, we, too, can find it helpful to face the past in order to understand the present and move into the future with God's fullest blessing.

Two days after the last joyous day of the Feast of Booths, the people of Judah and Jerusalem gathered once again in Jerusalem (vs. 1). Earlier, Ezra and Nehemiah had discouraged mourning over sin during the festival days when the people were to draw spiritual strength from the joy of knowing the Lord (see 8:9-10). Now they came again to explore another aspect of being the people of God through fasting, separation from idolatry, and confession of sin.

Rough goat-hair garments and dust-covered heads illustrated the state of mourning the Jews adopted as the proper approach to confession of their sins. They were prepared to connect their personal sins with the obvious rebelliousness of their ancestors before the Captivity.

The sackcloth worn by people in mourning could have simply been two rectangular pieces sewn together, with holes for the head and arms. Or, it could have been nothing more than a loincloth. The physical characteristics of this course material served as a powerful symbol of how the wearer felt. Mourners wore sackcloth as a form of self-abasement and to illustrate how their sorrow chafed their spirit.

The sackcloth worn by the confessing Jews was probably a coarsely woven cloth of goat hair (Neh. 9:1). Sackcloth irritated the skin; it was too rough for ordinary clothing. Because of its durability, this material was typically used to create bags.

B. Confessing and Worshiping: vss. 2-3

Those of Israelite descent had separated themselves from all foreigners. They stood in their places and confessed their sins and the wickedness of their fathers. They stood where they were and read from the Book of the Law of the LORD their God for a quarter of the day, and spent another quarter in confession and in worshiping the LORD their God.

The people stood for three hours of reading from the law and three hours of confession and worship, just as they had stood all morning on the first of the month to hear Ezra read the law (Neh. 9:2-3; see 8:3, 5). They stood in reverence because the law had come through Moses from "the LORD their God" (9:3).

Probably the assembly of Judah gathered for confession before the same platform in the square at the Water Gate where Ezra had read the law (see 8:1). The steps on which the Levites stood as worship and confession guides probably were the stairs to the platform. Two groups of eight Levites are named in Nehemiah 9:4-5. The first group of Levites called on the Lord while the people watched. The second group led the mass of worshipers in praising God. Five Levites—Jeshua, Bani, Kadmiel, Shebaniah, and Sherebiah—participated in both acts of worship.

The Levites called on the people to stand for worship (vs. 5a). This worship consisted of praise that focused on the covenant relationship between God and His people Israel. "The LORD"—Yahweh—was God's covenant name, and indeed the following recitation of Israel's history is an account of God's covenant faithfulness and Israel's covenant faithlessness.

Jewish tradition and many Christian commentators attribute the beautiful prayer of Nehemiah 9:5b-37 to Ezra. The prayer is structured carefully to guide the worshipers of Judah and Jerusalem in contrasting themselves with the Lord.

Worship at its best always does that. We stand in awe before God in His infinite majesty and power while we acknowledge our limitations. We stand mourning because He is pure and holy while we are stained by the effects of sin. We stand in hope because He is gentle and loving toward undeserving sinners who cast themselves on His mercy.

The emphasis throughout these verses is on God. They are addressed to Him, so the pronoun "you" peppers every sentence as the subject who acted decisively. The pattern is something like "You did this, and You did that, as You proved Your faithfulness again and again." No wonder the sequence begins with a blessing on God's glorious name to the effect that His name be lifted above the highest pinnacle of blessing and praise (vs. 5b).

The next 10 verses rehearse God's faithful works from Creation to the giving of the law on Mount Sinai (vss. 6-15). Their wording reflects the vocabulary of Genesis and Exodus at several points. This characteristic also suggests that Ezra, the accomplished student of the Scripture, composed this prayer.

On behalf of the Jews, Ezra confessed that God alone created the heavens with its stars, the earth and seas with all that is in them, and life in all its forms. Accordingly, the angelic multitude adored Him. They rejoiced in God's choice of Abraham and in the covenant that God made with the patriarch, which formed the

As God heard the groanings of His chosen people who suffered under the oppression of the Egyptians, He "remembered his covenant with Abraham, with Isaac and with Jacob" (Exod. 2:24). God's covenant with Abraham consisted of two parts. God promised to provide Abraham a homeland for his descendants (Gen. 15:18-21), and later promised to make him "the father of many nations" (17:4). God affirmed those promises to Isaac and to Jacob (vs. 21; 35:10-12). Ezra reminded Israel of these promises in his prayer of confession (Neh. 9:8).

basis of all His invariably faithful dealings with their nation (vss. 6-8). This is the only Old Testament reference outside Genesis to God renaming Abraham.

The Jewish assembly next recited God's mighty works of the Exodus. He heeded their anguish in Egypt and at the Red Sea when escape seemed hopeless. By means of the 10 plagues, God earned a lingering reputation among the nations. Then the barrier of the sea opened to save Israel and swallow the pursuing Egyptians (vss. 9-11). The phrase "like a stone into mighty waters" (vs. 11) echoes the victory song of Moses and Miriam sung on the shores of the Red Sea (see Exod. 15:5).

The Jews confessed how the Lord led their ancestors from the Red Sea to Mount Sinai with a pillar of cloud by day and a pillar of fire by night. They recalled the way He personally descended to address Israel through Moses. They acknowledged the justice, righteousness, and goodness of every kind of command they received from God on Sinai. They expressed special gratitude for the gift of the Sabbath through God's revelation to Moses (Neh. 9:12-14).

The confessing congregation acknowledged the physical sustenance that God gave Israel in the desert along with the spiritual food of the law. He gave them manna from heaven every day, water from the rock in emergency circumstances, and the opportunity to enter Canaan and enjoy its riches (see Exod. 16:4; 17:6; Num. 14:8-9; 20:7-13). At that moment, the Jews confessed, their ancestors had been poised to receive a fulfillment of God's promise to Abraham (Neh. 9:15).

Ezra praised God for leading the Israelites with a pillar of cloud by day and a pillar of fire by night (Neh. 9:12). Cloud and fire are often used as symbols of God's presence in the Hebrew Scriptures. Indeed, God gave Moses the 10 Commandments on Mount Sinai in the midst of smoke and fire (Exod. 19:18). Fire symbolizes God's holiness in Deuteronomy 4:24, His protective presence in 2 Kings 6:17, His wrath against sin in Isaiah 66:15-16, His glory in Ezekiel 1:4-13, and His righteous judgment in Zechariah 13:9. Clouds symbolize God's mystery and hidden glory in 1 Kings 8:10-11.

Discussion Questions

1. Why did God's people think it was necessary to take time out to hear the law read?
2. When the people learned about the festival of booths, what did they do? Why?
3. What was the basis for the people's joy?
4. Why did God's people think it was important for them to gather together to confess their sins?
5. Why did the people make God's Word the basis for their confession?

Now Ask Yourself . . .

How much attention do I give each day to God's Word?

When the Spirit prompts me to heed the truths of Scripture, how do I respond?

Do I experience joy from the Lord when I seek to follow His Word?

What place does the confession of sin have in my life?

Do I seek the counsel and company of other believers when I am dealing with the presence of sin in my life?

Illustrations

Nehemiah and his fellow Jews understood the importance of launching their resolve to obey God with the strongest possible beginning. Do your students have the same attitude about obeying God? This week's lesson stresses that when a strong commitment is absent, believers are more prone to violate His Word.

Missionaries tell stories that resemble Nehemiah's account about the public reading and teaching of God's Word. People who have never heard it before are amazed and overcome. They seek God's forgiveness for their sins and welcome Jesus Christ as their Lord and Savior.

On the other hand, people who have heard the Bible read and taught again and again sometimes find it hard to be moved. The Word of God becomes so familiar to them that it loses its initial forcefulness on their consciences.

We also face the problem of Bible ignorance and neglect. Public opinion polls show that among Christians regular Bible reading is largely neglected. Yet we can be thankful that local Bible study groups flourish in many churches and communities.

Those who hunger and thirst for righteousness will be spiritually satisfied (Matt. 5:6). When we seek God, and put Him first in our lives, we will listen to, study, obey, and teach God's Word. Compared to the upright remnant in Nehemiah's day, we are surfeited with Bibles and Scripture study materials. Therefore, our judgment will be severe if we neglect these gifts and opportunities from the Lord.

Actions Follow Beliefs

DEVOTIONAL READING

Psalm 27:1-8

DAILY BIBLE READINGS

Monday May 1
  Esther 3:1-7
  Haman Wants to Destroy the Jews

Tuesday May 2
  Esther 3:8-15
  The Order Goes Out to Kill the Jews

Wednesday May 3
  Esther 4:1-8
  Esther Talks to Mordecai

Thursday May 4
  Esther 4:9-17
  Esther Decides to Help Her People

Friday May 5
  Esther 5:1-8
  Esther Makes a Request of the King

Saturday May 6
  Esther 5:9-14
  Haman Is Invited to the Banquet

Sunday May 7
  Esther 6:1-9
  The King Wants to Honor Mordecai

Scripture

Background Scripture: *Esther 3—4*

Scripture Lesson: *Esther 3:2-3, 5-6a; 4:7-16*

Key Verse: *"If you remain silent at this time, relief and deliverance for the Jews will arise from another place, but you and your father's family will perish. And who knows but that you have come to royal position for such a time as this?" Esther 4:14.*

Lesson Aim

What we believe shows in our actions.

Lesson Setting

Time: 486–465 B.C.

Place: Susa, capital of the Persian Empire

Lesson Outline

Actions Follow Beliefs

  I. Haman's Plot: Esther 3:2-3, 5-6a
    A. *Mordecai's Refusal: vss. 2-3*
    B. *Haman's Revenge: vss. 5-6a*
  II. Mordecai's Challenge: Esther 4:7-16
    A. *Mordecai's Request: vss. 7-8*
    B. *Esther's Answer: vss. 9-11*
    C. *Mordecai's Insistence: vss. 12-14*
    D. *Esther's Response: vss. 15-16*

Introduction

Stand Up!

Harry thought he was the only Christian in his graduate class at the university. One day an especially critical professor began to attack Christians and their beliefs. He asked whether anyone in his class believed what Christianity taught. Harry looked around when he gingerly raised his hand and was delighted to see another fellow raise his, too. They became good friends and mutual encouragers.

Neither one risked their lives by raising their hands, but they risked experiencing ridicule. Sometimes in the rough and tumble of life that can be the hardest thing to take. Nevertheless, by taking a stand for our faith, we help others to consider their own faith or lack of it.

Generally, people respect Christians who make their beliefs clear with love and tact. And our fears of ridicule and persecution seldom materialize.

Lesson Commentary

I. Haman's Plot: Esther 3:2-3, 5-6a

A. Mordecai's Refusal: vss. 2-3

All the royal officials at the king's gate knelt down and paid honor to Haman, for the king had commanded this concerning him. But Mordecai would not kneel down or pay him honor. Then the royal officials at the king's gate asked Mordecai, "Why do you disobey the king's command?"

Esther is the exciting account of a wicked plot to wipe out the entire Jewish community during the reign of the Persian King Xerxes (Ahasuerus). The book may be divided into three parts. The first section deals with the *plight* of the Jews (1:1—3:15). Through the course of events, enemies plot for the execution and extinction of the Jewish people.

The Book of Esther is a third-person account of the events involving Esther and her older cousin Mordecai. No indication of the writer's identity appears in the book. The author's familiarity with Persia suggests Esther was written in Persia probably around 460 B.C., just before Ezra returned to Jerusalem.

The second section deals with the *plan* of the Jews (4:1—5:14). Through the intervention of Mordecai and Esther's appeal to the king, the deliverance of God's people is set in motion. The third section deals with the *preservation* of the Jews (6:1—10:3). Haman's plot is overturned and God's people are rescued from potential slaughter.

At the beginning of Esther, the Jews faced the threat of doom. At the end of the book they experienced the triumph associated with deliverance. In the midst of persecution there was impending ruin for the Jews. God, nevertheless, remained in control. He preserved His people by providing an incredible release from danger. Throughout all the events of the book, God miraculously displayed His care.

Concerning Xerxes, his empire stretched from what is now India through Persia (Iran), Turkey, the Middle East, across North Africa, and as far south as Sudan. The winter capital of the empire was in Susa, located about 150 miles east of Babylon.

During his reign, Xerxes gave a huge feast to climax a six-month display of his wealth and power. For some unknown reason Queen Vashti decided not to go along with his show and the king deposed her (chap. 1). Sometime later the king got around to finding a new queen. Esther was among the women to be chosen for the honor. Because she surpassed all of them, King Xerxes selected her to be his queen and threw a great banquet in her honor (chap. 2).

Esther had been raised by her cousin Mordecai, and he kept a close eye on her in the court. He had strictly admonished her not to reveal that she was a Jew (vss. 10, 20). One day Mordecai overheard a plot by two assassins against the king and he reported it to Esther, who told it to the king, attributing the information to her cousin (vss. 19-23).

After these events, Ahasuerus selected Haman to be the second most powerful official within the Persian Empire. Mordecai claimed an ancestor named Kish; Haman, one named Agag (3:1; see 2:5). King Saul had been the son of Kish; Agag had been the Amalekite king God ordered Saul to kill as part of a holy war against the Amalekites 500 years before the time of Esther (see 1 Sam. 15).

The Lord had sworn lasting enmity against the Amalekites after they attacked the Israelites leaving Egypt another 400 years before the time of Saul and Agag (see Exod. 17:8-16; Deut. 25:17-19). This historical background would explain Mordecai's disregard for Haman and Haman's hatred for not only Mordecai but for all the Jews.

The king was so impressed with Haman that he commanded that all the servants who were at the "king's gate" (Esth. 3:2) bow down and do obeisance (an attitude of respect or reverence) to

In the summer Susa's weather was unbearably hot, but its winters were relatively mild. The city's climate made Susa the winter capital of the Persian Empire. Cyrus made Susa one of the capitals of Persia. Darius I built his palace here. This palace, restored by Artaxerxes I, played a major role in the events of Esther's life. The territory of Susa is now in modern-day Iran about 150 miles north of the Persian Gulf and due east of Babylon. Archaeologists discovered that this city was occupied since at least 4000 B.C.

Some think the Book of Esther was written simply to explain the Jewish holiday of Purim. However, Esther is also an account of the way God uses His people, of all economic and social statuses, to accomplish His purposes. In particular, a woman is the "hero" of this narrative.

Haman. Mordecai, however, refused to revere Haman. There was no justification for Mordecai's behavior based on the Mosaic law (in other words, misplaced worship; Exod. 20:4) or scriptural precedent (Gen. 23:7; 33:3; 44:14; 1 Sam. 24:8; 2 Sam. 14:4; 1 Kings 1:16). Perhaps Mordecai's disobedience was based on the hatred that existed between the Jews and the Amalekites.

Mordecai, motivated by a strong sense of patriotism, defied Haman because he was an enemy of God's people and ultimately a menace to their existence (Esth. 3:10; 7:6; 8:1; 9:10, 24, 26). The king's servants noticed Mordecai's belligerent conduct regarding Haman and asked him why he refused to obey "the king's command" (3:3). Undoubtedly, Mordecai could not bring himself to bow before one who was descended from the Amalekites, the bitter enemies of the Jews.

B. Haman's Revenge: vss. 5-6a

When Haman saw that Mordecai would not kneel down or pay him honor, he was enraged. Yet having learned who Mordecai's people were, he scorned the idea of killing only Mordecai.

When Mordecai's peers spoke to him "day after day" (Esth. 3:4), he refused to listen to them. They finally told Haman about Mordecai's insubordination in an effort to determine whether this behavior was permissible or intolerable. When Haman verified what he had learned, he was "enraged" (vs. 5). Mordecai's actions threatened Haman's inflated ego. Thus he became obsessed with the determination to retaliate against Mordecai.

When Haman was told who "Mordecai's people were" (vs. 6), Haman spurned the idea that killing this rebel would be sufficient. Haman determined that all the Jews living within the Persian Empire had to die, perhaps as a fitting punishment for Mordecai's insolence. Haman's anger drove him to devise a scheme whereby all of the Jews in the Persian Empire would be exterminated.

In the twelfth year of King Ahasuerus (vs. 7), the court astrologers and magicians cast a lot for Haman to determine when to exterminate the Jews. The Persian word for "lot," *pur*, is highlighted because it plays an important part in events at the end of Esther (see 9:23-28). The lot fell on the last month of the Jewish calendar, giving Haman about 11 months to establish and implement his plan. He next presented his case to the king, and the monarch readily agreed and issued the decree (3:8-13). The edict was then dispatched to all of the provinces giving orders to annihilate all of the Jews in one day (vss. 14-15).

II. Mordecai's Challenge: Esther 4:7-16

A. Mordecai's Request: vss. 7-8

Mordecai told him everything that had happened to him, including the exact amount of money Haman had promised to pay into the royal treasury for the destruction of the Jews. He also gave him a copy of the text of the edict for their annihilation, which had been published in Susa, to show to Esther and explain it to her, and he told him to urge her to go into the king's presence to beg for mercy and plead with him for her people.

When Mordecai learned about the decree, he began to go through the city streets dressed in sackcloth and ashes (the clothing of mourning) and wept loudly (Esth. 4:1-3). Esther's maids told her what Mordecai was doing, and she sent one of her attendants to find out from him what was happening (vss. 4-6).

Mordecai then reviewed the details of all that had happened to him (vs. 7). He even stated the enormous sum of money that Haman would place in the royal treasury for those who helped massacre the Jews. Mordecai also gave the official a copy of the king's decree (vs. 8). Mordecai asked the queen to go into the king's presence and seek his favor and mercy concerning her fellow Jews.

The dangerous part of this conversation was that Mordecai trusted a palace servant with the secret that Queen Esther too was a Jew condemned under Haman's decree. Mordecai had to trust Hathach to explain everything to Esther.

B. Esther's Answer: vss. 9-11

Hathach went back and reported to Esther what Mordecai had said. Then she instructed him to say to Mordecai, "All the king's officials and the people of the royal provinces know that for any man or woman who approaches the king in the inner court without being summoned the king has but one law: that he be put to death. The only exception to this is for the king to extend the gold scepter to him and spare his life. But thirty days have passed since I was called to go to the king."

Mordecai, upon discovering the fate that Haman had decreed for the Jews in Xerxes' name, could see no escape from destruction. Humanly speaking, he and Esther and all their relatives and friends were nothing but dead people getting their affairs in order. Mordecai could have given up and fallen into despair, but he kept hoping that God would save His people.

Some have wondered why the Book of Esther makes no reference to God or to prayer. In fact, there is a conspicuous absence of any overtly religious vocabulary or concepts in the book. Most likely this was a rhetorical device the author used to indirectly underscore the fact that God truly was active throughout the entire account.

285

The Greek historian Herodotus recorded an incident from the reign of Xerxes' father, Darius, that led to the execution of one of seven heroes who had put down a rebellion of the caste of magicians (the Magus): "Now the law was that all those who had taken part in the rising against the Magus might enter unannounced into the king's presence, unless he happened to be in private with his wife. So Intaphernes would not have anyone announce him, but, as he belonged to the seven, claimed it as his right to go in. The doorkeeper, however, and the chief usher forbade his entrance, since the king, they said, was with his wife." Intaphernes insisted on entering the throne room. When he did, he and his family were immediately taken away to be executed.

The official explained to Esther the situation and she in turn sent back a reply to Mordecai (Esth. 4:9-10). Esther reminded her uncle that her life would be placed in jeopardy if she did what he had requested. The king might execute her for trying to seek an interview with him without being specifically summoned.

The king would only spare Esther's life (in other words, clear her of guilt) if he held out his "gold scepter" (vs. 11) and granted her permission to see him. She reasoned that this possibility was remote, for the king had not summoned her into his presence for over "thirty days."

C. Mordecai's Insistence: vss. 12-14

When Esther's words were reported to Mordecai, he sent back this answer: "Do not think that because you are in the king's house you alone of all the Jews will escape. For if you remain silent at this time, relief and deliverance for the Jews will arise from another place, but you and your father's family will perish. And who knows but that you have come to royal position for such a time as this?"

"When Esther's words were reported to Mordecai" (Esth. 4:12), he would not take no for an answer. He did not deny that Esther would take a great risk in approaching the king. What she said was true, but the well being of the Jews was so serious that Mordecai insisted that she appeal to the king.

Mordecai gave two reasons. First, he told the queen that she would not escape death when the edict was carried out (vs. 13). Her Jewish background would be revealed and she would perish with the rest of them.

Mordecai was confident that the Jews would be delivered in some way, and when they were, Esther and her family would be taken anyway. Divine punishment would come if the queen disobeyed the Lord. "From another place" (vs. 14) implies that Mordecai had God's intervention in mind.

Second, Mordecai raised a question in Esther's mind. The cousin speculated that she had been made queen specifically to bring about the deliverance of her people. Mordecai did not directly give God credit for bringing Esther to the throne, but there is the strong assumption that the cousin had this in mind.

"And who knows" implies that Esther's position was ultimately due to divine providence. In other words, the highly unlikely possibility that she had been made queen was more than what people call good luck. Mordecai put two and two together and told Esther that she had been selected from all the women in the empire specifically to ensure the well being of her people.

Mordecai's words prompted Esther to think about why she was queen. In her case, much more was involved than satisfying the whims and pleasures of the king. Hers was a much larger responsibility. She thus decided to place herself at risk for the good of her people.

D. Esther's Response: vss. 15-16

Then Esther sent this reply to Mordecai: "Go, gather together all the Jews who are in Susa, and fast for me. Do not eat or drink for three days, night or day. I and my maids will fast as you do. When this is done, I will go to the king, even though it is against the law. And if I perish, I perish."

Mordecai's persistence paid off. Esther reconsidered her options and courageously decided to see King Xerxes. However, before the queen did so, she asked for the help of all the Jews in Susa. She called for a three-day fast, and she and her maids would do the same (Esth. 4:15).

Fasting was the traditional Jewish way of asking for God's help in times of national crisis. Esther thus followed a long line of leaders who had called God's people to fasting and prayer. Normally, fasts lasted from sunrise to sunset, but Esther called for a much longer one.

After this time of fasting, Esther would break with Persian regulations by requesting an audience with the king. She resigned herself to the possibility of losing her life over this decision (vs. 16). Esther's attendants notified Mordecai, and he responded by heeding the queen's instructions (vs. 17).

Esther's reply was a sterling display of devotion to God and commitment to His people. Her bravery was also a demonstration of living trust in the Lord, especially at a critical time for the Jewish people.

Mordecai faced the pivotal moment of his life as an old man. Esther faced this time of crisis as a young woman. No Christian can say he or she is too old, too young, too disadvantaged, too troubled, too busy, or too unimportant to have something crucial to do in God's plan. We need to be available to Him and willing to accept His challenge whenever it arises.

In what may be the key statement of the Book of Esther, Mordecai pointed out to Esther that the dangerous challenge she faced may offer the key to understanding the incredible string of tragedies and surprises that had marked her entire life. Orphaned, adopted, forced into Xerxes' harem, pampered for a year to please a vain man, and then made queen of all Persia. Was this gamble with her life the key that made sense of it all as part of God's design?

Esther's attitude was not fatalistic. She had accepted that going to the emperor was God's will. Esther also knew that following His will did not guarantee her personal safety.

Discussion Questions

1. Who were the servants at the king's gate in Susa?
2. Why do you think the king's servants asked Mordecai again and again for the reason he refused to bow down before Haman?
3. What was it that intensified Haman's vindictive attitude toward Mordecai?
4. What do you think Mordecai said to Esther that made her determine to approach the king, unbidden, on behalf of her people?
5. How did you feel at times in your life when you needed God's strength and courage to face issues and circumstances, even when others misunderstood you?

Now Ask Yourself . . .

When someone has hurt me, what am I inclined to do?
How likely is it that I would pray for such a person?
Do I really believe the hand of God is at work in all the circumstances of my life?
When was the last time I faced the choice of speaking up for God or remaining silent?
How has God used me despite my weaknesses or deficiencies?

Illustrations

All of us face problems and situations in life that require courage. Occasionally we must face extremely challenging situations alone. Sometimes the issue is controversial, and friends and loved ones may discourage us or be critical of what we feel we must do. God often wanted those whom He chose to perform difficult tasks for Him to be courageous. He promised them He would be with them and provide the required strength at the moment of their need.

As in the case of Mordecai, a time may come when our spiritual convictions force us to choose between obeying a humanly constructed law or the law of God. Of course, such a stand does not permit us becoming violent. Nevertheless, as with Mordecai, a firm stand for what we believe is the proper thing to do may result in others harming us. This possibility is especially strong in places where Christianity is despised. We should thank God daily for the religious freedoms we enjoy in our country.

Mordecai's courageous refusal to bow before Haman no doubt was reflected in the attitude of Esther, whose life was influenced by her godly cousin. Godly parents and relatives can be role models of courage before their children. These character traits are absorbed in subtle and progressive ways. Esther's respect for Mordecai was such that she was willing to risk her life and throw herself at the mercy of the king. God honored her act of courage and it saved her people from annihilation. The results of our acts of courage may not be as dramatic, but they can accomplish much for the glory of God.

Finding the Celebration

DEVOTIONAL READING

Psalm 98:1-9

DAILY BIBLE READINGS

Monday May 8
Esther 6:10-14
Haman Helps Honor
Mordecai

Tuesday May 9
Esther 7:1-10
Esther Exposes Haman,
and He Is Hanged

Wednesday May 10
Esther 8:1-8
Queen Esther Receives
Haman's Estate

Thursday May 11
Esther 8:9-17
The Jews Rejoice at Their
Good Fortune

Friday May 12
Esther 9:1-15
The Jews Triumph against
Their Enemies

Saturday May 13
Esther 9:16-28
The Jews Celebrate

Sunday May 14
Esther 9:29—10:3
Mordecai Spreads
Goodwill and Assurance

Scripture

Background Scripture: *Esther 8—9*
Scripture Lesson: *Esther 8:3-8; 9:18-23*
Key Verse: *As the time when the Jews got relief from their enemies, and as the month when their sorrow was turned into joy and their mourning into a day of celebration. He wrote to them to observe the days as days of feasting and joy and giving presents of food to one another and gifts to the poor. Esther 9:22.*

Lesson Aim

God can turn sorrow to celebration.

Lesson Setting

Time: 486–465 B.C.
Place: Susa, capital of the Persian Empire

Lesson Outline

Finding the Celebration

I. Esther's Plea: Esther 8:3-8
   A. *Esther's Approach: vss. 3-4*
   B. *Esther's Case: vss. 5-6*
   C. The King's Answer: vss. 7-8
II. The Jews' Celebration: Esther 9:18-23
   A. *Nationwide Feasting: vss. 18-19*
   B. *The Annual Celebration: vss. 20-23*

Introduction

Don't Remain Afraid!

The syndicated news column that gives advice to readers who write to Ann Landers is more popular today than when it began many decades ago. Tens of thousands of readers write in each month asking for advice for the problems that confront them.

One time Ann Landers was asked what the most dominant theme was that characterized the letters that readers would ask her advice upon. She replied that, easily, the most dominant problem that her readers faced was fear. People are afraid of everything, she said, afraid of losing their health, their wealth, and their friends or loved ones. And most of all, she went on, they are afraid to do anything about it. They need someone to tell them not to be afraid, and to take action in the direction that they should go.

It's natural for us, as Christians, to be afraid at times. And it is *supernatural* for us to overcome paralyzing fears with God's help. His sustaining presence can enable us to do.

Lesson Commentary

I. Esther's Plea: Esther 8:3-8

A. Esther's Approach: vss. 3-4

Esther again pleaded with the king, falling at his feet and weeping. She begged him to put an end to the evil plan of Haman the Agagite, which he had devised against the Jews. Then the king extended the gold scepter to Esther and she arose and stood before him.

As we enter this week's lesson, Haman's plot to exterminate the Jews seemed to be progressing as planned. There was a reversal of fortunes, however, when the king honored Mordecai and ordered Haman to be hanged on the gallows he intended for Mordecai's execution.

Especially noteworthy is the information contained in Esther 7. While Xerxes and Haman were dining with Esther, the king again asked her what she wanted from him. The queen implored Xerxes to spare her life and that of her people, explaining that they had been bartered away (by means of the bribe Haman offered) to be slaughtered. She would not have bothered the king if the Jews had been sold as slaves (vss. 1-4).

When Xerxes asked who would do such a thing, Esther fingered Haman. Filled with rage, the king went into the palace garden. In the monarch's absence, Haman kneeled before Esther and begged her to save his life. Somehow he lost his balance and stumbled onto the couch where Esther was reclining. Just then Xerxes returned, saw what was happening, and accused Haman of trying to rape his queen in his own palace (vss. 5-8).

The king's servants covered Haman's head. The king's execution order signaled that the face of the condemned criminal be covered to hide his shame. Then Harbonah, one the king's personal servants, noted the gallows Haman had built to hang Mordecai. Xerxes ordered that Haman be hanged on the tower, and when this was done, the king's anger was appeased (vss. 9-10).

Although Haman was no longer a threat to the Jews, the king's decree against them remained in force. God used Esther and Mordecai to get Ahasuerus to issue a new set of decrees in which he permitted the Jews to defend themselves. They commemorated their victory over their enemies by establishing the Feast of Purim.

The Persians did not hang people by putting a rope around their necks. They impaled victims on wooden posts and left them to die. Alexander the Great would later import this type of crucifixion to Europe, and the Romans modified it from the Greeks.

Some view this series of events as bloodthirsty revenge. From the Jewish perspective, however, the honor of God was at stake when the welfare of His people was threatened. That is why Esther and Mordecai wanted God's enemies punished for their cruelty.

Esther 3:7 reveals that, in March or April of 474 B.C., the court astrologers and magicians cast a lot for Haman to determine when the extermination of the Jews was to take place. "Pur" was the Babylonian word for lot, and "purim" is the plural form. Chapter 9:18-32 reveals that the Feast of Purim became one of the traditional Jewish feasts established by God's people. The Jews normally observed this sacred holiday between February and March (that is, the month of Adar). The festival involved a day of joyous celebration, feasting, and giving of presents. It was intended to remind the Jews of their remarkable deliverance as a people during the time of Esther.

According to 8:1-2, the king gave Esther all that had belonged to Haman. Xerxes also made Mordecai one of his highest officials and gave him the ring Haman had worn. Esther then put Mordecai in charge of Haman's property. After that, Esther entered the king's chambers and fell at his feet, weeping and pleading with him on behalf of her people, the Jews, who were still under the death sentence (vs. 3).

A scepter was a staff or rod that ancient monarchs used to symbolize their authority and power. The objects could be either long (as in the case of the one used by Darius) or short. In the hands of a ruthless tyrant, the latter type could be used as a weapon of punishment and oppression. Many depictions of monarchs in ancient Near Eastern art include a scepter of some kind.

Sometimes it is easy to quit before a job is truly done. And some challenges are so intimidating that a partial success seems enough. Once Esther and Mordecai had escaped the threat of personal destruction and Haman had been executed, Esther could have thanked the emperor Xerxes and concluded that she had done all she could. But Esther did not consider her victory complete until the safety of her people was secured.

Moved by Esther's display of concern for her people, the king held out his golden scepter to her (vs. 4). The situation now was different from the previous time the king had extended his scepter to Esther (5:2). On that occasion, Esther risked her life to come into the king's presence uninvited. This time she had already made her emotional appeal before the king. His gesture in extending his scepter was an indication that Esther should rise from her prostrate position and continue to speak to him.

B. Esther's Case: vss. 5-6

"If it pleases the king," she said, "and if he regards me with favor and thinks it the right thing to do, and if he is pleased with me, let an order be written overruling the dispatches that Haman son of Hammedatha, the Agagite, devised and wrote to destroy the Jews in all the king's provinces. For how can I bear to see disaster fall on my people? How can I bear to see the destruction of my family?"

Esther based her case on her relationship with Xerxes and on his judgment to do "the right thing" (Esth. 8:5). Everything depended on what pleased the king. The queen, of course, followed the strict rules of court formality and addressed the king with the utmost respect. Esther knew that only the king's pleasure and his decision could bring about the deliverance of the Jews from their enemies.

Esther was wise to remind the king that Haman had instigated the destruction of the Jews (vs. 5). While the queen knew how the king felt about Haman, she carefully avoided blaming Xerxes for any part he may have unwittingly played in the conspiracy.

The queen, instead, appealed strongly to Xerxes' acceptance of her: "If he regards me with favor . . . if he is pleased with me." Then Esther explained how horrible it would be for her to see her people destroyed (vs. 6). Here we find Esther speaking with courage, wisdom, and passion for her people. She staked everything on the king's sense of justice and his appreciation for her as his queen.

Xerxes could hardly be moved by the extermination of a subject people, for he had built his empire by ruthless subjugation of millions from India to Ethiopia. What difference would it make to him to see the Jews die? But in this case the king saw a real Jew standing before him, not an abstract community of people. Esther's personal pain gave Xerxes something to think about on more than the bureaucratic level.

C. The King's Answer: vss. 7-8

King Xerxes replied to Queen Esther and to Mordecai the Jew, "Because Haman attacked the Jews, I have given his estate to Esther, and they have hanged him on the gallows. Now write another decree in the king's name in behalf of the Jews as seems best to you, and seal it with the king's signet ring—for no document written in the king's name and sealed with his ring can be revoked."

Xerxes summoned Esther and Mordecai and favorably accepted Esther's plea for her people. He reminded them that their enemy Haman had been executed (Esth. 8:7). Then the king told them to write a new decree "as seems best to you" (vs. 8). Xerxes would seal it and it would become law. Haman's decree would not be carried out, and the Jews were given authority to defend themselves against would-be attackers (vs. 11). The irrevocability of Haman's decree made it necessary for Mordecai to duplicate in reverse all of its provisions.

The emperor had made a great mistake when he let Haman write the terms of the first decree. He trusted the queen and Mordecai to write a law that wouldn't come back to haunt him in the future. Esther and Mordecai had shown by their loyalty to their people and their wisdom in approaching Xerxes that they could be relied on. We, too, can demonstrate our ability to handle authority responsibly by the way we handle smaller, less serious matters.

Great celebrations broke out among the Jews in Susa the capital and elsewhere throughout the empire. It included many Gentiles as well as Jews (vss. 15-17). Happiness, joy, and gladness were the orders of the day. Thus through Mordecai's irrepressible faith and Esther's courage and wisdom, the Jews were preserved.

The lesson of this portion of the Book of Esther concerns our source of joy. While we do not literally fight our persecutors, we have a stronghold in our heavenly Father to which we can run for protection (see Ps. 46). We rejoice because we are more than conquerors (see Rom. 8:37).

A signet was a seal engraved with a personal insignia that left an impression when it was pressed into soft wax or clay. It was typically worn as a ring on the finger or on a cord around the neck. A monarch's signet ring was a symbol of royal authority. In ancient times, it was used instead of a written signature to seal official documents.

The presence of a seal on a document, container, or storage compartment guaranteed that the contents had not been tampered with. The seal was considered powerful protection in the Near East because it was believed that anyone who misused the seal or broke a seal without the proper authority would be summarily cursed.

II. The Jews' Celebration: Esther 9:18-23

A. Nationwide Feasting: vss. 18-19

The Jews in Susa, however, had assembled on the thirteenth and fourteenth, and then on the fifteenth they rested and made it a day

God is just, and His justice shows in many of the details of the final chapters of Esther. For each of Haman's hateful deeds at the beginning of the Book of Esther there is a corresponding protective deed at the end. In fact the author went out of his way to echo chapters 3 and 4 in chapters 8 and 9. Mordecai the deliverer replaces Haman the destroyer. Regal robes replace sackcloth. Gathering for self-defense replaces gathering to fast. Finally, celebration replaces mourning.

of feasting and joy. That is why rural Jews—those living in villages—observe the fourteenth of the month of Adar as a day of joy and feasting, a day for giving presents to each other.

Great victories for the Jews swept the country (Esth. 9:1-15). Then the Jews who lived in Susa, the capital city, "had assembled on the thirteenth and fourteenth, and then on the fifteenth they rested and made it a day of feasting and joy" (vs. 18). The author added these words to explain that the Jews living in the city kept the Feast of Purim on the fifteenth day of Adar.

Those living in the rural areas observed it on the fourteenth day (vs. 19). Apparently the Jews in Susa were permitted two days to kill their enemies, whereas the Jews living elsewhere had only one day to carry out their defense. Thus they celebrated the feast on the fourteenth of Adar.

This celebration reminds us of earlier times when the Jews gathered to thank God for His deliverance. The songs of Moses and Miriam are one such example (Exod. 15:1-21). Similar celebrations marked the day the ark of God came to Jerusalem (1 Chron. 13—16), the dedication of the temple (2 Chron. 5—7), Hezekiah's Passover (chaps. 30—31), and Nehemiah's reading of the Word of God (Neh. 8:1-18). Such celebrations also formed the basis for worship expressed in the Book of Psalms.

B. The Annual Celebration: vss. 20-23

Mordecai recorded these events, and he sent letters to all the Jews throughout the provinces of King Xerxes, near and far, to have them celebrate annually the fourteenth and fifteenth days of the month of Adar as the time when the Jews got relief from their enemies, and as the month when their sorrow was turned into joy and their mourning into a day of celebration. He wrote them to observe the days as days of feasting and joy and giving presents of food to one another and gifts to the poor. So the Jews agreed to continue the celebration they had begun, doing what Mordecai had written to them.

Mordecai "recorded these events, and he sent letters" (Esth. 9:20) to his fellow Jews throughout the provinces of Persia. In the letters he recorded the high points of the past days, particularly that the Jews in Susa, after overcoming their enemies, rested on the fifteenth of Adar, while the Jews in the other provinces rested on the fourteenth of the month. Those days both groups kept as times of rejoicing.

Mordecai further stated that they were to observe these days of rejoicing year by year (vs. 21). Adar was to be remembered as the month during which the Jews gained relief from their enemies (vs. 22). In addition to this, they were to send gifts of food to one another and presents to the poor. When the Jews in the provinces received Mordecai's letter instructing them to establish an annual feast of rejoicing to commemorate their deliverance from their enemies, they adopted as a custom what they had begun to do (vs. 23).

Time and again throughout the Old Testament we see the importance of keeping special times for worship, sacrifice, fasting, and feasting. The Jews had so many significant milestones in their history—beginning with their exodus from Egypt—that their calendars were filled with reminders of God's goodness and mercy. Moses had laid down the laws for regular feasts, starting with the Passover, and Purim was added much later. Purim, of course, does not have the authority of Moses behind it, but it became an important part of Jewish history and tradition.

Readers wonder why Mordecai and Esther did not mention God when they established Purim. The most likely explanation is that, since the account was written in Persia soon after the events occurred, the author did not want to risk offending the Persians by directly mentioning God.

The account reveals much about God's hand in saving His people. That's why Purim has been such a popular celebration. It encourages people in difficulties to pray for deliverance even when their situations appear to be hopeless. Also, when we celebrate God's goodness regularly—not just when we're reaping His blessings—we honor Him and confess our faith, hope, and trust in Him. Our celebrations point to God as our great Deliverer.

We learn from the remainder of Esther 9—10 that Purim became an inclusive holiday, one that welcomed Gentiles to convert to faith in the living God, as many did in the days of Esther and Mordecai. Moreover, the queen communicated with the Jews throughout the Persian Empire to reinforce the establishment of Purim. Meanwhile, the status of Mordecai in Xerxes' government continued to increase. His deeds on behalf of the Jews could be read in official Persian annals right along with the accomplishments of the emperor himself.

Discussion Questions

1. What was the difference between the gesture of the king in extending his scepter to Esther the first time and the second time?
2. Why was Esther so distressed about the edict promoted by Haman?
3. Why did the Jews of Susa celebrate victory over their enemies on the fifteenth day of Adar, while the Jews in the other provinces celebrated on the fourteenth day of the month?
4. What specific activities were to accompany the Jews' time of feasting?
5. What are some practical ways that we can show gratitude to God for our victory in Christ?

Now Ask Yourself . . .

What is my attitude toward those in authority over me?

How patient am I to proceed cautiously in making big changes in my life?

How have I seen God demonstrate His power over powerful people?

What gives me the greatest joy in my Christian life?

If I were going to pick out two or three important events in my Christian life to mark with annual celebrations, what would they be?

Illustrations

In life threatening situations, people are prone to think of themselves first and others last. Esther and Mordecai responded differently to their circumstances. They were more concerned for the welfare of their people than for their own well being. They are role models for us as we encounter terrifying situations.

Consider, for example, the life challenges believers tend to face. In the midst of difficult circumstances, it might be easy for them to feel discouraged and frustrated. You can use this week's lesson to remind your students how God enabled His people in the Old Testament to prevail in the most difficult situations.

Another area of concern relates to God's perfect timing. Believers sometimes can become impatient when they do not receive the recognition they think they deserve. Encourage your students to look at life from an eternal perspective. Even if others fail to notice all the good things they have done, God is not ignorant of their deeds. In due time, He will bestow His heavenly riches on them in Christ.

A third area for consideration deals with the matter of expressing forgiveness. The jealously and pride that brought down Haman can unexpectedly trip up even the mature Christian. It is easy to magnify real or imagined slights and to strike back at them. Instead of seeking revenge, believers are to forgive those who wrong them. Although forgiving offenses is never easy, God can give His people the strength to do what is right.

The Problems of Obedience

DEVOTIONAL READING

1 John 2:15-17

DAILY BIBLE READINGS

Monday May 15
   2 Chronicles 32:1-8
   Be Strong and Courageous

Tuesday May 16
   Psalm 16
   The Lord Is Always There

Wednesday May 17
   Daniel 1:1-7
   The King Orders Noble
   Israelites to Him

Thursday May 18
   Daniel 1:8-16
   Daniel and His Friends
   Refuse the Rich Meals

Friday May 19
   Daniel 1:17-21
   God Blesses the Four
   Faithful Israelites

Saturday May 20
   James 1:1-11
   Consider Trials Pure Joy

Sunday May 21
   James 1:12-18
   Persevere under All Kinds
   of Trials

Scripture

Background Scripture: *Daniel 1*

Scripture Lesson: *Daniel 1:3-5, 8-16*

Key Verse: *But Daniel resolved not to defile himself with the royal food and wine. Daniel 1:8.*

Lesson Aim

We can obey God even in complex situations.

Lesson Setting

Time: 604 B.C.

Place: Babylon

Lesson Outline

The Problems of Obedience

   I. A Difficult Dilemma: Daniel 1:3-5
      A. *Captives in the Babylonian Court: vs. 3*
      B. *Education for Royal Service: vss. 4-5*
  II. Daniel's Solution: Daniel 1:8-16
      A. *The Request Made by Daniel: vs. 8*
      B. *The Official's Alarm: vss. 9-10*
      C. *The Suggestion Offered by Daniel: vss. 11-14*
      D. *The Blessing of God: vss. 15-16*

Introduction

Handling Temptation

Every temptation promises us relief from some form of "hunger" inside us. What allures us in our weakest moments can include such enticements as eating, spending, and lusting (to name a few things).

One way to get through temptation is this: look steadily at what is being offered and ask yourself, *Is this what I really want?* If we let that question sink in, we can discover a deeper need beneath our pressing desire of the moment: our hunger for unconditional love and fulfillment. It's a need only God can meet.

Perhaps it will also help to view sin in a different light—not as something we must constantly steel ourselves against, but as something we can finally gain the freedom to abandon, especially as we recognize its self-destructive effects. We find a glorious New Testament promise to encourage us: 1 Corinthians 10:13. Consider that Scripture as a promise to your life today. As He did with Daniel, God will always show us a way out—if we'll be open to taking it.

Lesson Commentary

I. A Difficult Dilemma: Daniel 1:3-5

A. Captives in the Babylonian Court: vs. 3

Then the king ordered Ashpenaz, chief of his court officials, to bring in some of the Israelites from the royal family and the nobility.

The Book of Daniel is simply titled in the Hebrew Bible, "Daniel," meaning "God is my judge." The reason for the name is twofold. First, Daniel is the chief character in the events unfolded. Second, it was Hebrew custom to identify a book by the name of the author. The author of this book is identified as "Daniel" (Dan. 12:4).

While Ezekiel prophesied to the exiles on the outskirts of Babylon, Daniel became one of King Nebuchadnezzar's most trusted advisors in the royal court. Though he was highly favored and greatly honored by the king, Daniel's ministry at the highest levels of government was characterized by humility and a complete lack of interest in personal power or prestige. It was on his knees that Daniel conquered kings and prophesied the rise and fall of world empires. Daniel's life is a model of what persistent prayer and unwavering faith can accomplish.

Daniel was born in the middle of good King Josiah's reign, and grew up under his religious reforms (see 2 Kings 22-23). During that time, Daniel probably heard Jeremiah, whom he later quoted (see Dan. 9:2). When Judah fell and Josiah was killed in a battle with Egypt in 609 B.C., Josiah's eldest son Jehoiakim was made king of Judah by Pharaoh Neco. For four years Judah was an

Egyptian vassal nation until Nebuchadnezzar defeated Egypt at Carchemish in 605 B.C.

That same year, the Babylonian king swept into Judah and captured Jerusalem. He had Jehoiakim, who was in the third year of his reign, carried off to Babylon. Nebuchadnezzar also ordered treasures from the temple in Jerusalem sent back home and placed in "the temple of his god" (1:1-2). The "god" referred to was probably the chief Babylonian god Bel, also called Marduk.

In keeping with a common practice of the time, Nebuchadnezzar had the best educated, most attractive, most capable and talented among Judah's citizens sent back to Babylon. In essence, only the poorer, uneducated people were left behind to populate conquered lands (see 2 Kings 24:14). Included among those deported from Judah to Babylon, were Daniel, Hananiah, Mishael, and Azariah (Dan. 1:3, 6).

Nebuchadnezzar commanded Ashpenaz, who was in charge of the king's court officials, to bring in some of the Israelites. The king specifically wanted to see members of the "royal family," referring to princes descended from David, and others who came from the ranks of nobility. Nebuchadnezzar was obviously looking for the "cream of the crop" (so to speak) among the captives. He wanted young men of such physical and mental superiority that they would be "qualified" for service to him (vss. 3-4a).

B. Education for Royal Service: vss. 4-5

Young men without any physical defect, handsome, showing aptitude for every kind of learning, well informed, quick to understand, and qualified to serve in the king's palace. He was to teach them the language and literature of the Babylonians. The king assigned them a daily amount of food and wine from the king's table. They were to be trained for three years, and after that they were to enter the king's service.

Ashpenaz was charged with teaching the young men the "language and literature of the Babylonians" (Dan. 1:4) with the intent of assimilating them into their new culture. In addition to this, they were to undergo an intensive three-year study program to prepare them for royal service. The course of study most likely included mathematics, history, astronomy, astrology, agriculture, architecture, law, and magic. During the course of their education,

Daniel and his friends were among those who were deported from Jerusalem to Babylon by Nebuchadnezzar (Dan. 1:3-6). The majority of the greatest Middle Eastern empires of ancient times routinely deported or dispersed large segments of the population of conquered nations.

Often, deportees from the upper classes were incorporated into the population of the ruling empire. This was done for a variety of reasons. First, it nourished the loyalty of subject peoples as they were gradually absorbed into the new culture. Second, it improved the conquering nation's pool of upper class workers. Finally, and perhaps most importantly, it denied the lower class citizens left behind in conquered countries the leadership of those most likely to plot rebellion.

Daniel, meaning "God is judge," was changed to Belteshazzar, translated "May Bel protect his life." Hananiah, meaning "Yahweh is gracious," became Shadrach, possibly translated "Command of Aku" (the moon god). Mishael, meaning "Who is what God is?," was changed to Meshach, which may mean "Who is what Aku is?" Azariah, meaning "Whom Yahweh helps," became Abednego, "Servant of Nebo" (god of writing and vegetation). If changing the names was a ploy to shift the young men's allegiance from the God of Israel to the gods of Babylon, it proved to be a miserable failure.

the young men would receive "food and wine" rations directly from the table of the king (vss. 4b-5).

The number of captives enrolled in the king's educational program is not stated. Only the names of the four young men from Judah are given. All four of the names referred to and honored the God of Israel in some way. In Hebrew, the ending "-el" means "God" and "-iah" is an abbreviation for "Yahweh," commonly translated, "Jehovah." The God-honoring names of the four men could indicate that they all had God-fearing parents. But since their captors wanted their gods to be honored rather than the God of Israel, the names of the four youths were changed (vss. 6-7).

II. Daniel's Solution: Daniel 1:8-16

A. The Request Made by Daniel: vs. 8

But Daniel resolved not to defile himself with the royal food and wine, and he asked the chief official for permission not to defile himself this way.

Those who were being groomed for service in the king's court were treated like athletes in training. They received the best of everything, including food and drink from the king's own table. But because Daniel was certain the king's provisions would bring ritual defilement, he resolved not to partake of them.

Daniel knew full well what God's law said concerning acceptable food and drink. He therefore resolved not to defile himself by breaking that law. The word "resolve" (Dan. 1:8) is a strong term signifying a determined, committed stand. When Daniel took this stand, it was simply the natural result of a life-long determination to be obedient to God's will in every situation.

With boldness and courage Daniel asked Ashpenaz for permission not to eat the king's food or drink his wine. Evidently, Daniel's three companions shared his resolve and made the same commitment as well. It is clear from this that the exceptional intelligence and physical appearance of the four young men from Judah were more than matched by their fidelity to God and devotion to divine principles (Dan. 1:8).

Daniel's concern undoubtedly centered on the realization that the king's food was not prepared in compliance with the law of Moses. Even the simple fact that it was prepared by Gentiles rendered it unclean. The king's diet surely included pork and other entrees that were forbidden by the Mosaic law (see Lev. 11). Furthermore, the Gentile monarch's food and wine would have been offered to Babylonian gods before they reached his table. Consuming anything offered to pagan gods was strictly forbidden in Exodus 34:15.

B. The Official's Alarm: vss. 9-10

Now God had caused the official to show favor and sympathy to Daniel, but the official told Daniel, "I am afraid of my lord the king, who has assigned your food and drink. Why should he see you looking worse than the other young men your age? The king would then have my head because of you."

Even though God had caused Ashpenaz to be favorably disposed toward Daniel, he was nevertheless reluctant to grant the Israelite's request. The physical well-being, as well as the intellectual development of the court trainees, had been entrusted to Ashpenaz by the king. So the chief official knew that if their health failed, as their poor physical appearance would indicate, his head would roll, and so would theirs (Dan. 1:9-10).

C. The Suggestion Offered by Daniel: vss. 11-14

Daniel then said to the guard whom the chief official had appointed over Daniel, Hananiah, Mishael and Azariah, "Please test your servants for ten days: Give us nothing but vegetables to eat and water to drink. Then compare our appearance with that of the young men who eat the royal food, and treat your servants in accordance with what you see." So he agreed to this and tested them for ten days.

Since he got nowhere with Ashpenaz, Daniel asked the guard placed over them by the chief official to put he and his friends on a 10-day trial diet of vegetables and water. The Hebrew word for vegetables meant "sown things," thus grains would also have been included. Since no vegetables were designated unclean by the law of Moses, there was no danger of defilement with this diet (Dan. 1:11-12).

The guard agreed to Daniel's proposal. Perhaps he was reassured by Daniel's confidence that the Israelites would fare better on the vegetarian diet than those who ate the king's food. In any case, he probably reasoned that 10 days was not enough time for the health of the four youths to suffer any permanent damage (vss. 13-14).

Without compromising his principles or lowering his standards, Daniel managed to negotiate his way to an acceptable solution to a difficult problem. Daniel undoubtedly petitioned the Lord for divine guidance in this matter. That he received God's assistance is

Both Daniel 1:8 and 9 contain a phrase that can be rendered "the commander of the officials" or as "the chief of the eunuchs." The earliest-known eunuchs lived in Mesopotamia, where they worked as servants in the women's quarters of the royal household. They could also serve as palace or government officials, even generals. They were castrated in the belief that this would make them more compliant to their superiors.

While the Hebrew term for "eunuch" appears 47 times in the Old Testament, it is used in the technical sense of a castrated man on only 28 of those occasions. The rest of the time it appears to be used more broadly to refer to an official representative of the king. Its use in Daniel is probably meant to emphasize the official capacity of those who cared for Daniel, rather than their physical state.

obvious. Daniel's lesson to us in this passage is to trust the Lord's leading in difficult situations without compromising biblical principles.

D. The Blessing of God: vss. 15-16

At the end of the ten days they looked healthier and better nourished than any of the young men who ate the royal food. So the guard took away their choice food and the wine they were to drink and gave them vegetables instead.

At the end of the 10-day trial, the four on the vegetarian diet were the picture of health. They looked more vigorous and fit than those who had eaten the king's food. Thus reassured, the guard allowed the young men to continue eating their choice of food rather than the king's provisions (Dan. 1:15-16).

This incident illustrates the truth that God blesses those who obey and trust Him. Perhaps the lesson was not lost on the Israelite people as a whole. They had disobeyed God's laws and were severely judged because of it. Their nation was destroyed and they were now captives.

Daniel and his friends, on the other hand, obeyed God by refusing to eat Nebuchadnezzar's food. They did this even though they knew their stand might cost them their lives. But because of their faithfulness and obedience, the four youths experienced God's blessing, and continued to thrive even in a hostile, ungodly environment.

While Daniel and his three friends were being groomed for service in the royal court, God was preparing them for service to Him and to His people. The Lord gave the four Israelites "knowledge and understanding." They had a special ability to reason clearly and logically, and to approach any subject with insight and discernment. Under royal tutelage and with divine assistance, the four youths excelled in a wide range of subjects in the arts and sciences. Daniel, however, surpassed all the other students in a special field. God enabled him to "understand visions and dreams of all kinds" (vs. 17).

Through the ages, people's fascination with dreams and visions has focused especially on omens and oracles which supposedly reveal the future. Regrettably, such activity has most often been associated with occultic practices. Thus when God's people

Daniel's very life depended on his faith. Since he requested a specific amount of time, a specific method, and a specific result, he knew that only God could bring the necessary results. In one sense Daniel was pitting God against the Babylonian king himself. Daniel would have seen in the Babylonian literature he was being taught many stories in which the gods and goddesses affirmed the king as a deity. So God was the ultimate reason for the success of Daniel's plan.

entered the land of Canaan, where the occult permeated all areas of pagan society, they were strictly forbidden to adopt those practices (see Deut. 18:9-13). Yet in Babylon, Daniel found himself immersed in a culture where that kind of occultic activity was woven into the fabric of everyday life. By God's Spirit and special commission, Daniel was able to interpret dreams without being tainted by any occultic associations.

At the conclusion of the three-year educational program implemented by Nebuchadnezzar, Ashpenaz brought all the court trainees, including Daniel, Hananiah, Mishael, and Azariah, before the king for their "final exam." On the basis of the oral examination that followed, the king graduated the four Israelites at the top of their class and enrolled them in his service. The Babylonian monarch found these four godly young men not only to be the "best and brightest" among the trainees, but also "ten times better than all the magicians and enchanters in his whole kingdom" (Dan. 1:18-20).

In addition to "magicians" and "enchanters," in the next chapter and elsewhere, reference is made to "sorcerers," "astrologers," and "diviners." But all of these seem to be covered by the ironic designation "wise men" (Dan. 2:12-14). Most cultures in the ancient world had an elite group of well-educated men whose counsel and advice was highly regarded and widely sought after, especially by kings. The "wisdom" of such men was usually derived from many sources, most of which were connected with the occult or other pagan rites and rituals.

Such men were among the king's closest advisors. They were glib, master communicators who knew how to impress the king with high-sounding messages from phony gods. Next to the true wisdom and knowledge imparted by the God of Israel, the best the occult specialists could offer looked anemic and uninspired.

Daniel, Hananiah, Mishael, and Azariah achieved prominence even though forced to live in a foreign land and culture. They honored God by applying themselves to their studies and striving for excellence in everything they did. But they honored Him most by their dedicated prayer, unwavering trust, and steadfast loyalty to godly convictions.

The term "ten times" was an expression in the Old Testament meaning "many times" (see Gen. 31:7; Num. 14:22; Job 19:3). "Magicians" was perhaps a general designation for all practitioners of the occult. "Enchanters" may refer to men who performed exorcisms by reciting special spells.

Daniel's service in the royal court continued until Cyrus overthrew the Babylonian empire in 539 B.C. (Dan. 1:21). Other kings would come and go between Nebuchadnezzar and Cyrus. But it mattered little to Daniel which earthly monarch he was compelled to serve at any given time. His allegiance was to the King of all the earth. To God alone would Daniel kneel in prayer, bow in worship, and look for wisdom and guidance.

303

Discussion Questions

1. Why were Daniel and his friends chosen for court service?
2. What are some reasons why eating food from the king's table would violate God's law?
3. Why was the chief official unwilling to make changes in Daniel's diet?
4. What were the reasons for the success of Daniel's resistance?
5. How was Daniel's faith in God evident throughout the entire episode?

Now Ask Yourself . . .

How does my response to stressful situations compare with the way Daniel responded?

How does my faith in God compare with Daniel's faith?

How has my spiritual resolve been tested recently?

Am I, like Daniel, willing to obey God no matter what situation I'm in?

How can I determine what is the right thing to do when I'm in a complex situation?

Illustrations

The first chapter of Daniel teaches several important practical lessons. The first lesson is the value of discernment. The four youths knew exactly what was wrong with eating the king's food. Most likely, they learned this from pious parents (Deut. 6:4-9).

Because of their early training in godly living, the young men knew precisely what they had to do the moment the crisis presented itself. Resisting temptation is easier and more effective if our principles are established ahead of time. The very moment at which enticement to sin presents itself is a poor time to take a crash course in convictions.

The second lesson we learn from Daniel and his friends is the true character of courage. They were not afraid to speak up when their principles were

challenged. But it was more then just talk. The guard was right. Their refusal to eat the king's food could have cost them their lives. The same courage of conviction was revealed later in a fiery furnace and den of lions.

The third lesson is the power of perseverance laced with humility and common sense. Daniel and his companions were determined to overcome any obstacle in order to follow God. With respect and humility, Daniel presented his request to Ashpenaz that he not be made to defile himself with the king's food. But when Ashpenaz refused, in quiet persistence, Daniel went to the guard and proposed a test that was both reasonable and feasible. Then as now the Lord honors such faith and courage.

A Time for Courage

What's Right—Regardless!

DEVOTIONAL READING

Psalm 27:7-14

DAILY BIBLE READINGS

Monday May 22
Psalm 106:1-5
Constantly Do What Is
Right

Tuesday May 23
Proverbs 1:1-7
Do What Is Right, Just,
and Fair

Wednesday May 24
Daniel 3:1-7
The King Makes a Statue
in His Image

Thursday May 25
Daniel 3:8-15
The Jews Don't Worship
the Statue

Friday May 26
Daniel 3:16-25
Three Men Thrown into a
Fiery Furnace

Saturday May 27
Daniel 3:26-30
God Keeps the Three Safe

Sunday May 28
1 Peter 3:13-22
Despite Suffering, Do
What Is Right

Scripture

Background Scripture: *Daniel 3*
Scripture Lesson: *Daniel 3:14, 16-25*
Key Verse: *"They neither serve your gods nor worship the image of gold you have set up."* Daniel 3:12b.

Lesson Aim

We should stand for what is right regardless of the consequences.

Lesson Setting

Time: 580 B.C.
Place: Babylon

Lesson Outline

What's Right—Regardless!

  I. Standing Up for What Is Right: Daniel 3:14, 16-18
     A. *One Last Chance to Compromise: vs. 14*
     B. *A Refusal to Compromise: vss. 16-18*
 II. Willing to Face Death: Daniel 3:19-25
     A. *The Infuriated King: vs. 19*
     B. *The Fiery Inferno: vss. 20-23*
     C. *The Miraculous Rescue: vss. 24-25*

Introduction

Doing What's Right—
Regardless!

When new offices or shopping centers are built today, they can be "instantly" landscaped with bushes, rolls of sod, and even large trees. That kind of portable landscaping is not what the prophet Jeremiah described when he told his audience to "plant" themselves in God (Jer. 17:7-8). Like firmly rooted trees, those who trusted God could remain faithful to Him regardless of the circumstances.

Always standing for what is right challenges our faith. It is tempting to follow the crowd instead. Yet just as a tree burrows its roots deep into the soil to brace itself against the storm and rain, so we believers can anchor ourselves in the Lord Jesus to withstand attacks against us. In this week's lesson, we see how three Hebrew men stood against the wrath of King Nebuchadnezzar. Just as the Lord was with them, so He will be with us, especially as we honor Him in all that we say and do.

Lesson Commentary

I. Standing Up for What Is Right: Daniel 3:14, 16-18

In earliest times, the traditional view among Jews and Christians alike was that Daniel wrote the book bearing his name, and that it was composed in the sixth century in Babylon. However, from at least the third century of the church age, the authorship and date of Daniel have been hotly disputed. Many arguments are set forth by critics for rejecting the traditional view, but their underlying reason is usually a rejection of miraculous prophecy.

A.   One Last Chance to Compromise: vs. 14

And Nebuchadnezzar said to them, "Is it true, Shadrach, Meshach and Abednego, that you do not serve my gods or worship the image of gold I have set up?"

Daniel was not the only one determined to act with integrity while living in Babylon. His three friends—Shadrach, Meshach, and Abednego—were just as strong in their convictions. Their names had been changed from Hebrew to Babylonian (Dan. 1:6-7), but their hearts had not lost any of their initial resolve to stay true to the God of Israel.

Sometime during the reign of Nebuchadnezzar (around 580 B.C.), the king became obsessed with his own power and grandeur. He decided to make a 90-foot image of gold and ordered that everyone must fall down and worship it. According to 3:1, Nebuchadnezzar's giant statue sat on the plain of Dura. It is unclear where this plain was located, but several sites have been suggested. One was the spot where the Harbor and Euphrates

Rivers met. Others have suggested that Dura was located near Apollonia, north of Babylon and east of the Tigris River. The name "Dura" could also have referred to a circular enclosure or fortress.

We do not know which pagan god was honored by this statue. Outside of this account, there is no information about it anywhere. Perhaps Nebuchadnezzar's dream, which is recorded in Daniel 2, motivated him to build the great statue. On the other hand, perhaps his idea of building the idol precipitated his dream, which told of kingdoms that would follow his.

Whatever the case, the king's three Hebrew administrators refused to worship this monstrous idol. Of course, some of the king's astrologers reported this to him, partly out of spite and jealousy, because they deeply resented having these young Hebrews placed over them. They reminded the king that he had put them in positions of responsibility, and now they were being disrespectful to him (3:12).

Overcome with rage because of the Hebrews' disobedience to his decree, Nebuchadnezzar summoned Shadrach, Meshach, and Abednego to his royal court (vs. 13). There he questioned them sharply, to be sure that his informers had told him the truth (vs. 14). Obviously, it was incomprehensible to him that anyone would disobey him, especially his trusted administrators. They were supposed to set the example for others, not break the laws.

As loyal citizens, the Hebrews' were expected to serve Nebuchadnezzar's gods and worship the image of gold. Of course, he had no idea that their first duty was to the God of Israel, not to Nebuchadnezzar's gods. Good polytheist that he was, the king couldn't understand why the Hebrew nobles could not worship his gods along with theirs. That was the way everybody did it.

B. A Refusal to Compromise: vss. 16-18

Shadrach, Meshach and Abednego replied to the king, "O Nebuchadnezzar, we do not need to defend ourselves before you in this matter. If we are thrown into the blazing furnace, the God we serve is able to save us from it, and he will rescue us from your hand, O king. But even if he does not, we want you to know, O king, that we will not serve your gods or worship the image of gold you have set up."

The king's question, "Is it true . . . ?" (Dan. 3:14) went unanswered. Nebuchadnezzar charged ahead and repeated his original command and his warning of execution by burning if the Hebrews did not obey (vss. 5-6). The list of instruments, plus "all kinds of music" (vss. 5, 7, 15), shows how important music was in the worship at ancient temples and palaces. The zither, harp, and pipes were Greek instruments, showing Greek influence in Babylon.

The term rendered "furnace" in Daniel 3 probably comes from a Babylonian word for "oven." Ovens in biblical times were used for smelting and refining metals, firing pottery, or cooking. Some ovens were constructed by digging a pit in the ground and covering its sides with mud, potsherds, or plaster. Such a pit would be several feet deep. People built fires on the oven floor, which was covered with a layer of stones to retain the heat. Fuel for the oven came from wood, charcoal, straw, grass, or even animal dung.

Where was Daniel during this episode? We can only speculate that perhaps he had been sent on a mission somewhere else in the empire. At any rate, Nebuchadnezzar had confessed that Daniel's God was the "God of gods and the Lord of kings" (Dan. 2:47). Daniel had a secure position at the royal court (vs. 49). Despite this, the issue boiled to a head, and in his rage Nebuchadnezzar apparently forgot all about Daniel's God. His anger overcame his logic.

Execution by burning in a furnace was well known in those days. The blast furnaces were made of bricks. There were many brick fields around Babylon. Most bricks were sun-dried, but many were fired in kilns.

After threatening to kill his three young Hebrew officials (vs. 15), Nebuchadnezzar threw down his final challenge. He dared them to even think that their god could save them from the wrath of his judgment. In other words, if they did not worship his god, they were doomed.

Was Nebuchadnezzar really jealous for the worship of his gods, or was he outraged because they had defied his order? Probably his authority was at stake. He could not tolerate the idea that even his choicest appointees could violate his decrees and get away with it.

Therefore, the king made the issue clear once again. The Hebrews could either worship the golden idol or be thrown into the blazing furnace. He would show them no special favors. Despite their privileged position in his kingdom, he would execute them.

Here is the beginning of a remarkable confession. The three Hebrew officials were not daunted by the king's threats (vs. 16). Note that initially they did not make any excuses for their refusal to worship the golden idol. In fact, their answer was a courageous acknowledgment that what their enemies had said about them was indeed true.

Logic and survival would dictate that the Hebrew officials had to defend themselves before the king. But they punctured the king's pride and power by telling him that they did not need to answer to him for their conduct in this matter. Of course, if they had placed top priority on their lives, they would have come up with some weak explanation and begged for mercy.

Instead of defending themselves and trying to save their lives, Shadrach, Meshach, and Abednego chose the path of unwavering faith. In effect, they challenged Nebuchadnezzar to put their God to the test. Now the king had to decide. The ball was in his court: "If we are thrown into the blazing furnace . . . ." (vs. 17).

Such astounding courage shows what faith is made of. The Hebrew officials professed to believe in God; now they were putting their faith on the line. They testified that God was able to save them, and that He would rescue them.

How did the Hebrew officials come by their strong faith? They had walked in obedience to God. They saw God as personal, as someone whom they were bound to serve. They did not waffle, trying to worship Nebuchadnezzar and God. When the chips were down, they went with God. To do otherwise would amount to idolatry.

Of course, the Hebrew officials were strengthened by standing together. They supported each other in their momentous decision. When the law was first passed, they had decided not to worship the idol. They probably had time to think, discuss, and pray together before being hauled before the king. They assured each other that they would remain faithful to Israel's God, no matter how terrible the punishment. Mutual support and encouragement are vital to unwavering faith.

These men were prepared to die for their convictions. The bottom line for them was refusal to engage in false worship of any kind. Even though they owed their positions to the king, they would not compromise and worship his gods.

Part of the Hebrew officials' strong faith must have sprung from their firsthand experience of being captured and deported. They probably knew how the prophets Isaiah and Jeremiah had warned Israel that idolatry would bring certain judgment from the Lord. Although Israel and Judah failed to repent, the lessons taught by the prophets had begun to take hold. After the captivity in Babylon, Israel was never again as prone to idolatry.

Although these Hebrew officials might die, it was not worth it to compromise. Israel and Judah had tried to mix idolatry with worship of God. That effort had brought catastrophe. Therefore, it was not worth trying the same thing again. Regardless of what Nebuchadnezzar might do, Shadrach, Meshach, and Abednego stood firm in their faith in God and their obedience to His laws about worshiping other gods (vs. 18).

Although Shadrach, Meshach, and Abednego were confident in their reply to the king, they were not presumptuous. They were personally convinced that God would rescue them, but recognized the possibility that they may have misunderstood His plans. Either way, their response would be the same. Whether it meant deliverance or death, they would never compromise in their faith (Dan. 3:17-18).

II. Willing to Face Death: Daniel 3:19-25

A. The Infuriated King: vs. 19

Then Nebuchadnezzar was furious with Shadrach, Meshach and Abednego, and his attitude toward them changed. He ordered the furnace heated seven times hotter than usual.

Perhaps Nebuchadnezzar had never before encountered such stiff resistance. Didn't these young Hebrew officials understand what the powerful Babylonian king could do with them? He was in no mood to back down, and in fact because of his pride and position he could not back down. Therefore, to give vent to his furious anger he ordered his people to heat up the furnace seven times hotter than usual (Dan. 3:19).

B. The Fiery Inferno: vss. 20-23

And commanded some of the strongest soldiers in his army to tie up Shadrach, Meshach and Abednego and throw them into the blazing furnace. So these men, wearing their robes, trousers, turbans and other clothes, were bound and thrown into the blazing furnace. The king's command was so urgent and the furnace so hot that the flames of the fire killed the soldiers who took up Shadrach, Meshach and Abednego, and these three men, firmly tied, fell into the blazing furnace.

To make sure that nothing could upset his plans, the king ordered his toughest soldiers to bind Shadrach, Meshach, and Abednego and hurl them into the firey furnace (Dan. 3:20). Perhaps even then Nebuchadnezzar wasn't totally sure about his scheme. He certainly wasted no time on reflection or logic. He had put himself in a corner, and there was no way out.

We don't know how long it was between the initial interrogation and the king's decision. While the king raged on, no doubt the three young Hebrew officials possibly were deep in prayer, asking for God's intervention and for courage to remain true to their convictions. Faced with the prospect of certain death, they did not cave in, recant their faith, and beg for mercy.

Consequently, the three Hebrews were tied up and tossed into the superheated oven (vs. 21). The king's command was so urgent and the furnace so hot that the flames leaped out and incinerated the soldiers as they threw the three men in (vs. 22). Humanly speaking, nothing now seem to prevent Shadrach, Meshach, and Abednego from experiencing a similar gruesome end.

There is no indication in the narrative that the three Hebrew officials had any kind of spiritual vision or revelation that they would be saved from the furnace. They simply trusted in God and refused to bow down to the angry king who ordered their execution (vs. 23).

That Nebuchadnezzar was willing to sacrifice his strongest soldiers to carry out the execution shows the intensity of the king's fury. It was probably the monarch's anger more than a sense of duty that compelled the soldiers to endanger their lives in this way. The death of the soldiers underscored the hopelessness of Shadrach, Meshach, and Abednego's situation and prepared for the surprise that would greet the miraculous deliverance to follow.

C. The Miraculous Rescue: vss. 24-25

Then King Nebuchadnezzar leaped to his feet in amazement and asked his advisers, "Weren't there three men that we tied up and threw into the fire?" They replied, "Certainly, O king." He said, "Look! I see four men walking around in the fire, unbound and unharmed, and the fourth looks like a son of the gods."

"Seven times hotter" (Dan. 3:19) was enough to consume the soldiers, but not enough to destroy Shadrach, Meshach, and Abednego. Nebuchadnezzar realized that something astounding had taken place. He had to check his arithmetic. He was sure that he had sentenced three men to die in the furnace, and his advisers said this was true.

Even though the king's soldiers had cast three men into the fire (vs. 24), Nebuchadnezzar saw four unharmed, unbound men in the fiery furnace. The fourth figure he described as "a son of the gods" (vs. 25). This answer fit his theology, which included the possibility of many gods.

The monarch did not have a name for this person in the furnace, but he was sure the one he saw was not a mere mortal, but a supernatural being. According to verse 28, it was an angel. Some think the Lord Jesus Christ made a special preincarnate appearance to save these faithful men.

In any case, God had vindicated the unwavering faith of these Hebrews with a mighty miracle. By definition this was an act performed in the external world by the supernatural power of God, contrary to the ordinary course of nature, and designed to be a sign. In this incident, the deliverance of the three men from the fiery furnace was intended to show God's sovereignty over the Babylonians who had captured Israel.

After the three men walked out of the fire (the fourth did not for he had evidently disappeared), the king and his officials crowded around them and marveled that the ropes binding them were the only things scorched. Not a hair on the Hebrews' heads was singed. There was not even the smell of fire on them (Dan. 3:27). Instead of losing their ability to influence the king, Daniel's three friends—who were willing to die rather than serve another god—were given a promotion, and God was honored throughout Babylon (vss. 29-30).

311

Discussion Questions

1. What consequences did Shadrach, Meshach, and Abednego face for not worshiping the image?
2. How strongly committed were the three to not worshiping the image?
3. What details show the severity of the three men's punishment and Nebuchadnezzar's anger with them?
4. Why did seeing a fourth person in the fiery furnace astonish Nebuchadnezzar?
5. Who are some Christians you know who have stood up for what is right?

Now Ask Yourself . . .

How do I feel about standing up for what is right?

Are there certain situations when I might not stand up for what is right?

How do I handle fears I might have about taking a stand for what is right?

How can I help my Christian brothers and sisters stand up for godly principles?

Who are some believers I can remember in prayer as they stand up for what is right?

Illustrations

Shadrach, Meshach, and Abednego clearly understood that King Nebuchadnezzar would punish them if they refused to submit to his demand to commit idolatry. Yet despite the severe consequences, they were unwavering in their devotion to God.

Christians around the world today are suffering and even dying for their faith. Most of us, however, will never face a deadly threat as a result of standing for our Christian convictions. But we are often in situations where we must pay some kind of price for our faith when we stand up for what the Bible teaches to be true and right. At times the price may be as costly as losing a job or alienating a loved one, but more often we may suffer a smirk or a derisive laugh.

When we put our religious beliefs on the line, we must always stand on our Christian principles regardless of the consequences. After all, Jesus was resolute in saving us from God's wrath despite encountering every kind of hostility and indignation. Therefore, we must have the same kind of attitude as His apostles, who rejoiced "because they had been counted worthy of suffering disgrace" (Acts 5:41) for Christ.

Keeping an unwavering faith in Christ when we are alone can be difficult. We need to remember that one straw can easily be broken, but many straws joined together are unbreakable. That is why God provides us with Christian brothers and sisters to strengthen us when we stand up for what is right in the Lord.

June 4, 2006

Our Heavenly Father

Share the Blessings

DEVOTIONAL READING

Psalm 24

DAILY BIBLE READINGS

Monday May 29
  Genesis 12:1-9
  God Blesses Abram

Tuesday May 30
  Psalm 119:1-8
  Blessed Are Those Who Seek God

Wednesday May 31
  Psalm 128
  Walk in God's Ways and Be Blessed

Thursday June 1
  Matthew 5:1-12
  Jesus Shares with the Crowds

Friday June 2
  Matthew 5:13-16
  Be Salt and Light

Saturday June 3
  Ephesians 1:1-14
  Jesus Christ Has Blessed Us

Sunday June 4
  Ephesians 1:15-23
  Pray for Others to Be Blessed

Scripture

Background Scripture: *Matthew 5:1-16*
Scripture Lesson: *Matthew 5:1-16*
Key Verse: *"In the same way, let your light shine before men, that they may see your good deeds and praise your Father in heaven." Matthew 5:16.*

Lesson Aim

Receive God's blessings and share them.

Lesson Setting

Time: A.D. 28
Place: Galilee

Lesson Outline

Share the Blessings

  I. The Sermon's Setting: Matthew 5:1-2
  II. The Sermon's Blessings: Matthew 5:3-12
     A. *For the Poor in Spirit: vs. 3*
     B. For the Mournful: vs. 4
     C. *For the Meek: vs. 5*
     D. *For the Spiritually Hungry: vs. 6*
     E. *For the Merciful: vs. 7*
     F. *For the Pure in Heart: vs. 8*
     G. *For the Peacemakers: vs. 9*
     H. *For the Persecuted: vss. 10-12*
  III. The Sermon's Challenges: Matthew 5:13-16
     A. *To Be Salt: vs. 13*
     B. *To Be Light: vss. 14-16*

Introduction

*Finding Supreme
Happiness*

With the proliferation of legalized gambling, more and more people think they can find happiness by winning lots of money. Players envision paying off their debts and buying a new home, car, or boat. They also dream of traveling to distant lands and enjoying idyllic vacations.

Occasionally, we read stories about the troubles that have plagued overnight millionaires. This should not surprise us, for as Christians we know that money cannot buy happiness. Perhaps that's why Jesus, in His Sermon on the Mount, did not pronounce His blessings on the materially rich.

While we acknowledge the perils of money, we find it hard not to define our lives in terms of how much we have. It should come as no surprise, then, that we need the Sermon on the Mount for our eternal wellness. In it Jesus strikes at the heart of our desires and values. By taking His spiritual medicine, we will make our souls vibrant and strong.

Lesson Commentary

I. The Sermon's Setting: Matthew 5:1-2

Now when he saw the crowds, he went up on a mountainside and sat down. His disciples came to him, and he began to teach them, saying:

Jesus announced that God's kingdom was drawing near (Matt. 4:17). What attitudes and actions were appropriate for a citizen of God's kingdom? Christ answered this question in what is known as the Sermon on the Mount (chaps. 5—7). Although Jesus' primary audience would have been His disciples, there was a larger crowd of people who listened to Him teach (7:28).

The "crowds" of Matthew 5:1 who came to hear Jesus' sermon are presumably the same as the "large crowds" of 4:25 who followed Jesus. They came from at least a 100-mile radius of the territory to listen to Jesus teach. God's supreme Old Testament revelation—the law—was given by Moses, accompanied by thunder and lightning, from Mount Sinai. One greater than Moses gave this sermon also from a mountain region probably near the Sea of Galilee.

As the Master Teacher, Jesus employed the normal sitting posture of a Jewish rabbi. The ethics that He taught in His sermon

There are two views regarding when and where the Sermon on the Mount was preached. One group asserts that it is a compilation of various teachings that were given on different occasions in several places. A second group believes the sermon was delivered at one time early in Jesus' ministry and in one location (for example, on the side of a mountain near Capernaum).

contrasted sharply with the legalism of His religious opponents. They were absorbed with external righteousness. Jesus launched His sermon by overthrowing such an approach to life.

II. The Sermon's Blessings: Matthew 5:3-12

A. For the Poor in Spirit: vs. 3

"Blessed are the poor in spirit, for theirs is the kingdom of heaven."

At various times in history, there have been common misconceptions made about the Sermon on the Mount. Some have said it is nothing more than a call to social action, while others regard it simply as a list of things to do to be happy. Still others say the sermon is not applicable for this age, but rather only for the Kingdom age to come. As we read the sermon, we should be careful to put it in its first-century context and let the lessons appearing in it speak for themselves.

For instance, consider Matthew 5:3. In this verse we are immediately struck by the presence of the word "blessed." This refers to the spiritual wellness of believers. The term conveys the idea of being the privileged recipient of God's favor, and thus enjoying a happier end than the wicked. (Jesus' various declarations of blessedness are commonly called the Beatitudes.)

Jesus pronounced His first blessing on the "poor in spirit," which is a reference to humility. These are believers who have been stripped of their own securities and thus feel deeply their need for God. The Savior's redemption, not their own goodness, is the basis for their citizenship in heaven.

B. For the Mournful: vs. 4

"Blessed are those who mourn, for they will be comforted."

Jesus pronounced His second blessing on the mournful, who will receive God's comfort. "Those who mourn" (Matt. 5:4) weep because they know they have transgressed against the Lord. And they cry in confession and repentance, which are a reflection of their humble spirit.

These believers do not look to the world for satisfaction, joy, or comfort. Rather, they find these things in the Savior alone. They come to Jesus in humility and faith, confessing their sins, and He

Portions of the Sermon on the Mount are similar to Jesus' Sermon on the Plain (Luke 6:20-49). Some experts think these passages represent two different messages given on separate occasions, while others think the two passages represent the same message. According to the second view, Luke presented an abbreviated version of the longer sermon recorded in Matthew.

enters their lives and stays there with the sweet assurance of His forgiveness.

C. For the Meek: vs. 5

"Blessed are the meek, for they will inherit the earth."

Jesus gave His third blessing to the meek and promised them the earth as an inheritance (Matt. 5:5). Meekness has two aspects. On the one hand, the meek bear up under provocations, control their feelings, and refuse to get even. On the other hand, they are courageous, generous, and courteous. They put others, not themselves, first.

Here we find Jesus explaining the values of the Kingdom. Relationships, possessions, information, prayer, money, and power are a few of the categories He redefined from God's perspective. Jesus showed that following Him involves radical change. For most of us this means undoing the way we've always acted and reconsidering traditional sources of wisdom from our family, friends, and culture. To become like Jesus requires us to do a tough-minded review of our moral values and lifelong goals and dreams.

Just as in the preamble to the Ten Commandments God presented Himself to Israel as their Redeemer (Exod. 20:1-2), so in the prologue to Jesus' Sermon He presented Himself to Israel as their Messiah (Matt. 5:1-2). Also, as Moses received the law on a mountain, so Jesus taught the "new law" from a mountainside.

D. For the Spiritually Hungry: vs. 6

"Blessed are those who hunger and thirst for righteousness, for they will be filled."

Jesus next blessed those who longed for righteousness and promised to fulfill their desires (Matt. 5:6). The attitude is one of desiring God above all things and seeking to be in a right relationship with Him and others. While greed, injustice, and violence consume the unsaved, believers yearn for justice and goodness to be established.

In these first four beatitudes there is a logical progression. First, we admit our spiritual bankruptcy (vs. 3). Seeing ourselves as "poor in spirit" causes us to "mourn" (vs. 4) our condition. Because we grieve over our sorrowful state, we come to a correct notion of ourselves, which is to be humble and meek (vs. 5). Thus, by accepting the appraisal arrived at in verses 3 through 5, we are ready to "hunger and thirst for righteousness" (vs. 6).

E. For the Merciful: vs. 7

"Blessed are the merciful, for they will be shown mercy."

Jesus then blessed the merciful and said they will be treated with mercy (Matt. 5:7). This verse is talking about having a gracious disposition toward others. The merciful are kind, charitable, and ready to sympathize with the sufferings of the afflicted. They long for justice, but are not harsh and cruel. And they seek to be generous to all by showing the love of God without partiality or preconditions.

F. For the Pure in Heart: vs. 8

"Blessed are the pure in heart, for they will see God."

Jesus gave His sixth blessing on the pure in heart and promised that they would see God. The focus here is on being genuine and honest in all one's dealings. Such purity requires spiritual discipline and self-control. It renounces self-love for the love of God.

Sin is the enemy of moral purity, and popular ideas and activities conspire to undo it. Furthermore, the world ridicules and taunts the virtuous for not having fun. But instead of fun, the pure receive the greatest gift of all, namely, a personal encounter with the living God. When we come to know Him through faith in Christ, we are truly fulfilled.

G. For the Peacemakers: vs. 9

"Blessed are the peacemakers, for they will be called sons of God."

In the seventh beatitude, Jesus pronounced a blessing on "the peacemakers" (Matt. 5:9). In saying they "will be called sons of God," Jesus meant they will become spiritual children in God's heavenly family (John 1:12; Eph. 1:5). Peacemakers do not merely stay cool, calm, and collected but also work for peace in their families, schools, churches, businesses, and communities.

Jesus is the ultimate peacemaker, for He destroyed the enmity between sinners and God (2 Cor. 5:18-19; Eph. 2:13-18). Jesus not only brings us peace with God, but also heals our broken relationships.

H. For the Persecuted: vss. 10-12

"Blessed are those who are persecuted because of righteousness, for theirs is the kingdom of heaven. Blessed are you when people

We don't know exactly where Jesus preached the Sermon on the Mount. The traditional site, however, is on a hillside near Capernaum, on the northwest shore of the Sea of Galilee. Part of the "crowds" (Matt. 4:25; 5:1) Jesus drew came from the thousands of people who lived in the cities and smaller settlements that dotted the coastline of the Sea of Galilee during the first century A.D.

insult you, persecute you and falsely say all kinds of evil against you because of me. Rejoice and be glad, because great is your reward in heaven, for in the same way they persecuted the prophets who were before you."

In the final beatitudes, Jesus blessed the persecuted and promised them the kingdom of heaven (Matt. 5:10). He taught that when Christians stand up for truth, righteousness, and goodness, they will be slandered and insulted (vs. 11). Such persecution arises because of taking a stand for righteousness and being known as a follower of Christ.

Jesus gave two reasons His harassed followers could accept their circumstances with an attitude of joy (vs. 12). First, they ought to realize that their eternal reward will exceed their wildest expectations. Second, they can remember that God's enemies also mistreated His prophets.

As followers of Christ, we should not be shocked when we are slandered, physically harmed, or targeted for malicious rumors. Although we feel the intense pain of such injustices, we can persevere by holding to the promise of God's richest blessings.

For instance, Jesus said that heaven belongs to the persecuted. By this He meant they would have a place of distinction in the kingdom of God. In this present world, many believers are harassed and abused by others for the cause of Christ. The world might regard them as nobodies, but God considers them as people of honor who should be given nothing less than unending joy in His presence.

III. The Sermon's Challenges: Matthew 5:13-16

A. To Be Salt: vs. 13

"You are the salt of the earth. But if the salt loses its saltiness, how can it be made salty again? It is no longer good for anything, except to be thrown out and trampled by men."

Jesus next compared believers to salt (Matt. 5:13). In ancient times, the Jews obtained their salt from the Dead Sea and from mineral deposits they found in the soil. The salinity of the chemical could be lost due to overexposure to the sun and excessively damp conditions. People used salt to season and preserve their food and to bring out its flavor. Ingesting salt also helped people to maintain their electrolytes and prevent dehydration from occurring.

Jesus noted that when salt becomes contaminated with foreign substances, it can lose its distinctive flavor and preservative qualities. When this happened, people would discard such a worthless chemical. Jesus was figuratively referring to the spiritual qualities that should be present in His disciples. In other words, they needed to have a wholesomeness about them that enabled them to be a blessing and a moral preservative in the world.

B. To Be Light: vss. 14-16

"You are the light of the world. A city on a hill cannot be hidden. Neither do people light a lamp and put it under a bowl. Instead they put it on its stand, and it gives light to everyone in the house. In the same way, let your light shine before men, that they may see your good deeds and praise your Father in heaven."

Jesus explained that a city located at the top of a hill cannot escape detection (Matt. 5:14). Likewise, believers who are fully devoted to Jesus could not remain hidden, for the spiritual light of their lives will be visible to everyone. They are to radiate the knowledge and presence of God to people living in spiritual darkness or ignorance.

Christ noted that people in His day did not light a lamp and place it under a wooden basket or clay bowl, which was used to measure ground meal or flour. Rather, they placed the lamp on a stand so that it might radiate its light to every person in the house (vs. 15).

The lamp symbolized the believers' works of righteousness, the light of which shone far into the darkness of the world and gave glory to God. When the unsaved saw the good that believers performed, they were more inclined to praise the "Father in heaven" (vs. 16).

In Bible times, cities on hills often were built out of white limestone. These towns gleamed in the sun and could not easily be hidden. Furthermore, at night the oil lamps used by the inhabitants could be seen glowing over the surrounding area.

Discussion Questions

1. In what ways does God bless the "poor in spirit" (Matt. 5:3)?
2. What did Jesus promise to those who mourn and to those who desire righteousness?
3. What do the merciful receive?
4. What blessings come to the persecuted?
5. What distinguishes believers as "the light of the world" (vs. 14)?

Now Ask Yourself . . .

How has my Christian faith given me contentment with life?

What are some of God's blessings in my life that I can share with others?

How do I usually respond when someone unfairly criticizes me or questions my motives in serving the Lord?

What are some things I can do to encourage other Christians to rejoice when they feel mistreated?

What does it mean to me to be salt and light to the world?

Illustrations

Jesus began the Sermon on the Mount with the Beatitudes. These blessings list the rewards of poverty of spirit (humility), mournfulness (grieving over sin), meekness (keeping power under control), hunger and thirst after righteousness (spiritual seeking), mercy (being gracious), purity of heart (being forgiven), peacemaking (reconciliation), and persecution (suffering for taking a stand).

Contentment is at the heart of such character qualities. Satisfaction and joy is difficult in our society because so many things tell us we're lacking this or that—a bigger house, a more luxurious car, another television, a thinner figure, a better job, a gorgeous boyfriend or girlfriend, and so on. Yet we know from the teachings of Scripture that God can fill us with contentment despite lacking these things (Phil. 4:11-13).

A godly character is the foundation upon which contentment rests. We know that as Christians, our character should be godly because that's who we are. For instance, if someone asks why we are being peacemakers, our answer should be "It's just my character in Christ." At the same time, we need to cultivate a godly character each day by committing ourselves to being all Christ taught. When we do, we will grow in godly character.

The Right Reflection

DEVOTIONAL READING

Amos 5:4-15

DAILY BIBLE READINGS

Monday June 5
Genesis 22:1-8
God Tests Abraham

Tuesday June 6
Genesis 22:9-19
Abraham's Character Is
Strengthened

Wednesday June 7
1 Samuel 16:1-13
God Looks on the Heart

Thursday June 8
Matthew 5:17-26
Jesus Came to Fulfill the
Law

Friday June 9
Matthew 5:27-37
Jesus Says to Think
Differently

Saturday June 10
Matthew 5:38-48
Be Like Your Heavenly
Father

Sunday June 11
Romans 5:1-11
Character Is Developed
through Suffering

Scripture

Background Scripture: *Matthew 5:17-48*

Scripture Lesson: *Matthew 5:17-20, 38-48*

Key Verse: *"Be perfect, therefore, as your heavenly Father is perfect." Matthew 5:48.*

Lesson Aim

Jesus wants us to reflect God's character.

Lesson Setting

Time: A.D. 28

Place: Galilee

Lesson Outline

The Right Reflection

I. A Call to Extreme Righteousness: Matthew 5:17-20
   A. *Affirming the Importance of the Law: vss. 17-19*
   B. *Affirming the Importance of Righteousness:*
     vs. 20

II. Responding to Evil: Matthew 5:38-42
   A. *The Sinful Way: vs. 38*
   B. *The Godly Way: vss. 39-42*

III. Responding to Our Enemies: Matthew 5:43-48
   A. *The Sinful Way: vs. 43*
   B. *The Godly Way: vss. 44-47*
   C. *The Divine Standard: vs. 48*

Introduction

Fulfilling the Commandments

Everyone who has gone through military basic training knows what the drill sergeant's idea of "perfection" means. One speck of dust anywhere in the barracks can bring down the wrath of the inspectors. In civilian industry this attitude used to be called "zero defects."

When we consider our lives, we know that we have not reached such a high standard, especially in terms of morality. But that is not an excuse to slack off and settle for second best. Whether it's our character, our maturity, or our compassion for others, we should make every effort to grow in these areas.

The Christian life means growth over a lifetime in obeying the teachings of Scripture. Because we are joined to Jesus by faith, we have the resources we need to be upright in thought and virtuous in conduct. With the Lord's help and the encouragement of His people, we can aim for the goal of being holy in our lives.

Lesson Commentary

I. A Call to Extreme Righteousness: Matthew 5:17-20

A. Affirming the Importance of the Law: vss. 17-19

"Do not think that I have come to abolish the Law or the Prophets; I have not come to abolish them but to fulfill them. I tell you the truth, until heaven and earth disappear, not the smallest letter, not the least stroke of a pen, will by any means disappear from the Law until everything is accomplished. Anyone who breaks one of the least of these commandments and teaches others to do the same will be called least in the kingdom of heaven, but whoever practices and teaches these commands will be called great in the kingdom of heaven."

"The Law" (Matt. 5:17) refers to the specific code of rules and regulations that God gave to Moses on Mount Sinai. The law was part of the covenant that set Israel apart as God's people. It governed their worship, their relationship to God, and their social relationships with one another.

God's moral and ceremonial laws were given to help people love God and be compassionate to people. However, throughout Israel's history, these laws had often been misquoted and misapplied. Sadly, by Jesus' time, the religious leaders had turned the laws into a confusing mess of rules.

In the Sermon on the Mount, Jesus talked about a better way to understand God's law. Because of this, some of His antagonists falsely accused Him of trying to set aside the teachings of the Hebrew Scriptures (the Law and the Prophets, as they were commonly referred to in ancient times). Jesus countered by declaring that He did not stand in opposition to the Mosaic law. In fact, He was trying to bring people back to the law's original purpose.

Thus, Jesus did not speak against the law itself, but rather against the abuses and excesses to which it had been subjected. Likewise, His goal was not to set aside, negate, or annul God's commands. Rather, Jesus came to fulfill the truth of the Old Testament. All that was written in the law pointed to Him, and everything He did underscored His deep commitment to it (Matt. 5:17).

When Jesus said "I tell you the truth" (vs. 18), He was making a solemn statement. "The smallest letter" (the Hebrew letter *yodh*) and the "least stroke of a pen" (the slight extension on the Hebrew letter *daleth*) refer to the minutest part of the law. Jesus declared that as long as heaven and earth continued to exist, so would the smallest detail of God's Word until its purpose was achieved.

There were some in the crowds who loved to tell others what to do, even though they failed to live up to the law's commands. Jesus made it clear to these hypocrites that obeying God's laws is more important than just explaining them.

Thus, Jesus condemned those who set aside what they considered the least of the commandments of Scripture and taught others to do the same. Jesus declared that any of His followers who ever committed such an offense would be considered least in the divine Kingdom (vs. 19). In this case, the punishment fit the crime. Conversely, those who obeyed Scripture and taught others to do the same would have an important place in the Kingdom. The contrast between the two options could not be greater.

Though the law was given specifically to Israel, it rests on eternal moral principles that are consistent with God's character. Thus, it is a summary of fundamental and universal moral standards. It expresses the essence of what God requires of people.

B. Affirming the Importance of Righteousness: vs. 20

"For I tell you that unless your righteousness surpasses that of the Pharisees and the teachers of the law, you will certainly not enter the kingdom of heaven."

The religious leaders of Israel were exacting and scrupulous in their efforts to follow their laws. It's understandable why many in Jesus' day would see the Pharisees and scribes as icons of virtue. But Jesus declared that even they were not sufficiently good to merit God's approval. In fact, a person's righteousness had to go

Jesus came as the fulfillment of the Law and the Prophets, not as their destroyer. He established a standard of righteousness for people that can only be attained through Him.

Though the religious leaders of Jesus' day (such as the Pharisees) are often looked down upon by Christians, there were some, like Nicodemus, who genuinely sought God (see John 3:1-21). To exceed the righteousness of these men would be considered impossible by the standards of the day.

In the rest of Matthew 5, Jesus discussed how His followers were to surpass the religious leaders in righteousness. He dealt with anger (vss. 21-26), lust (vss. 27-30), divorce (vss. 31-32), vows (vss. 33-37), revenge (vss. 38-42), and loving enemies (vss. 43-48).

well beyond that of the Jewish leaders. Unless a person did a better job at being religious, entrance into the kingdom of God would be denied (Matt. 5:20).

We might well ask ourselves how we can be more righteous than people like the Pharisees, who devoted their lives to learning and obeying the law. The answer is that we can have such righteousness through faith in Christ (Phil. 3:9). Moreover, real righteousness surpasses legalistic devotion in that it is not merely external rules-keeping. We can be right with God and enjoy His favor by submitting to Jesus in our heart.

II. Responding to Evil: Matthew 5:38-42

A. The Sinful Way: vs. 38

"You have heard that it was said, 'Eye for eye, and tooth for tooth.' "

When Jesus said, "But I tell you" (vss. 22, 28, 32, 34, 39, 44), He was not doing away with the law or adding His own beliefs. Rather, He was clarifying why God instituted the law. For example, the Mosaic law taught a code of retribution known as *lex talionis,* a Latin phrase meaning "the law of the tooth." This is based on the maxim "an eye for an eye, and tooth for tooth" (vs. 38), which the law affirmed (Exod. 21:24; Lev. 24:20; Deut. 19:21). Although in our day this principle seems unnecessarily harsh, it was actually more lenient than the code of retribution practiced by many of Israel's neighbors.

During the Old Testament era, the principle of *lex talionis* helped to deter evil and limit retribution. For instance, if people knew that whatever they did to hurt someone would be done to them, this might make them hesitate before deliberately inflicting injury. Also, if one person put out the eye of another, the victim was not allowed to murder in retaliation. In other words, the punishment had to fit the crime. Such a limitation curbed the custom of blood feuding that was all too common in the ancient world.

This principle of retaliation was never intended to be implemented on a personal level, but appeared in Old Testament passages addressed to civil officials. Sadly, many people eventually reversed its limiting intent to such an extent that by Jesus' day some used it as a guideline for their personal relationships. Those who did so kept track of offenses and looked for an opportunity to retaliate.

B. The Godly Way: vss. 39-42

"But I tell you, Do not resist an evil person. If someone strikes you on the right cheek, turn to him the other also. And if someone wants to sue you and take your tunic, let him have your cloak as well. If someone forces you to go one mile, go with him two miles. Give to the one who asks you, and do not turn away from the one who wants to borrow from you."

Jesus sought to restore the legal standard to its original intent. He thus stated that instead of retaliating, His followers were not to resist at all (Matt. 5:39). Jesus supported this amazing command with four examples taken from the everyday life of believers.

The first example told believers who were slapped on the right cheek to offer the offender the other cheek as well. The mention of the right cheek possibly suggests that Jesus had in mind a back-handed slap, a particularly vicious kind of insult in that culture.

By this example, Jesus was telling His disciples not to seek revenge or retaliate. Rather than try to get even, they were to be loving, kind, and considerate. They were to show compassion to those who hated them, goodwill to those who spoke abusively to them, and patience to those who harassed them. Clearly, only God could enable believers to live in this way.

The second example is set in the court of law. If someone sued Jesus' followers for their tunic, they were to give the "cloak as well" (vs. 40). The tunic was a long undergarment of cotton or linen. The cloak was a heavier outer garment worn as a robe and used as a blanket at night. A person usually had only one cloak, and the law said it could not be taken (Exod. 22:26).

By this example, Jesus was urging His followers to be generous and sympathetic to those in need. If someone asked for food or water, they were to give it readily and willingly. Or if someone asked His disciples for other kinds of help, they were to respond freely and generously. Such responses required an attitude of humility on the part of believers.

The third example was drawn from Israel's experience with the occupying Roman army. Roman soldiers had the authority to seize civilians and force them to carry military equipment the length of one Roman mile. Those who were drafted for such a task did not have the luxury of saying no, but instead had to drop whatever they were doing and comply immediately. Obviously, the tendency would have been to obey only to the limit of the law. Jesus, how-

In Matthew 5:17-48, Jesus appears to make some stark, seemingly impossible demands. For instance, God's people should never use force in self-defense (vs. 39), comply with all types of demands (vs. 41), and lend without reserve (vs. 42). It's helpful to remember that, in this part of the Sermon, Jesus was addressing the issue of morality. He spoke in stark contrasts and strong hyperboles (overstatements for the sake of emphasis) in order to stress that good should prevail over evil, grace over vengeance, and love over hatred. In the midst of this teaching, Jesus challenged His followers to be people of grace and integrity. He thus gave them several examples of ways that He expected them to surpass the religious leaders in virtue.

325

In summary, Matthew 5:38-42 illustrates numerous aspects of Kingdom living. For instance, Jesus commands His followers to love everyone, even those who hate and abuse them. By loving everyone, the believer imitates God's love for all people. Jesus also noted that even unbelievers loved those who loved them, so believers must do more than that. Ultimately, Jesus' followers must strive to be like God Himself.

ever, urged His disciples to go two miles (Matt. 5:41).

The fourth example involved a loan. According to the law of Moses, a loan could be made to a fellow Israelite, but no interest could be charged (Exod. 22:25). Jesus' followers, however, were to give without any thought of return (Matt. 5:42).

Although these four examples relate to a variety of situations drawn from human as well as divine law, they all require the believer to forgo certain rights. They also call on the follower of Jesus to go beyond the normal standard. The essential principle behind the commands is that of putting other people first.

III. Responding to Our Enemies: Matthew 5:43-48

A. The Sinful Way: vs. 43
"You have heard that it was said, 'Love your neighbor and hate your enemy.'"

Leviticus 19:18 commanded God's people to love their neighbor. The Pharisees undercut the original intent of this law by asserting that they should love only those who love in return. Some even rationalized away this obligation by defining the concept of "neighbor" narrowly to include only the upright. They also said that Psalms 139:19-22 and 140:9-11 validated their desire to hate their enemies (Matt. 5:43). Clearly, such an attitude contradicted what God had revealed in the law.

B. The Godly Way: vss. 44-47
"But I tell you: Love your enemies and pray for those who persecute you, that you may be sons of your Father in heaven. He causes his sun to rise on the evil and the good, and sends rain on the righteous and the unrighteous. If you love those who love you, what reward will you get? Are not even the tax collectors doing that? And if you greet only your brothers, what are you doing more than others? Do not even pagans do that?"

Jesus commanded His followers to reject the popular misinterpretation of the law and replace it with an accurate understanding. For instance, Jesus urged the disciples to love their enemy as well as their neighbor and pray for anyone who mistreated them (Matt. 5:44). Like their Savior, Christ's disciples were to act in the best interests of those who treated them badly.

Verse 45 reveals that Christian love is to be a reflection of God's own love. The motive Jesus gave for obeying these principles was that His followers would be acting like their Father in heaven, who showered His kindness and blessings on all people regardless of who they were. This was the language of evidence. Believers were to act toward their enemies as the Father in heaven has acted toward us.

According to Jesus, those who love only those who love them follow a standard no higher than that of the tax collectors (vs. 46). These people were widely regarded as extortionists who enriched themselves at the expense of their neighbors. To say that someone was doing no more than a tax collector implied that the person's behavior was unrighteous and self-centered.

Jesus mentioned the custom of greeting one's neighbor because a typical greeting involved the pronouncement of a blessing (vs. 47). Jesus' contemporaries greeted one another with the word *shalom*— a prayer for the bestowal of God's peace upon the recipient.

C. The Divine Standard: vs. 48

"Be perfect, therefore, as your heavenly Father is perfect."

The standard Jesus' followers were to adopt was that of God Himself. As His children, they were to reflect His image. The New Testament term rendered "perfect" (Matt. 5:48) can also be translated "complete" or "having attained the end or purpose." In other words, Jesus was focusing on moral purity and spiritual maturity, which were demonstrated by the believer's willingness to heed God's commands.

Ultimately, our standard of behavior is the perfect example of Jesus Christ. His life and teaching shows that the call to perfection is a command to love as inclusively and completely as God does. Obviously obedience to such a command requires the transforming work of the Holy Spirit. We cannot love others as Christ does apart from the grace of God.

An overview of Matthew 5:21-48 indicates that Jesus gave a total of six examples of ways that He expected His followers to surpass the religious leaders in righteousness. His examples are as follows:

- *Go beyond avoiding murder to avoiding anger.*
- *Go beyond avoiding adultery to avoiding lustful looks.*
- *Go beyond avoiding illegal divorce to avoiding divorce itself (except for unfaithfulness).*
- *Go beyond avoiding the breaking of your oath to avoiding the taking of an oath.*
- *Go beyond avoiding taking unreasonable retribution to giving unreasonable help.*
- *Go beyond loving your neighbors to loving your enemies as well.*

Discussion Questions

1. What was Jesus' intent with respect to the law?
2. What moral standard of righteousness was needed to enter the divine kingdom?
3. How did Jesus say His followers should respond to those who wronged them?
4. How is it possible for believers to love their enemies?
5. According to Matthew 5:48, in what sense does God want us to be perfect?

Now Ask Yourself . . .

What is my attitude toward God's commands in Scripture?

How has my life been enriched by heeding God's Word?

How does Jesus want me to respond to evil people and to those in need?

Do others see from my actions that I am a member of God's spiritual family?

What can I do to help new believers to grow in Christ?

Illustrations

Every small group has certain individuals who invariably demand extra grace on our part to accommodate their personality. Even in a Christian setting, they require a soft answer and patience. Maybe some people have come to mind as you read this. They are not enemies, just frustrating people who do not return the grace you extend toward them.

Part of the reason we have difficulty responding in love to those who have irritated us is that we don't want to appear like a doormat to others. Thus we become defensive instead of exhibiting the fruit of the Spirit. It's natural for us to feel angry, hurt, and sometimes bitter when others sin against us. The choice to forgive will not automatically cancel out these emotions. What, then, should we do?

First, we can begin by showing love to those who have hurt us, regardless of our feelings. It is possible to act lovingly toward an enemy even while we are struggling with the bitterness or anger we feel. Second, we should acknowledge such emotions to God and ask for His help. There is no need to hide such feelings from God, for He knows the thoughts and intents of our hearts even better than we do.

Third, we should entrust ourselves to the care of God. Jesus' words remind us that God is the only one who can ensure that true justice will be done. As long as our eyes are on the offense of the one who has hurt us, we will be drawn into the vortex of bitterness. But when our focus is on Jesus, we find both an example of forgiveness and the motivation to follow His example.

Stop Worrying

DEVOTIONAL READING

Philippians 4:4-9

DAILY BIBLE READINGS

Monday June 12
  Philippians 4:6-9
  Don't Be Anxious

Tuesday June 13
  Philippians 4:10-12
  Be Content in All
  Circumstances

Wednesday June 14
  Luke 12:22-26
  Consider the Ravens

Thursday June 15
  Luke 12:27-34
  Seek His Kingdom

Friday June 16
  Matthew 6:19-24
  Serve God, Not Money

Saturday June 17
  Matthew 6:25-27
  Don't Worry about Your
  Life

Sunday June 18
  Matthew 6:28-34
  Seek God First

Scripture

Background Scripture: *Matthew 6*

Scripture Lesson: *Matthew 6:25-34*

Key Verse: *"Seek first his kingdom and his righteousness, and all these things will be given to you as well."* *Matthew 6:33.*

Lesson Aim

Focus on God, not the worries of this world.

Lesson Setting

Time: A.D. 28

Place: Galilee

Lesson Outline

Stop Worrying

  I. Lessons from Nature: Matthew 6:25-30
    A. *Anxiety about Life: vs. 25*
    B. *Our Value to God: vs. 26*
    C. *The Futility of Worry: vs. 27*
    D. *The Lesson from Nature: vss. 28-30*
  II. God's Prescription for Anxiety: Matthew 6:31-34
    A. *God's Awareness of Our Needs: vss. 31-32*
    B. *Kingdom Priorities versus Future Concerns: vss. 33-34*

Introduction

Worrying Needlessly

It's common knowledge that excessive and prolonged worrying is not good for our health. We also know that worrying can rob us of peace and contentment. It should come as no surprise, then, that Jesus told us not to worry. He saw it as an exercise in futility. How then can we stop worrying?

Many books and sermons on tape give us good practical advice. The simplest answer, of course, is to focus our attention on the Lord. When we start the day with praise and thanks to God as well as meditation on His Word, we are in good shape to deal with the problem of worrying.

It also helps to have some good friends. These would not be people who dream up more stuff for us to worry about, but rather those who are good listeners and who can draw us back to our resources in Christ. Occasionally, we all need encouragement to let go of our worries and give them to the Lord.

Lesson Commentary

The second half of Jesus' Sermon on the Mount begins with three don'ts and a do. First, He said, "Don't store up earthly treasures, don't worry about your life, and don't judge others" (see Matt. 6:19—7:6). Then He said, "Do ask what you want of God" (see 7:7-12). The sermon comes to its conclusion with advice to stay away from false teaching and embrace Jesus' teaching (see 7:13-27).

I. Lessons from Nature: Matthew 6:25-30

A. Anxiety about Life: vs. 25

"Therefore I tell you, do not worry about your life, what you will eat or drink; or about your body, what you will wear. Is not life more important than food, and the body more important than clothes?"

In our age of consumerism and materialism, the first don't Jesus mentioned is terribly important for us to hear. Jesus told His followers not to spend their time hoarding greater and greater amounts of earthly treasures. After all, He indicated, fine clothes can be eaten by moths, metal jewelry and utensils can rust, and money and valuables can be stolen (Matt. 6:19). Worldly wealth is never entirely secure.

Instead of hoarding, Jesus' followers were to invest their lives in accumulating heavenly riches. Perhaps Jesus was referring to rewards from God for such things as serving others in love and forgiving those who have inflicted harm. In heaven there is no depreciation and no theft; the treasures stockpiled there are safe (vs. 20).

With penetrating insight, Jesus declared, "Where your treasure is, there your heart will be also" (vs. 21). People who spend their time accumulating earthly possessions have their interests anchored on temporal concerns. People who spend their time storing up spiritual treasures are focused on eternal matters.

Jesus switched from talking about one body part, the heart, to talking about another, the eye. But He was still on the topic of problems associated with greed for worldly wealth. In first-century A.D. Palestine, the setting of the sun meant it was time to light the lamps. Jesus said that just as a lamp spreads a glow in a room at night, so the eye brings light into the body. As long as the eyes work, the body has light; but if they don't work, the body is in darkness (vss. 22-23a).

The Lord had a strong word for the spiritually blind. Using a paradox, He said that the "light" of these people is "darkness," and He commented, "How great is that darkness!" (vs. 23b).

Jesus changed His metaphor again, this time to slavery. He pointed out that it wouldn't work for a slave to have two owners, for the slave would inevitably favor the one over the other (vs. 24ab). That means one slave owner would be disappointed in the service given by the slave. Jesus was still talking about financial matters. He stated plainly, "You cannot serve both God and Money" (vs. 24c). If our top goal in life is to accumulate wealth, God won't get the worship and obedience from us He deserves.

We can imagine Jesus' listeners on the hillside wondering what would happen to them if they chose to serve God rather than money. Perhaps they also fretted over whether their basic material needs would go unmet if they no longer were zealous to earn material wealth. Jesus' answer, in effect, was not to worry about such things (vs. 25). This is the second of Jesus' three don'ts in the Sermon on the Mount.

Worry, or anxiety, is characterized by such emotions as fear and distress. External circumstances or internal causes can bring it on. When left unchecked, worry can decrease our awareness of things, diminish our ability to cope with life's traumas, and leave us feeling isolated.

Perhaps with this awareness in mind, Jesus told His followers not to fret about maintaining their life by getting food, or about protecting their bodies by getting clothing. Furthermore, the Lord rhetorically asked, "Is not life more important than food, and the

Jesus was not saying that money is evil, or even that being rich is necessarily evil. He was concerned about greed—the desire to acquire greater wealth no matter what.

Jesus was using physical vision metaphorically to stand for spiritual vision. His point apparently is that people who are intent on amassing worldly wealth are spiritually blind, while those who are most concerned about deserving heavenly rewards have acute spiritual vision.

Laying up treasures in heaven forms the conceptual backdrop for Jesus' admonitions in Matthew 6 (see vs. 20). Scripture teaches that heaven is the dwelling place of God and the abode of His sanctuary (Ps. 102:19; Isa. 63:15). God's throne is in heaven—at times heaven is called the throne of God (Ps. 103:19; Isa. 66:1).

As God's dwelling place, heaven is not a cosmic shelter where the Lord isolates Himself from the earth. Rather, it is the divine workplace, where He sends blessings to His people and punishment on His enemies (Deut. 26:15; Ps. 11:4-7). Heaven is also a channel of communication between God and humans (Gen. 28:12; Neh. 9:13). As God's creation, the heavens praise Him and display His glory, righteousness, and creativity (Ps. 19:1; 50:6; 69:34).

body more than clothes?" In other words, by worrying about food and clothing, the people were focusing on insignificant things. Jesus wanted His followers to be focused on what really matters.

B. Our Value to God: vs. 26

"Look at the birds of the air; they do not sow or reap or store away in barns, and yet your heavenly Father feeds them. Are you not much more valuable than they?"

Despite His admonitions, Jesus recognized that His disciples would still be tempted to worry. Thus, He used examples from the natural world to reassure them that God would indeed meet their needs.

Christ likely pointed to some common barn sparrows flying in the sky as He stated that these creatures did not plant or harvest crops, nor stockpile grain in storehouses, and yet the heavenly Father amply supplied their need for food (Matt. 6:26). All about them, the birds could find the insects that they needed to eat—all provided by God. He cared for these little creatures, and so He would certainly provide for the needs of His people, who were of greater value to Him.

C. The Futility of Worry: vs. 27

"Who of you by worrying can add a single hour to his life?"

Some think Matthew 6:27 should be translated as it appears in the NIV, where the emphasis is on time. Others think the phrase "add a single hour to his life" should be rendered "add a single cubit to his height." (A cubit was a unit of measure roughly equal to 18 inches.) In either case, Jesus' point is essentially the same. Worrying is pointless, for it doesn't change anything.

The Bible teaches that because of God's love and unlimited power, we don't have to worry. The implication is that only God can run the world; thus being anxious about things not under our control is senseless. In fact, a preoccupation with ourselves is a form of self-reliance. It's no wonder that when we seek anything other than God as the first priority in our lives, the meeting of our needs is not assured.

D. The Lesson from Nature: vss. 28-30

"And why do you worry about clothes? See how the lilies of the

field grow. They do not labor or spin. Yet I tell you that not even Solomon in all his splendor was dressed like one of these. If that is how God clothes the grass of the field, which is here today and tomorrow is thrown into the fire, will he not much more clothe you, O you of little faith?"

Jesus asked His followers why they worried about having clothes to wear. He probably pointed to some lilies growing in the nearby fields as He asked His audience to consider how such delicate flowers grew. These plants did not "labor or spin" (Matt. 6:28) to obtain protective covering; rather, God graciously supplied their glorious color and texture. Solomon the son of David was very wealthy and could afford to dress in the most magnificent clothing available. And yet the lilies carpeting the fields of Palestine were more gloriously dressed than Solomon ever was (vs. 29).

Jesus next directed the attention of His followers to the field of grass surrounding them. The life span of such vegetation was short, and grass was of little value. For instance, people in Bible times would use grass as a cheap and abundant source of fuel to heat their clay ovens. Yet God so decorated these seemingly insignificant plants with beautiful flowers. Jesus asked rhetorically, "Will [the Father] not much more clothe you, O you of little faith?" (vs. 30).

Here Jesus was raising a serious charge. The people lacked faith. This was the first time He mentioned faith in His sermon. He knew that faith is the antidote to being consumed by possessions (vss. 19-23). Faith keeps us from serving money (vs. 24). Faith also protects us from worry (vss. 25-30).

By faith we are compelled to answer *yes* to all the questions Jesus asked. Faith affirms that God will provide our necessities. Faith agrees that we are more valuable than birds and lilies. Faith rises up as a bulwark against worry.

We learn in Jesus' Sermon that all nature depends on God's provision. Meanwhile, people worry about where their provisions will come from. Their trust in God will grow if they observe how God provides His creation what it needs. This truth is also underscored in Acts 14:17. As Paul and Barnabas proclaimed the Gospel in Lystra, they declared that God has shown humanity "kindness by giving [people] rain from heaven and crops in their seasons." Moreover, He provides humankind "with plenty of food and fills [their] hearts with joy."

II. God's Prescription for Anxiety: Matthew 6:31-34

A. God's Awareness of Our Needs: vss. 31-32
"So do not worry, saying, 'What shall we eat?' or 'What shall we drink?' or 'What shall we wear?' For the pagans run after all these things, and your heavenly Father knows that you need them."

Having concluded His nature examples, Jesus returned to directly urging His listeners not to worry. They did not need to wonder about where they would get their food and clothing (Matt. 6:31). To do so was to be like the pagans (vs. 32).

It should come as no surprise that the unsaved are given to excessive worry. Day after day they obsess over where they will obtain the basics of life. Such anxiety indicates their focus is on themselves, not God and other people. In contrast, Jesus' followers can rest in the knowledge that their heavenly Father is aware of and will provide for their needs.

These verses make up one of the most frequently cited passages of Scripture in discussions involving money and work. Sadly, there are some who insist that Jesus was against earning money and that He considered work a distraction from things that really matter. Nothing could be further from the truth. Jesus was condemning worry, not work. He called us to make God the object of our faith, for He is the one who ultimately supplies our needs. There are many ways that God provides for us, but perhaps the most common is through everyday work.

B. Kingdom Priorities versus Future Concerns: vss. 33-34

"But seek first his kingdom and his righteousness, and all these things will be given to you as well. Therefore do not worry about tomorrow, for tomorrow will worry about itself. Each day has enough trouble of its own."

"Kingdom" in Matthew 6:33 translates *basileian*, from which we get our English word *basilica*. The term refers to the rule of God over His creation. The Bible describes God's kingdom as being heavenly (2 Tim. 4:18), unshakable (Heb. 12:28), and eternal (2 Pet. 1:11).

Scripture describes the richness of God's kingdom in a variety of ways. It is inseparably linked to righteousness, peace, and joy (Rom. 14:17). The kingdom of God is associated with suffering and patient endurance (Rev. 1:9), supernatural power (1 Cor. 4:20), promise (Jas. 2:5), glory (1 Thess. 2:12), and the "renewal of all things" (Matt. 19:28).

God's kingdom is not the product of human striving or invention (John 18:36). It is given as a gift (Luke 12:32) and humbly received (Mark 10:15). The Lord brings His people into His kingdom (Col. 1:13), makes them worthy of it (2 Thess. 1:5), and pre-

---

Several places in the Sermon on the Mount Jesus referred to the "kingdom of heaven" (for instance, Matt. 5:3, 10, 19; 6:33), and He told those who would be His followers to bring that kingdom "on earth as it is in heaven" (vs. 10). Jesus was not speaking about a geographical area, such as the Holy Land, or a political entity, such as the Roman Empire. Rather, the divine kingdom is independent of those.

Elsewhere in Matthew, Jesus' parables spoke of the Kingdom metaphorically, as being like a farmer (Matt. 13:24), a mustard seed (vs. 31), yeast (vs. 33), a treasure (vs. 44), a pearl merchant (vs. 45), and a dragnet (vs. 47).

The Kingdom embraces all who walk in fellowship with the Lord and do His will. It is governed by God's laws, which are summed up in our duty to love God supremely and love others as ourselves. This Kingdom will one day displace all the kingdoms of this world.

serves them for it (2 Tim. 4:18).

Jesus told His followers to value God's kingdom and righteousness above anything else (Matt. 6:33). In fact, God's kingdom is defined by His righteousness. The latter means that God acts justly and fairly in all His decisions and actions (Dan. 9:14).

God declares as righteous those who acknowledge their sin and put their faith in Christ for forgiveness and eternal life (Mark 2:17; Luke 18:14). In contrast, the unsaved have a false sense of righteousness, for they trust in their moral accomplishments to make others think they are living in accordance with God's holy standard (Matt. 23:28; Luke 18:9).

Thus, rather than assert their own goodness, the life goal of God's people should be to submit to His rule and to call others to do the same. As they do, "all these things" (Matt. 6:33)—meaning food and clothing and other items they need—will be given to them as well.

In light of these truths, Jesus urged His followers not to be filled with distress about what lay ahead. He explained that "tomorrow will worry about itself" (vs. 34). By this Jesus meant that each new day brings with it plenty of anxiety-producing situations, and undue worry about what might happen is pointless. If God's people cannot control the present with its problems, what point is there in being preoccupied with the future? We cannot control our happiness; that is in God's hands.

At least seven reasons are given in Matthew 6:25-34 for why we should not worry:

- *The same God who created life in us can be trusted with the details of our life (vs. 25).*
- *Worrying about the future impedes our efforts for today (vs. 26).*
- *Worrying is more harmful than helpful (vs. 27).*
- *God does not ignore those who depend on Him (vss. 28-30).*
- *Worrying shows a lack of faith in and understanding of God (vss. 31-32).*
- *Worrying keeps us from real challenges God wants us to tackle (vs. 33).*
- *Living one day at a time keeps us from being consumed with worry (vs. 34).*

Discussion Questions

1. Why is it far wiser to store up treasures in heaven rather than on earth?
2. Why is our heart an accurate indicator of what we treasure most?
3. What is worry, and why is it futile?
4. What lessons about trust can we learn by observing nature?
5. What is the difference between worry and proper concern for the future?

Now Ask Yourself . . .

Am I a person who worries a lot? If so, why?

What would it take to set me free from worry and anxiety?

In light of what Jesus taught, what are some practical things I can do to manage my anxiety?

What can I do to give God first priority in my life?

How can I help other Christians not to become victims of worry and anxiety?

Illustrations

In his book *Come Before Winter,* Chuck Swindoll writes, "I don't have many temptations to worship evil things. It's the good things that plague me. It isn't as difficult for me to reject something that is innately bad or wrong as it is to keep those good and wholesome things off the throne."

Although many adults try to meet the demands of living, they seem to pile up like unfolded laundry. Since each day has only 24 hours, believers need to be selective. Meanwhile, their use of the time and energy that God gives them indicates where their priorities lie. Jesus' teaching in this week's lesson Scripture will help them to understand how they can spend their time and energy in ways that have eternal value.

Consider this. In the financial world investors use money to make more money. In a sense the Spirit is like a broker who is continually reinvesting God's resources in His children's lives. God first invested in us when He sent Christ to buy us back from Satan's kingdom. Now the resulting "dividends" include the fruit of the Spirit (Gal. 5:22-23).

Since everything we have belongs to God, we are stewards, obligated to use our possessions, time, and energy as investments for our Master. Every act of faithful stewardship adds to our spiritual treasure. Where, then, is our heart focused? Do our spiritual lenses need cleaning? Are we using our resources to invest in God's kingdom? Where have we stockpiled our treasures? The answers to these questions indicate that the contents of our character matter more to God than the size of our stock portfolio.

The Sweet Fragrance of Forgiveness

DEVOTIONAL READING

2 Corinthians 5:16-21

DAILY BIBLE READINGS

Monday June 19
  Genesis 45:1-11
  Joseph Shows Genuine
  Forgiveness

Tuesday June 20
  Genesis 45:12-28
  Forgiveness Brings
  Blessings

Wednesday June 21
  Matthew 18:21-27
  Peter Asks about
  Forgiveness

Thursday June 22
  Matthew 18:28-35
  The Servant Refused to
  Forgive Another

Friday June 23
  John 20:19-23
  Jesus Urged Us to Forgive

Saturday June 24
  Romans 12:9-21
  Forgiveness Marks a
  Christian Life

Sunday June 25
  1 John 1:5-10
  Forgiveness Is Complete

Scripture

Background Scripture: *Matthew 18*

Scripture Lesson: *Matthew 18:21-35*

Key Verses: *"If you forgive men when they sin against you, your heavenly Father will also forgive you. But if you do not forgive men their sins, your Father will not forgive your sins." Matthew 6:14-15.*

Lesson Aim

God's forgiven must forgive.

Lesson Setting

Time: A.D. 28–30

Place: Capernaum

Lesson Outline

The Sweet Fragrance of Forgiveness

I. A King's Pity: Matthew 18:21-27
  A. *Jesus' Response to Peter: vss. 21-22*
  B. *The King's Demand: vss. 23-25*
  C. *The Servant's Plea: vss. 26-27*

II. A Servant's Revenge: Matthew 18:28-35
  A. *A Stern Demand: vss. 28*
  B. *A Rejected Plea: vss. 29-31*
  C. *A Harsh Reprimand: vss. 32-34*
  D. *A Sobering Truth: vs. 35*

Introduction

Forgiving Each Other

Every Sunday millions of Christians pray, "Forgive us our sins, for we also forgive everyone who sins against us" (Luke 11:4), as part of the Lord's Prayer. It's easy to say that prayer without thinking about whether we have really forgiven all those who have offended us.

Forgiveness is extremely difficult to grant others because it costs us so much. When we forgive someone, we accept the loss or the hurt without demanding any reimbursement, revenge, or satisfaction of any kind. Forgiveness means we suffer so that the offending party can be restored to fellowship with us.

To forgive means we hold no grudges and nurse no resentments. To forgive means to yield a claim that might rightfully be ours. It means to excuse a penalty that might be justified. This is why forgiveness, if genuine, goes far beyond saying a rote prayer.

Lesson Commentary

I. A King's Pity: Matthew 18:21-27

A. Jesus' Response to Peter: vss. 21-22

Then Peter came to Jesus and asked, "Lord, how many times shall I forgive my brother when he sins against me? Up to seven times?" Jesus answered, "I tell you, not seven times, but seventy-seven times."

According to Matthew 17:24, Jesus and His followers had arrived in Capernaum. This was the home of some of the disciples. The city also served as the Lord's headquarters during a large portion of His public ministry. It was a fishing village built on the northwest shore of the Sea of Galilee.

Capernaum hosted a Roman garrison that maintained peace in the region. Major highways crisscrossed at Capernaum, making it militarily strategic. Because of its fishing and trading industries, the city was something of a melting pot of Greek, Roman, and Jewish cultures.

After the incident involving the temple tax (vss. 24-27), there follows the fourth of five great discourses in the Gospel of Matthew (chap. 18). While Jesus was teaching His disciples about what to do when a fellow believer mistreats them in some way, Peter approached the Savior and asked, in effect, "What about the person who keeps on wronging me over and over? How many times do I have to let someone like that off the hook before I'm justified in telling him or her that the well of my forgiveness has run dry?"

When Peter suggested forgiving a person seven times (vs. 21), he was being generous, at least in light of the tradition of the day. The rabbinic rule of thumb was that a person could be forgiven up to three times, but there was no forgiveness for the fourth offense. Thus, forgiving a person seven times seemed remarkable.

Jesus' response, however, was even more remarkable. Not until seven times, but until "seventy-seven times" (vs. 22). Some Bible scholars think Jesus actually meant "seventy times seven" (KJV). Whether the figure was 77 or 490, the amount Jesus named implied an unlimited number of times. A stingy soul keeps track of how often it forgives, but a loving soul forgives time and time again.

Jesus' answer exceeded any amount anyone might have imagined. And it set a new standard—not of numbers, but of principle. We should always forgive. Of course, this new standard was not intended to encourage free sinning, but free forgiving. At times it might be better to ignore those little offenses that we experience on a daily basis, like being tailgated by an impatient driver. Under other circumstances God certainly does not want a wrong to be repeated over and over without trying to resolve the problem as Christ would have.

Jesus' reply to Peter probably alluded to the accounts of Cain and Lamech (Gen. 4:1-24). When Cain murdered Abel, God put on Cain a mark of some kind and said that anyone who killed Cain would "suffer vengeance seven times over" (vs. 15). Cain and his wife later had their first child, Enoch, and a descendant of Enoch was Lamech.

Lamech is credited in Scripture with humanity's second known murder. He proclaimed to his wives, "I have killed a man for wounding me" (vs. 23). Then he proudly told them that "if Cain is avenged seven times, then Lamech seventy-seven times" (vs. 24). In some way, Lamech believed that by taking vengeance into his own hands he had outdone God. In His response to Peter, Jesus reversed this old cycle of retribution by saying that believers should always bring forgiveness, not revenge, to situations where they feel wronged.

B.   The King's Demand: vss. 23-25
"Therefore, the kingdom of heaven is like a king who wanted to settle accounts with his servants. As he began the settlement, a

Jesus used parables as a favorite teaching technique. The parables are effective because they appeal to the entire person, touching emotions, challenging the mind, and igniting the imagination. The Gospels of Matthew, Mark, and Luke record 40 parables Jesus told. They are short stories and sayings drawn from familiar events of daily life, but Jesus used these stories to communicate spiritual truths that may have been unfamiliar to His audience.

Jesus would start by commenting on something in the physical world and then compare it to something in the spiritual world. Jesus' parables usually emphasized one primary concept that could be applied in a variety of ways. Not all the details of a parable necessarily had significance. This serves as a caution against reading too much into a parable. The parables motivated interested listeners (such as the disciples) to find out more about what was being taught. At the same time, the parables hid the truth from disinterested listeners (such as proud religious leaders).

man who owed him ten thousand talents was brought to him. Since he was not able to pay, the master ordered that he and his wife and his children and all that he had be sold to repay the debt."

Perhaps Jesus' words—until "seventy-seven times" (Matt. 18:22)—to Peter were met with incredulous stares and a "But Lord . . ." or two, for Jesus immediately launched into a parable to help His listeners grasp the reason behind His instruction. Jesus compared the kingdom of heaven (that is, God's rulership in the hearts of His people) to an earthly kingdom. The monarch of this kingdom represents God and the servants represent His people.

In this parable the king called the servants of his realm together to settle accounts with them (vs. 23). These servants, the parable implies, had been put in charge of portions of the king's money. Some Bible scholars think that the servants in this story were high-ranking officials whose duty it was to collect royal taxes and to bring their collections to the king at appointed times.

One by one the servants appeared before the monarch until one servant was brought into his presence. This hapless fellow owned the king "ten thousand talents" (vs. 24). By today's standards that would have been millions and millions of dollars. At the time of Christ, if a man were a governor employed by a king (which apparently this servant was), he could earn only about 1,000 talents in his lifetime. A debt of 10,000 talents was insurmountable.

How had the servant come to owe such a huge amount to the king? What had he done with the 10,000 talents he was to present? Had he been enjoying a lifestyle beyond his means, all at the king's expense? Flaunting wealth that wasn't his? Living for the moment, never giving a thought to his day of reckoning that was certain to come? Whatever the use or misuse of his master's funds, the servant was not able to repay them. Thus, he was to be sold into slavery along with his family, and his possessions were to be sold as well. All the proceeds would go to the king (vs. 25). The servant was doomed!

C. The Servant's Plea: vss. 26-27

"The servant fell on his knees before him. 'Be patient with me,' he begged, 'and I will pay back everything.' The servant's master took pity on him, canceled the debt and let him go."

A talent was not a coin but a measurement of weight. It was the largest unit of weight in the New Testament era and was used for measuring out gold and silver. The most basic unit of weight was the shekel. It took 3,000 shekels to equal one talent.

We get a sense of the enormous size of the debt owed by the servant in Jesus' parable when it is compared to the amount of revenue received by rulers in New Testament times. According to the Jewish historian Josephus, the annual tax revenue received by Herod the Great amounted to approximately 1,000 talents. When his daughter married, Herod gave her a dowry of 300 talents.

Although the money from the sale of the servant, his family, and his belongings likely couldn't begin to pay the sum of the debt, the punishment was acceptable by the standards of the time. Thus the servant's only hope was to beg for mercy. In his desperation the servant groveled before the king, even promising to repay all he owed—a ridiculous proposition (Matt. 18:26).

Despite his servant's wrongdoing and foolishness, the king's compassion was stirred. Not only did he let his servant go free, but he also released him from the obligation of the impossible debt (vs. 27). The king's forgiveness was a demonstration of grace and flowed from the compassion he felt for the plight of his servant. The monarch's actions symbolized God's forgiveness of believers' sins.

II. A Servant's Revenge: Matthew 18:28-35

A. A Stern Demand: vss. 28

"But when that servant went out, he found one of his fellow servants who owed him a hundred denarii. He grabbed him and began to choke him. 'Pay back what you owe me!' he demanded."

It isn't directly stated how much time elapsed between the first servant's being forgiven and his attack on his co-worker, but Matthew 18:28 leads the reader to believe that the events occurred one right after the other. It's hard to imagine that the first servant could so quickly forget the mercy shown to him, but suddenly his fingers were wrapped around the throat of a fellow servant, demanding immediate payment of a debt owed him.

And what was the amount of the debt? It came to exactly "a hundred denarii." The denarius coin was considered a day's wage for a laborer in the time of Jesus. One hundred denarii was approximately three months' wages for the average worker. It was a tiny sum compared to the debt pardoned by the king. By some estimates the former was about 600,000 times less than the latter.

B. A Rejected Plea: vss. 29-31

"His fellow servant fell to his knees and begged him, 'Be patient with me, and I will pay you back.' But he refused. Instead, he went off and had the man thrown into prison until he could pay the debt. When the other servants saw what had happened, they were

The forgiven servant was unaffected by the king's compassion. He seems to have gone straight from the king's presence to find a colleague who owed him a much smaller debt and have him thrown into prison. Ironically, the second debtor uttered nearly the same words when asking for mercy that the forgiven servant had used when pleading his own case before the king. One difference, however, was that the fellow servant's promise to pay his debt was realistic. Given time, he likely could pay up.

341

The borrowing and lending done in this parable seem to go beyond the restrictions the Old Testament placed on lending to ensure that no one took advantage of the borrower. Among the Israelites, lending was supposed to be a means of showing mercy to the poor. As a result, an Israelite could not charge interest on a loan made to a fellow Israelite (Lev. 25:35-38). However, interest could be collected from a Gentile (Deut. 23:20).

A lender who took a borrower's cloak as collateral could not keep it overnight but had to return it at sunset (Exod. 22:26-27). Nor could a lender take a borrower's millstone as security for a loan because that would also be taking away the borrower's means for repaying the debt (Deut. 24:6). Every seven years, as part of the year of Jubilee, all debts were supposed to be forgiven (15:1-2). We might draw the application that for the Christian every year is a year of Jubilee when it comes to forgiveness for our unpayable debt of sin.

greatly distressed and went and told their master everything that had happened."

The fellow servant fell on his knees and began begging the servant who had been forgiven to be patient. The debtor even promised to repay what he owned (Matt. 18:29). The forgiven servant, however, took no notice of the relative smallness of his fellow servant's debt. And even the imploring cries of his co-worker did nothing to penetrate his outrage (vs. 30).

Tragically, neither pleas nor promise of repayment softened the temper of the forgiven servant. He would be satisfied with nothing less than immediate settlement. He thus took full advantage of his legal rights to have the debtor thrown into prison until he could somehow pay off the debt. The forgiven servant failed to recognize and acknowledge that his fellow servant's need paralleled his own, which showed that he was a callous, self-centered person. By promptly dismissing the great kindness shown him by the king, he showed that he was also a grossly ungrateful and unmerciful person.

The incident between the two servants did not go unnoticed by their peers. Certainly it was well known among the courtiers that the king had let the one servant off the hook (so to speak) in a big way. And so this servant's actions toward his fellow servant were an insult to the king's graciousness. Consequently, the other servants made sure the king learned about the situation (vs. 31).

C. A Harsh Reprimand: vss. 32-34

"Then the master called the servant in. 'You wicked servant,' he said, 'I canceled all that debt of yours because you begged me to. Shouldn't you have had mercy on your fellow servant just as I had on you?' In anger his master turned him over to the jailers to be tortured, until he should pay back all he owed."

After hearing the account in full detail, the king summoned the forgiven servant again. Earlier, even when the servant's debt had been discovered, the king had not berated him, but now the monarch's righteous anger was stirred (Matt. 18:32).

The king had presumed that his example of compassion would be taken as a cue by the servant to be forgiving to others as well. By bringing the situation back to the servant's remembrance, the ruler, in essence, said, "Where did you get the idea you could be so cruel to your co-worker? After all, didn't I forgive your huge debt?"

(see vs. 33). The king's words imply a lasting obligation on the servant's part to be merciful to others.

The servant's cruelty, however, revealed his glaring ingratitude to the king, and for the first time the monarch called his servant "wicked" (vs. 32). The ruler then sentenced him to be turned over to the tormentors, whose job it was to torture subjects who had committed the worst kinds of crimes, until he could repay the debt (vs. 34). For the wicked servant, this was a life sentence, since he would never be able to repay his debt.

D. A Sobering Truth: vs. 35

"This is how my heavenly Father will treat each of you unless you forgive your brother from your heart."

The king had expected the servant to treat others as he himself had been treated. In Jesus' application, He pointed out that this is also what God expects of those who have experienced His forgiveness (Matt. 18:35). Since our heavenly Father has forgiven us, we must forgive others who have wronged us. If we refuse, we will incur the wrath and punishment due us from God. Expressed differently, we will be shown the same measure of mercy that we have extended to others.

Jesus saw nothing inappropriate in the actions of a king who can be full of mercy and forgiveness and can also become angry and call for punishment. Mercy was not the servant's birthright. The king offered mercy as he desired, and he gave it generously. The ruler's mercy could not be earned. It was given because the monarch was good, not because the servant had done something to deserve it.

The servant, however, responded to the king's mercy ungratefully by refusing to act mercifully to others. He demonstrated that he was either unable or unwilling to live and act in the spirit of mercy. Therefore, he could live and be dealt with only in the spirit of justice—just recompense for actions. In this case the just reward for the servant's wickedness was punishment.

Jesus' parable of the unforgiving servant emphasizes two themes. First, God will always forgive sins, no matter how serious, as long as there is sincere repentance. Second, our refusal to forgive others shunts our ability to fully appreciate and appropriate the forgiveness that God freely and unconditionally offers us in Christ.

If Peter understood when Jesus told him to forgive his peers up to 77 times (Matt. 18:21-22), he undoubtedly felt overwhelmed when he heard the parable that followed (vss. 23-34). Perhaps in some way, after Jesus finished commenting on that parable (vs. 35), 77 times probably didn't look too extreme to Peter!

Discussion Questions

1. What did Jesus' answer to Peter's question mean?
2. Why did the king cancel his servant's debt?
3. How did the servant respond to the king's compassion?
4. What did the king do when he learned about the forgiven servant's behavior?
5. How could the king be compassionate toward his servant at one point and later filled with anger, punishing him without mercy?

Now Ask Yourself . . .

When was the last time someone committed a gross injustice against me? How did I respond?

In light of Jesus' parable, how would I respond now? What would characterize the difference in my response?

How is my relationship with God affected when I refuse to forgive someone who has wrong me?

Why do I need God's help in order to forgive some wrongs done to me?

How does my forgiving others help me draw closer to the Lord?

Illustrations

Who could actually be as calloused as the servant in Jesus' parable? The story seems exaggerated. It's hard to believe anyone could be so blinded to his shortcoming as this servant seems to have been. But that is exactly Jesus' point. He was uncovering a blind spot in His listeners' thinking as well.

An unfaithful spouse, a rebellious child, an abusive parent, a traitorous friend—no doubt any one of these can cause inexpressible pain. When these kinds of people devastate our hopes and expectations, we wrestle with deep anger and sorrow that threatens to become bitter. How can we possibly forgive? Jesus gave the only answer that can motivate us to forgive even when it hurts. We can and must do so, for we have been forgiven.

The offended holiness of God is no light matter. Though we can hardly imagine the greatness of our offense against Him, we can get an idea of it when we look at what it cost Him to forgive us. A bleeding, suffocating Jesus crying out from a cross, forsaken by His Father, to whom He had been unswervingly faithful. Darkness. Death. This is the picture of pain of an offended God, deeply wounded by our sin yet willing to bear that pain for the sake of reconciling us to Himself.

In light of this, our question "How can we possibly forgive? becomes "How can we possibly *not* forgive?" No one—not even Jesus—said it would be easy. God forgave us by way of the Cross, and we dare not deceive ourselves by thinking we will escape the pain of having to forgive the offenses committed against us in this life. But as our gratefulness for God's forgiveness grows, our willingness to forgive others will grow as well.

Made for Each Other

DEVOTIONAL READING

Psalm 150

DAILY BIBLE READINGS

Monday June 26
  Genesis 2:4-9
  Man Is Created

Tuesday June 27
  Genesis 2:10-18
  God Decides Man Should
  Not Be Alone

Wednesday June 28
  Genesis 2:19-25
  Woman Is Created

Thursday June 29
  Matthew 19:1-12
  Jesus Explains the
  Marriage Relationship

Friday June 30
  1 John 3:11-15
  Love One Another

Saturday July 1
  1 John 3:16-24
  Loving One Another
  Requires Action

Sunday July 2
  1 John 4:7-12
  Loving Relationships
  Come from God

Scripture

Background Scripture: *Genesis 2*
Scripture Lesson: *Genesis 2:7-9, 15-25*
Key Verses: *The LORD God said, "It is not good for the man to be alone." Genesis 2:18.*

Lesson Aim

God made us for relationships.

Lesson Setting

Time: The dawn of human history
Place: Eden

Lesson Outline

Made for Each Other

  I. Privilege and Responsibility: Genesis 2:7-9, 15-17
     A. *The Breath of Life in Man: vs. 7*
     B. *The Planting of the Garden: vss. 8-9*
     C. *The Man in the Garden: vs. 15*
     D. *The Lord's Warning: vss. 16-17*
  II. Companionship: Genesis 2:15-25
     A. *The Lord's Decision: vs. 18*
     B. *The Absence of a Suitable Companion: vss. 19-20*
     C. *The Lord's Creation of a Woman: vss. 21-22*
     D. *The Man's Joy: vss. 23-24*
     E. *The Absence of Shame: vs. 25*

Introduction

Discovering Our Value

Wouldn't it be wonderful to live in the Garden of Eden, to be satisfied with a life of contemplation and light gardening, enjoying luscious fruits, and being married to the perfect spouse with whom we had no differences? Does the fact that this picture was ruined prevent us from discovering our value in God's creation, even as it exists now?

Some people disregard this thought as irrelevant to modern life, and many prefer to fill their mind with pictures of violence and perversion. But reading and discussing God's purpose for our good is like taking a hot shower. Afterward you come away feeling clean and refreshed. So, let's learn and enjoy God's purpose for us. And let's, in turn, look to Him for refreshment and instruction as we seek to do His will.

Lesson Commentary

Most conservative Bible scholars credit Moses as the author of the Pentateuch, including Genesis. No less an authority than Jesus Christ provided warrant for this view (John 7:19). Unquestionably, Moses had the ability to write the Pentateuch. He would have learned, among other things, languages, history, and law (Acts 7:22). We don't know if Moses worked alone on the Pentateuch. He may have had one or more assistants. Certainly someone else added the story of his death (Deut. 34).

I. Privilege and Responsibility: Genesis 2:7-9, 15-17

A. The Breath of Life in Man: vs. 7

The LORD God formed the man from the dust of the ground and breathed into his nostrils the breath of life, and the man became a living being.

Genesis is the book of beginnings. Here we find the beginning of the material universe, human life and sin, divine judgment on human sin, covenant promises, and the Israelite tribes. Since God was about to establish His people in the promised land, Moses undoubtedly felt they needed a written record to guide them. The people needed to know where they had come from. They needed to know how they had been chosen by God. They needed a law to show them how to live. These are just some of the purposes for Genesis.

Starting with Genesis 2:4, we have a second account of Creation. The material, unlike what precedes it, focuses narrowly on the first humans and the special place God prepared for them. The Hebrew term rendered "account" is one of 10 literary markers indicating the major sections of the Book of Genesis. The first three accounts pertain to the pre-Flood world and the last seven deal with the post-Flood period.

The terms "Lord God" are also significant in that verse 4 is the first place in Scripture where they appear together. (These terms also appear throughout Genesis 2.) The Hebrew word *Elohim*, which is rendered "God," is the same term used in 1:1. The plurality of the name underscores God's majesty and power. Beginning in 2:4, *Elohim* is combined with *Yahweh*, which is rendered "Lord." This is the personal name for God used by His covenant people, the Israelites (see Exod. 3:14-15).

With respect to the main narrative, initially when the sovereign Lord created the heavens and the earth, He did not send any rain; also, there were no people to tend the soil. Consequently, such vegetation as grass and grains were not growing anywhere (Gen. 2:5). According to verse 6, the planet was watered from a mist rising up from the ground. It was at that time that the sovereign Lord formed the body of a man from the elements of the soil and breathed life into him.

Verse 7 contains a number of important details worth considering. First, *adam* is the Hebrew word for "man" used here, while *adamah* is the term used for "ground." The idea is that man's physical elements came from the soil of the earth.

Second, the word rendered "formed" was commonly used for a potter's work (see Isa. 45:7-9). The idea is that God was like a potter, and the first man, being formed from the dust of the ground, was like a pot made from clay (see Rom. 9:20-21).

Third, the man was formed out of the ground like the rest of the animals (compare Gen. 2:7 and 19). He became "a living being" (vs. 7) just as all the animals became "living creatures" (1:24)—the same words in Hebrew. All this goes to show that, in regard to his earthly body, Adam was much like the animals; yet he was also different from the animals because he was made in the image of God (see 1:26-27).

B. The Planting of the Garden: vss. 8-9

Now the Lord God had planted a garden in the east, in Eden; and there he put the man he had formed. And the Lord God made all kinds of trees grow out of the ground—trees that were pleasing to

Genesis 2:7 complements what is revealed in 1:26-27. We learn that God created humankind in His image. Theologians have long debated what it means to be made in the image of God. Three common opinions focus on human reason, ethics, and dominion.

Some theologians say humans are in the image of the all-knowing God because we have high mental abilities. Others say people reflect God's image when we behave morally, as God always does. Still others believe we are in God's image because we rule over the rest of creation, just as God rules over all creation.

The image of God in humans was defaced through sin. But Genesis 9:6 and James 3:9 suggest that all people still bear God's image to some degree. The apostle Paul wrote that believers are having the image of God restored in them as they become more and more Christlike (Rom. 8:29; 2 Cor. 3:18; Eph. 4:22-24; Col. 3:9-10).

the eye and good for food. In the middle of the garden were the tree of life and the tree of the knowledge of good and evil.

God had lovingly prepared a home for Adam. This was a garden occupying part of a place called "Eden" in Mesopotamia (Gen. 2:8). The name *Eden* means either "delight" or "a plain," perhaps both. The Garden of Eden itself was a lovely place with pleasing trees and abundant food (vs. 9).

The author of Genesis clearly meant his readers to understand Eden as a real place, since he provided many geographic details (vss. 10-14). He named the rivers that flowed from Eden's river, along with lands watered by those rivers. He even mentioned some of the natural resources of those lands. Some of the names can no longer be linked with known geographic features, but we can guess that they were all known at the time Genesis was written.

Down through the centuries commentators have debated where Eden was located. The mention of the Tigris and Euphrates rivers suggests that the garden was situated somewhere in Mesopotamia. More specific locations include the possibility of Babylonia (in Mesopotamia proper), Armenia (north of Mesopotamia), and an island in the Indian Ocean. In later biblical usage, Eden came to symbolize the blessedness and fruitfulness of God's people in His life-giving presence.

C. The Man in the Garden: vs. 15

The LORD God took the man and put him in the Garden of Eden to work it and take care of it.

No matter how idyllic Eden seemed, Adam's stay there was no vacation. He was expected to "work [the garden] and take care of it" (Gen. 2:15). The Hebrew terms behind the NIV rendering imply priestly activity within a special place, namely, the sanctuary of the garden. In essence, Adam's responsibilities represented worshipful service to the Lord.

Our command to subdue the earth (see 1:28) is not inconsistent with the stewardship and conversation of nature. Christians should have a clearer understanding than anyone else of the human responsibility to take care of the world God has given us.

D. The Lord's Warning: vss. 16-17

And the LORD God commanded the man, "You are free to eat from any tree in the garden; but you must not eat from the tree of the knowledge of good and evil, for when you eat of it you will surely die."

Eden was filled with trees, but two were special. One of these was the tree of life (Gen. 2:9). The other was "the tree of the knowledge of good and evil" (vs. 17). The meaning of this tree's name has been disputed. It probably has something to do with the tree's ability to convey moral discernment; but the most impor-

348

tant fact to note about the tree is that it was forbidden.

God permitted Adam to eat freely from the fruit growing on any of the trees, except for the tree that gave the ability to discern the difference between moral right and wrong. This tree was God's tool for testing the man.

The Lord thus gave Adam only one restriction. If he ate from this tree, he would suffer death (physically and spiritually). As revealed in Genesis 3, the man did eat from the forbidden fruit. The fact that Adam had so many alternatives to choose from makes his eventual disobedience of God all the more condemnable.

II. Companionship: Genesis 2:15-25

A. The Lord's Decision: vs. 18

The LORD God said, "It is not good for the man to be alone. I will make a helper suitable for him."

At first God made only one human—Adam; but the Lord never planned for Adam to be a loner, the only one of his kind. All along God intended to make a woman for Adam. Thus, marriage and the family were part of God's plan from the start.

It is true that Eve was created to be Adam's helper (Gen. 2:18); but there is nothing in the language to suggest that this made the woman in some way less than Adam. On the contrary, the same word is used elsewhere to refer to the kind of help God provides (Ps. 30:10; 121:2). Thus, though Eve differed from Adam, she was not less than he was. Eve was Adam's feminine counterpart, companion, and co-laborer.

B. The Absence of a Suitable Companion: vss. 19-20

Now the LORD God had formed out of the ground all the beasts of the field and all the birds of the air. He brought them to the man to see what he would name them; and whatever the man called each living creature, that was its name. So the man gave names to all the livestock, the birds of the air and all the beasts of the field. But for Adam no suitable helper was found.

God wanted to prepare Adam for the change that would come into his life, but because he had not ever known another creature of his kind, Adam needed to learn that there was a void in his life. Thus, to have Adam recognize his need for a woman, God had

When God finished His creation activity, He declared that what He had made was "very good" (Gen. 1:31). This included His creation of humankind. As those who bore His image (vss. 26-27), they existed to be in relationship with Him and with one another. It is understandable, then, why the Lord declared in 2:18 that it is "not good for the man to be alone."

The idea behind this statement is that Adam's lack of companionship prevented him from realizing his full potential as a human being. A corresponding truth is that the believers' commitment to God does not demand celibacy (that is, the condition of being unmarried). In fact, in the Old Testament the persons regarded as being most holy (or dedicated in their service to God)—the high priest (Lev. 21:13) and the Nazirites—were not commanded to be celibate (Num. 6:1-4).

Adam name the animals, which the Lord had formed from the soil of the earth (Gen. 2:19). God then listened to what Adam named each creature.

The naming activity had at least a couple of purposes. First, it was a way for Adam to exercise his God-given dominion over the rest of creation (see 1:26, 28). Just as God had named day and night and other basic features of creation, so Adam named the animals.

Second, the naming was a way for Adam to review the whole of the animal kingdom and discover at the end what God already knew. Adam was alone as a human being; there was no one else like him. Not one of the animals was a suitable companion for the man to complement and complete him (2:20).

C. The Lord's Creation of a Woman: vss. 21-22

So the LORD God caused the man to fall into a deep sleep; and while he was sleeping, he took one of the man's ribs and closed up the place with flesh. Then the LORD God made a woman from the rib he had taken out of the man, and he brought her to the man.

Now that Adam knew he needed a mate, God caused a deep sleep to come over him (Gen. 2:21). The woman was not created from the dust as Adam had been; instead, Eve was formed from one of Adam's ribs, that is, a part of Adam himself. By sharing the same life as Adam, Eve was fully a part of the human race God had started. Eve, along with Adam, bore the image of God (see 1:27).

The Hebrew word translated "ribs" (22:21) can also rendered "side." For example, in Exodus 25:12, it refers to the sides of the ark of the covenant. Such usage has prompted some to suggest that God took more than a rib from Adam when He made the first woman. The Lord may have taken some flesh along with some bone (Gen. 2:22).

D. The Man's Joy: vss. 23-24

The man said, "This is now bone of my bones and flesh of my flesh; she shall be called 'woman,' for she was taken out of man." For this reason a man will leave his father and mother and be united to his wife, and they will become one flesh.

When Adam woke after his operation, God led the woman to him. Judging by the fact that Adam's declaration on this occasion is the first piece of poetry in the Bible, Adam was overjoyed to see

---

The New Testament reveals that all human relationships should be characterized by Christian submission. Paul illustrated this truth by pointing to three familiar, household relationships— between husbands and wives (Eph. 5:22-33), children and parents (6:1-4), and slaves and masters (vss. 5-9). Then he concluded by ironically pointing to our position of power that comes through such submission (vss. 10-19).

Clearly when God led Paul to call all believers to submit to one another, human standards of superiority and inferiority were irrelevant. As Christ Himself exemplified, submissively humbling ourselves is an act of unselfish love. So selfishly wielding our rights and personal status have no place in the context of Christian submission (see Phil. 2:1-8).

Eve. The man exclaimed, "This is now bone of my bones and flesh of my flesh" (Gen. 2:23). Adam completed his naming activity by calling the new human "woman." She alone was truly comparable to Adam and thus a suitable companion for him.

Verse 24 explains that, because men and women are made for each other, a man will leave his parents, be united to his wife, and be physically intimate with her. In the case of Adam and Eve, they were married from their first moment together and remained united for life. Their marriage set a pattern for the marriages of their descendants.

Here we see that the divine ideal for marriage was monogamy (that is, a man and a woman being joined only to each other in matrimony). They equally and mutually formed an unbreakable unit, one that is as inseparable as the union between a biological parent and child. The latter share the same blood kinship (see Gen. 29:14). Likewise, a husband and wife are bound together as "one flesh" (2:24) for as long as they live.

Genesis 2:24 says that the husband is "united to his wife." Supporting this union is the notion of a covenant-like commitment. The idea is that when a man and woman enter into holy matrimony, they solemnly pledge to let nothing disrupt or destroy their partnership in marriage. Their union is a picture of God's relationship to His people (Hos. 2:14-23; Eph. 5:22-23).

E.   The Absence of Shame: vs. 25
The man and his wife were both naked, and they felt no shame.

At this time, the husband and wife did not need any clothing (Gen. 2:25). Sin had not entered in, bringing with it a sense of shame and guilt. We are not told how long the two of them enjoyed the paradise in which their fellowship with God and each other was unhindered by sin. It is enough to make one wistful, thinking of all that sin has cost the human race.

Discussion Questions

1. What is significant about the phrase "LORD God" (Gen. 2:7)?
2. What differentiated man from the rest of the creatures?
3. How do we know that marriage and the family were part of God's plan from the start?
4. How did God prepare Adam for the change that would come into his life?
5. Why does a man willingly leave his parents?

Now Ask Yourself . . .

Have modern scientific theories or contradictory opinions ever shaken my belief in the Creator?

While I enjoy the beauty of nature, do I think of the Creator and praise Him for His wondrous works?

Do I get satisfaction from the work that I do? Why or why not?

What would my life be like without family and friends?

What would my life be like without the opposite gender?

Are my relationships with others as deep and enduring as I would like them to be?

Illustrations

The creation of the first woman emphasizes our need as human beings to be in relationships. God declared in Genesis 2:18 that it was not good for Adam to be alone. Thus the Lord created from man himself a woman. Adam needed someone like himself to share with, someone so much a part of him that he could call her bone of his bones and flesh of his flesh (vs. 23). Because men and women were created for each other, they can unite in a marriage and become like one person—knowing each other's thoughts, finishing each other's sentences, and sharing each other's hopes and dreams.

But we also need relationships beyond marriage. God made us all with the desire to be lovingly related to others. Consider Margaret. She is a single woman—no husband, no children. But Margaret says she isn't lonely. Within her church, Margaret has found a supportive "family" with whom she can be honest and open about her ups and downs.

"I have key relationships in my life that help to fill up the places that might otherwise be hollow and empty. There's no doubt that my most significant relationship is with God, but He's also put tangible demonstrations of His love for me in my life.

"By that I mean I have a relationship with people who care for me with the kind of love God has for me. I believe God made us to be in community with other believers and to have meaningful relationships within the church.

"No one is perfect; least of all me. That's why there will always be some pain involved in closeness with others. But the good I experience in the relationships I have now far outweighs the bad that sometimes happens."

Deceit's Destructive Force

DEVOTIONAL READING

Proverbs 17:7-28

DAILY BIBLE READINGS

Monday July 3
   Genesis 25:19-28
   Jacob and Esau Are Born

Tuesday July 4
   Genesis 25:29-34
   Jacob Deceives Esau

Wednesday July 5
   Genesis 27:1-10
   Rebekah Plots to Deceive
   Isaac

Thursday July 6
   Genesis 27:11-17
   Jacob Pretends to Be Esau

Friday July 7
   Genesis 27:18-29
   Jacob Deceives Issac

Saturday July 8
   Genesis 27:30-35
   Esau Discovers Jacob
   Stole His Blessing

Sunday July 9
   Genesis 27:36-40
   Esau Weeps with
   Bitterness

Scripture

Background Scripture: *Genesis 25; 27*

Scripture Lesson: *Genesis 25:29-34; 27:30-37*

Key Verses: *"Your brother came deceitfully and took your blessing." Esau said, "Isn't he rightly named Jacob? He has deceived me these two times; He took my birthright, and now he's taken my blessing!" Genesis 27:35-36.*

Lesson Aim

Deceit can destroy relationships.

Lesson Setting

Time: 1929 B.C.

Place: Canaan

Lesson Outline

Deceit's Destructive Force

  I. A Birthright Despised: Genesis 25:29-34
     A. *The Demand Made by Esau: vss. 29-30*
     B. *The Counter-Demand Made by Jacob: vss. 31-33*
     C. *The Completion of the Transaction: vs. 34*
  II. A Blessing Lost: Genesis 27:30-37
     A. *The Arrival of Esau: vs. 30*
     B. *The Request Made by Esau: vs. 31*
     C. *The Affirmation of Blessing on Jacob: vss. 32-33*
     D. *The Desperation of Esau: vss. 34-37*

Introduction

Deceit's Destructive Force

One of the guiding principles of modern business is this: "Fool me once, shame on you. Fool me twice, shame one me." In other words, it should take only one hard-won lesson to make us forever wary. If we fail to be sufficiently on our guard after that, it is clearly our own fault.

Not surprisingly, that attitude does not lead to mutually satisfying business partnerships. It makes even less sense when it becomes the guiding principle of our personal lives. It turns once-loving, trusting relationships into bitter disappointments. Relationships are built on trust. Once deception enters the picture—infidelity, a violated promise, an outright lie—trust is broken, and the memory of the deceit taints everything that follows.

Genesis describes how Jacob brought such deceit into his relationship with his brother, Esau, and his father, Issac. As this week's lesson explains, Jacob's deception would leave its mark on the family for many years to come.

Lesson Commentary

From start to finish, Genesis is a book of history, and its historical account is trustworthy because it was inspired by God. But we should not expect the book to provide a complete or systematic history of time from its origin until the Hebrews' Egyptian sojourn. The author's concern was not history for history's sake. He used true historical figures and events to teach truths about God and humankind. We should read Genesis, the book of beginnings, in that light.

I. A Birthright Despised: Genesis 25:29-34

A. The Demand Made by Esau: vss. 29-30
Once when Jacob was cooking some stew, Esau came in from the open country, famished. He said to Jacob, "Quick, let me have some of that red stew! I'm famished!" (That is why he was also called Edom.)

In Genesis 25:1-11, we read about the final years and the death of Abraham. He lived 35 years after Isaac and Rebekah were married. He also had children through another marriage. But finally, at the age of 175, Abraham died. Isaac and Ishmael cooperated in burying their father. The mention of Ishmael leads to the mentioning, in verses 12-18, of his descendants and his death at the age of 137.

Beginning with verse 19, the focus shifts to "Abraham's son Issac." Undoubtedly, Isaac knew about the covenant concerning him and his descendants. But for a while it looked as though he might not have any descendants. He did not marry until he was 40 (vs. 20). Then for many years his wife, Rebekah, bore no children.

As time wore on, Isaac became more and more concerned about his lack of children. The Lord was testing Isaac's faith as He had previously tested the faith of Isaac's father. Many years earlier, Abraham also had waited impatiently for Isaac's birth. The text tells us that Isaac prayed for a son (vs. 21). The Lord responded to this plea. God knew all along what He would do, but He waited to do it in cooperation with the prayers of Isaac.

God gave Isaac not one son but two. Prior to birth, "the babies jostled each other within [their mother Rebekah]" (vs. 22). Although it is common for pregnant mothers to feel their children move about within them, Rebekah sensed that the motion of her children had a special meaning. But she didn't know what meaning.

Both Isaac and Rebekah displayed faith by bringing their matters of concern before God. Isaac prayed diligently, and Rebekah sought an answer from the Lord concerning her situation. In response, the Lord said that just as the babies jostled one another in her womb, so they would be rivals as adults (vs. 23). The two sons within Rebekah would be the fathers of great nations. But contrary to custom, the older would serve the younger. The younger son's people would be the stronger. The younger son would receive the blessings of the covenant.

The birth of Esau and Jacob was the first biblically recorded birth of twins (vs. 24). But there was nothing identical about them. They were different in behavior and in appearance. The name *Esau* probably means "hairy" (vs. 25), referring to the fact that he was covered with hair from birth. But he was also called *Edom*, which means "red." That was a reference to his appearance at birth and to the red lentil stew for which he traded his birthright (vs. 30). The nation that came from Esau was named Edom.

The name *Jacob* means "he grasps the heel," a reference to Jacob's position at birth, holding on to Esau's heel (vs. 26). The name also carried the idea of outwitting or deceiving another person. Jacob's life would give new meaning to that idea.

By the time the twins reached adulthood, Esau became the sportsman of the family (vs. 27). He loved to be outdoors hunting game. He also became the favorite of Isaac, who enjoyed eating the wild game Esau brought him (vs. 28). Jacob was different from his brother. He enjoyed the quiet life with his mother among the tents, where he evidently became a good chef. Rebekah enjoyed the company of Jacob over that of Esau.

The importance of the Lord's statement recorded in Genesis 25:23 cannot be overemphasized. In His sovereignty, God chose Jacob over Esau (Rom. 9:10-13). Although it would be many years before Jacob displayed maturity in his relationship with God, the characters of Esau and Jacob would eventually confirm the wisdom of the Lord's decision.

The displays of favoritism by the parents caused great problems in the home. It deepened the rivalry between the brothers, and eventually broke the family apart. The sad results of the partiality in Isaac's family serve as a warning to parents today. Human nature has not changed since the time of Isaac and Rebekah. It is easy to play favorites with children, and the resulting strife from such actions still occurs today. Favoritism is almost a guarantee of trouble.

In Bible times it was customary for the firstborn son (whether a child of a legal wife or a concubine) to inherit the rights, or privileges, of the family. This typically included receiving the family name and titles. It also included becoming the leader of the family and the one through whom the line was continued. Further, because a child was the firstborn, he usually inherited a double portion of the family estate.

Archaeologists discovered that these customs were not absolutely observed by people in the ancient Near East, and the Bible gives evidence of this as well. A father could ignore the rights of the firstborn and give the inheritance to a younger son (Gen. 48:13-20). A father could also disregard the firstborn son of a concubine in favor of a son he had through a legal wife (21:10).

One day Esau came in from the fields feeling ravenous (vs. 29). He saw that Jacob was cooking lentil stew, and demanded that supper be served immediately (vs. 30). Because he was impulsive, he thought his hunger would not wait. Jacob did not hesitate to exploit Esau's hunger to his own advantage.

B. The Counter-Demand Made by Jacob: vss. 31-33

Jacob replied, "First sell me your birthright." "Look, I am about to die," Esau said. "What good is the birthright to me?" But Jacob said, "Swear to me first." So he swore an oath to him, selling his birthright to Jacob.

Jacob was a schemer. He typically would make situations work to his advantage, even though it might hurt another person. He probably also knew that Esau was more pragmatic in his character. Thus Jacob took advantage of his brother's fatigued and famished condition by requesting that he sell him his "birthright" (Gen. 25:31), namely, his inheritance privileges as the firstborn. Jacob knew it would be to his long-term advantage if he could wrestle away the birthright from Esau.

Perhaps by now Esau was even more famished. No doubt seeing little immediate value in his birthright, he willingly discarded it for a quick bite to eat (vs. 32). Perhaps Jacob had heard that "the older will serve the younger" (vs. 23). If so, Jacob was ready for this prophecy to come true; he wanted to secure the birthright.

Before Jacob would give his famished brother some stew, he insisted that Esau swear to him at that moment that the birthright was his (25:33). Esau gave in by swearing an oath. In ancient times this would have been a solemn statement that both parties used to confirm a promise. Such pledges were taken seriously.

C. The Completion of the Transaction: vs. 34

Then Jacob gave Esau some bread and some lentil stew. He ate and drank, and then got up and left. So Esau despised his birthright.

Once his demands had been met, Jacob gave Esau some bread and lentil stew. He in turn "ate and drank, and then got up and left" (Gen. 25:34). He seemed indifferent to the fact that he had given up his birthright. In short, he had despised it.

In Isaac's family, the birthright also included the promises of

Abraham's covenant made by God. Thus we can see how foolish Esau was to barter his birthright for a bow of lentils. If he had been patient, someone would have fed him. It is difficult to believe that he was really close to death from starvation. And later, he demonstrated his ability to prepare a meal (27:31).

In Hebrews 12:16 we read, "See that no one is sexually immoral, or is godless like Esau, who for a single meal sold his inheritance rights as the oldest son." The writer of Hebrews attached spiritual significance to Esau's giving up of the birthright. God regarded the sale as a valid transaction.

II. A Blessing Lost: Genesis 27:30-37

A. The Arrival of Esau: vs. 30
After Isaac finished blessing him and Jacob had scarcely left his father's presence, his brother Esau came in from hunting.

Isaac is overshadowed in Genesis by his father, Abraham, and his son Jacob. But in Genesis 26, we read about one period in Isaac's life. A famine struck. Isaac moved his clan to the Philistine town of Gerar. Evidently, he was planning to keep going all the way to Egypt, but the Lord told him to stay where he was. The Lord also reviewed the covenant blessings.

While in Gerar, Isaac became involved with the Philistine king in a conflict over Isaac's wife, Rebekah. Nevertheless, Isaac grew wealthy in Gerar. For this reason, Isaac was forced to move back to the vicinity of Beersheba. There he built an altar to the Lord and reestablished peaceful relations with the Philistines.

Toward the end of Isaac's life, he intended to pass on the family blessing to Esau, his first born. But Rebekah wanted to see the blessing go to Jacob, her favorite, so they cooked up a scheme in which Jacob pretended to be Esau. Jacob wore goatskins so he would feel like his hairy brother to his nearly blind father, and he brought cooked meat and bread to Isaac, who then blessed Jacob, thinking he was Esau (27:1-29).

Isaac and Esau were attempting to do the wrong thing—to give Esau his father's blessing. Rebekah and Jacob were seeking the right thing—to get Jacob the blessing—but in the wrong way. We do not know how God would have handled the matter without the scheme Rebekah devised. But under other circumstances, He could have diverted the blessing to Jacob without the serious con-

If Esau had valued the great covenant blessings given to Abraham and Isaac, he would not have considered selling his birthright under any circumstances. Although there were material benefits to the covenant, the promises revolved mainly around God's redemptive program. We can assume that Jacob wanted to be a part of that; he desired a place in God's plan to bless the whole world. But Esau had little regard for God's work.

To her credit, Rebekah believed what the Lord said about Jacob. But when she stepped in to "help" God, she went astray. God does not condone the use of deception. Ephesians 4:25 says, "Each of you must put off falsehood and speak truthfully to his neighbor, for we are all members of one body." The standard for believers is to be truthful at all times.

357

Jacob received the blessing because God wanted him to have it, not because of his trickery. The Lord had many lessons to teach Jacob in the days ahead. As the years passed, He slowly removed the crust from Jacob's life to reveal a heart that sought the Lord.

sequences of the deception.

While Jacob may at first have been hesitant about deceiving his father, once he agreed to his mother's plan, he worked hard to make the deception successful (Gen. 27:18-25). Many of his statements to Isaac were completely false. He even associated God's name in one of his lies. Clearly, that was not the way God wanted him to receive the blessing.

Although Isaac thought he was blessing Esau, his inspired words brought Jacob the clearest indication yet of what God would do through the younger son. Isaac's words called for Jacob to be blessed by God and by people, and to have a position of superiority (vss. 26-29).

Once Jacob had secured his father's blessing, he left the scene. In fact, he had scarcely departed from his father's presence when Esau returned from his hunting expedition (vs. 30). Of course, he had no way of knowing the elaborate deception Jacob had just pulled off to steal away the family blessing.

B. The Request Made by Esau: vs. 31

He too prepared some tasty food and brought it to his father. Then he said to him, "My father, sit up and eat some of my game, so that you may give me your blessing."

As Esau anticipated receiving the family blessing, he must have invested a considerable amount of time and effort to prepare his father's favorite dish. Once it was ready, Esau brought the meal to Isaac. Esau invited his father to sit up from his reclining position and eat the wild game. Then afterward he could give his son his blessing (Gen. 27:31).

In Bible times the family blessing consisted of the father orally conveying his authority and possessions to his children sometime before his death. The father usually followed an informal ceremony in which he first prayed that God's favor would rest upon one of his descendants (most often the firstborn). The father then would divide his power and property among his children. Once the family blessing was confirmed, it was considered irrevocable.

C. The Affirmation of Blessing on Jacob: vss. 32-33

His father Isaac asked him, "Who are you?" "I am your son," he answered, "your firstborn, Esau." Isaac trembled violently and said, "Who was it, then, that hunted game and brought it to me? I ate it just before you came and I blessed him—and indeed he will be blessed!"

At first Isaac was confused and shocked by the presence of Esau and asked the person before him to identify himself (Gen. 27:32). Esau must have also been perplexed and worried by his father's apparent lapse in memory. When Esau stated his name and relationship to his father, Isaac began to tremble uncontrollably and asked who had just served him wild game. Just before Esau's arrival, Isaac had finished consuming the meal and giving his irrevocable blessing to Jacob (vs. 33).

D. The Desperation of Esau: vss. 34-37

When Esau heard his father's words, he burst out with a loud and bitter cry and said to his father, "Bless me—me too, my father!" But he said, "Your brother came deceitfully and took your blessing." Esau said, "Isn't he rightly named Jacob? He has deceived me these two times: He took my birthright, and now he's taken my blessing!" Then he asked, "Haven't you reserved any blessing for me?" Isaac answered Esau, "I have made him lord over you and have made all his relatives his servants, and I have sustained him with grain and new wine. So what can I possibly do for you, my son?"

Isaac felt the grief of his son Esau, but though Esau begged him, he could do nothing to change what had happened (Gen. 27:34-35). Oral blessings given on a deathbed were considered legally binding. They possessed the same force as a signed contract would today. Presumably, Isaac also knew that God had directed the blessing to Jacob.

Referring to the symbolic meaning of Jacob's name, Esau complained about his brother's deceiving nature (vs. 36). But the real tragedy was his ignorance of the sacredness of the blessing. He desired only the material blessing. He did not realize that God was watching when he sold the birthright.

Even Esau's pleading for a blessing from his father could not change what had happened. Isaac had made Jacob the master of Esau and declared that all Jacob's relatives would serve him. Isaac even guaranteed Jacob an abundance of grain and wine (vs. 37). It's no wonder that the firstborn broke down and wept.

Esau realized from what had occurred that he had lost much to his younger brother. He had lost both the family birthright and the blessing to Jacob (vs. 38). But perhaps Jacob was the biggest loser, for he allowed his selfish desires to virtually destroy his relationship with his brother. And though Jacob gained much from his actions, he brought anguish and division to his family.

Isaac's excessive trembling may have stemmed primarily from a fear of God. The Lord had overruled Isaac's plot to give Esau the blessing. Isaac may have realized that he had brought the deception upon himself through his foolish choice to favor Esau.

Discoveries at the town of Nuzi in Mesopotamia have verified the importance of an oral blessing. A Nuzi court record tells the story of a man named Tarmiya who inherited a slave girl from his father. Tarmiya's two older brothers, however, contested the claim. Tarmiya argued that his father gave the girl to him while the father was sick and lying on a couch. After an examination of witnesses, the judges decided in favor of Tarmiya. They ruled that the oral promise of the father, before his death, was legally binding.

Discussion Questions

1. How did Esau show that he was impulsive and shortsighted?
2. How did Jacob show that he could be insensitive and scheming?
3. How did Isaac show that he was distressed over what Jacob had done?
4. What was the outcome of Jacob's trickery?
5. How did Esau show his alarm over what Jacob had done?

Now Ask Yourself . . .

How have I felt when others deceived me?

What relationships have I seen destroyed by the presence of deceit?

How can I be more fair in my dealings with my family and friends?

Is seeking the kingdom of God really the driving force in my life?

What is my real motive for serving God? Do I desire to know Him above all else?

Illustrations

The great Scottish novelist Sir Walter Scott once wrote, "Oh, what a tangled web we weave, when first we practice to deceive!" His point was that a lie can't live alone; it must breed other lies in order to survive. Jacob first lied to his father about who he was and then had to lie about God in order to dupe Isaac and steal the blessing (Gen. 27:18-20).

I saw a such a layer of lies created when John, a church treasurer, was found to have embezzled money from the church for years and built a façade of lies to cover what he was doing. When the facts came out, his wife left him, and his reputation was ruined. Fragmentation within the church followed, as did an exodus of disillusioned members. As the web of lies unraveled, it destroyed not only John but also the church he had pledged to serve.

Then there's the example of Vernon Pierce.

According to *Today in the Word* (September 29, 1995), he needed a notebook to keep track of the stories he told his four wives and the other women he was dating. But even that wasn't enough. His tangled love life began to unravel when one of the four women to whom he was married sent the police to Pierce's home to check up on him. The police found another wife knocking on the door.

There was a lot of lying going on. Police said Pierce was dating other women and keeping track of some of them on a 3-by-5 inch card labeled "Who to Marry." Pierce also carried a little black book in his wallet to keep his stories straight.

Many of us are involved in one or more relationships in which we are entangled in a web of deceit. The deceits may be small or great, but they still do our relationships no good.

The Folly of Favoritism

DEVOTIONAL READING

Psalm 5:1-8

DAILY BIBLE READINGS

Monday July 10
   Genesis 37:1-8
   Jacob Loves Joseph Most

Tuesday July 11
   Genesis 37:9-11
   Joseph's Brothers Are
   Jealous

Wednesday July 12
   Genesis 37:12-18
   The Brothers Plot to Kill
   Joseph

Thursday July 13
   Genesis 37:19-24
   Joseph Is Thrown into the
   Cistern

Friday July 14
   Genesis 37:25-30
   Joseph Is Sold to
   Merchants Going to Egypt

Saturday July 15
   Genesis 37:31-36
   The Brothers Tell Jacob
   Joseph Was Killed

Sunday July 16
   James 2:1-10 Favoritism Is
   Forbidden

Scripture

Background Scripture: *Genesis 37*

Scripture Lesson: *Genesis 37:3-4, 17b-28*

Key Verse: *When his brothers saw that their father loved him more than any of them, they hated him and could not speak a kind word to him. Genesis 37:4.*

Lesson Aim

Favoritism can have devastating effects.

Lesson Setting

Time: 1898 B.C.

Place: Canaan

Lesson Outline

The Folly of Favoritism

  I. The Favored Son and Hated Brother: Genesis 37:3-4
      A. *The Supreme Love of Israel for Joseph: vs. 3*
      B. *The Extreme Hatred of Joseph's Brothers: vs. 4*
  II. The Favored Son in a Pit: Genesis 37:17b-24
      A. *The Plot to Murder Joseph: vss. 17b-18*
      B. *The Brothers' Disdain for Jospeh's Dreams:*
          vss. 19-20
      C. *The Alternate Plan Proposed by Reuben:*
          vss. 21-22
      D. *The Execution of Reuben's Plan: vss. 23-24*

Introduction

The Folly of Favoritism

"WANTED: Mother. Salary: $00. No retirement, no insurance, no guarantees. Bonuses for a job well done may include a few hugs and kisses. Skills required: Must love children, cats, dogs, hamsters, and fish. Must have nursing experience for kissing 'owies,' and lots of bandages. Must be able to love a kid, even when he's rotten."

This tongue-in-cheek advertisement, from *What Kids Need Most in a Mom* by Patricia Rushford, is a good beginning of a never-ending job description. An equally overwhelming one would apply to a father.

Parents know that each child has a "love tank" that requires daily refueling. If this is neglected for any child, his or her "engine" can cut off. The same thing happens in other areas of life when we show undue partiality to particular co-workers, relatives, or even Sunday school students. Pray this week that God would disclose any people in your life whom you are paying more attention to at the expense of others.

Lesson Commentary

I. The Favored Son and Hated Brother: Genesis 37:3-4

A. The Supreme Love of Israel for Joseph: vs. 3

Now Israel loved Joseph more than any of his other sons, because he had been born to him in his old age; and he made a richly ornamented robe for him.

Commentators take different views of Joseph's reporting to his father. Some blame him, calling him a tattletale. Other commentators defend Joseph, saying he was only acting as a son should.

The first 11 verses of Genesis 37 explain the friction that developed between the teenage Joseph and other members of his family. First, we learn that Joseph, at the age of 17, told on his brothers. The brothers had done something they shouldn't have (we have no idea what) while away from home tending the flocks. Joseph saw the wrongdoing and let Jacob know about it (vss. 1-2).

The brothers must have had hard feelings toward Joseph because of his reporting on them. Jacob increased the friction between the older brothers and Joseph by showing his preference for Joseph (vs. 3). Jacob loved Joseph more because Joseph was born in his old age. As a matter of fact, Joseph was his youngest son, next to Benjamin. Jacob may also have preferred Joseph because Joseph was the first son of his favorite wife, Rachel.

B. The Extreme Hatred of Joseph's Brothers: vs. 4

When his brothers saw that their father loved him more than any of them, they hated him and could not speak a kind word to him.

Jacob revealed his favoritism by giving Joseph a special outer garment. As Joseph wore the robe, it must have become a constant irritation to the other brothers. It reminded them that their father loved Joseph best. They were jealous (Gen. 37:4). When Jacob had been younger, his mother had liked him better than Esau, while his father had preferred Esau. This show of parental favoritism had led to threats of murder and to a deep rupture between Jacob and Esau. Having seen the damage favoritism can do, Jacob should have known better than to show favoritism to Joseph.

Next, we read about two dreams (vss. 5-11). In the ancient world, dreams were widely believed to foretell the future. This belief was right in the case of Joseph's dreams. God sent the dreams to show the superior blessings He would give Joseph.

In the first dream, Joseph saw himself and his brothers binding sheaves of grain in a field. This was a normal harvest scene. But suddenly, his brothers' sheaves bowed down to Joseph's sheaf. When Joseph told his brothers about his dream, the brothers correctly interpreted it to mean that one day they would bow down to Joseph. This literally happened when Joseph became a ruler in Egypt. Of course, the brothers did not like the idea of serving their younger brother. Because of the dream, the brothers' hatred of Joseph rose a notch higher.

In Joseph's second dream, he saw the sun and moon and 11 stars bow down to him. This time Joseph described the dream to his father as well as to his brothers. Now even his father was upset with Joseph. Jacob accurately interpreted the dream to mean that he and his wife Leah (Joseph's mother, Rachel, had died by this time) and his sons would all bow down to Joseph. This dream, too, referred to the future when Joseph would be a ruler in Egypt. The biblical text says that Jacob did not forget his son's dreams. But the next event in Joseph's life made their fulfillment seem impossible.

Most of the narrative in the last 14 chapters of Genesis is devoted to the life of Joseph. The faith this son of Jacob showed in the midst of distressing circumstances has encouraged believers through the centuries.

In relating the dreams, Joseph was only telling the truth. But some commentators suggest that he was unwise to mention them, being motivated by pride. Joseph had the ability to interpret dreams, so he probably knew what these dreams meant. Joseph could have kept his mouth shut about them, but he did not. (Of course, regardless of whether Joseph was wrong to tell about the dreams, the brothers were wrong to nurse feelings of jealousy and hatred against him.)

II. The Favored Son in a Pit: Genesis 37:17b-24

A. The Plot to Murder Joseph: vss. 17b-18

So Joseph went after his brothers and found them near Dothan.

But they saw him in the distance, and before he reached them, they plotted to kill him.

Shortly after Joseph's dreams, most of Jacob's sons took his flocks many miles to the north (Gen. 37:12). A desire to get away from Joseph may have been one reason why they traveled so far from their home in the Valley of Hebron. But if so, it did no good. Jacob sent Joseph after them to find out how they were doing (vss. 13-14). Neither the son nor the father could have known that more than 20 years would pass before they laid eyes on each other again.

The biblical text notes the arrival of Joseph at Shechem. This ancient fortified city was located in the hill country of Ephraim in north central Palestine. Shechem was primarily built on the slope, or shoulder, of Mount Ebal. Long before the Israelites occupied Canaan, this town was important because of its location between main highways and ancient trade routes.

According to verse 15, a man found Joseph wandering around the countryside. When Joseph was asked what he was looking for, the adolescent stated he was trying to find his brothers and wanted to know where they were grazing their flocks (vs. 16). The man, upon further questioning, indicated overhearing Jospeh's brothers say they were going to Dothan, which was located about 13 miles north of Shechem. Joseph thus traveled to Dothan, where he found his brothers (vs. 17).

The brothers saw Joseph approaching from a distance wearing his special coat and plotted to kill him (vs. 18). The specific Hebrew words in verse 3 describing this piece of clothing are unclear to us today. The coat or tunic could have been multicolored, or long-sleeved, or extravagantly ornamented. Though the precise description of the coat is uncertain, it's clear its special appearance loudly proclaimed Jospeh's favored status with his father.

Dothan was already over a thousand years old when Jacob's sons tended their sheep near it (Gen. 37:17). The city lay on a major route between Damascus and Egypt, so it was not surprising that a caravan came near the city and took Joseph to Egypt. Its location caused Dothan to be destroyed and rebuilt a number of times. For example, it was nearly destroyed when the king of Aram (Syria) besieged the city to capture Elisha (2 Kings 6:13-19).

B. The Brothers' Disdain for Jospeh's Dreams: vss. 19-20

"Here comes that dreamer!" they said to each other. "Come now, let's kill him and throw him into one of these cisterns and say that a ferocious animal devoured him. Then we'll see what comes of his dreams."

The sight of Joseph prompted his brothers to exclaim, "Here comes that dreamer!" (Gen. 37:19). The Hebrew term rendered "dreamer" conveys the idea of "dream expert" or "master of dreams." The disdain behind the statement of Joseph's brothers was fueled by uncontrolled jealously and hatred.

The apostle Paul wrote, "Get rid of all bitterness, rage and anger . . . . Be kind and compassionate to one another, forgiving each other, just as in Christ God forgave you" (Eph. 4:31-32). We must learn to deal with jealousy and hatred before they destroy us.

The brothers' contempt for Joseph turned to calculated rage. Perhaps they reasoned that if they murdered him, his dreams of them being in a subservient role to him would never come true.

The plan the brothers adopted called for tossing Joseph's body in a nearby cistern (Gen. 37:20). This would have been a pear or bottle-shaped pit for catching and storing runoff rainwater. In contrast, a well would have been fed by underground water seepage. Most cisterns were made from limestone. The porous nature of this material led to a lot of the accumulated water escaping from the reservoir.

The plan called for the brothers blaming the death of Joseph on a wild animal. They could get away with such a claim because Joseph was away from their father's protection. Also, there no witnesses were nearby to refute their tale.

C.   The Alternate Plan Proposed by Reuben: vss. 21-22

When Reuben heard this, he tried to rescue him from their hands. "Let's not take his life," he said. "Don't shed any blood. Throw him into this cistern here in the desert, but don't lay a hand on him." Reuben said this to rescue him from them and take him back to his father.

Not all the brothers wanted to murder Joseph and stash his corpse in a dry cistern (Gen. 37:21). Reuben, the oldest son, came to Joseph's rescue (in a manner of speaking) when he urged the others not to shed innocent blood. Instead, Reuben suggested they throw Joseph into the deep pit alive. This meant they would not be directly responsible for his death. Verse 22 says that Reuben secretly planned to help Joseph escape and then bring him safely back to his father. The unfolding of events, however, would foil this ill-conceived scheme.

Joseph's conflict with his brothers is not the only case of rivalry between brothers recorded in the Book of Genesis. A jealous Cain murdered his brother Abel (4:1-16). Ishmael was sent away from his father, Abraham, to make room for his brother Isaac (21:8-14). Jacob fled for his life when his brother, Esau, threatened to kill him (27:41-45).

Often the parents were active participants in these conflicts. Hagar's struggle with Sarah for dominance in Abraham's clan led to Ishmael's teasing of Isaac and Ishmael's expulsion (16:4; 21:8-10). Isaac's blatant preference of Esau, and Rebekah's favoring of Jacob, ensured the brothers' near-fatal rift (25:28). Jacob carried on Rebekah's tradition by blatantly favoring Joseph over his brothers. The coat Jacob gave Joseph was a public proclamation of carrying on this unwise tradition of favoritism (37:3-4).

Perhaps because Reuben was Jacob's firstborn son, he felt responsible for the welfare of Joseph. In a sense, Reuben assumed the role of the father while the brothers were away from home. It's also possible that Reuben wanted to prevent upsetting his father by failing to protect Joseph.

In an earlier episode in which Reuben slept with Bilhah, one of Jacob's concubines (35:22), the eldest son undoubtedly had diminished his status as the firsborn. It's possible Reuben wanted to prevent any further erosion of his standing in the family. And by saving his father's favorite son, Reuben thought he might be able to regain the trust of his father as well as look more worthy of leading the family.

D. The Execution of Reuben's Plan: vss. 23-24

So when Joseph came to his brothers, they stripped him of his robe—the richly ornamented robe he was wearing—and they took him and threw him into the cistern. Now the cistern was empty; there was no water in it.

The brothers adopted Reuben's plan (Gen. 37:23). But before they put Joseph in the pit, they took from him the robe that had so inflamed their jealousy. Thankfully, the cistern had no water in it at this time (vs. 24). Otherwise, Joseph would have been less likely to survive for any lengthy period.

A large caravan could number over 3,000 people and animals. As it journeyed from town to town, some persons and merchandise would leave the caravan, while other persons and merchandise would replace them. Often, slaves would be a part of the merchandise. The wealthier persons in a caravan would ride camels. The beasts of burden would also carry trading goods. The poorer travelers would walk or ride on donkeys.

The lack of compassion the brothers felt toward Joseph shows in their causally sitting down to eat after leaving him to die in the pit (vs. 25). While dining, they saw a caravan of Ishhmaelite traders passing nearby on their way to Egypt. Not wanting to bear the burden of murdering a brother, and seeing the opportunity to make a little financial profit, Judah suggested they sell Joseph to the traders instead of killing him (vss. 26-27).

Travel was extremely dangerous in ancient times. The threat of robbers and wild animals discouraged most people from traveling alone or even in small groups. For safety on the unmarked roads between Syria and Egypt, caravans such as the one that Joseph was sold into were often formed.

Judah's recommendation was probably motivated by two desires. First, Judah could have believed that God would punish them for committing such a heinous crime as killing their own brother. God's judgment on Cain for murdering Abel may have been in Judah's thoughts at that moment. Apparently, selling a brother into slavery was not considered to be so dreadful. Second, Judah saw an opportunity to be rid of Joseph and make some money on the side.

All the brothers except Reuben eagerly agreed to the plan. Reuben was elsewhere at the time (vs. 29). Perhaps he was with a different part of the flock, or he was formulating his own plans to rescue Joseph when his other brothers were not around.

In any case, Joseph's brothers sold him into slavery for 20 shekels of silver (vs. 28). Dealing in slaves was a common practice in the Arabian desert, and archaeological records tell us that the amount paid for Joseph was the usual price for a boy between the ages of five and 20. (Older boys would bring a higher price.) And the Egyptians were always open to purchasing slaves, as well as other commodities, from traders such as the Ishmaelites, who were now taking Joseph on the first step of an incredible journey.

Since it was too late to help Joseph, Reuben went along with his brothers in their plan to trick Jacob, the great trickster. They dipped Joseph's robe in goat's blood and, when they returned home, showed it to their father (vss. 30-31). They knew full well that Jacob would interpret the bloodied robe to mean that a wild beast had killed Joseph.

Thinking his favorite son dead, Jacob went into mourning. His grief was uncommonly powerful. No one could comfort him. He looked forward to his own death, because he imagined that then he would be reunited with his beloved Joseph (vss. 32-35).

But, of course, Joseph was not dead. He was in Egypt, where the Midianites resold him. Far from home, Joseph found himself the slave of Pharaoh's "captain of the guard" (vs. 36). This title perhaps means that Potiphar was in charge of the soldiers who guarded Pharaoh's jail and carried out executions as ordered.

The biblical text calls the traders who bought Joseph both "Ishmaelites" (Gen. 37:25, 27) and "Midianites" (vs. 28). Since Midian and Ishmael were both sons of Abraham (25:2, 12), the terms probably generally described an interrelated group of people who lived in the Sinai Peninsula and the Arabian Desert east of the Red Sea. It was to this area called Midian that Moses fled after he killed the Egyptian who was beating a Hebrew slave (Exod. 2:15).

In fact, there is evidence in Scripture that the Midianites and Ishmaelites worked together. The "Midianites" who later conquered the Israelites during the period of the judges (Judg. 6:1-6) were described as part of a coalition of "eastern peoples" (vs. 3) who included the Ishmaelites (8:24).

Discussion Questions

1. Why did Jacob favor Joseph over his other sons?
2. What motivated the brothers to kill Joseph?
3. Why did Reuben keep the brothers from murdering Joseph?
4. Was the brothers' plan well thought out or spontaneous?
5. Why did Judah suggest selling Joseph to the traders instead of killing him?

Now Ask Yourself . . .

What examples of favoritism have I encountered in my family, workplace, or church?

What are some negative feelings I have when others I know are the recipients of favoritism?

What are some negative results I've observed connected with showing favoritism?

What are some ways that God can use me to heal the damage caused by playing favorites?

What are some ways I can show God's love to people who have been victims of favoritism?

Illustrations

Whether or not you are aware of it, you may be showing favoritism toward one person at the expense of someone else. If one person receives most of the attention, others will go unnoticed. The favored one develops a "me first" attitude. And ignored child may cry "Notice me!" through rebellious behavior.

Overlooked people, like Joseph's brothers, can become withdrawn and resentful. The employee who knows that the boss's favorite will get all of the recognition eventually says "Why bother?" The student who is overlooked by his or her teacher stops learning or caring about an education.

The effects of favoritism may be hidden for years, especially if those not favored are afraid to voice their feelings. Accumulated hatred and bitterness almost caused Esau to kill Jacob (Gen. 27:41) and certainly motivated Joseph's brothers to sell him as

a slave. Anger about preference may produce a root of bitterness that can contaminate families, groups, or even entire communities for a long time.

Perhaps you are the one who has been overlooked or ignored. Or perhaps you know someone who has been rejected by a parent or superior. God's Spirit can heal even the most damaged person. And all Christians can help heal the victims of favoritism by loving them as God loves. Your friendship may help someone who has been rejected feel like a person of value.

Parents, pastors, teachers, bosses, and grandparents are just some of the people who should examine how they are treating others to see if they are playing favorites—and then change that attitude to God's attitude. In heaven's eyes no one is overlooked or insignificant.

July 23, 2006
Our Human Family

God Means It for Good

DEVOTIONAL READING
Romans 11:33-36

DAILY BIBLE READINGS
Monday July 17
  Genesis 44:1-13
  The Silver Cup Is Found
Tuesday July 18
  Genesis 44:14-24
  Joseph's Brothers Return
Wednesday July 19
  Genesis 44:25-34
  The Brothers Plead with
  Joseph
Thursday July 20
  Genesis 45:1-7
  Joseph Reveals His
  Identity
Friday July 21
  Genesis 45:8-13
  Joseph Invites His Family
  to Egypt
Saturday July 22
  Genesis 45:14-20
  Pharaoh Agrees with
  Joseph
Sunday July 23
  Genesis 45:21-28
  Jacob Hears the Good
  News

Scripture

Background Scripture: *Genesis 44—45*
Scripture Lesson: *Genesis 44:18-20, 33—45:7*
Key Verse: *"You intended to harm me, but God intended it for good to accomplish what is now being done, the saving of many lives." Genesis 50:20.*

Lesson Aim

God's purposes exceed our plans.

Lesson Setting

Time: 1876 B.C.
Place: Egypt

Lesson Outline

God Means It for Good

I. Joseph Tests His Brothers: Genesis 44:18-20, 33-34
    A. *Judah's Request: vs. 18*
    B. *Judah's Explanation: vss. 19-20*
    C. *Judah's Petition: vss. 33-34*
II. Joseph Reveals His Identity: Genesis 45:1-7
    A. *Joseph's Weeping: vss. 1-2*
    B. *Joseph's Declaration: vss. 3-4*
    C. *Joseph's Explanation: vss. 5-7*

Introduction

God Means It for Good

Jim Elliot, Nate Saint, Pete Flemming, Ed McCulley, and Roger Youderian were martyred in 1956 shortly after they arrived in the jungles of Ecuador to bring the Gospel to the Auca Indians. It was a witness that could not be ignored. They were a testimony that properly placed faith is more precious than life itself.

Five years after she watched those martyrdoms, a woman named Dawa became the first Auca Christian. Other conversions followed, and 36 years later the Aucas (properly called the Huaoranis) received their first complete New Testament.

Some wonder if Elliot and his associates could have planned their missionary outreach better and thus worked longer for the Lord. Yet God allows some candles to burn fast and brilliantly, while others burn long and steady. Both are a part of His mysterious and wonderful plan.

Lesson Commentary

I. Joseph Tests His Brothers: Genesis 44:18-20, 33-34

A. Judah's Request: vs. 18

Then Judah went up to him and said: "Please, my lord, let your servant speak a word to my lord. Do not be angry with your servant, though you are equal to Pharaoh himself."

In the years following Joseph's enslavement in Egypt, he went from being a prisoner to becoming the second in command. Pharaoh charged him with managing the nation's grain supply during a famine. Joseph's position gave him the means to preserve the lives of his family, through whom the blessings of the covenant would be transmitted to the world. This was why God had established Joseph in Egypt.

We learn in Genesis 42 through 44 that a severe famine extended from Egypt to Canaan. This forced Jacob to send 10 of his sons (not including Benjamin) to Egypt with money for food. Appearing before Joseph, they did not recognize their brother. But he recognized them.

Joseph pretended to think his brothers were spies. He kept one brother as a hostage, but sent the others home with grain as well as the money they had brought. Their instructions were to bring their youngest brother, Benjamin, to Joseph to verify their claim of identity. At first, Jacob refused to give up Benjamin. But when the family's Egyptian grain was gone, he relented. The brothers went back to Egypt with Benjamin.

This time Joseph received his brothers graciously. But before they left, he hid his silver cup (a prized possession in that day) in Benjamin's sack of grain. Then he sent his steward after the brothers to "discover" the cup. The steward had orders to arrest Benjamin but to tell the other brothers they could go on home. This was a test. Would the brothers abandon Benjamin as long ago they had abandoned Joseph? They did not; they passed this test.

As the 11 brothers reentered Joseph's presence, they threw themselves to the ground. This was their way of showing humility and begging for mercy (44:14). They were afraid of what Joseph might do to them because, as it appeared, Benjamin had stolen Joseph's silver cup.

At first, Joseph justified their fears by speaking roughly to them (vs. 15). He intimidated them by telling them they shouldn't have thought they could get away with the crime, since he had a diviner's powers to know the truth. Divination was a common practice in Egypt and other parts of the ancient world. Speaking to his brothers, Joseph may have hinted at greater involvement in divination than he actually had, so as to frighten them.

Judah spoke for the whole group. He admitted that he could not disprove the allegation of theft. He even said, "God has uncovered your servants' guilt" (vs. 16). Some commentators point out that it is unclear whether Judah was here talking about guilt for the stealing of the cup or guilt for the selling of Joseph.

In addition, Judah said the brothers were all willing to become slaves as punishment for the theft. Judah probably felt that it would be better for all the brothers to remain in Egypt as slaves than for some of them to return to Jacob without Benjamin. The fact that all the brothers had returned to Joseph when they had the chance to get away proves that they felt the same way.

Joseph would have none of Judah's suggestion of slavery for all the brothers. Instead, Joseph repeated the offer to let all the brothers except Benjamin go home to Canaan (vs. 17). Joseph was testing them again.

Then Judah arose to make one of the most moving intercessions recorded in the Bible. In this capacity he represented all of the brothers. His tribe would later become preeminent among the Israelites. In the presence of Joseph, Judah was extremely deferential as he referred to himself as Joseph's "servant" (vs. 18) and to Joseph as his "lord." This is one of the episodes in which the brothers fulfilled the dreams they had scorned years earlier (see 37:8).

Divination is the attempt to discover hidden truths. In the ancient world many kinds of divination were practiced. Some kinds, such as necromancy (consulting the dead), were condemned in Scripture (Lev. 19:31). Other kinds of divination, such as cleromancy (casting lots), were accepted by Scripture—with the understanding that God determined the outcome (Prov. 16:33).

Joseph practiced a kind of divination called oneiromancy (interpreting dreams). God not only gave him predictive dreams of his own but also gave him the ability to know the meaning of others' dreams. If the steward's words recorded in Genesis 44:5 are true, then Joseph also practiced hydromancy (examining liquids). Probably Egyptian hydromancy involved dropping objects into liquids, or adding one liquid to another, and then interpreting the resulting pattern in a way thought to reveal truths.

371

In ancient times those in subservient positions risked much to speak before a dignitary without first being invited. Judah realized this when he implored Joseph not to be angry with him for doing so. Judah tried to ingratiate himself further with the flattering statement that Joseph was "equal to Pharaoh himself" (44:18). Of course, the Genesis account makes it clear that Pharaoh was Joseph's superior (see 41:40, 43).

B. Judah's Explanation: vss. 19-20

"My lord asked his servants, 'Do you have a father or a brother?' And we answered, 'We have an aged father, and there is a young son born to him in his old age. His brother is dead, and he is the only one of his mother's sons left, and his father loves him.' "

After first flattering Joseph, Judah recalled an earlier discussion between the brothers and Joseph about Jacob their father and Benjamin their youngest brother (who was probably then in his twenties or thirties). On that occasion, Joseph had asked whether the group had a "father or a brother" (Gen. 44:19). The response was that they did have the former, who was quite aged by then, as well as a child in his old age, who was his youngest son (vs. 20).

The group did not know what had happened to Joseph. They hadn't seen him in over 20 years. They assumed he was already dead. Also, they wouldn't have recognized him now due to his new Egyptian appearance. For these reasons the brothers and their father thought that Benjamin alone was left of his mother Rachel's children. That is why Benjamin's father loved him very much. The thought of losing him would have crushed Jacob's spirit. Nevertheless, the prolonged famine threatened Jacob's family with starvation. And so he reluctantly allowed Benjamin to return with his other sons to Egypt.

C. Judah's Petition: vss. 33-34

"Now then, please let your servant remain here as my lord's slave in place of the boy, and let the boy return with his brothers. How can I go back to my father if the boy is not with me? No! Do not let me see the misery that would come upon my father."

Judah concluded by pleading with Joseph to be kept in Egypt as a slave in place of Benjamin. The young man, in turn, would be permitted to return with his other brothers to their home in

Judah's speech proved that he was not the same man who earlier had come up with the idea of selling Joseph to Midianite traders. It had taken a long time, but the Lord had worked changes in his heart.

Often we are tempted to become impatient with God over the pace of spiritual development in our own life or in the lives of other believers. Yet quietly and invisibly, God is at work. When we look back over a lengthy period of time, we often can see great improvement. And even when we don't detect much spiritual growth, we still can wait faithfully for God to operate in the lives of His people.

Canaan (Gen. 44:33). Judah explained that the alternative would involve him returning to his aged father without Benjamin, and Judah could not bear to witness the devastation Jacob would feel (vs. 44).

Judah's offer to be come a substitute in slavery for his brother Benjamin can remind us of how Jesus Christ became our substitute on the cross. While Benjamin, not Judah, was thought to be guilty of stealing a cup, Judah was willing to take the punishment for the crime. Similarly, the innocent Jesus has taken on Himself the punishment we deserve for our sins. Now all who believe in Him may receive His righteousness through faith, and be reconciled to the Father.

The apostle Peter wrote to a group of Christians, "[Jesus Christ] himself bore our sins in his body on the tree, so that we might die to sins and live for righteousness; by his wounds you have been healed" (1 Pet. 2:24). At the right time the Messiah came into this world as a descendant of Judah.

II. Joseph Reveals His Identity: Genesis 45:1-7

A. Joseph's Weeping: vss. 1-2

Then Joseph could no longer control himself before all his attendants, and he cried out, "Have everyone leave my presence!" So there was no one with Joseph when he made himself known to his brothers. And he wept so loudly that the Egyptians heard him, and Pharaoh's household heard about it.

As Judah was telling about Jacob's sorrow and was offering himself as a substitute for Benjamin, Joseph must have listened with rising emotion. Finally, he could hide his feelings no more. Not for a minute longer could he stand in front of his brothers and pretend to have a merely official interest in them (Gen. 45:1).

Joseph decided to reveal his identity to his brothers there and then, since they had proved themselves to be changed men. But first he ordered his Egyptian attendants out of the room. The tender reunion about to occur would be a family matter, and presumably he didn't want any outsiders around to distract him and his brothers. The biblical writer describes Joseph's emotional release as so powerful that his weeping could even be heard outside his household (vs. 2).

Joseph had wanted to find out if the selfish, vengeful brothers he had known in his youth had changed. They had no qualms about making Joseph a slave, even though it hurt their father deeply.

Years later, instead of saving themselves, Joseph's brothers risked their lives by returning to Egypt to plead for Benjamin's freedom. Judah even offered to take Benjamin's place as Joseph's slave. They had passed the test. They had placed the good of their father and the family ahead of their own selfish interests.

The biblical text portrays Joseph as an emotional, sensitive man. The moment when he revealed his identity to his brothers (Gen. 45:3) is not the first time in the narrative that he cried. He did so briefly but secretly when he had Simeon taken from his brothers and held prisoner (44:24). Then he showed even more emotion when he first saw his brother Benjamin. So his brothers would not see him cry, he left them and wept by himself for a while in his private room (43:30). Later, he would weep "for a long time" (46:29) when he saw and embraced his father Jacob for the first time in at least 20 years.

B. Joseph's Declaration: vss. 3-4

Joseph said to his brothers, "I am Joseph! Is my father still living?" But his brothers were not able to answer him, because they were terrified at his presence. Then Joseph said to his brothers, "Come close to me." When they had done so, he said, "I am your brother Joseph, the one you sold into Egypt!"

The brothers must have been puzzled by the ejection of the attendants. Probably all along Joseph had been talking to them through an interpreter, disguising the fact that he could understand their Hebrew speech. The interpreter would have left the room with the other attendants. How could they communicate with Joseph now?

Then to the brothers' amazement, Egypt's second most powerful man said to them in their own language, "I am Joseph!" (Gen. 45:3). For more than 20 years they had thought of Joseph as enslaved or dead. Since meeting Joseph, they had never for a moment suspected that the ruler dressed in Egyptian finery and speaking the Egyptian language was their brother. But here he stood, saying in Hebrew that he was their brother.

Joseph quickly followed up his self-revelation by asking about the father he had not seen for many years. This was the concern closest to his heart; he was eager to have more news of his father. Until this point he would have aroused suspicion by showing too much interest in Jacob.

Joseph's brothers made no reply to his question. They were still in shock over finding themselves in the presence of Joseph. They apparently had not mentioned the name of the brother who—as the cover-up story went—had been killed by an animal (see 42:13; 44:28). So perhaps Joseph's using his own name convinced them that he really was their brother. Now they were terrified and with good reason. They had coldly sold Joseph into slavery after being hostile toward him for years.

Thinking that perhaps the brothers did not believe he was who he said he was, Joseph called them to him so that they could take a closer look at his face (45:4). Then he repeated his claim to be Joseph, whom long ago they had sold into slavery. Only Joseph himself could have known the secret that they had mistreated him so shamefully. But that was not all; Joseph had much more to tell the brothers.

C. Joseph's Explanation: vss. 5-7

"And now, do not be distressed and do not be angry with your-selves for selling me here, because it was to save lives that God sent me ahead of you. For two years now there has been famine in the land, and for the next five years there will not be plowing and reaping. But God sent me ahead of you to preserve for you a remnant on earth and to save your lives by a great deliverance."

Joseph reassured his terrified brothers that he was not interested in revenge. He was able to forgive his brothers because he had learned to look at his trials from a godly perspective. Instead of Joseph concentrating on his brothers' evil intentions, he focused on God's intentions of blessing him with success and saving people from destruction.

Thus Joseph urged his brothers not to be angry with themselves for their past misdeeds. Ultimately God had been working in the circumstances that had brought Joseph to Egypt. Though the brothers' actions in the past were despicable, God had used their decisions to place Joseph in a position of authority so that he could rescue Egypt and his own family (Gen. 45:5).

Joseph explained that the two years of famine that had already past would extend to seven. During this time the drought would be so severe that neither plowing nor harvesting would occur (vs. 6). God would use Joseph to preserve a "remnant" (vs. 7) of His people. Joseph's words reminded his brothers of the great peril they had put the family in and implied that they had been saved only because God had something special in store for this family.

Joseph told his brothers to bring all of his father's family to Egypt, where he would settle them in Goshen (vss. 9-11). This region was located in the northeastern section of the Nile River delta. Although the area is not large (about 900 square miles), it is considered some of the best land in Egypt. With irrigation, it is an excellent area for grazing and for growing certain crops.

Joseph's plan would enable Jacob's family to survive the five more years of famine that were approaching. Jacob lived out the rest of his life happily in Egypt, near his favored son. When Jacob died, his body was taken back to Canaan for burial (50:12-14). The Hebrew people were still living in the land of Goshen at the time of the Exodus, four centuries after Joseph.

In the ancient Near East there was no greater goal than preserving the family line and no greater family sin than endangering the family line. Joseph's brothers endangered the family line by robbing the family of Joseph, a male member. Jacob endangered the family line by hesitating to let Benjamin go to Egypt to get grain (Gen. 42:38). His selfish desire to protect Benjamin might have caused the starvation of the entire family and the family line would end.

Later, both Jacob and his sons began to put the good of the family ahead of their own desires. Jacob gave in to Judah's powerful plea that Benjamin return to Egypt with them (43:11-14). The brothers were willing to all become slaves because of the silver cup they did not steal (44:16). Most dramatically, Judah offered to exchange himself for Benjamin—the ultimate act of placing his family's welfare ahead of his own (vss. 33-34).

Discussion Questions

1. Why did Joseph conceal his identity from his brothers and threaten to keep Benjamin as a slave?
2. How had Joseph's brothers changed since they had sold him into slavery?
3. What was the reason for Joseph's emotional outburst?
4. Why were Joseph's brothers terrified of him?
5. How could Joseph forgive his brothers for what they had done to him?

Now Ask Yourself . . .

When was the last time I was treated unfairly? How did I react?

How willing am I to forgive those who have hurt me?

Have I had a test of my character lately? If so, how did I do?

In the last year, how has God worked to make me more like His Son?

How have I seen God turn an evil into a good?

How can I trust God more even when I don't understand what He is doing?

Illustrations

No good was inherent in the plans of Joseph's brothers to sell him into slavery in Egypt. All of their intentions were self-serving and hateful. But God's good purposes for Joseph far exceeded the evil plot of his brothers. Even as Joseph lay in the dry cistern near Dothan, God was in control.

Egypt turned out not to be Joseph's place of doom but instead the site of his finest hour. Eventually he would be able to look back on all the things that had happened to him and tell his brothers, "You intended to harm me, but God intended it for good" (Gen. 50:20).

At some point Joseph may have wondered, *Has God forgotten me?* God is sometimes strangely silent when we are in the middle of a crisis. But at that time we need to think back to what God has already done. His past blessings provide us with evidence of His loving purpose.

We must remember that God's ways are not our ways (Isa. 55:8), and we have many biblical examples of that. For instance, God took the evil of the Crucifixion and turned it into the eternal good of the Resurrection. From this we see that our earthly vision is dim and limited. We often cannot see beyond today. Frequently, it isn't until after the struggle is over that we can say, "I see what God was doing."

So even when it seems no good can come out of a situation, we must continue to believe that God knows what He is doing. Faith is seeing light with your heart when all your eyes see is darkness. When you can't see God's hand, you can trust His heart.

A Perfect Imitation

DEVOTIONAL READING
Luke 6:43-49

DAILY BIBLE READINGS

Monday July 24
Ephesians 5:1-7
Live a Life of Love

Tuesday July 25
Ephesians 5:8-14
Live as Children of Light

Wednesday July 26
Ephesians 5:15-20
Live Wisely

Thursday July 27
Ephesians 5:21-32
Submit to One Another

Friday July 28
John 15:9-17
Love One Another

Saturday July 29
Philippians 1:3-11
May Your Love Abound

Sunday July 30
Philippians 2:1-11
We Should Be Like Christ

Scripture

Background Scripture: *Ephesians 5—6*
Scripture Lesson: *Ephesians 5:1-5, 21-29; 6:1-4*
Key Verse: *Submit to one another out of reverence for Christ. Ephesians 5:21.*

Lesson Aim

Imitate Christ in your personal relationships.

Lesson Setting

Time: A.D. 60–62
Place: Rome

Lesson Outline

A Perfect Imitation

I. Maintaining High Standards of Morality: Ephesians 5:1-5
   A. *Following the Divine Example: vss. 1-2*
   B. *Shunning All Forms of Evil: vss. 3-5*

II. Showing Mutual Respect: Ephesians 5:21-29
   A. *The Responsibility of Wives to Husbands: vss. 21-24*
   B. *The Responsibility of Husbands to Wives: vss. 25-29*

III. Nurturing Good Parent-Child Relationships: Ephesians 6:1-4
   A. *The Responsibility of Children: vss. 1-3*
   B. *The Responsibility of Parents: vs. 4*

Introduction

A Perfect Imitation

When Animal Kingdom, Walt Disney World's newest Orlando, Florida, attraction, was under construction throughout most of the 1990s, park developers struggled with some unique problems. One was dealing with the intelligence of their new residents.

Although nearly all of the other animals would be free to roam vast spaces during the day, at night they were all brought into their paddocks for safekeeping. Despite being well cared for, these animals yearned to be free. And they realized that one way to attain that freedom was to imitate the actions of their human caretakers with the intent of exploiting any weaknesses they could find in their captors' behavior.

In this week's Scripture passage, Paul suggested that believers also should have a strong desire to be truly free spiritually. Unless we wish to remain captive to the evil that surrounds us, we need to imitate Christ in every aspect of our lives.

Lesson Commentary

I. Maintaining High Standards of Morality: Ephesians 5:1-5

A. Following the Divine Example: vss. 1-2

Be imitators of God, therefore, as dearly loved children and live a life of love, just as Christ loved us and gave himself up for us as a fragrant offering and sacrifice to God.

In Ephesians 4:29-32, we read about some of the issues involved in replacing the old self with the new self: unwholesome talk versus edifying talk and malice versus love. Then in 5:1, we read about how we ought to imitate God.

More than just in the matter of forgiveness, Christians are to imitate God in all aspects of His character (Eph. 5:1). As children try to copy their parents, so we should try to copy our heavenly Father. And to imitate God means to "live a life of love" (vs. 2). Our whole life should be characterized by acts and signs of love shown to family, friends, and strangers.

Paul referred to the example of Christ to illustrate how we should love. Jesus showed us His love by giving Himself up as a sacrifice for our sins. Just as Old Testament sacrifices of animals sent up a pleasing aroma to the Lord (see Exod. 29:18), Christ's death was a fragrant offering. It was an acceptable sacrifice to God because of the Savior's perfection of love. His love is unselfish, pure, and active.

B. Shunning All Forms of Evil: vss. 3-5

But among you there must not be even a hint of sexual immorality, or of any kind of impurity, or of greed, because these are improper for God's holy people. Nor should there be obscenity, foolish talk or coarse joking, which are out of place, but rather thanksgiving. For of this you can be sure: No immoral, impure or greedy person—such a man is an idolater—has any inheritance in the kingdom of Christ and of God.

A life filled with God's love will not include the sins that the Ephesians saw in their pagan neighbors and that, indeed, they themselves had committed before coming to faith. In Ephesians 5:3-7, Paul named some of those sins.

The apostle's readers were to have nothing to do with sexual immorality, impurity, and greed (vs. 3). These three sins were only some of the sins practiced by unbelievers in Paul's day. But they were serious ones then, and they are still serious today. Sad to say, immorality, impurity, and greed even creep into the church.

Paul followed up the first list of three sinful behaviors with another list of three behaviors unsuitable for Christians: obscenity, foolish talk, and coarse joking (vs. 4; compare 4:29). These kinds of speech are sinful because they harm both those who speak them and those who hear them. In place of improper speech, the Ephesians were to give thanks to God. Expressing gratitude is beneficial to all who speak it and hear it.

Next, Paul returned to the three sins he had mentioned first: sexual immorality, impurity, and greed (5:5; compare vs. 3). It also crossed the apostle's mind to mention that greed is idolatry. The greedy, in effect, worship wealth; wealth occupies the highest place in their affections—the place God alone ought to occupy. Paul wanted to make sure his readers realized that greed and other sins are marks of people who will not enter the kingdom of God.

The present aspect of the divine kingdom is the Lord's everlasting rule and the working out of His loving and wise plan for the ages. As such, God's kingdom is not always apparent and unbelievers do not always acknowledge it. However, one day the divine kingdom will come in all its fullness and be evident to all (Matt. 6:10; 25:31-34). At that time God's glorious power will conquer the forces of evil and unbelief.

Evidently, Paul expected some people in the Ephesian church to say that his standards of morality were higher than necessary. The

As one studies Ephesians, it's good to keep in mind the thematic development of this letter. Paul depicted the Church as God's new humanity, a colony where the Lord of history has established a foretaste of the renewed dignity and unity of the human race (1:9-14; 2:11-22; 3:6, 9-11; 4:1—6:9). The Church is a community where God's power to reconcile people to Himself is experienced and shared in transformed relationships (2:1-10; 4:1-16; 4:32—5:2; 5:22—6:9). It is a new temple, a building of people, grounded in the sure revelation of what God has done in history (2:19-22; 3:17-19).

The Church is an organism where power and authority are exercised after the pattern of Christ (1:22; 5:25-27), and its stewardship is a means of serving Him (4:11-16; 5:22—6:9). The Church is an outpost in a dark world (5:3-17), looking for the day of final redemption. Above all, the Church is the bride, who is preparing for the approach of her groom, the Lord (5:22-32).

The Greek verb rendered "submit" (Eph. 5:21) was used in literature outside of the Bible in the sense of soldiers subordinating themselves to their superior, or of slaves yielding to their masters. Here, the verb does not mean a forced submission, but rather a voluntary giving up of one's right or will.

At least as early as Aristotle, Greek writers—especially Stoic philosophers—offered rules for governing households. They hoped to build a stable society. Hellenistic (Greek-influenced) Jewish teachers frequently made lists of household rules. They believed that these moral laws applied equally to Jews and Gentiles.

Probably, early Christian writers were influenced by the Hellenistic Jewish teachers. Besides Ephesians 5:22—6:9, household codes can be found in Colossians 3:18—4:1; 1 Timothy 2:8-15; 6:1-2; Titus 2:1-10; and 1 Peter 2:18—3:7. Several Christian leaders from the post-apostolic period listed household codes.

apostle called the arguments employed by such people "empty words" (vs. 6). The moral standards Paul taught were not his own but God's, and the Lord does indeed judge those who disobey His standards. Thus the Ephesians were not to be deceived by people with low moral standards or "be partners with them" (vs. 7) by joining in their sin.

II. Showing Mutual Respect: Ephesians 5:21-29

A. The Responsibility of Wives to Husbands: vss. 21-24

Submit to one another out of reverence for Christ. Wives, submit to your husbands as to the Lord. For the husband is the head of the wife as Christ is the head of the church, his body, of which he is the Savior. Now as the church submits to Christ, so also wives should submit to their husbands in everything.

In Ephesians 5:8-14, Paul used the analogy of darkness and light to contrast the state of believers before and after salvation. Furthermore, he said believers are to seek the Lord's will and to expose sin. Then in verses 15-20, the apostle stated that living for Christ in a corrupt environment requires us to make a habit of watching our conduct. We're to live in a wise, opportunistic manner, governed by God's will. Such a Spirit-led life expresses itself in thankfulness and music-filled worship.

Paul continued his instructions on specific lifestyle issues by instructing all believers to submit to one another (vs. 21). Mutual submission means yielding or adapting to each other. Because of our selfish human nature, we do not naturally want to yield or adapt to anyone. But since we love and respect Christ, and since He asks us to submit to one another, we must submit. Paul developed what he meant about submission by discussing three sets of household relationships—those between wives and husbands (vss. 22-33), between children and parents (6:1-4), and between slaves and masters (vss. 5-9).

Offering his first example of submission among Christians, Paul said that wives are to submit to their husbands (vs. 22). He did not, however, provide a detailed explanation of what he meant. Since this instruction has given rise to widely differing interpretations, we might wish the apostle had said more.

Perhaps it is helpful to consider what Paul did not mean by

380

wives submitting to their husbands. He was not saying that women are inferior to men or that all women must submit to all men. And even though Paul said wives should submit "in everything" (vs. 24), the teaching of Scripture as a whole indicates that a wife should not submit when her husband wants her to act in a way that is clearly contrary to God's will (compare Acts 5:29).

Instead of explaining what he meant by wifely submission, Paul made a comparison (Eph. 5:23-24). He said a wife is to submit to her husband just as she—indeed, just as all the Church—submits to Christ. That's because a husband is the head of his wife just as Christ is the Head of the Church.

This comparison helps us only if we understand what Paul meant by Christ's being the Head of the Church. New Testament scholars have taken different positions on this. According to one group of experts, Jesus is the Head of the church in the sense that He is the church's source and origin. On the basis of this interpretation, these scholars conclude that a wife must honor and love her husband, but the two may share decision making equally.

According to another group of experts, however, Christ is the Head of the church in the sense that He is its leader and authority. Based on this interpretation, these scholars suggest that a wife should honor and love her husband, but he should oversee family decisions.

B. The Responsibility of Husbands to Wives: vss. 25-29

Husbands, love your wives, just as Christ loved the church and gave himself up for her to make her holy, cleansing her by the washing with water through the word, and to present her to himself as a radiant church, without stain or wrinkle or any other blemish, but holy and blameless. In this same way, husbands ought to love their wives as their own bodies. He who loves his wife loves himself. After all, no one ever hated his own body, but he feeds and cares for it, just as Christ does the church

The wife is not the only partner in a marriage who has a duty to the other. While she must submit to her husband, he must love her (Eph. 5:25). In a male-dominated Roman society, the news that husbands owe their wives any duty must have sounded revolutionary. Once again, Paul put husbands in the place of Christ and wives in the place of the church to help clarify his meaning. A husband

Interpreters of Ephesians 5:21-33 tend to take one of two views concerning what this passage says about marriage. One group says that wives should submit by obeying their husbands, and husbands should submit to God by loving their wives. Advocates of this view note that Jesus' sacrifice and love for the Church establishes His authority. They conclude that while husbands should be kind and considerate toward their wives, they should also exercise authority when necessary.

Another group says that Paul's command for wives to submit to their husbands is essentially equivalent to his command for husbands to love their wives. Proponents of this view emphasize Jesus' abandonment of authority on the cross and the mutuality of love between the Savior and the Church. They conclude that in a marriage, both partners are equals and should equally share authority.

381

In Ephesians 5:31, Paul quoted Genesis 2:24 to show how a married couple are joined. Adam realized that Eve was, quite literally, bone of his bones and flesh of his flesh. She had been made from him. This illustrates that the bond of marriage is strong. In fact, the Greek word translated "united" (Eph. 5:31) literally means "glued." Paul's implication was that a man must love the woman to whom he is glued (in a manner of speaking) by marriage.

Genesis 2:24 has a dual implication. People have always known that it refers to the relationship between husbands and wives. But only after Christ's coming to earth did some realize that it also refers to the relationship between Jesus and the church. That's what Paul meant when he called it a "profound mystery" (Eph. 5:32)—a deep secret that had been revealed through Christ.

is to love his wife even as Christ loves the Church.

Verses 25-31 contain the apostle's description of how Christ loves the church and how husbands should love their wives. The Greek word translated "love" in these verses is *agape*. The term refers to an unselfish and active concern for another. This is the appropriate word, since Jesus' love for us motivated Him to give up His life for us (vs. 25).

Throughout this passage, Paul used wedding and marriage terms to picture Christ's love for the Church. Before a wedding ceremony in ancient times, the bride would carefully wash herself and put on clean clothes. Similarly, Christ cleanses His bride, the Church, "by washing with water through the word" (vs. 26). (Some think this statement is part of a reference to early baptismal practices.) After this washing, the bride of Christ is "radiant . . . without stain or wrinkle or any other blemish" (vs. 27). Expressed differently, the redemption Jesus won on the cross cleanses members of the Church of sins, making us "holy and blameless" in God's sight.

In modern wedding ceremonies it is traditional for the bride's father to present the bride to the groom. But in ancient weddings, ordinarily a friend of the groom would present the bride to the groom. According to Paul's description neither the modern nor the ancient traditions will be followed in Christ's wedding ceremony with the church, which will take place at the end of time. Jesus will act as both the presenter and as the groom, since He will present the Church to Himself.

Why does Christ love the church so much that He gave Himself up for it, washes it, and will present it to Himself? It's because the church is His body (vs. 30). A person naturally loves his or her own body, and shows that love by taking care of it (vs. 29). Similarly, "husbands ought to love their wives as their own bodies. He who loves his wife loves himself" (vs. 28).

III. Nurturing Good Parent-Child Relationships: Ephesians 6:1-4

A. The Responsibility of Children: vss. 1-3
Children, obey your parents in the Lord, for this is right. "Honor your father and mother"—which is the first commandment with a promise—"that it may go well with you and that you may enjoy long life on the earth."

The second set of household relationships Paul addressed included children and their parents. We may not often think of children reading the apostle's letters (or listening as they were read aloud) along with adults in the churches. But Ephesians 6:1-3 is one place where Paul addressed children directly. He told them plainly that it is proper for children to obey their parents (vs. 1).

This obedience by children is to take place "in the Lord." Paul imagined a family in which parents and children believe in Christ. Neither mother nor father but Jesus is the family's ultimate authority. Therefore, the parents make rules consistent with Christian principles, and the children obey their parents as they would obey Jesus.

This instruction for children to obey their parents was hardly unusual. The same instruction may be found at several places in the Bible. Paul quoted the fifth commandment to back up his instruction (vss. 2-3; compare Exod. 20:12; Deut. 5:16).

Perhaps to make the requirement of child obedience sound less like a duty and more like an opportunity, Paul pointed out that the fifth commandment comes with a promise attached: "That it may go well with you and that you may enjoy long life on the earth" (Eph. 6:3). The promise does not give absolute assurance that those who are obedient to their parents will have a long and easy life on earth. But generally, the promise indicates that God blesses those who honor their parents.

B. The Responsibility of Parents: vs. 4

Fathers, do not exasperate your children; instead, bring them up in the training and instruction of the Lord.

In God's way of thinking, parents don't have absolute power over their children. When parents operate under the lordship of Christ, they will consider their children's feelings and provide them with godly instruction. The Greek word rendered "training" (Eph. 6:4) refers to discipline or instruction. The word rendered "instruction" refers to correction or encouragement by word of mouth.

Instead of frustrating, enraging, or ridiculing their children, parents should adopt rules and policies that are objective, fair, and sensible. Moreover, parents should use all appropriate methods to teach their children about God, with the goal that they will receive Christ and become His faithful disciples.

Can the fifth commandment be the "first" (Eph. 6:2) with a promise if the second commandment also seems to have one (Exod. 20:5-6; Deut. 5:9-10)? The fifth may have been "first" in the sense that it was the initial (and primary) one taught to children. Or the fifth is at least one of the first divine injunctions in importance.

Paul's teaching concerning the responsibility of parents was truly unusual. According to the Roman law of patria potestas ("the father's power"), fathers had absolute power over their families. They could murder their unwanted newborns, make their children work in the fields wearing chains, or sell their children into slavery. Far from advocating such parental tyranny, Paul told fathers to provide for their religious training (Eph. 6:4).

Discussion Questions

1. What aspects of God's character are believers to imitate?
2. What is the connection between greed and idolatry?
3. What is the basis for believers submitting to one another?
4. How should spouses relate to each other?
5. How should parents relate to their children?

Now Ask Yourself . . .

Which character traits mentioned by Paul do I most need to work on improving in my life?

What is one definite step I can take to be more loving toward others?

Have I accepted biblical morality once and for all, or do I sometimes rebel against it?

Does mutual love and respect characterize my relationship with my family and friends?

How can I better imitate Christ in my personal relationships?

Illustrations

We are called to imitate Christ in our relationships, but some people seem impossible to get along with. They just rub us the wrong way or maybe even go out of their way to make our lives difficult.

Whenever Claire got to church on Sunday morning, there was Arnold right in her face. He was overbearing and hardly gave her space to talk to anyone else. Claire endured him because Arnold was a brother in Christ and was part of a ministry team in which Claire also served.

Though on the surface Claire appeared to be kind, inside she was seething with rage at Arnold's inability to take what she was sure was obvious clues—verbal and otherwise—that she was not comfortable with his attentiveness. After church, Arnold would become the target for Claire's mocking remarks and jeering comments as she related to a friend the latest happenings at church.

However, Claire became increasingly guilt-ridden about being nice to Arnold and then ridiculing him behind his back. Claire knew she should do what Jesus did in His relationships with people—be honest and forthright with Arnold, but with gentleness and respect. Also, Claire needed to end her cruel remarks to others about Arnold.

After resolving to do what was right, Claire talked to Arnold the following Sunday. While it was a difficult discussion to initiate, Claire felt relief as she was able to understand Arnold's intentions and relate her own discomfort. As the truth came out, Claire felt her resentment leaving. In its place was a new respect and appreciation for Arnold, who graciously received her message.

Showers of Blessings

DEVOTIONAL READING

Psalm 136

DAILY BIBLE READINGS

Monday July 31
Psalm 103:1-8
God's Blessings Are for Us

Tuesday August 1
Psalm 103:9-18
God's Blessings Are Always with Us

Wednesday August 2
Psalm 103:19-22
Continue to Praise the Lord

Thursday August 3
Ephesians 1:1-10
Spiritual Blessings Come from Christ

Friday August 4
Ephesians 1:11-14
We Have Hope in Christ

Saturday August 5
Ephesians 1:15-23
Pray Blessings for Others

Sunday August 6
James 1:12-18
Every Gift Is From God

Scripture

Background Scripture: *Ephesians 1*
Scripture Lesson: *Ephesians 1:1-14*
Key Verse: *Praise be to the God and Father of our Lord Jesus Christ, who has blessed us in the heavenly realms with every spiritual blessing in Christ. Ephesians 1:3.*

Lesson Aim

Praise God for every spiritual blessing.

Lesson Setting

Time: A.D. 60–62
Place: Rome

Lesson Outline

Showers of Blessings

  I. Greetings from Paul: Ephesians 1:1-2
    A. *The Sender and the Recipients: vs. 1*
    B. *Grace and Peace: vs. 2*
  II. Blessings in Christ: Ephesians 1:3-10
    A. *Praise to the Father: vs. 3*
    B. *Chosen by God: vss. 4-6*
    C. *Redeemed by God: vss. 7-8*
    D. *God's Plan Centered in Christ: vss. 9-10*
  III. Brought Together in Christ: Ephesians 1:11-14
    A. *Jewish Believers in Christ: vss. 11-12*
    B. *Gentile Believers in Christ: vs. 13a*
    C. *Sealed by the Spirit: vss. 13b-14*

Introduction

In the classic 1930s movie comedy *Christmas in July,* a young, financially-strapped couple are told they have won a contest that offers them a department-store shopping spree. Suddenly they go from down-on-their-luck to downright well-off. They fill their small apartment with new furniture. They buy presents for all of their friends. Their neighbors celebrate their good fortune.

Then the terrible news: the announcement they had won the contest was a practical joke. They hadn't won a thing. As the store's truck pulls up to take back all of their new belongings, the couple feel lower than ever. Perhaps they should have tried Thanksgiving in July, rather than Christmas.

In this week's Scripture passage, the apostle Paul discusses many of the spiritual blessings for which we can praise God. As the old hymn says, truly He is the God "from whom all blessings flow."

Lesson Commentary

I. Greetings from Paul: Ephesians 1:1-2

A. The Sender and the Recipients: vs. 1

Paul, an apostle of Christ Jesus by the will of God, to the saints in Ephesus, the faithful in Christ Jesus.

Paul evangelized the city of Ephesus toward the end of his second missionary journey (Acts 18:18-21). When he departed, he left a Christian couple named Priscilla and Aquila to continue his work (vs. 26). When Paul wrote the Letter to the Ephesians, he was no longer an evangelist on the move; he was a prisoner in Rome. And the church he was now writing to was not opposing him and his teaching; it was a basically sound congregation that was ready to receive advanced teaching in theology and ethics.

Paul began the epistle by identifying himself as an apostle. Although Paul was always ready to admit his unworthiness to receive grace, he never underrated his role as an apostle, or ambassador, for Christ since it had been given him "by the will of God" (Eph. 1:1).

Not all early Greek manuscripts of this letter have the words "in Ephesus" in verse 1. Bible scholars have explained this omission in

The Letter to the Ephesians encourages believers to expand their concept of what God designed the universal church to be. This epistle contains language that is majestic and positive. It describes the church as a place where a little bit of heaven is brought down to earth.

various ways. But probably the letter was sent to the church in Ephesus, and then passed around to other congregations in the Roman province of Asia Minor (now western Turkey). Also, the general nature of most of the epistle's teaching may indicate that from the start Paul meant for the letter to be read by more than one church.

Whoever the apostle wrote to, he called his recipients "saints"—literally, "holy ones." Paul was not addressing certain Christians who were holier than others; he was addressing all his readers. All Christians are saints because Jesus has set us apart as His own special people and has made us holy with His own righteousness. Paul also called his readers "the faithful in Christ Jesus." They were faithful in the sense that they had expressed faith in Christ for their salvation and also in the sense that they were faithfully following Him.

B. Grace and Peace: vs. 2

Grace and peace to you from God our Father and the Lord Jesus Christ.

The apostle concluded his greeting with a blessing on his readers (Eph. 1:2). He wished them "grace and peace." The essence of the Gospel is the grace of God given to undeserving people. Peace is the harmony felt by those in a restored relationship with the Lord.

The general nature of Ephesians makes it difficult to determine the specific circumstances that gave rise to the letter. Nevertheless, it is clear that the recipients were Gentiles (3:1) who were estranged from citizenship in the kingdom of Israel (2:11) but devout followers of the Lord (1:1). Now, thanks to the gracious gift of God, they enjoyed the spiritual blessings that come through faith in Christ, including peace with God.

II. Blessings in Christ: Ephesians 1:3-10

A. Praise to the Father: vs. 3

Praise be to the God and Father of our Lord Jesus Christ, who has blessed us in the heavenly realms with every spiritual blessing in Christ.

Ordinarily in his letters, Paul immediately followed up his greeting to his readers with thanksgiving for them. In this epistle,

Not all Bible scholars accept the idea that Paul wrote Ephesians. Some note that parts of the letter closely resemble other portions of the New Testament, especially Colossians. Therefore, they have concluded that when the body of Paul's letters were collected, an unnamed admirer of Paul penned Ephesians as an introduction to his writings. Other experts note that Ephesians has unique wordings and features and thus conclude from this that Paul did not write it. Neither of these theories is convincing. The resemblance of Ephesians to other New Testament letters can be explained on the basis that Paul penned some of those other epistles and that he shared the perspective of other New Testament writers. And unique wordings and features of Ephesians may be due to its distinctive purpose and to the timing and conditions of its writing. Many early Christian writers ascribed Ephesians to Paul. The letter's style and content are similar to those of other epistles that the apostle wrote. And Paul twice referred to himself in the letter (1:1; 3:1). Thus, it is reasonable to conclude that Paul wrote Ephesians.

387

Ephesians 1:3 is only one of many places in Scripture where the word "blessing" appears. It refers to an act of declaring (or wishing) favor and goodness upon others. In the Old Testament, important people blessed those with less power or influence. For example, the patriarchs declared God's favor upon their children (Gen. 49:1-28). Leaders frequently blessed their subordinates, especially when preparing to leave them (for instance, Moses and Joshua, Deut. 31).

The Lord's people bless Him by showing gratitude and singing songs of praise (Ps. 103:1-2). God also blesses His people through spiritual and physical enrichment. For example, He showers them with life and fruitfulness (Gen. 1:22, 28). Of course, God's foremost blessing is turning people from their wicked ways and pardoning their sins (Acts 3:25-26). The atoning sacrifice of Christ is the basis for the Lord's favor and goodness to believers (Eph. 1:3).

however, he delayed the thanksgiving so that he could offer extended praise to God (Eph. 1:3-14). The apostle extolled our heavenly Father for the spiritual blessings He has given to Christ's followers (vs. 3). God has blessed us, among other ways, by choosing us (vss. 4-6), by redeeming us (vss. 7-8), and by revealing His eternal plan of redemption to us (vss. 9-10).

God often blesses His people materially as well as spiritually, but in verse 3 Paul chose to focus on spiritual blessings. These are certain, for they have been secured for us "in heavenly realms." They flow from God the Father, through God the Son, to us.

B. Chosen by God: vss. 4-6

For he chose us in him before the creation of the world to be holy and blameless in his sight. In love he predestined us to be adopted as his sons through Jesus Christ, in accordance with his pleasure and will. To the praise of his glorious grace, which he has freely given us in the One he loves.

The first spiritual blessing Paul mentioned is that God "chose us" (Eph. 1:4) and "predestined us" (vs. 5). These terms are parallel but have different shades of meaning. Just as God chose the Jewish nation to be His own and to receive as an inheritance the promised land, so He chose Christian believers to be His own people and to receive the inheritance of eternal life. It can "never perish, spoil or fade" (1 Pet. 1:4), for it is "kept in heaven" for us eternally.

God chose believers "to be holy and blameless in his sight" (Eph. 1:4). To be holy means to be distinctly different from the world so that God can use us for His purposes. Our holiness is the *result* of our having been chosen, not the *reason* we were chosen. To be "blameless" means to be free of the immoral and selfish lifestyle that marks people apart from God.

God also predestined believers "to be adopted as his sons" (vs. 5). Through Jesus Christ, God's Son, we become sons or daughters of God. Under Roman law, adopted sons enjoyed the same privileges as natural sons. Similarly, God reckons believers as His true children and as recipients of all the benefits that go with that status. It's no wonder that believers give God praise for the wonderful grace He has poured out on them in His Son, whom He dearly loves (vs. 6).

C.   Redeemed by God: vss. 7-8

In him we have redemption through his blood, the forgiveness of sins, in accordance with the riches of God's grace that he lavished on us with all wisdom and understanding.

Despite the greatness of our having been chosen by God, this spiritual blessing is not the only one we receive. Paul also mentioned the blessing of redemption (Eph. 1:7-8). Through redemption God makes His choosing effective in our lives. The Greek word translated "redemption" (vs. 7) refers to a ransom. It was used in ancient times of buying back one who had been sold into slavery or had become a prisoner of war. It also described the freeing of a person from the penalty of death.

Because we were born with a sinful nature, God was not attracted to us due to any goodness He saw in us. Despite our sinful condition, He rescued us from our state of separation from His holiness. He did this by sending His Son to become the sacrifice for our sins. By His blood, Christ ransomed us from slavery to sin and from the sentence of death under which we languished.

Closely related to redemption is "forgiveness." The Greek word Paul used had a variety of meanings including "to send off," "to release," "to give up," "to pardon," and "to hurl." The idea is that when we receive the effect of Jesus' redemption through faith, God releases us from the penalty of our sins and hurls our sin debt far away from us. What the Father did for us through His Son was in harmony with the riches of His grace.

In addition to showering us with His unmerited favor, God has also lavished us "with all wisdom and understanding" (vs. 8). Before we believed, we did not have spiritual insight. But since coming to a knowledge of the truth, we can now see how things really are and can get an idea of how God wants us to live.

D.   God's Plan Centered in Christ: vss. 9-10

And he made known to us the mystery of his will according to his good pleasure, which he purposed in Christ, to be put into effect when the times will have reached their fulfillment—to bring all things in heaven and on earth together under one head, even Christ.

Another spiritual blessing Paul listed is our ability to know the "mystery of [God's] will" (Eph. 1:9). For the apostle, a "mystery" is a truth that was once hidden but has now been revealed through

There are at least two distinct views of what predestination means when it is discussed in Scripture. Some think that people are so debased by sin that they are unable to respond to the offer of salvation made available in Christ. It is argued that those who believe have the ability to do so only because God previously chose them for redemption. In other words, the Lord gives them grace, and this enables them to believe the truth.

Others think that God gives all people enough grace to accept the offer of salvation. This remains true even though many reject His grace. In this way, the Lord predestines some for redemption in the sense that He knows beforehand those who will choose of their own free will to believe the truth.

Christ. The Lord's disclosure to us of His will was in accordance with His good pleasure, which He centered in His Son.

Paul declared that God's eternal plan was to head up all things in Christ at the divinely appointed time (vs. 10). This includes everything "in heaven and on earth." The Greek word translated "bring . . . together" means to sum up. In Paul's day, when a column of figures was tallied, the total was placed at the head of the column. In a similar fashion, at the end of history all things will be seen to add up to Christ.

From eternity, the Father has intended to give the Son possession of all things. But from our viewpoint within history, we can see that God set His plan in motion at just the right time, namely, when Jesus came into the world at His Incarnation. And the Father will bring His plan to a glorious conclusion at just the right time, namely, when the Son comes into the world at His Second Advent. On that day, our sorrows will be over, our conflicts will be at an end, and our weakness will be replaced by strength.

III. Brought Together in Christ: Ephesians 1:11-14

A. Jewish Believers in Christ: vss. 11-12

In him we were also chosen, having been predestined according to the plan of him who works out everything in conformity with the purpose of his will, in order that we, who were the first to hope in Christ, might be for the praise of his glory.

Previously in Ephesians 1:4-5, Paul had mentioned God's plan for believers. Now the apostle returned to that theme. He noted that God causes all things to happen in accordance with "the purpose of his will" (vs. 11). This included Jews such as Paul coming to faith in Christ. The divine purpose was that their conversion would bring the Lord eternal praise (vs. 12). Similarly, according to Romans 8:28, "in all things God works for the good of those who love him, who have been called according to his purpose."

The historical record is that the apostles and other Jews were the first to trust in Christ. Admittedly, the majority of Jews who were contemporaries of Paul rejected the Messiah. Nevertheless, a remnant of that generation of Jews formed the nucleus of the church. Through them, the Gospel went out to the entire world. Those early Jewish believers were walking testimonies of God's glory.

The language of Ephesians (particularly the first half) is richer and more effusive than the language in other letters by Paul. The apostle's style is demonstrated in this phrase: "the plan of him who works out everything in conformity with the purpose of his will" (Eph. 1:11). The phrase contains an inclusive term ("everything") and several synonyms ("plan," "works out," "purpose," "will"). This style suits Paul's subject of God's grand plan for believers, the church, and the universe.

B. Gentile Believers in Christ: vs. 13a

And you also were included in Christ when you heard the word of truth, the gospel of your salvation.

With Ephesians 1:13 Paul changed pronouns from "we" to "you." He was now referring to the Ephesian believers specifically. Although Jewish Christians had been chosen for their role in starting the church, this should not make the Ephesians feel like outsiders. They, too, were included in Christ. Jewish and Gentile believers formed one united church, the body of Christ.

Paul noted the stages of development by which the Gentiles had become "included in Christ." It is the same process through which anyone is born again. First, the Gentiles had "heard the word of truth" when Paul or others had proclaimed the Gospel to them. Then they "believed" the truth they had heard. The result was their spiritual regeneration.

C. Sealed by the Spirit: vss. 13b-14

Having believed, you were marked in him with a seal, the promised Holy Spirit, who is a deposit guaranteeing our inheritance until the redemption of those who are God's possession—to the praise of his glory.

Paul noted that when his readers trusted in Christ, they were "marked . . . with a seal" (Eph. 1:13b), which is the Holy Spirit. In other words, the Lord identified believers as His own by giving them the Spirit, whom He promised long ago.

By calling the Spirit a seal, Paul may have raised a number of images in the minds of his readers. At that time, seals were put on documents to guarantee their genuineness. They were also attached to goods during transportation to indicate ownership and ensure protection. Sometimes they represented an office in the government. Any of these uses of seals might symbolize a part of the Holy Spirit's work in the lives of those who follow Christ.

But for Paul, the Spirit is not only a seal. He is also a "deposit" (vs. 14). In the apostle's day a deposit was a token payment or first installment assuring a seller that the full purchase price would follow. At the end of time believers will receive the full installment of eternal life from the riches of God's grace. In the meantime, the Spirit's presence in our lives assures us of coming glory. This giving of the Spirit is also to "the praise of his glory" (compare vs. 12).

It's clarifying to note that all three persons of the Trinity are involved in the lives of believers. The Father has blessed us because of our spiritual union with His Son (Eph. 1:3). Further, the gift of the Spirit identifies us as God's spiritual children. Moreover, the Spirit is the believers' guarantee that they belong to the Father and that He will do for them what He has promised in His Son. The Spirit's abiding presence confirms that one's faith is genuine and that one's adoption into God's family is real. These are excellent reasons for us to give unending praise to God!

391

Discussion Questions

1. What did Paul say that God had bestowed on the believers in Ephesus?
2. To what extent did Paul say that God has blessed Christians?
3. What spiritual blessings from God did Paul mention in Ephesians 1:4-12?
4. When did Paul say that God would bring all things under the headship of Christ?
5. What role does the Spirit serve in the life of believers?

Now Ask Yourself . . .

How set apart am I to do the will of God?

What are some ways I can thank God for making me His child?

What difference has the forgiveness and redemption I have in Christ made in my life?

What characteristics of God's Son are becoming more evident in my life?

How aware am I of the presence of the Holy Spirit in my life?

Illustrations

When Marty received God's gift of salvation, he had no idea he'd hit the mother lode of spiritual blessings. At that time, Marty was quite young and really only aware that God had forgiven his sins and would one day welcome him into heaven. As far as Marty was concerned, that's all that mattered. Those two blessings alone—forgiveness and eternal life—would have been enough for him.

As Marty got older, however, and could understand more of what he was reading in Scripture, it began to dawn on him that he had far more in Christ than he'd ever imagined. Instead of being just a forgiven person, Marty came to see that God viewed him as holy and blameless in Christ.

It came as news to Marty that the Lord was not constantly frustrated with Marty's faltering steps. Quite to the contrary, God's glorious grace was poured out in Marty's life to pick him up, assure him of unconditional love, and encourage him to keep on growing in that grace. In addition, Marty was not, as he had at times imagined, some tolerated tag-along among the saints. He was an adopted, cherished son in God's great family.

How do people usually respond to good news? When Paul tried to describe these incredible blessings to the Ephesians, he himself got excited and burst into a pen-to-paper shout of praise. What Marty had in Christ was a fantastic life of freedom and intimacy with God to be lived in the present— right now!—along with much, much more to come.

Do your students know what it means that they have been granted immense spiritual blessings by God? If they do, they will respond, heart and soul, to Him in unbridled praise.

All Together Now

DEVOTIONAL READING

1 Peter 2:4-10

DAILY BIBLE READINGS

Monday August 7
Galatians 3:23-29
We Are All Children of God

Tuesday August 8
Ephesians 2:1-10
We Are Alive with Christ

Wednesday August 9
Ephesians 2:11-16
We Are One in Christ

Thursday August 10
Ephesians 2:17-22
Christ Is Our Cornerstone

Friday August 11
Ephesians 3:1-6
We Are Members of One Body

Saturday August 12
Ephesians 3:7-13
We Have Equal Access to God

Sunday August 13
Ephesians 3:14-21
May We Be Grounded in Love

Scripture

Background Scripture: *Ephesians 2*
Scripture Lesson: *Ephesians 2:8-22*
Key Verse: *You are no longer foreigners and aliens, but fellow citizens with God's people and members of God's household. Ephesians 2:19.*

Lesson Aim

God's grace breaks down the walls of prejudice.

Lesson Setting

Time: A.D. 60–62
Place: Rome

Lesson Outline

All Together Now

  I. Christ—Our Salvation: Ephesians 2:8-10
     A. *Saved by Grace through Faith: vss. 8-9*
     B. *Saved to Do Good Works: vs. 10*
  II. Christ—Our Unity and Peace: Ephesians 2:11-18
     A. *Excluded from the Community of Faith: vss. 11-12*
     B. *Included in the Community of Faith: vs. 13*
     C. *Peace between Saved Jews and Gentiles: vss. 14-15a*
     D. *Unity among Saved Jews and Gentiles: vss. 15b-16*
     E. *Joint Access to the Father: vss. 17-18*
  III. Christ—Our Cornerstone: Ephesians 2:19-22
     A. *Members of God's Family: vss. 19-20*
     B. *A Holy Temple for the Lord: vss. 21-22*

Introduction

All Together Now

"All for one and one for all" is a great rallying cry for French musketeers, political movements, and football teams. It sounds so wonderful. It assumes that each individual will lay aside his or her own preferences for the sake of others.

But when we allow Jesus to break down barriers, we do much more than paper over our differences. We have to confess and acknowledge that hostility does exist. We also have to admit that unless we allow Jesus to change us from within, we won't be able to achieve oneness in human relationships.

Because Jesus gives us new hearts and new motivations, we can seek His help and power to get along with everyone, regardless of our differences. We accept people as they are, and see them as objects of God's love in the Gospel. We also show humility and love—demonstrating Christlikeness to people who are very different from ourselves—so that we can all become one family in Christ.

Lesson Commentary

I. Christ—Our Salvation: Ephesians 2:8-10

A. Saved by Grace through Faith: vss. 8-9

For it is by grace you have been saved, through faith—and this not from yourselves, it is the gift of God—not by works, so that no one can boast.

The Letter to the Ephesians contains three elements: autobiography—the apostle gave information about himself, particularly concerning his ministry; instructions—Paul used the letter to teach the Ephesians what to believe and how to act; and argument—the letter defends a true understanding of the Gospel and tries to guard the church against heresy.

In Ephesians 2:1-3, Paul reminded his readers that they were spiritually dead before trusting in Christ. They had been enslaved to the world, the devil, and the flesh, and thus had been objects of God's wrath. Then, in verses 4-7, Paul noted that the Lord extended His mercy to the Ephesians through Christ, making them spiritually alive and giving them honor.

Verses 8 and 9 reveal that when it comes to salvation, believers have no room to boast. After all, their redemption is by God's grace through faith in Christ. Some mistakenly think that the act of believing is a good work that earns one a place in heaven. Rather, faith is simply putting one's trust in Christ for salvation. Accordingly, God receives all praise for this incredible gift of salvation. He made it possible for us to turn away from our sin and receive Christ by faith.

The implication is that God saves all Christians by His grace. This is His free act of doing something good for us, even though we don't deserve it. God's grace is activated in our lives through faith. Paul said that when we put our trust in Christ, we become the recipients of His grace, and so we enjoy salvation.

B. Saved to Do Good Works: vs. 10

For we are God's workmanship, created in Christ Jesus to do good works, which God prepared in advance for us to do.

Though believers' good works did not produce our salvation, our salvation is indended to produce good works (Eph. 2:10). The Greek term rendered "do" is the same word translated "live" in verse 2. It means "walk about." While unbelievers walk about doing evil deeds, believers are to walk about doing good deeds.

Through grace, we are God's "workmanship" (vs. 10). He created us, and He created the jobs He wants us to accomplish. We need not live our lives aimlessly, but can seek to discover and fulfill God's plan for our lives. When we do the will of God as His obedient servants, we show the world that we are His work of art, namely, those whom He has created anew in Christ to His eternal praise.

II. Christ—Our Unity and Peace: Ephesians 2:11-18

A. Excluded from the Community of Faith: vss. 11-12

Therefore, remember that formerly you who are Gentiles by birth and called "uncircumcised" by those who call themselves "the circumcision" (that done in the body by the hands of men)—remember that at that time you were separate from Christ, excluded from citizenship in Israel and foreigners to the covenants of the promise, without hope and without God in the world.

After reminding the Ephesians about their former need for God to raise them from spiritual death to spiritual life by His grace (Eph. 2:1-10), Paul reminded them of their former disadvantages in contrast with the Jews (vss. 11-13). The Jews' privilege was due solely to God's grace in making a covenant with them, but many Jews identified their privilege with their circumcision, which was merely a sign of the covenant.

The grace Paul referred to (Eph. 2:8) is the Lord's favor that He shows without regard to the recipient's worth or merit. God bestows His kindness despite what the person deserves. This is possible because of what Jesus did at Calvary.

God's grace is one of His key attributes. For instance, Exodus 34:6 reveals that the Lord is "the compassionate and gracious God." His redemption of His people from Egypt and His establishment of them in Canaan was a superlative example of His grace. He did this despite their unrighteousness (Deut. 7:7-8; 9:5-6).

Christ is the supreme revelation of God's grace. Jesus not only appropriated divine grace but also incarnated it (Luke 2:40; John 1:14). Christ died on the cross and rose from the dead so that believing sinners might partake of God's grace (Titus 2:11). Their entrance into God's kingdom is not based on their own merit.

Jews are the descendants of Abraham, Isaac, and Jacob. God entered into a covenant with these people to make them the channel through which His truth would be declared to the world. Gentiles are all peoples other than Jews. Old Testament law permitted Gentiles to become members of the covenant community if they were circumcised and agreed to obey the law. But Gentiles never joined the Jewish faith in large numbers.

Some Jews considered themselves superior to Gentiles, not because of what God had done for the Jews but simply because of who they were. This prejudice carried over into the early church, as Jewish believers reckoned Gentiles as second-class Christians unless they adopted Jewish practices. Paul had to deal with this problem often.

The Jews called themselves "the circumcision" (vs. 11) and used the insulting term "uncircumcised" of Gentiles, such as the Ephesians. Paul stated the use of this contemptuous term without himself meaning any contempt. In fact, the apostle affirmed that, under the Gospel, circumcision holds no spiritual significance. As he said elsewhere (see Rom. 2:29), true circumcision is of the heart.

Many Jews went too far in evaluating their privileges; nevertheless, it is true that Gentiles—such as those living in Ephesus—were under some disadvantages. Paul thus described the Ephesians' condition before they were saved. First, they had been without the Messiah (Eph. 2:12). The promises of the coming Redeemer had been made to the Jews, and so Gentiles did not expect Him.

Second, Paul's readers had been alienated from the citizenship of Israel and strangers to the covenants of promise. While membership in the covenant community of Israel was not a guarantee of salvation, it was of significant value, for God had made promises of blessing to the physical descendants of Abraham and Isaac.

Third, the Ephesians previously had no hope and were without God in the world. Though God had not forgotten the Gentiles, most of them knew nothing about Him. Their pagan religious practices did not put them in touch with Him, and so left them with no hope of finding peace and immortality.

B. Included in the Community of Faith: vs. 13

But now in Christ Jesus you who once were far away have been brought near through the blood of Christ.

Paul next turned from the dismal picture of the Ephesians' former condition of once being far away from God. Now, by means of Christ's shed blood, they had been brought near to God (Eph. 2:13). The Son was the meeting point with the Father for all who believed the Gospel. Thus, the grace of God in the sacrifice of His Son was the reason for the change in status of the Ephesians.

C. Peace between Saved Jews and Gentiles: vss. 14-15a

For he himself is our peace, who has made the two one and has destroyed the barrier, the dividing wall of hostility, by abolishing in his flesh the law with its commandments and regulations.

When the Ephesian believers were reconciled with God (Eph. 2:11-13), they were also brought together with Jewish believers (vss. 14-18). Of course, Jews and Gentiles were still distinct groups; but as far as the church was concerned, Christ had merged the two groups (vs. 14). Previous religious and ethnic backgrounds did not matter for their status in the church, for all were equals in Christ.

Paul described this union as Christ tearing down the middle wall of partition, a barrier of hostility, which once separated Jews and Gentiles. Paul may have been thinking of the wall at the Jerusalem temple mount that separated the court where anyone was welcome from the courts where only Jews could go. The Court of the Gentiles, in particular, permitted non-Jews to come near the sanctuary and worship God; but a barrier separated this enclosure from another section where only Jews could go. Paul was saying that in the church, Jewish believers and Gentile Christians could mingle freely.

Because sin entered the human race and controlled the lives of people, God in His pure righteousness could not permit human beings in His presence. Also, sin caused people to rebel against God and live without any consideration of their Creator. Because of Christ's work on the cross, God has dealt with sin and entered into a relationship with believers. For reconciliation to be applied individually, it is necessary that each person accept Christ's work for herself or himself.

Thus Jesus, through His atoning sacrifice, united believing Jews and Gentiles. Paul noted in verse 15a that Christ's death nullified, or rendered inoperative, the commandments and ordinances of the law of Moses. This does not mean that God had cast off the upright principles of the law; rather, Christ makes it possible for the righteous standards that people could never achieve to be attained.

The Mosaic law had been given to the Jews, and because of that many felt superior to Gentiles, but Jesus, by dying on the cross, became the means of salvation for all people. Thus salvation by faith in Christ superseded the law.

The physical arrangement of the temple in Jerusalem was the dominant image in Ephesians 2:14. In addition to a wall that separated Jews and Gentiles, there were also signs that threatened punishment by death for any Gentiles who entered the Holy Place. This was the spot where it was thought that God dwelt. This locale was also where sacrifices for sin were offered.

D. Unity among Saved Jews and Gentiles: vss. 15b-16

His purpose was to create in himself one new man out of the two, thus making peace, and in this one body to reconcile both of them to God through the cross, by which he put to death their hostility.

Paul personified Jewish and Gentile believers, and said Christ had made one new body out of those two groups (Eph. 2:15b). From a spiritual perspective there were no longer Jews and Gentiles. A new body had come into existence—the church—resulting in peace. Here we see that God's grace has been poured out on all of us—no one has been left out. The Lord, in turn, wants us to imitate Him and to embrace all people with His love and acceptance.

The apostle noted that Jesus' death reconciled Jews and Gentiles to God as well as to each other (vs. 16). Christ brought an end to the hostility between sinners and God as well as to the hostility between Jews and Gentiles. Because Christ died on the cross, the enmity between people and God can die there too.

E. Joint Access to the Father: vss. 17-18

He came and preached peace to you who were far away and peace to those who were near. For through him we both have access to the Father by one Spirit.

Since Christ never made Gentiles the prime focus of His earthly ministry, Ephesians 2:17 must refer to the spread of the Gospel to Gentiles. The apostles and other Christians were responsible for this evangelistic effort. Thus, through Jesus' early followers, He proclaimed peace through the Gospel to Gentiles (who were far away from God) and to Jews (who were somewhat nearer to God).

Jews had been, in a sense, nearer to God than Gentiles because they had the Old Testament revelation and because the Messiah had ministered among them; but now both Jews and Gentiles—indeed, all people—have equal access to the Father through the same Holy Spirit because of what Christ has done at Calvary. All three persons of the Trinity make this possible (vs. 18).

III. Christ—Our Cornerstone: Ephesians 2:19-22

A. Members of God's Family: vss. 19-20

Consequently, you are no longer foreigners and aliens, but fellow citizens with God's people and members of God's household, built on the foundation of the apostles and prophets, with Christ Jesus himself as the chief cornerstone.

Centuries earlier Isaiah had foretold a day when the peace of God would be proclaimed to those near and far (Isa. 57:19). Paul declared the fulfillment of Isaiah's prophecy through Christ and the proclamation of the Gospel. As the Good News was heralded, the Spirit brought Gentiles—those "far away" (Eph. 2:17)—and Jews—those "near"—together before the Lord in a community of faith.

After all Paul had written about the new status of both Gentiles and Jews in Christ, the apostle next drew his conclusion. To do this, he used a construction metaphor. He said Gentiles and Jews form a single building with Christ as the cornerstone.

Paul told the Ephesians that they were no longer outcasts. The word rendered "foreigners" (Eph. 2:19) refers to transients who had no rights or privileges; and the word rendered "aliens" describes residents who, by the payment of a minor tax, received protection but not full citizenship. Both terms indicate an inferior status. This was the standing of Gentiles before coming to Christ.

Instead of being inferior, the Ephesians were now fellow citizens with the saints (all of God's holy people) and members of God's household (His spiritual family); in other words, like Jewish believers, saved Gentiles now were in a personal relationship with God. The Lord's household of believers is like a building that has been erected on the foundation of the New Testament apostles and prophets (see 3:5). The Messiah is the cornerstone, or capstone, of the entire structure (2:20). This means the church is based on Christ and the work He performed through the leaders of the church.

In ancient times it was common practice for builders to place a stone at the corner where two walls of an edifice came together. The intent was to bind together and strengthen the intersecting walls. This practice was augmented by the fact that builders made their more permanent structures out of stone that was precisely cut and squared. Jesus, as the "chief cornerstone" (Eph. 2:20), is the foundation of the believer's faith.

B. A Holy Temple for the Lord: vss. 21-22

In him the whole building is joined together and rises to become a holy temple in the Lord. And in him you too are being built together to become a dwelling in which God lives by his Spirit.

Like a cornerstone joining two walls together, Christ is the one in whom the entire structure is united (namely, the community of the redeemed). Moreover, Jesus enables it to grow into a holy temple for the Lord (Eph. 2:21). The word for "temple" that Paul used did not stand for the entire sanctuary complex, but only for the inner sanctum where God's presence dwelt. In keeping with this designation, Paul told the Ephesians that they, as well as the Jewish believers, were part of a dwelling—the church—in which God lives by His Spirit (vs. 22).

Discussion Questions

1. What is the relationship between grace and faith?
2. What is the relationship between salvation and good works?
3. In what way had Christ united believing Jews and Gentiles?
4. What impact did Jesus' death have on the relationship between people and God?
5. How does trusting Christ change one's status in relation to God?

Now Ask Yourself . . .

What difference has the grace of God made in my life?

What good works has God prepared for me to do in the coming week?

What types of prejudice have I personally encountered among Christians?

What specific things can I do to promote harmony and eliminate prejudice within the Church and in society?

How can I encourage other believers to embrace all people with the love and acceptance of God?

Illustrations

In 1959, a Caucasian man named John Howard Griffin changed his appearance to make himself look as though he were an African American. Feeling that he never could glimpse the plight of blacks unless he experienced life from a different vantage point, he altered the pigment of his skin with oral medication, sunlamp treatment, and various kinds of stains. He then set out on travels throughout the South. The results, he found, were unbelievable.

Griffin reported receiving treatment that was almost inhuman. There were vehicles in which he was not allowed to ride. There were restaurants where he could not eat. There were hotels that would not give him a room for the night. And there were rest rooms he was not permitted to use. He was persecuted, slighted, and cheated. Griffin wrote about his treatment in his book entitled *Black Like Me.*

This man's experience helped him to become more aware of the wicked ways in which racial prejudice was being expressed in North America prior to the civil rights movement. And while the civil rights movement did not wipe out racial prejudice, it did help to sensitize many people to the need for justice and equality for all people, regardless of race, color, or creed.

Often it is not until we ourselves feel the sting of an injustice or inequity that we take notice of the existence of prejudice. But God's people are called to be free from prejudices of all kinds, regardless of whether we have experienced them. As we actively ask God to make known and eradicate our own prejudices, then we can see clearly to lead others into prejudice-free living.

Body Building

DEVOTIONAL READING

Romans 12:1-8

DAILY BIBLE READINGS

Monday August 14
Ephesians 4:1-6
There Is One Body and
One Spirit

Tuesday August 15
Ephesians 4:7-16
We Need to Be United in
Faith

Wednesday August 16
Ephesians 4:17-24
Do Not Live in Darkness

Thursday August 17
Ephesians 4:25-32
Be All God Wants You to
Be

Friday August 18
1 Thessalonians 3:6-10
Be Encouraged by Others

Saturday August 19
1 Thessalonians 5:1-11
Encourage One Another

Sunday August 20
1 Thessalonians 5:12-28
Do Good to One Another

Scripture

Background Scripture: *Ephesians 4*
Scripture Lesson: *Ephesians 4:1-16*
Key Verse: *To each one of us grace has been given as Christ apportioned it. Ephesians 4:7.*

Lesson Aim

We are each responsible to build up other Christians.

Lesson Setting

Time: A.D. 60–62
Place: Rome

Lesson Outline

Body Building

I. Living in Unity: Ephesians 4:1-6
   A. *The Characteristics of a Christlike Life: vss. 1-3*
   B. *The Common Aspects of the Believers' Faith: vss. 4-6*

II. Serving in Unity: Ephesians 4:7-13
   A. *Spiritual Gifts from Christ: vs. 7*
   B. *Christ's Authority to Bestow Spiritual Gifts: vss. 8-10*
   C. *A Diversity of Spiritual Gifts: vs. 11*
   D. *A Common Purpose for the Spiritual Gifts: vss. 12-13*

III. Growing in Unity: Ephesians 4:14-16
   A. *Spiritual Instability: vs. 14*
   B. *Spiritual Stability: vss. 15-16*

Introduction

Building Others Up

An officer parachuting off a plane was so intent on leaping out at the right coordinates that he ordered silence to the lower-ranking soldier beside him. "But, lieutenant—" continued the private. "Not another word!" snapped the officer. As the lieutenant made ready to jump, the private pulled him to the floor. "Like I've been trying to tell you, your chute's torn!" shouted the soldier to his now-grateful superior.

Although this story is fictional, it isn't too far-fetched. In real life, words heard and heeded can and do make tremendous differences. Have you ministered beneath or beside someone who, because he or she "knew it all," would not listen to others? Worse, have you exhibited that kind of behavior yourself?

Building others up in love requires us to graciously listen to them. God wants our work with fellow believers to edify, not diminish, the body of Christ.

Lesson Commentary

Paul was incarcerated quite often during his apostolic ministry. For instance, he noted that he had been "in prison more frequently" (2 Cor. 11:23) than his opponents. Paul and Silas were cast into a Roman prison at Philippi (Acts 16:23-24). The apostle endured at least two years of incarceration at Caesarea (24:27) and a minimum of two years of house arrest in Rome before being released (28:30). Many scholars believe that Paul was imprisoned a second time in Rome, which ended in his execution (2 Tim. 4:6-8).

I. Living in Unity: Ephesians 4:1-6

A. The Characteristics of a Christlike Life: vss. 1-3

As a prisoner for the Lord, then, I urge you to live a life worthy of the calling you have received. Be completely humble and gentle; be patient, bearing with one another in love. Make every effort to keep the unity of the Spirit through the bond of peace.

Paul was most likely under house arrest in Rome when he wrote this letter (Acts 28:30-31). This explains his reference to being "a prisoner for the Lord" (Eph. 4:1). Despite his confinement, the apostle could still maintain an active involvement in the lives of his Christian friends in Ephesus through his letters.

The apostle's status as an evangelist imprisoned for the cause of Christ lent weight to his appeal to the Ephesians. Since Paul had been faithful to the point of being imprisoned, they (who were under less pressure) could be faithful too. Specifically, the apostle urged his readers to live a life worthy of the calling they had received (Eph. 4:1). Having been given saving grace, they should do no less than respond to the Lord by living faithfully. This does not mean that they were to earn their salvation by leading a worthy life. Rather, they conducted themselves uprightly as a result of their spiritual rebirth.

So that the Ephesians would know what he meant by a life worthy of their calling, Paul mentioned four virtues that ought to be theirs (and ours as Christians): humility, gentleness, patience, and forbearance (vs. 2). Each of these terms is worth considering further.

The Greek word translated "humble" was adapted by Christians to describe an attitude of lowliness. The term rendered "gentle" refers not to weakness but to submission to others for the sake of Christ. The word rendered "patient" indicates the refusal to avenge wrongs committed against oneself. And the phrase for "bearing with one another" refers to putting up with others' faults and peculiarities.

The four virtues Paul cited can all contribute to the church's harmony. This goal was uppermost in the apostle's mind. In his day, Jewish and Gentile believers sometimes didn't understand one another. And Gentile Christians from different backgrounds or with different temperaments sometimes didn't get along. Paul wanted to see all believers united and harmonious.

But unity is something we must work at. As the apostle noted in verse 3, we are to "make every effort to keep the unity of the Spirit through the bond of peace." Here we see that Christians are united through the Spirit, but our unity can be damaged if we allow our relations to become hostile rather than peaceful. That's why it's sensible to add peacemaking to the list of virtues believers ought to possess.

B. The Common Aspects of the Believers' Faith: vss. 4-6

There is one body and one Spirit—just as you were called to one hope when you were called—one Lord, one faith, one baptism; one God and Father of all, who is over all and through all and in all.

After exhorting the Ephesians to preserve spiritual unity, Paul went on to show the role that unity plays in various aspects of the Christian faith. In fact, the apostle's mention of the "unity of the Spirit" (Eph. 4:3) prompted him to give more attention to the matter. First, Paul noted that there is one spiritual body of Christ and that its members have the same Spirit. Believers also have been called to the same glory-filled future (vs. 4).

The "body" is the church. Just as a human body has many parts

While under house arrest in Rome, Paul had the time to write many letters. He seems to have penned epistles to the churches in Ephesus and Colosse, as well as to Philemon of Colosse, at about the same time. Paul's companions Tychicus and Onesimus could have dropped off one letter at Ephesus on their way to delivering the other two in Colosse (Eph. 6:21-22; Col. 4:7-9; Philem. 10-12). It's clear that Paul didn't want his imprisonment to come between him and the Christians he love!

Ephesians has been called "The Heavenly Epistle" and "The Alps of the New Testament." In it the apostle takes the reader from the depths of ruin to the heights of redemption. The letter contains two distinct, though related parts. Chapters 1—3 remind the readers of their privileged status as members of Christ's Body, the Church, which occupies an important place in God's plan for the universe. Chapters 4—6 appeal to the readers to live in a way consistent with their godly calling rather than to conform to the ungodly society in which they lived.

Paul included quotations from a variety of sources in his writing and speaking. Some scholars believe Ephesians 4:4-6 came from a Christian confession used during the apostle's day. As evidence, they point to its content and to its Trinitarian construction of three groups each containing three items. There is:

1) one body and
2) one Spirit—just as you were called to
3) one hope when you were called—

1) one Lord,
2) one faith,
3) one baptism;
one God and Father of all, who is

1) over all and
2) through all and
3) in all.

but is one entity, so the church has many members but is one group. Indwelling all members of the church is the Holy Spirit. As we learned from Ephesians 1:14, the Spirit's presence in our lives is the guarantee of our common hope to live eternally with God in heaven. This became our hope and expectation when we accepted the call to faith.

Second, there is only "one Lord, one faith, one baptism" (4:5). All believers serve one Lord, namely, Jesus Christ. We serve this Lord because we have made the same profession of faith in Him. And baptism identifies us with Christ. The reference to baptism could be either to that of water or the Spirit (Rom. 6:3-4; 1 Cor. 12:13).

Third, there is only "one God and Father" (Eph. 4:6) who alone is sovereign over us all, in us all, and living through us all. In a culture that recognized many gods, Paul affirmed that there is only one true God whom Christians worship and serve. He is the Father of all who believe in Him. In His relationship to His people He is both transcendent ("over all") and immanent ("through all and in all"). Paul's mention of all three persons of the Trinity in verses 3-6 shows us that all three persons harmoniously work together to bring about the unity of believers in everyday life.

II. Serving in Unity: Ephesians 4:7-13

A. Spiritual Gifts from Christ: vs. 7

But to each one of us grace has been given as Christ apportioned it.

Although there is one church and there is to be unity in the church, that doesn't mean all Christians are clones of one another or think and act alike. Accordingly, Paul followed up his strong message about church unity with an equally strong message about gift diversity. The apostle noted that Jesus supplies His followers with grace, making some Christians leaders who prepare the rest for ministry so that the whole church may achieve unity and maturity.

When Paul said that Christ gives "grace" (Eph. 4:7), the apostle was referring to the grace by which believers are equipped, or enabled, to perform ministries in the church. We don't earn grace; we are given it. Neither can we pick the kind of grace we will receive. Christ assigns it as He sees fit. We are to receive this grace thankfully and use it for God's glory.

B. Christ's Authority to Bestow Spiritual Gifts: vss. 8-10

This is why it says: "When he ascended on high, he led captives in his train and gave gifts to men." (What does "he ascended" mean except that he also descended to the lower, earthly regions? He who descended is the very one who ascended higher than all the heavens, in order to fill the whole universe.)

To support what he had said about Christ's giving grace, Paul quoted from Psalm 68:18 (see Eph. 4:8). The picture is one of a triumphal procession in which the victor both received and distributed gifts. When applied to the Savior, this verse shows how He has given gifts to His followers ever since His ascension.

Lest anyone doubt that the one who "ascended on high" was Jesus Christ, Paul added the explanation in verses 9 and 10. The apostle noted that the person who ascended had previously descended "to the lower, earthly regions" (vs. 9). The main emphasis is that Jesus completely conquered sin, death, and Satan through His resurrection and ascension.

Despite the clarity of emphasis, scholars have different opinions about what Paul actually meant. Some think the apostle was referring to Jesus' entrance into Hades (the underworld or realm of the dead) after His crucifixion to take saints to heaven when He rose from the dead. Others say that Christ's descent refers to His burial in the grave. Still others claim that Paul was talking about Jesus' incarnation, in which He came to earth as a human being.

This person "who descended is the very one who ascended" (vs. 10). Expressed differently, Jesus is not only a man who lived on earth, but also the Lord whose eternal dwelling is in heaven. Jews of the day believed there were seven heavens. But Paul said that Christ ascended "higher than all the heavens." In fact, now He fills "the whole universe." This means Jesus' lordship over the universe is absolute and complete because of His resurrection and ascension. He thus has the power and authority to be generous in bestowing gifts of grace to His followers.

C. A Diversity of Spiritual Gifts: vs. 11

It was he who gave some to be apostles, some to be prophets, some to be evangelists, and some to be pastors and teachers.

All believers have at least one spiritual gift (1 Pet. 4:10). But in

Scholars note that the wording of Paul's quote in Ephesians 4:8 differs somewhat from that of Psalm 68 both in the Hebrew text and the Septuagint (an ancient Greek rendering of the Old Testament). The most significant alteration is the reading "gave gifts to" in place of "received gifts from." Some think the apostle was citing a variant of Psalm 68 that has not survived outside its quotation in Ephesians 4:8. Others think Paul's citation was part of any early Christian hymn. A third possibility is that the apostle intentionally rendered the text he quoted in the way he did to better support his point.

405

The Greek word often rendered "gifts" (1 Cor. 12:4) is charismata. *The singular form of this word is* charisma. *Both terms relate to the word* charis, *which means "favor" or "grace." While* charisma *denotes a personal endowment of grace,* charismata *refers to a concrete expression of grace. The main idea is that the Spirit bestows His gifts of grace on Christians to accomplish God's will.*

Paul listed three categories of spiritual gifts through which the Holy Spirit manifests Himself in the church. There are "different kinds of gifts," "different kinds of service" (vss. 4-5), and "different kinds of working" (vs. 6). Despite the diversities and differences, all spiritual gifts have the same source—the triune Godhead: the Spirit (vs. 4), the Lord Jesus (vs. 5), and God the Father (vs. 6; see 2 Cor. 13:14; Eph. 4:3-6).

Ephesians 4:11 Paul focused on those who have received special abilities to be leaders in the churches. He mentioned apostles, prophets, evangelists, pastors, and teachers. The Greek word rendered "apostle" is used in various ways in the New Testament. In this case, Paul was probably using the term in a restricted sense, to refer to a group of people (including himself) whom Jesus had personally chosen to found the church.

The "prophets" Paul had in mind were probably not Elijah, Isaiah, and the other Old Testament spokespersons. The church of Paul's day had its own prophets. These people delivered messages from God, and sometimes foretold the future. Before the New Testament books were written, about the only way God had to communicate to the church was through His special speakers.

The other three kinds of leaders have related functions. "Evangelists" in the early church were people who conducted outreach in areas where the church had not yet been established. In other words, they were pioneers for the faith. In the wake of the evangelists, "pastors and teachers" served already established congregations. Pastors shepherded churches, while teachers instructed them. Of course, these two roles could be combined in one person.

D. A Common Purpose for the Spiritual Gifts: vss. 12-13

To prepare God's people for works of service, so that the body of Christ may be built up until we all reach unity in the faith and in the knowledge of the Son of God and become mature, attaining to the whole measure of the fullness of Christ.

Despite the presence of different, uniquely gifted believers, they all have a common goal. The Lord wants them to equip believers to do God's work so that the Church might be strengthened (Eph. 4:12). Christians use their gifts to help one another become united in their faith and intimate in their knowledge of God's Son. The entire Body benefits when each of its members is mature, fully grown in the Lord, and measuring up to the full stature of Christ (vs. 13).

III. Growing in Unity: Ephesians 4:14-16

A. Spiritual Instability: vs. 14

Then we will no longer be infants, tossed back and forth by the waves, and blown here and there by every wind of teaching and by the cunning and craftiness of men in their deceitful scheming.

Children tend to be gullible, vulnerable, and easily victimized. This is true both in the physical and spiritual realms. As along as believers remain immature, they will be like a ship tossed on a stormy sea. As the winds of opinion blow in one direction, some Christians are easily swayed by it. Then as another gust of ideas blasts across their bow, they change their mind about what they believe. According to Ephesians 4:14, Jesus' followers are not to be characterized by spiritual immaturity and ignorance.

B. Spiritual Stability: vss. 15-16

Instead, speaking the truth in love, we will in all things grow up into him who is the Head, that is, Christ. From him the whole body, joined and held together by every supporting ligament, grows and builds itself up in love, as each part does its work.

Paul did not want God's people to be fooled by the cleverly worded lies of religious imposters. Instead, the apostle urged believers to hold to the truth in love (Eph. 4:15). In other words, honesty, veracity, and compassion should characterize all that believers say and do. Believers are also to become more like Christ in every area of their lives. This is as it should be, for He is the head of the Church. Under His direction, this spiritual body is fitted together perfectly.

By calling Jesus "the Head," Paul was returning to his familiar analogy between the church and the body. Believers make up the members of Christ's body, with Him as our Head. Paul liked this analogy because it indicates the organic connection between Jesus and His followers.

As each part does its own unique and special work, it helps the other parts to grow (vs. 16). Each member of Christ's spiritual body is to work together in harmony to promote the growth and vitality of the Church. As a result, the entire Body becomes healthy, mature, and full of love. Every believer should operate with one another so that all might mature and come to know Christ more fully.

Paul's frequent sea voyages, including his harrowing trip to Rome (Acts 27:1—28:14), may have prompted the seafaring metaphor he used in Ephesians 4:14. Navigation of ocean-going vessels was achieved by means of a side rudder, which was nothing more than an oversized oar that pivoted in a slanting position near the stern. A series of ropes were fitted to the mast and sails to help steer the ship.

The pilot of the vessel had limited tools to help navigate the ship. These included manuals with brief notes on distances, as well as information about landmarks, harbors, and anchorages. Mid-May to mid-September was the best time to sail in the Mediterranean. After that, the severity of winter storms and the poor visibility due to fog and cloudiness made navigation by compass nearly impossible. Sailing during the late fall and winter was used only for delivering urgent messages, transporting essential supplies, and relocating desperately needed troops.

Discussion Questions

1. What did Paul urge the Ephesians to do?
2. Which godly virtues did Paul want to see characterize their lives?
3. What areas of unity did they have with each other?
4. Why are the spiritual gifts Paul mentioned given to the Church?
5. What is the goal of all believers in the Church?

Now Ask Yourself . . .

In which of the four areas—humility, gentleness, patience, forbearance—am I strongest? In which am I weakest?

What can I do to help keep unity in my church?

What enabling grace has Christ given me to share with others?

How can I encourage other believers to grow in spiritual maturity?

Illustrations

The community church Erin attends knows how to build up believers. The benefits of this, she finds, includes the visible and the invisible. Pastors, teachers, and musicians build up the body during the Sunday worship service—a visible aspect of ministry. But Erin sees more going on behind the scenes during the week.

Small groups meet weekly, ministering to one another, challenging each other, and encouraging and affirming recognized spiritual giftedness. Also, people expressing interest in a ministry area are encouraged to train and try their hand at it. When Erin expressed an interest in music ministry, she was encouraged to attend practices and was soon playing her instrument in worship.

Erin is amazed at the creativity that flows from people who are encouraged to exercise their giftedness. New worship music comes out of the music ministry, and members regularly write original dramas, holiday presentations, and thematic songs. The church's publications are always eye-catching and well-designed.

Church activities are designed not only for member fellowship, but also to make outsiders feel welcomed and comfortable. Erin has felt open to invite people from her work to these activities. Also, those who are gifted in evangelism lead a class series for non-believers interested in investigating Christianity.

When Erin tells these things to others, the typical response is, "That's easily done in a large church like yours." Erin responds, "Though it is growing, it's a relatively new and relatively small body of believers." Erin realizes that this group, however, has learned the secret of building one another up for effective ministry in Christ.

The Battle Belongs to the Lord

DEVOTIONAL READING

Colossians 2:20-23

DAILY BIBLE READINGS

Monday August 21
John 16:29-33
*Jesus Has Overcome the
World*

Tuesday August 22
Ephesians 6:1-4
*Wisdom for Children and
Parents*

Wednesday August 23
Ephesians 6:5-9
*Our Interaction with
Authority*

Thursday August 24
Ephesians 6:10-17
Wear the Armor of God

Friday August 25
Ephesians 6:18-24
Always Pray in the Spirit

Saturday August 26
2 Timothy 2:1-7
Be Strong in Christ

Sunday August 27
1 John 5:1-12
*With God We Can
Overcome the World*

Scripture

Background Scripture: *Ephesians 6*
Scripture Lesson: *Ephesians 6:10-24*
Key Verse: *Be strong in the Lord and in his mighty power.
Ephesians 6:10.*

Lesson Aim

God alone can equip us for spiritual warfare.

Lesson Setting

Time: A.D. 60–62
Place: Rome

Lesson Outline

The Battle Belongs to the Lord

I. Putting on the Armor: Ephesians 6:10-12
   A. *Donning Our Spiritual Armor: vss. 10-11*
   B. *Recognizing Our True Enemy: vs. 12*

II. Standing with the Armor: Ephesians 6:13-17
   A. *Victory as the Goal: vs. 13*
   B. *Our Spiritual Arsenal: vss. 14-17*

III. Fully Using the Armor: Ephesians 6:18-24
   A. *Praying in the Spirit: vs. 18*
   B. *Praying for Other Believers: vss. 19-20*
   C. *Dispatching Tychius: vss. 21-22*
   D. *Final Greetings: vss. 23-24*

Introduction

The Battle Belongs to God

In the movies, fighting evil is simply a matter of having the right equipment. But in real life, spiritual warfare involves a far more powerful weapon—faith in God. Anything less, and it is like waving a plastic wand over an empty top hat and expecting "magic" to happen. There's no power in the plastic. It's a mere prop. Only the trained illusionist can take that empty hat and amazingly fill it with a living rabbit.

When it comes to combating evil and sin in our world, the real power is in the sovereign Lord of all creation. Thus, to be victorious, we must put ourselves in God's hand. When we do, He promises to give us the spiritual tools we need to stand our ground when the day of evil comes.

The Book of Acts tells us that's what happened in the ancient Ephesus (19:11-20), especially as "the name of the Lord Jesus" (vs. 17) triumphed over evil. We can witness those same results today.

Lesson Commentary

I. Putting on the Armor: Ephesians 6:10-12

A. Donning Our Spiritual Armor: vss. 10-11

Finally, be strong in the Lord and in his mighty power. Put on the full armor of God so that you can take your stand against the devil's schemes.

Some people say that Satan and demons are a myth invented by primitive, ignorant people. In contrast, the Bible indicates that the devil and his fallen angels are real and pose a threat to the Christian way of life. Paul said that to withstand their attacks, believers must depend on God's strength and use every item that He makes available (Eph. 6:10).

Paul understood the power of evil as much as anyone. He had often been the object of satanic efforts to hurt him and hinder his work. And he knew the Ephesian Christians were on Satan's list of targets too. So in bringing his letter to a close, the apostle focused on the spiritual struggle that lay before them.

In verse 11, the apostle exhorted his readers to "put on the full armor of God" so that they could stand firm against all the strategies and tricks of the devil. We should not be surprised that Satan is deceptive, for Jesus called him a "liar and the father of lies" (John 8:44). Paul, too, said that the devil "masquerades as an angel of light" (2 Cor. 11:14).

B. Recognizing Our True Enemy: vs. 12

For our struggle is not against flesh and blood, but against the rulers, against the authorities, against the powers of this dark world and against the spiritual forces of evil in the heavenly realms.

The battle Paul described is not a human one, but rather a supernatural one. It involves a hierarchy of evil rulers and authorities in the unseen world, and wicked spirits in the heavenly realms (Eph. 4:12). The Greek words translated "rulers" and "authorities" indicate that demons have a certain amount of power and influence at this stage in history. But of course such is far less than Christ's.

The Greek term rendered "powers" once indicated those who aspire to world control. In pagan religions it was often used of gods and especially of the sun, which was considered a deity. Paul's use of the term in connection with the phrase "dark world," therefore, may have been meant to suggest that while the demons masquerade as light (good), they are in fact darkness (evil).

The phrase translated "the spiritual forces of evil in the heavenly realms" reflects the language of astrology in Paul's day. Astrologers taught that demons live in the heavenly bodies, and from there control the destiny of people. The apostle's use of the phrase in this context indicates that believers are not dominated by demons but are able to fight against them.

But let us not forget that this is a powerful demonic army whose prime objective is to defeat the followers of Christ. In this battle, Satan and his subordinates use whatever devices they have to turn us away from the Lord and back to sin. Christians today are engaged in a spiritual struggle no less fierce than the one that raged in the early years of the church. In fact, our battles are really the continuation of a war begun long ago.

Satan and his demons have adapted their strategies to current situations, but their goals have not changed. They want to prevent unbelievers from hearing the Gospel; they want to undermine the faith of believers; and they want to prevent Christians from contributing to God's work in the world.

The devil certainly is far stronger than we are, but he is infinitely weaker than God. So if we fight Satan in God's strength and not in our own, we can be victorious. In fact, Christ's death and resurrection ensure that eventually we will win. As John explained, "For everyone born of God overcomes the world. This is the victory that has overcome the world, even our faith" (1 John 5:4).

In other places besides Ephesians, the Bible describes cosmic forces that are at work in the world against God (Rom. 8:38; 1 Cor. 15:24; Col. 2:15; 1 Pet. 3:22). Most often they are called "powers" and "spiritual forces" (Eph. 6:12). Satan is called the "ruler of the kingdom of the air" (2:2), and he has this world in his power (1 John 5:19). Believers fight against evil spiritual beings who are part of a hierarchy of power in heavenly and earthly places. Their ultimate goal is to destroy the relationship between God and humanity. But one of the major themes of Ephesians is that Christ is the ultimate power in the universe. Once we believe in Him, we can escape defeat by the ruler of this world (1:21; 2:2).

II. Standing with the Armor: Ephesians 6:13-17

A. Victory as the Goal: vs. 13

Therefore put on the full armor of God, so that when the day of evil comes, you may be able to stand your ground, and after you have done everything, to stand.

Paul told the Ephesians not to delay preparing for spiritual battle. They should put on the "full armor of God" (Eph. 6:13) right away. Then they would be ready in the time of evil, that is, when Satan launches his attack. Paul was convinced that with the right preparation (and of course courageous fighting), his readers would be still standing and retained their ground when the battle was over. According to traditional military doctrine, the army in possession of the field after a battle is the victor.

In Paul's discussion we are not told to take the offensive against Satan. But he is attacking us. Therefore, we need to look to our defenses and make sure we do not lose any ground to him. Our spiritual successes have been hard-won, and so we should stand firm and fight to hold on to them.

B. Our Spiritual Arsenal: vss. 14-17

Stand firm then, with the belt of truth buckled around your waist, with the breastplate of righteousness in place, and with your feet fitted with the readiness that comes from the gospel of peace. In addition to all this, take up the shield of faith, with which you can extinguish all the flaming arrows of the evil one. Take the helmet of salvation and the sword of the Spirit, which is the word of God.

Having made his plea for preparedness, Paul began describing the six pieces of equipment that the Christian should take into spiritual battle (Eph. 6:14-17). The apostle listed them in the order in which they naturally be put on by a soldier getting ready for a battle.

The first piece of equipment is the "belt of truth" (vs. 14). A Roman soldier's belt held in his tunic and breastplate, and became a place to hang his sword. For Christians, our belt is "truth." This general term may refer to the truth of the Gospel and to our truthfulness in everyday life. Satan is a liar and hates the truth.

The second piece of equipment Paul describe is the "breastplate of righteousness." Roman soldiers wore over the entire front of their torso a large protective plate made of bronze, or, if they were

As a prisoner in Rome, Paul was chained to a Roman soldier at all times. Thus it was natural for him to see his guard as a model and to think of the spiritual struggle in military terms. But undoubtedly the Old Testament influenced the apostle too, since the Hebrew Scriptures frequently use military images for spiritual realities (for example, see Isa. 11:5 and 59:17).

Paul's guards probably did not wear full battle dress. But they could easily bring to Paul's mind the times he had seen Roman soldiers fully armed. As every Roman soldier knew, the time to put on his armor was not when the arrows began to fly. Before the battle, he prepared himself by taking up armor and weapons.

wealthy, of chain mail. The Christian's breastplate is "righteousness." As we draw on the Savior's righteousness, we are able to live devout and holy lives. An upright life is an effective defense against Satan's attacks.

Paul didn't quite come out and say what the third piece of equipment is. But he obviously was referring to footgear. Roman soldiers wore strong sandals or boots studded underneath with nails for traction while marching. Similarly, Christians are to be shod with "the readiness that comes from the gospel of peace" (vs. 15). This phrase probably was meant to suggest that our peace with God, won by Christ, gives us sure footing in our spiritual battle with Satan.

The fourth piece of equipment is the "shield of faith" (vs. 16). Roman soldiers carried large shields made of wood covered with hide and bound with iron. These shields provided effective protection from blows and even from the flaming darts fired at them by their enemies. Faith is more effective than a Roman shield in defending us against Satan's attack, especially as we steadfastly maintain our trust in Christ.

The fifth piece of equipment is the "helmet of salvation" (vs. 17). Roman soldiers wore helmets of bronze and leather to protect their heads. And just as Roman soldiers received their helmets from their armor-bearers to put on, so Christians receive salvation from the Lord to use in their conflict with Satan. We look forward to a time when our salvation will be complete and Satan will be utterly defeated.

The last piece of equipment in the Christian's armory is the "sword of the Spirit." For some reason Paul did not mention the long spear that was the Roman soldier's chief offensive weapon. Instead, he referred to the short two-edged sword Roman legionaries carried. Paul compared this weapon to "the word of God." When Christ was tempted in the wilderness, He used Scripture as a weapon against Satan. The Spirit can help us use God's Word against the same foe.

"Flaming arrows" (Eph. 6:16) were often used in sieges of cities. Bows and arrows would effectively hit targets from long range (300–400 yards). If a solider became terrified of flaming arrows stuck in his shield, he might throw down his shield and be more vulnerable to attack. Therefore, shields were sometimes dipped in water to extinguish flaming arrows.

III. Fully Using the Armor: Ephesians 6:18-24

A. Praying in the Spirit: vs. 18

And pray in the Spirit on all occasions with all kinds of prayers and requests. With this in mind, be alert and always keep on praying for all the saints.

Prayer is not a piece of spiritual armor for believers. We are not to use prayer just when under attack, but rather we are always to keep in touch with God through prayer, and receive power and strength from Him. Accordingly, Paul urged his readers to pray "in the Spirit" (Eph. 6:18). This probably means either to pray in communion with the Spirit or to pray in the power of the Spirit.

Paul described some qualities associated with prayer in the Spirit. First, it is frequent. We are to pray "on all occasions" and "always keep on praying." Second, prayer in the Spirit has room for variety. We are to pray "with all kinds of prayers and requests." Third, prayer in the Spirit is well informed. We are to "be alert," that is, on the lookout for needs. Fourth, prayer in the Spirit is unselfish. We are to pray not only for ourselves "but for all the saints," meaning for all Christians.

B. Praying for Other Believers: vss. 19-20

Pray also for me, that whenever I open my mouth, words may be given me so that I will fearlessly make known the mystery of the gospel, for which I am an ambassador in chains. Pray that I may declare it fearlessly, as I should.

As an example of a saint for whom the Ephesians could pray, Paul offered himself (Eph. 6:19-20). He did not ask his readers to pray for his release from imprisonment. Instead, he requested prayer for a courageous spirit in proclaiming the Gospel while imprisoned. (vs. 19).

Ambassadors are usually afforded the privilege of diplomatic immunity from arrest. Yet even though Paul was "in chains" (vs. 20), he saw himself as an ambassador for Christ. There was no doubt in his mind that his imprisonment was a God-given opportunity. It would enable him to convey the Gospel to officials high in the Roman government—people he would not otherwise have had an opportunity to meet. The emperor might even have heard his case personally.

Since the government officials had the power of life and death over Paul, he naturally felt some anxiety. But he didn't want unease to prevent him from preaching the Gospel clearly and powerfully. So his primary prayer request was for fearlessness and

When Paul arrived in Rome as a prisoner about A.D. 60, he was not kept in one of the civil or military prisons. He was permitted to rent his own home, to receive visitors, and to preach the Gospel (Acts 28:30-31). Soldiers of the Praetorian guard, the emperor's bodyguard unit, took turns watching the apostle while chained to him. Paul was able to share Christ with these soldiers as well as others associated with his case (Phil. 1:12-14). The imprisonment lasted about two years. During this period the apostle wrote Philemon, Colossians, and Philippians, as well as Ephesians.

reliance upon God when it came time for him to witness at the risk of his life.

C. Dispatching Tychicus: vss. 21-22

Tychicus, the dear brother and faithful servant in the Lord, will tell you everything, so that you also may know how I am and what I am doing. I am sending him to you for this very purpose, that you may know how we are, and that he may encourage you.

Beyond mentioning that he was a prisoner, Paul didn't tell the Ephesians much about his condition. He knew they would be interested in his condition, though. And surely he would have written more to them if he hadn't known that the letter carrier, Tychius, could satisfy their curiosity about him. Tychius had been with Paul in Rome and knew all about his situation.

Tychius is mentioned several times in the New Testament. He seems to have been a loyal assistant to Paul for several years. The apostle sent Tychius on several important errands, including another one to Ephesus, which may have been his hometown (Acts 20:4; Col. 4:7-8; 2 Tim. 4:12; Titus 3:12).

Ephesus was not the final destination in Tychius's itinerary. He and his traveing companion, Onesimus (Col. 4:9), went on to Colosse to deliver other letters. But surely they stopped awhile in Ephesus, resting and enjoying the fellowship of the believers. During this period they would tell the Ephesians about, among other things, Paul's living conditions and his freedom to share the Gospel (Eph. 6:21). Since Tychius would be able to tell the Ephesians that Paul was comfortable and in no immediate danger, he would put their minds at rest about the apostle (vs. 22).

D. Final Greetings: vss. 23-24

Peace to the brothers, and love with faith from God the Father and the Lord Jesus Christ. Grace to all who love our Lord Jesus Christ with an undying love.

Paul concluded his letter with a typical apostle's benediction. It was his desire that "God the Father and the Lord Jesus Christ" (Eph. 6:23) would give his readers peace as well as love with faith. Moreover, Paul desired that God's grace would be upon all whose love for the Savior was never-ending, incorruptible, and sincere (vs. 24).

Early traditions suggest that Paul was not martyred at the end of the Roman imprisonment during which he wrote Ephesians. One possible scenario for the last years of Paul's life, based on historical reports and inferences, goes like this:

About A.D. 62 Paul was released from house arrest in Rome, either because he was acquitted or because his case dragged on beyond the allowable limit. Then Paul achieved his long-held goal of taking the Gospel to Spain, the western limit of the Roman Empire. Next, the apostle turned east, revisiting cities in Crete, Asia Minor, and Greece. In one of these places or in Rome, Paul was rearrested and taken to the Mamertime Prison in Rome. The persecution of Christians under Nero was in full swing, so Paul's second Roman imprisonment was shorter and harsher than his first one. But he managed to get off the letters to Timothy and Titus. Between A.D 65 and 67 he was executed by beheading, and his body was buried along the Ostian Way outside Rome.

Discussion Questions

1. What should believers do when the devil and his subordinates attack?
2. When is the best time to put on God's spiritual armor?
3. What good is truthfulness when fighting against Satan?
4. Of what value is God's Word in the midst of the battle?
5. When did Paul envision believers praying?

Now Ask Yourself . . .

Where have I experienced some element of spiritual warfare?

What might be Satan's schemes for me and how can I take a stand against him?

From where do I obtain spiritual strength to battle the enemy?

Am I fully equipped for the spiritual struggle in which I'm engaged?

Are my prayers frequent, varied, well informed, and unselfish?

What is my top prayer request currently?

Illustrations

The "Got Milk?" ad campaign made a valid point: the necessity of an item is never so apparent as when it's missing. Consider the experiences of these individuals.

Loraine, a Christian, knew she lacked a certain degree that would give her an edge in getting a job she really wanted. On her application, she said she held the degree. However, someone who knew about Loraine's education saw her application. They were ready to hire her, but the company called and asked if she held the degree she indicated. In shame, Loraine had to admit that she didn't. Got your belt of truth?

Devon was busy with the demands of the Christmas season when his landlord came to his door to deliver a Christmas card. Devon hoped their visit would be brief, and it was. The landlord announced he had things to get done. Devon wished him Merry Christmas and got back to his work. But a few minutes after the landlord left, Devon noticed on his table an invitation to his congregation's Christmas candlelight service. In his self-centeredness, he'd forgotten that he had been praying for an opportunity to give his landlord the invitation. Got your boots of readiness?

Bill had been laid off from his job, and Tina's income was just barely paying the bills. Bill was always one of the final candidates for the jobs, but he was never hired. As difficulties pressed in on this young couple, they began to turn on one another in anger and frustration, straining their relationship. At church, they acted as if everything was all right, but in their hearts, they had begun to wonder if God had abandoned them. Got your shield of faith? Paul couldn't have stressed more strongly our need to put on spiritual armor.